CONTENTS AND METHODS OF CATECHIZATION

for the use of

LAY TEACHERS OF RELIGION, SISTERS, SEMINARIANS AND PRIESTS

by the

Right Rev. Msgr. Rudolph G. Bandas, Ph.D.Agg., S.T.D. et M.
Archdiocesan Director of the Confraternity of Christian Doctrine
Rector of the Saint Paul Seminary
Consultor of the Sacred Congregation of Seminaries and Universities

WIPF & STOCK · Eugene, Oregon

Wipf and Stock Publishers
199 W 8th Ave, Suite 3
Eugene, OR 97401

Contents and Methods of Catechization
For the Use of Lay Teachers of Religion, Sisters, Seminarians and Priests
By Bandas, Rudolph G.
ISBN 13: 978-1-60899-134-1
Publication date 9/28/2009
Previously published by The Confraternity of Christian Doctrine
of the Archdiocese of St. Paul, Incorporated, 1957

NIHIL OBSTAT:

GUALTERUS H. PETERS, S.T.L., Ph.D.,
Censor Librorum

IMPRIMATUR:

GULIELMUS O. BRADY, S.T.D., D.D.,
Archiepiscopus Sancti Pauli

Paulopoli, die 12ª, Junii, 1957

TABLE OF CONTENTS

PART I
CONTENTS OF CATECHIZATION

PART II
METHODS OF CATECHIZATION

ILLUSTRISSIMO, REVERENDISSIMO DOMINO

DOMINO

GULIELMO O. BRADY, S.T.D., LL.D.

ARCHIEPISCOPO SANCTI PAULI

GREGIS PASTORI VIGILANTI

CLERI POPULIQUE PATRI AMANTI

IN FILIALIS AMORIS TESTIMONIUM

AUCTOR

SACRA CONGREGATIO
DE SEMINARIIS
ET STUDIORUM UNIVERSITATIBUS

Roma, 25 aprile 1957

Prot. Num. 535/56/9
(Hic numerus in responsione referatur)

Ill.mo e Rev.mo Monsignore,

apprendo con viva soddisfazione che Ella sta per pubblicare il Suo nuovo lavoro sul Catechismo "Contents and Methods of Catechization", e me ne rallegro vivamente.

Gli argomenti trattati dalla S.V.Ill.ma e Rev.ma sono di suprema importanza, e dovrebbero essere appresi e meditati da tutti gli Ecclesiastici. Sin dai corsi teologici dovrebbero studiarsi le nozioni storiche e metodologiche che Ella illustra con rara competenza.

La prima parte è fondamentale, in quanto illustra gli inizi e le radici dell'attività catechistica nella Bibbia, nella Storia Ecclesiastica, nella Liturgia, nel canto e nella musica religiosa, nella preghiera pubblica e privata.

Vengono poi presentati i grandi Esempi. Gesù Cristo N.S. e con Lui, San Paolo, Sant'Agostino e le sue direttive, Giovanni Gersone apostolo dei bambini, l'Abbé Claude Fleury, J.J. Olier e Dupanloup, ed infine i metodi più scientifici di Monaco e di Stieglitz. Ottima l'idea di concludere con l'espositione del "Metodo Eucaristico" e del "Metodo del Seminatore".

Benedica il Signore questa Sua magnifica opera, in cui i principi sono mirabilmente intrecciati alla pratica, in modo che si diffonda largamente tra i Sacerdoti, tra i Religiosi e le Religiose, tra i laici di Azione Cattolica!

Con sensi di particolare stima ed ossequio torno a professarmi

della S.V.Ill.ma e Rev.ma
dev.mo in G.C.
G. Card. Pizzardo

+ C. Confalonieri, Segr.

Ill.mo e Rev.mo Signore
Mons. RODOLFO G. BANDAS
Rettore del Seminario di
= SAN PAOLO DI MINNESOTA =
w

PART I
CONTENTS OF CATECHIZATION

CHAPTER I

CONTENTS OF CATECHIZATION IN HISTORY THE CATECHISM

Before discussing the Catechism as we know it today, we shall first give a brief historical summary of catechization in the Church. It is true, of course, that many documents remain to be unearthed before a complete history of catechization, of catechetics and of the Catechism can be written. Yet, what recent research has brought forth is sufficiently interesting to deserve our attention.

The First Two Centuries

The term "catechesis" [1] is derived from the Greek verb κατηχέω, which means to instruct orally, to teach by word of mouth. It is in

[1] Cf. R. J. Jansen, *Canonical Provisions for Catechetical Instruction* (Washington, 1937), pp. 6 ff.; "Patristic Catechetics," in *St. Bonaventure Seminary Year Book, Vol. XXII* (St. Bonaventure Seminary, 1938), p. 9; Joseph H. Ostdiek, *Simple Methods in Religious Instruction* (Milwaukee, 1936), pp. 3 ff; *Simple Methods in Teaching Religion* (Milwaukee, 1936); F. H. Drinkwater, *Religion in School Again* (London, 1935), pp. 149 ff.; J. Hronek, *Vyučování Naboženství* (Praha, 1935), pp. 99ff.; A. N. Fuerst, *The Systematic Teaching of Religion*, 2 vols. (New York, 1939, 1942); John M. Bennett, *A Manual of Suggestions in Catechetics* (Toronto, 1948); Sister M. Berenice, *Course in Methods for Confraternity Teachers* (San Antonio, 1948); Fitzpatrick-Tanner, *Methods in Teaching Religion in Elementary Schools* (Milwaukee, 1939); Sister M. Frederic, *A Vade Mecum for Teachers of Religion* (Milwaukee, 1948); Aloysius J. Heeg, *Practical Helps for the Religion Teacher* (St. Louis, 1946); Sister M. Rosalia, *Teaching Confraternity Classes* (St. Paul, 1950); John K. Sharp, *Teaching and Preaching Religion to Children* (New York, 1936); J. T. McMahon, *Building Character from Within* (Milwaukee, 1940); C. E. Roy, *Organization Catechistique* (Montreal, 1945); *Lumen Vitae, International Review of Religious Instruction*, Oct.-Dec., 1950; entire issue; F. J. Sheed, *Are We Really Teaching Religion?* (New York, 1953).

this sense that the verb κατηχεῖν is used by New Testament writers, especially by St. Luke and St. Paul. Thus, Apollo is said to have been "instructed in the way of the Lord" (κατηχημένος τὴν ὁδὸν του κυρίου).[2] St. Luke wrote his Gospel to recall to Theophilus the truths in which he had been "instructed (περί ὧν κατηχήθης.[3] St. Paul speaks in the Church in order to instruct his hearers (ἵνα κατηχήσω),[4] and desires that he who "is instructed (ὁ κατηχούμενος) in the word communicate to him that instructeth him (τῷ κατηχοῦντι) in all good things. [5]

Hence, among early patristic writers the Greek term κατήχησις and the Latin word *catechesis* were predicated either of the instruction process itself or of its subject matter. In the measure in which the catechumenate developed, the term took on a more exact and restricted meaning; it was applied particularly to the oral instruction preparatory to the reception of Baptism. During the first centuries those to be catechized were mostly adults; since the beginning of the Middle Ages, however, they were generally children. Today the word "catechization" is used to denote the religious instruction of both youth and adults; it designates the religious training of pupils in both Catholic and secular schools and institutions, of adults through discussion clubs and religious inquiry classes, and of parents in their role as religious educators of their children in the home. Catechetics is a science which explains the rules to be observed and the aids to be used in the process of catechization.

Conformably to the precept of the Master,[6] the Apostles first taught and then baptized.[7] In all instances they tried to engraft the heavenly doctrine on the apperceptive masses of their listeners. To the Jews, who for centuries had been living in expectation of God's Anointed One, they announced that Christ was indeed the Divine Messias foretold by the Prophets.[8] When addressing the Jews of the Dispersion, St. Stephen extolled Christ above Moses, and declared the Christian religion independent of the Mosaic rites and

[2] Acts 18:25.
[3] Luke 1:4.
[4] I Cor. 14:19.
[5] Gal. 6:6.
[6] Mark 16:15.
[7] Cf. St. Leo the Great, *Epist.* xvi, 6 in *P. L.*, LIV, 702.
[8] Acts 2:22–36.

prescriptions.[9] According to St. Paul's Epistle to the Hebrews, the following elements constituted the primitive catechesis: repentance, faith in God as Author of the Beatific Vision and as Rewarder, Baptism, imposition of hands, resurrection of the dead, and eternal judgment.[10]

In addressing themselves to the Gentiles, the Apostles were confronted by a manifold and deep-seated paganism. As is evident from St. Paul's speech on the Areopagus,[11] the gospel of the uncircumcision comprised among others the following points: the existence of one God, Creator of heaven and earth; necessity of rejecting idolatry in all its forms ;the need of repentance with a view to the future judgment by the glorious Christ.

A valuable witness of the immediate post-apostolic age is the Didache.[12] In the first part of this work we find the model of a catechesis addressed to the catechumens before the conferring of Baptism. It takes the form of a short moral instruction on the Two Ways. The way of life[13] consists of the observance of the twofold Gospel precept of love and of the golden rule; the way of death[14] consists in committing the various sins enumerated. Although the catechesis does not comprise anything explicitly dogmatic, it certainly presupposes a renunciation of paganism and an elementary acquaintance with the fundamental doctrines of Christianity.

The *Epistle of Barnabas*,[15] the first *Apology* of Justin Martyr, and the *Exhortation to the Heathen* of Clement of Alexandria also give us some idea of the moral and dogmatic doctrines taught the candidates before Baptism.

Documents thus far available[16] show that up to the middle of

[9] Acts 6–7.

[10] Heb. 5:12, 6:1–2, 11:6.

[11] Acts 17:22–31.

[12] Cf. F. Prat, *La théologie de Saint Paul* (Paris, 1923), II, 41; *Catholic Encyclopedia*, IV, 779.

[13] Chapters I–IV.

[14] Chapters V–VI.

[15] Chapters XVIII–XX.

[16] Cf. Gatterer-Krus-Culemans, *The Theory and Practice of the Catechism* (New York, 1924), pp. 24 ff.; G. Bareille, art. "Catechèse," in Vacant's *Dictionnaire de Théologie Catholique* (Paris, 1905), p. 1877; E. Mangenot, "Catéchisme," *ibid.*, p. 1896; G. Bareille, "Catéchumenat," *ibid.*, p. 1868; Ch. Hézard, *Histoire de Catéchisme* (Paris, 1900). The writer wishes to acknowledge his indebtedness to Ch. Hézard and to the *Dictionnaire* for his first acquaintance with many of the references to Patristic and medieval catechetics, Cf. also M. Gatterer, *Katechetik* (Innsbruck, 1931), pp. 17 ff.

the second century the catechumenate was not so elaborately organized as it was afterwards. In the second half of the second century, however, we find references in the various writings to the gradual development of the catechumenate. The preparation for Baptism is carried on in an orderly manner according to set rules. The prospective converts are obliged to follow a well-defined course of instruction and submit to certain ascetical and liturgical practices. As the candidates for Baptism increase in number, the Church becomes more exacting in regard to the worthiness of the applicants. Apostasies in times of persecution lead to a tightening of the rules of the catechumenate, and in time of peace these regulations are further perfected. The catechumenate reached its highest stage of perfection in the fourth and fifth centuries and declined rapidly afterwards. Today the ritual of Baptism is the only echo of that once flourishing organization in the early Church.

From the Beginning of the Third to the Fifth Century

During this period the catechumenate functioned as an organized institution. The candidates received a preliminary instruction and underwent a certain probation before being admitted into the catechumenate, for the Church desired as candidates only those who were determined to abide by the lofty moral principles of the new state. Although no manuscript containing a model of this preliminary catechesis has come down to us, the existence of such instruction and training cannot be doubted. Valuable information in this regard is found in the *Constitutiones Apostolicæ* [17] and in the treatises of SS. Ambrose, Gregory of Nyssa, and Augustine.

St. Ambrose [18] demands that the attitudes of the Church's missionaries towards the heathen be the same as that of St. Paul on the Areopagus towards the Greeks. The pagans must be instructed to believe in one God, Ruler of the universe and Supreme Good, to reject idolatry and to accept Christ as Saviour, who through His deeds and His own Resurrection declared Himself as truly God.

St. Gregory's catechesis [19] embodies directions for Christian catechists in their dealings with different adversaries, especially the pagans, Jews and heretics. The method which he outlines is rather

[17] Book VIII.
[18] *In Lucam,* VI, 104–105, in *P. L.*, XV, pp. 1096–1097.
[19] *Oratio Catechetica Magna,* in P. G., XLV, pp. 9 ff.

that of a controversialist or apologist—confronted with certain objections against Christian dogmas—than that of a catechist.

It is especially to St. Augustine [20] that we are indebted for our knowledge of the method and subject matter of the catechesis in question. He carefully describes the attitude to be adopted, the plan to be followed and the matter to be treated. He shows successively how to deal, first, with the unlettered man, secondly, with a man possessing some knowledge of Holy Scripture and Christian literature, and, thirdly, with a man cultivated from the literary viewpoint but ignorant in matters of faith. He adds two model lessons, one long and the other short, to be used according to the time which one has at his disposal. Each lesson consists of an exordium, narration and conclusion.

1. *The Catechumens.* If they concluded satisfactorily the preliminary training and if their request for Baptism was found to be prompted by worthy motives, the candidates were enrolled among the catechumens. Their separation from their former associates was symbolized and effected by various liturgical functions, such as breathing on them while reading an exorcism, marking their forehead with the sign of the cross, imposition of hands, giving of blessed salt and anointing with oil. These ceremonies, as we know, still exist in a condensed form in the baptismal ritual. The candidates were then admitted into the assembly of the faithful. Here in a place specially reserved for them they listened to Bible readings and became acquainted with the lofty moral principles of Christianity. These scriptural passages were then, for their further instruction, explained in homilies which today are incorporated into our Breviary lessons. When the homily was ended, the deacon requested those present to pray for the prospective converts. The bishop with extended hands prayed over them, and they were dismissed from the service.

The catechumenate did not extend over the same length of time in all places. Three years were required in the Orient; two, in Spain. In some cases it was prolonged indefinitely, somctimes by abuse even to the moment of death.

[20] *De catechizandis rudibus*, in *P. L.*, XL, pp. 307 ff. For the influence of St. Augustine's catechetical method on the subsequent history of catechetics, see Part II, Chap. 3, *infra*, and Joseph V. Tahon, *The First Instruction of Children and Beginners* (New York, 1930). Cf. also J. P. Christopher, *De catechizandis rudibus* (Washington, 1926).

2. *The Competents.* When the catechumens were found to be sufficiently prepared, they were invited by the bishop at the beginning of Lent to register their names as candidates for Baptism. Thereafter they were no longer known as "catechumens" but as "competents" (*petere bapitismum*).

They now entered upon the immediate preparation for Baptism. The subject matter of the catechesis continued to be the same as that of the former stage—namely, the faith and the life of the Christian.[21] But it was explained in a more detailed, explicit and analytical manner. The instruction was no longer given by a member of the lower clergy or by a lay teacher (*didaskolos*), but by the bishop himself or by his delegate. The nature, method and subject of these instructions are best indicated in the series of eighteen popular catecheses delivered in Jerusalem in 348 by St. Cyril in the name of Bishop Maximus.[22]

The Creed was now taught the prospective converts for the first time; this ceremony was called the "giving of the symbol" (*traditio Symboli*) and in Rome took place on the Wednesday after *Laetare* Sunday. A few days later took place the "giving of the Lord's Prayer" (*traditio Orationis Dominicae*). These prayers were memorized, recited publicly, and afterwards thoroughly explained. Both prayers constituted a part of the "discipline of the secret."

The competents were questioned at the "scrutinies," which took place at the public assembly of the faithful, and they were required to give a satisfactory account of what they had learned. At liturgical functions they submitted to exorcisms and imposition of hands. In this way their severance of all connection with sin and with the author of sin was symbolized and effected.

3. *The Neophytes.* The competents were solemnly baptized and confirmed early on Easter morning, and clothed with a white tunic which they wore until the following Sunday. Their catechetical training, however, was not yet at an end. They continued for eight more days under the direction of their masters, and only then were they definitely aggregated to the body of the Christian faithful. The five mystagogical sermons delivered by St. Cyril[23] at Jerusalem represent the particular kind of instruction received by the

[21] Cf. *Constitutiones Apostolicae*, VII, 39, in *P. G.*, I, p. 1040.
[22] *P. G.*, XXXIII, pp. 332 ff.
[23] *P. G.*, XXXIII, pp. 1065 ff.

neophytes in the East. In the West the same custom of addressing certain complementary instructions to the neophytes after their baptism prevailed. At Milan St. Ambrose deferred until after Easter the explanation of the mysteries, since the concrete accomplishment of these mysteries prepared the way for their verbal explanation.[24] In Africa, especially at Hippo, most of these instructions preceded the conferring of Baptism; the week after Easter was employed in imparting certain supplementary teaching concerning the Mass and Communion, and in exhorting the neophytes to persevere in the new Christian life.[25]

That the untiring efforts of priests and catechists in the early Church were abundantly blessed by God is evident from the splendid results obtained. Even the heathens admired the exemplary lives of the Christians, and martyrs by the hundreds sealed their faith with their blood.

From the End of the Fifth Century to the Ninth

1. *Decline of the Catechumenate.* Although the ancient organization still continued during this period in certain parts of Africa,[26] Spain [27] and Gaul,[28] the catechumenate began on the whole to decline rapidly. The period of time required for catechumenal training was greatly abbreviated. The Sacrament of Baptism came gradually to be administered on many other days besides those prescribed by the catechumenate. Baptism of infants came slowly into vogue. The Church – which was now very powerful in Italy, North Africa, Spain and Gaul – began to receive into her bosom the barbarian peoples of the northern countries. Entire tribes were often converted *en masse* and were baptized before they received sufficient instruction. Such baptized adults – and children as soon as they reached the age of reason – were obliged to follow a course of Christian instruction in order to become acquainted with the obligations which they assumed at Baptism. This instruction was given by the sponsors, parents or priests.

[24] *De Myst.*, I, 2, in *P. L.*, XVI, 389.

[25] St. Augustine, *Sermo cclx*, in *P. L.*, XXXVIII, 1202; *Sermo cccliii*, ibid., p. p. 1560.

[26] Cf. Fulgentius of Ruspe, *Sermo lxxviii*, in *P. L.*, LXV, 950.

[27] Cf. St. Isidore, *De Offic.*, II, 21, in *P. L.*, LXXXIII, 814.

[28] Cf. Gennadius, *De Eccles. Dog.*; LXXIV, in *P. L.*, LVII, 997.

This elementary Christian instruction replaced the catechesis of the catechumenate. Just as formerly the Creed and the Lord's Prayer were "given" to the catechumens, so now these same formulas were memorized in Latin or in the native tongue, and explained by the priest or catechist. In the Carolingian Empire the same program prevailed everywhere. The Council of Frankfurt [29] in 794 ruled that the Creed and the Lord's Prayer [30] must be known by all. The Council of Aix-la-Chapelle [31] declared in 836 that children must be thoroughly acquainted with the Creed and the Lord's Prayer. In the tenth century Ratherius, Bishop of Verona, ordered his priests to explain the Creed and the Lord's Prayer in their sermons to the people.[32] Besides this, the adults were also made acquainted with the Athanasian Creed, with the duties of their state and with the different categories of sins and vices.

2. *First Catechism.* In a work by Alcuin (735–804) we meet for the first time with an arrangement resembling our modern Catechism; it is a Latin explanation, in the form of questions and answers, of the Creed and the Lord's Prayer.[33]

3. *Missionary Catechesis.*[34] We can also conjecture with some plausibility what were the catechetical methods in the missionary countries of this epoch. Since they had to adapt themselves to the intellectual capacity of their listeners, the missionaries did not write down in Latin the sermons which they addressed to the pagans. Hence, none of these primitive missionary catecheses have come down to us. The summary references which are found in contemporary documents, and which enable us partially to reconstruct the catechetical methods of missionary regions, indicate that the missionary catechesis comprised many elements of the patristic and apostolic catechesis. For while the surroundings were different, the chief obstacle – namely, paganism and its superstitiions – always remained the same. Although occasionally the vanquished

[29] Mansi, XIII, 908.

[30] Cf. F. Prat, *La théologie de Saint Paul* (Paris, 1923), II, 40.

[31] Mansi, XIV, 681.

[32] *Synodica*, 12, in *P. L.*, CXXXVI, 563.

[33] *Disputatio puerorum per interrogationes et responsiones*, in *P. L.*, CI, 1097–1144. Some historians attribute the treatise to a contemporary of Alcuin.

[34] Cf. *"Patristic Catechetics,"* in *St. Bonaventure Seminary Year Book, Vol. XXII*, (St. Bonaventure Seminary, 1938); J. Thauren, *Die religiöse Unterweisung in den Heidenländern* (Vienna, 1935).

people were forcibly obliged to accept the Christian faith, ordinarily the missionaries used the common means of suasion and confirmed their teaching by their own example, by the sanctity of their lives and by their devotion to duty.

The missionary catechesis comprised, in the first place, a condemnation of idolatry and paganism in all its forms. St. Eligius[35] mentions a great number of these superstitions, and the *Concilum Liptinense*[36] enumerates as many as thirty. Then followed the teaching on the existence of one God, Creator of heaven and earth, the doctrine of the Incarnation, a brief summary of the religious history of the world and of the economy of the Redemption, an explanation of Baptism and of the renunciations and responsibilities which it entails, a list of sins to be avoided and duties to be fulfilled and, finally, an emphatic reference to the last things of man, especially, eternal punishment or reward.

The catechetical method of St. Augustine in England may be determined to some extent from the letter addressed to him by Pope Gregory the Great upon the conversion of King Ethelbert in 597.[37] Another catechetical program is indicated in a letter written by Boniface V in 624 to Edwin, the pagan king of Northumberland, encouraging him and his whole household to embrace the faith.[38] The question of human origin and destiny seems to have played an important role in the catechization of these Anglo-Saxons.[39] The discourses of St. Eligius seem to be an echo of the Two Ways of the Didache and of St. Augustine's *De catechizandis rudibus*.[40] The discourses of St. Gall on the shores of Lake Constance likewise seem to suggest the *narratio* of St. Augustine.[41] In fact, the whole history of catechetics seems to bear an impress of St. Augustine's catechetical method.[42] The papal letter which St. Boniface, after having been consecrated bishop at Rome by Gregory II, brought to the tribes of Germany[43] and the discourses of St. Lebwinus at

[35] *Vita S. Eligii*, II, in *P. L.*, LXXXVII, 524–550.

[36] *Indiculus superstitionum et paganiarum*, in *P. L.*, LXXXIX, pp. 810 ff.

[37] *Epist.*, lib. XI, epist. xxvii, in *P. L.*, LXXVII, 1139.

[38] *Epist.*, III, in *P. L.*, LXXX, 438.

[39] St. Bede, *Hist. Eccles.*, II, 13, in *P. L.*, XCV, 104.

[40] *Vita S. Eligii*, II, 7, in *P. L.*, LXXXVIII, 513; II, 15, *ibid.*, 524–550.

[41] *Serm.*, in *P. L.*, LXXXVII, 13–26.

[42] Cf. Joseph V. Tahon, *The First Instruction of Children and Beginners*, (New York, 1930).

[43] *Epist.*, VII, in *P. L.*, LXXXIX, 504–505.

Merklo[44] also reveal interesting aspects of missionary activity in this region.

The Middle Ages

As we have noted above, instruction of children in the elements of Christian doctrine gradually replaced the instruction of catechumens and of adults. Upon parents, first of all, rested the important duty of imparting to their offspring the rudiments of the Christian faith. Hence, the Church required that godparents and those about to marry have a sufficient acquaintance with them. Those more immediately charged with this duty, however, were the clergy. On Sundays and feast days all children seven years old were brought to church in order to be instructed in Christian doctrine and to learn the Creed, the Lord's Prayer and the Hail Mary. Again, in the numerous schools which began to flourish in Charlemagne's reign not only was religious instruction imparted but religion was placed at the very basis of the curriculum and the spirit of faith pervaded all the different branches. Finally, the lengthy instruction which formerly preceded Baptism was now replaced by an extensive preparation for Confession and Holy Communion. Confession books, confession mirrors, explanations of the Ten Commandments, treatises on the different kinds of sin, and preparations for Holy Communion became very numerous. These instructions were often written on tablets and placed in parish churches, schools and other public places.

Two new methods, both of which enjoyed no small success and exercised a considerable influence on subsequent catechetical training, were inaugurated in the twelfth century. The first is the so-called *Elucidarium* of Honorius of Autun.[45] It is divided into three parts, and comprises an explanation of the "Symbol of the Apostles," of moral and physical evil, and of the last things of man, especially of the state of the blessed and the damned. The text is arranged in the form of questions and answers. The second method, the *Septenarium*, originated with Hugh of St. Victor.[46] It explains a doctrine under seven heads and then compares or contrasts these

[44] *Vita S. Lebwini*, XII, in *P. L.*, CXXXII, 890.
[45] *P. L.*, CLXXII, 1109–1176.
[46] *De quinque septenis seu septenariis opusculum*, in *P. L.*, CLXXV, 405–414.

with the seven points of another doctrine. Thus, the seven petitions of the Lord's Prayer are correlated with the seven beatitudes or the seven gifts of the Holy Spirit. The seven capital sins are contrasted with the seven principal virtues or the seven works of mercy. Borrowed undoubtedly from St. Augustine,[47] the *Septenarium* enjoyed a considerable vogue and its influence is felt in almost every catechetical work of the Middle Ages.[48] A Council held at Lambeth in 1281 ordered priests to explain to the faithful, among other things, the seven works of mercy, the seven principal virtues, the seven Sacraments, etc.[49] Among the poems inspired by the *Septenarium*, the *Floretus* is especially deserving of mention. It explains in verse the principal dogmas and virtues.[50]

For those to whom the written word was unintelligible, a means of instruction was provided in the stained glass windows, statues, carvings in wood, and pictures which adorned the churches and represented biblical scenes or the lives and deeds of saints.[51]

Then, again, there were the so-called "Bibles of the Poor." The appeal of the concrete to both the young and old induced some of the medieval artists to represent by means of pictures the principal events of the Bible. The invention of these picture books, which were eventually designated as *Biblia Pauperum*, is commonly attributed to St. Ansgar, Bishop of Bremen. These books represented scenes from Our Lord's life together with the corresponding prophetic types. The series usually consisted of forty or fifty pages. The page was divided into nine sections. The four corners were used for explanatory texts. The central scenes represented in chronological order events from Our Lord's life. Above and below were pictures of prophets, and on each side were scenes from the Old Testament. It was, therefore, a correlation of the Old and New Testaments based on the teaching of the Scriptures, the Liturgy, and the Fathers.[52] It is uncertain why these books were called

[47] *De Sermone Domini in Monte*, in *P. L.*, XXXIV, 1285–1286.

[48] Cf. for example, John of Salisbury, *De septem septenis* (*P. L.*, CXIX, 943–964), and Hugh of Amiens, *Super fide catholica et oratione dominica* (*P. L.*, CXCII, 1334, 1345–1346).

[49] Mansi, XXIV, 410–413.

[50] Cf. "Patristic Catechetics," in *St. Bonaventure Seminary Year Book, Vol. XXII* (St. Bonaventure's Seminary, 1938), pp. 62 ff.

[51] Cf. J. L. Huysmans, *The Cathedral* (London, 1898), chap. V.

[52] Cf. John 5:39; Luke 24:24–27, 44–45; Col. 2:16–17; Eusebius, *Demonstratio Evangelica*, Lib. IV; St. Thomas *Summa Theologica*, II–II, Q. ii, art. 7.

"Bibles of the Poor." Some think that the title originated from the ancient saying that pictures were the Bibles of the poor and uneducated. Others are of the opinion that the name came from their use by the mendicant orders as books of instruction. Others suppose that the term means "inexpensive;" manuscripts at that time were beyond the means of most people. Whatever be the case, it is certain that the "Bibles of the Poor" exercised a great influence in spreading the faith, affording themes for both preachers and artists. It was only when it became possible to issue the whole Bible with illustrations that the "Bibles of the Poor" fell into disuse.[53]

As a further development of the former, we find the "Catechisms in Pictures,"[54] presenting their teaching in so realistic and concrete a manner as to appeal to even the most unlettered. Other concrete means of instruction were the cribs set up in the churches at Christmas, the holy sepulchres at Easter, and the Stations of the Cross. Finally, recourse was had to mystery and miracle plays and to living religious tableaux corresponding to the liturgical season of the year.

Several writers of this period made important contributions to the catechetical science. Rabanus Maurus (d. 856), a disciple of Alcuin, embodied in his *De Disciplina Ecclesiastica* a long instruction for catechists which follows very closely the catechetical method of St. Augustine. St. Edmund of Canterbury (d. 1224) left us charming treatises on prayer, the seven deadly sins ,the Decalogue and the Sacraments. St. Thomas Aquinas (d. 1274)[55] prepared short commentaries on the Creed, the Sacraments, the Lord's Prayer, the "Hail Mary" and the Commandments. The outstanding characteristic of these writings is what catechists term "immanent recapitulation" – the intimate correlation of one doctrine with another.

Jean Charlier Gerson (d. 1429) occupies a special place among the catechists of this period. Being the oldest of several children in the family, he assumed the task of guiding spiritually his brothers

[53] Several facsimile reproductions have appeared with historical and bibliographical introductions, notably by Berjeau (1859), Camesina and Heider (Vienna, 1863), Unwin (London, 1884), Einsle (Vienna, 1890), P. Heitz (1902), and Leib and Schwarz (1892).

[54] Cf. *Catechism in Pictures* (La Bonne Presse, Paris).

[55] These commentaries have been published in English translations by Rev. Joseph Collins (St. Anthonys Guild, Paterson, N. J.).

and sisters. He also composed practical religious treatises for the instruction of the common people. When in 1395 he became chancellor of the University of Paris, he doubled his zeal for the religious instruction of the people and of the children. He provided for a more thorough instruction of those who later were to be leaders and teachers of the people, ordered that simple religious booklets be prepared for those who rarely heard a sermon, drew up a program of instruction for the children of Paris and strongly recommended the use of children's handbooks of religion which would explain to them the chief teachings of the Faith. His *Opus Tripertitum de praeceptis decalogi, de confessione et de arte moriendi*,[56] which he published for the French pastors, became very popular among the French bishops. When some contended that a man of his position should not be wasting his time with catechization, Gerson composed a small treatise, entitled *De Parvulis ad Christum trahendis*,[57] in which he justifies his conduct. In this work Gerson advocates the early religious training of children, dwells on the evil results of scandal, speaks of bringing children to Christ through confession and praises the high dignity of the catechist's office.

On the eve of the so-called Reformation we find a serious neglect of catechization and catechetical activities. Indifference in matters of belief and looseness in morals, which characterized the close of the medieval period, were inevitably reflected in the ministry of catechization. Respect for the bishops was being undermined. Priests and catechists were despised. Parents became oblivious of their sacred duties towards children. Religious instruction lost its attractive and historical form and became abstract and argumentative. God, however, who providentially guides His Church through all crises and trials, raised up holy men who would devote themselves to a renewal of the pristine catechetical spirit.

From the Sixteenth to the Nineteenth Century[58]

Although with the rise of Lutheranism and with the invention of printing the Catechism came to be known by the name it has pre-

[56] *Joannis Gersonii Opera Omnia* (Paris, 1728), I, 425–450.

[57] *Ibid.*, III, 277–291.

[58] Cf. A. Hézard, *Histoire du Catéchisme* (Paris, 1900); J. Tahon, *op. cit.*, pp. 105 ff.

served to this day, it cannot be said that Luther originated the Catechism in its form and contents. In the first place, we have already mentioned several works which, though they do not bear the title of "Catechism," were nevertheless "Catechisms" in content. The treatise attributed to Alcuin, the *Elucidarium* of Honorius, and the *Breve compendium* of the Council of Tortosa (1492) all preceded Luther.

At Luther's request, many of his immediate followers prepared manuals for the catechization of children, and their compositions are reproduced in the *Monumenta Germaniae paedagogica.* In composing his Catechism, Luther was influenced by a practice which had existed in the Church for many centuries. There is only this difference; whereas formerly the word "Catechism" was applied to all catechetical instruction imparted either orally or with the help of a book or in conjunction with the various liturgical ceremonies which preceded the reception of Baptism, since Luther's time the word has been used to designate a book explaining the principal Christian doctrines in the form of questions and answers.

The Catechism now became the common property of both Catholics and Protestants, and editions of the book literally poured from the press. As it is impossible to give a complete list of all the Catechisms printed,[59] we shall mention only a few of the most important. In 1563 Calvin composed a Catechism in French [60] and carefully embodied in it the chief points of his heresy. In England the first *Book of Common Prayer* (1549) contained a Catechism, with a brief explanation of the Commandments and the Lord's Prayer. In 1647 the Westminster Assembly of Divines drew up the Presbyterian "Larger" and "Smaller" Catechisms.

The restoration of the Church's catechetical work after the Reformation is due at once to several causes. In the first place, the zealous endeavor to instruct the children and the laity was due to the inner workings of the Holy Spirit, who never abandons the Church. It was due also to the religious reforms inaugurated a century before this. It received a further impetus from the very

[59] Cf. E. Mangenot, "Catéchisme," in *Dictionnaire de theologie catholique,* pp. 1895 ff.

[60] *Le Formulaire d'inistruire les enfans en la chrestiente, fait en maniere de dialogue ou le ministre interroge et l'enfant repond.*

excesses of the Reformation as well as from the efforts of holy and learned men and especially from the Council of Trent. The latter, in its Fifth and again in the Twenty-fourth Session, emphatically reminded the pastors of the flock to provide catechetical training for both young and old. Bishops were urgently requested to carry out these regulations and were given extensive faculties for this purpose. The frequent holding of synods, which concerned themselves with the education of youth, the foundation of new religious orders whose primary object was the training of children, and the establishment of the Confraternity of Christian Doctrine soon resulted in a renewal of the Christian spirit among the people.

Among Catholic writers of Catechisms of this period, St. Peter Canisius (d. 1597) undoubtedly occupies the place of honor.[61] His large Catechism was published in 1555 and bore the title of *Summa doctrinae christianae per quaestiones tradita.* In 1556 appeared his small Catechism "adapted to the understanding of the unlettered" (*ad captum rudiorum accommodata*). A third and medium-sized Catechism appeared in 1559 and was entitled *Parvus catechismus catholicorum.* The Canisian Catechisms are divided into the following sections: faith, hope, prayer, charity and the Commandments of God and of the Church, the Sacraments and Christian justice. Canisius explained, in a quiet and dispassionate manner, especially those doctrines which were being attacked by the heretics. His biographers tell us that he was careful to avoid all mechanical memorizing on the part of the children and that he strove to adapt his teaching to their capacity. He relied more on prayer than on threats and punishments, devoted special individual care to the weakest and poorest among the little ones and, like Gerson, advocated the frequent reception of the Sacraments by children.[62]

What St. Peter Canisius accomplished for Germany and Northern Europe, St. Robert Cardinal Bellarmine[63] did for Italy. In 1598, by order of Pope Clement VIII, St. Robert composed a short manual of Christian Doctrine to be learned by heart, entitled *Dottrina cristiana breve da imparasi a mente.* The work is arranged

[61] Cf. Otto Braunsberger, *Beati Petri Canisii Epistulae et Acta*, 8 vols. (Freiburg im B., 1896–1923); J. Tahon, op. cit., pp. 80 ff.

[62] Cf. *Catholic Encyclopedia*, XI, pp. 756 ff.

[63] Cf. James Brodrick, *The Life and Work of Blessed Robert Francis Cardinal Bellarmine*, 2 vols. (New York, 1928).

in the form of questions and answers, but its long sentences are a considerable disadvantage. For the use of catechists he published a *More Thorough Explanation of Christian Doctrine* (*Dichiarazione più copiosa della dottrina cristiana*). The books of St. Robert were not only used extensively in the city of Rome but were adapted in any other dioceses. At the Vatican Council (1870) Pius IX expressed the wish that Bellarmine's Catechism might be adopted as the uniform and official Catechism in the whole Church.

A large share in the revival of catechetical zeal must be ascribed to the *Catechismus Romanus*.[64] The Council of Trent (1545–1563) resolved to publish this Catechism, but it was not brought out until the year 1566 by St. Pius V under the title of *Catechismus ex decreto Concilii Tridentini ad parochos Pii V jussu editus Romae 1566*. St. Charles Borromeo was most prominently connected with the composition and publication of the book. The work explains in four parts the Apostle's Creed, the Sacraments, the Ten Commandments and the Lord's Prayer. It was not intended as a manual for children but was designed as a help to pastors and to those engaged in the teaching of the Catechism. It systematized and unified Christian Doctrine and dealt a staggering blow to Protestant pretensions.

Several writers of Catechisms of the seventeenth and eighteenth centuries are here deserving of mention. In 1686 Jacques Bossuet published a Catechism for his Diocese of Meaux and wrote several instructions concerning its contents, object and use.[65] His Catechism has the usual divisions. Realizing full well that intellectual activity is based on sense activity, Bossuet prefixed a historical narrative to each lesson. Worthy of note, too, is his *Catechism of Feasts* (*Catéchisme des Fêtes*).[66] This Catechism is also written in the form of questions and answers. It treats of the institution of the Sunday, the feasts of Our Lord and of the observances of the Church which have relation with the mysteries of Jesus Christ, and the feasts of the Blessed Virgin and of the Saints. The continuity of the liturgical year is unduly broken by the arrangement of the lessons. The explanations abound in allegories and in uninteresting

[64] Cf. McHugh-Callan, *Catechism of the Council of Trent for Parish Priests* (New York); J. Donovan, *Catechism of the Council of Trent* (Dublin, 1867).

[65] Cf. *Œuvres de Bossuet* (ed. F. Lachat, 1885), V.

[66] *Ibid.*, pp. 142–205.

references to local conditions. However, the work has many fine points, the chief of these being the idea of such a Catechism itself.

In Ireland the two famous and outstanding names are those of Dr. Reilly, Archbishop of Armagh (d. 1758), and Dr. James Butler, Archbishop of Cashel (d. 1791). Dr. Reilly's Catechism was used extensively up to the introduction of the so-called Maynooth Catechism. In regard to Dr. Butler's Catechism, which had become very popular in many Irish dioceses, it is interesting to note that, when the question of a uniform Catechism came before the Third Plenary Council of Baltimore, many of the bishops were in favor of a revised edition of Butler's Catechism.

Catechisms that have come into existence since the sixteenth century have the following points in common: (1) Christian Doctrine is not given in the form of a narration but in questions and answers. The new Augsburg Catechism, Fleury's Catechism,[67] and York's textbooks of religion offer a happy combination of the two methods. (2) All Catechisms, even the oldest ones, are built up around the four formulas constituting an outline of Christian Doctrine – the Creed, the Sacraments, the Commandments, and the Lord's Prayer. (3) Diocesan Catechisms are frequently published in two or three editions – small, medium and large. They are concentric; the second contains the questions of the first, and the third the questions of the two preceding ones. Questions of minor importance, which may be reserved for older and abler students, are marked with an asterisk.

Several writers of this period, although they did not compose Catechisms, nevertheless made important contributions to the catechetical science. St. Francis Xavier,[68] the great missionary to the Orient, has a right to be classed among the most zealous of catechists. Emulating the zeal of the Apostle of the Gentiles, he was untiring in his efforts to present the beauties of the Christian religion to new peoples. Like St. Paul, too, he made himself all things to all men. He mingled freely with sailors, soldiers, gamesters and the worst of sinners in order to win them for Christ. He would go through the streets of Goa ringing a little bell and calling children to the religion class. He would march before them, singing

[67] *Catechisme historique contenant en abrégé l'Histoire sainte et la Doctrine Chrétienne* (Lyons, 1747).

[68] Cf. *Œuvres de saint François de Sales* (Annecy, 1892).

aloud the Catechism and teaching them. His catechization was characterized by the greatest charity for those whom he instructed. He tried to make the memory work as attractive as possible by first explaining the truths in easily understandable and concrete terms. His instruction was accompanied by the singing of sacred hymns and by frequent acts of faith in the mysteries that were being expounded. As soon as he had taught the pagans a Christian truth or precept, he at once asked them to pray for grace so that they might be able to apply the doctrine in their daily lives.

The merits of St. Charles Borromeo, Archbishop of Milan (d. 1584), have already been mentioned when we spoke of the *Roman Catechism.* He convoked no less than six provincial councils which dealt with the management of Catholic schools and with the duties of catechists and religious teachers. He encouraged and aided the founder and leaders of the Confraternity of Christian Doctrine and sought to establish this instructional agency throughout his whole archdiocese.

St. Francis de Sales, Prince-Bishop of Geneva (d. 1622), who was also a zealous supporter of the Confraternity of Christian Doctrine, wrote a treatise on catechizing for the use of his priests and himself frequently went through the streets with a bell calling the children to religious instruction.[69]

No one contributed so effectively to the revival and spread of catechization in France as Jean Jacques Olier (d. 1657), the disciple and friend of St. Vincent de Paul. The large parish of St. Sulpice in Paris, of which he took possession in 1642, was at that time a very sink of immorality. But by means of Catechism classes, which he established throughout the parish and confided to the care of ecclesiastics from the seminary, the Babylon was soon converted into a flourishing religious center. The principal exercises of the method – the very foundation of the Catechism classes – are the recitation of the letter of the Catechism, the instruction, the reading of the Gospel, and the homily. Besides these, there are certain secondary exercises, namely, admonitions, singing of hymns, and prayers. Various rewards and attractions supply the condiment of the class, and maintain a spirit of emulation among the children.[70]

[69] Cf. *Œuvres de saint François de Sales* (Annecy, 1892).

Francis Fénelon, Archbishop of Cambrai (d. 1715), published several writings on Christian education.[71] His most important work, from our viewpoint, is his treatise on the *Education of Girls*, in which he lays down the principles to be followed in teaching Christian Doctrine to children. He demands that the whole process of education be made as pleasant and agreeable for the children as possible; that the instructor make generous use of sense-objects in order to appeal to the child's curiosity and imagination; that the children be given good example and protected against scandal; and that praise and rewards be given with discretion.[72] In the same treatise he also lays down special principles for the teaching of Bible History and of the Catechism.

The Abbé Claude Fleury (c. 1640), whose life and work is treated in Part II, Chap. 5, below, was a friend of Bossuet and Fénelon. Made preceptor of the Princes of Conti, whom Louis XIV wished to be educated with the Dauphin, Fleury began to take an active interest in pedagogy, and in 1686 composed his well-known *Catéchisme historique*. In this treatise he examines the various causes of religious ignorance among the people, advocates the Biblical-historical method of St. Augustine as the best means of instructing children and adults and lays down important rules to be observed by the catechist.

The sixteenth, seventeenth and the first half of the eighteenth century saw again the upward trend of catechization. The Catechism was taught thoroughly and perseveringly and became the household book in Catholic families. Catechisms were revised, improved and kept up-to-date. Especially was this the case with the Canisian Catechisms, which always remained models of their kind.

At the end of the eighteenth and at the beginning of the nineteenth century, however, a decline set in. Rationalism began to pervade a large portion of pedagogical and catechetical literature. The exponents of this philosophical system maintained that we should accept only those truths – whether revealed or not – which

[70] For an exposition of the method of St. Sulpice, see Part II, Chap. 6, *infra*; the well-known translation from the French, *Method of St. Sulpice* (London, 1896); Bishop Dupanloup, *The Ministry of Catechising* (New York); J. Bricount, *L'Enseignement du Catéchisme en France* (Paris, 1922); P. Boumard, *Formation de l'enfant par le Catéchisme* (Paris, 1927).

[71] Cf. *Œuvres de Fénelon* (Paris, 1843).

[72] *Ibid.*, II, pp. 475 ff.

man can grasp by his reason alone. This rationalism was the logical outcome of Luther's principle of private judgment and of his denial of all external authority in religion. If Scripture is interpreted by one's private judgment, man will gradually reject those truths which he cannot fully grasp or which are at variance with his private conduct. This will be all the more the case if there is no infallible authority which would guide him annd which he must obey. Furthermore, Luther minimized the intellectual and exaggerated the affective elements in faith. This view resulted necessarily in an obscuring and neglect of the intellectual and immutable character of dogma. Hence, many Catechisms of this period no longer carried the long-established and traditional division of the subject matter. In fact, it is hard to estimate what would have been the leakage in the Church, had not the Faith been kept alive by liturgical worship and by the liturgical year.

Modern Times

In the nineteenth century we find a new flowering of catechetical endeavor, which combines at once a Catholic spirit and correct pedagogical principles. The general revival of interest in catechization is to be attributed to the following factors: the urgent appeals of the popes, the decrees of provincial councils, the zeal of the priesthood ,and the activity of numerous religious bodies of men and women devoted exclusively to the work of Catholic education.

Catechization now becomes the subject of a distinct and separate theological science called catechetics. Catechetical periodicals and manuals multiply rapidly in various countries. The method of instruction is no longer the Socratic or heuristic method of the previous period – a method which takes for granted that the truths of religion have already been implanted in the child's reason and need only to be called forth to consciousness by progressive questioning – but the authoritative statement of revealed truths and the assertive exposition by an authorized teacher of the Church. Bible history, the history of divine revelation, is again given its due and proper place. The history, liturgy and organization of the Church are frequently brought before the child's mind. More value is attached to thorough understanding than to mere memorizing, and the will is not neglected in the interests of mere reason.

The center of this catechetical renaissance of the nineteenth century is to be found in the German-speaking countries. We cannot do more than indicate here some of the German writers who came to exercise a lasting influence on the catechetical science:

1. Augustin Gruber (d. 1835),[73] Archbishop of Salzburg, was instrumental in reviving and bringing into prominence the biblical and historical method of St. Augustine.

2. Joseph Deharbe (d. 1871) composed at the request of the Bavarian bishops a Catechism which has obtained wide circulation, not only in Germany but also in England and America. Deharbe's Catechism follows the traditional division and is written in a pleasant style. But it contains too many questions, definitions and abstract theological formulas unintelligible to the child.[74]

3. John Schuster is the author of a Bible History, which in its present revised form is used in Catholic schools of almost every country.[75]

4. Frederic Knecht is considered as a very high authority on both catechetics and Bible History.[76]

5. Early in the twentieth century, a strong movement to improve Catechisms and catechetical instruction was set on foot by the Society of Catechists of Munich and Vienna. Dissatisfied with the superficial procedure on the part of many catechists, with the difficult and abstract language of many Catechisms and with the wrong order of presentation, these men struck out in a relatively new direction. Their method is known as the "Stieglitz Method" (from its chief exponent) or as the "Munich Method," because it originated among the members of the Society of Catechists in Munich. The views of this group are expounded in the *Katechetische Blätter* of Munich and in the *Christlich-pädagogische Blätter* of

[73] Cf. Johann Eising, *Die katechetische Methode vergangener Zeiten in zeitgemässer Ausgestaltung* (Vienna, 1905).

[74] Cf. T. N. Busch, *Der Weg des deutschen katholischen Katechismus von Deharbe bis zum Einheitskatechismus* (Freiburg, 1936). Adaptations of Deharbe have been published by: Fander-Porter, *Catechism of the Catholic Religion* (London, 1883); G. Groenings and G. Rockliff. *A Catholic Catechism for the Parochial and Sunday Schools of the United States* (New York, 1921); J. Linden, *Catechism of the Catholic Religion* (St. Louis, 1934).

[75] Cf. Schuster-Holzammer, *Handbuch zur Biblischen Geschichte* (8th ed.; Freiburg im B., 1925).

[76] Cf. Knecht-Glancey, *A Practical Commentary on Holy Scripture* (London, 1910).

Vienna. The Munich Method emphasizes the following stages in the teaching process: preparation, aim, presentation, explanation, synthesis, application.

In France the outstanding catechist of this period is the famous bishop of Orléans, Bishop Dupanloup (d. 1878). This prelate made a lasting contribution to the science of catechetics by his masterly treatise entitled *The Ministry of Catechizing.*[77] This work is a fuller development of another well-known book which we mentioned before, *The Method of St. Sulpice,* published in Paris in 1832 [78] – a book explaining the system of Catechism classes carried out in the parish of St. Sulpice. The exponents of the Sulpician Method have adopted the following division of the Catechism, based on the difference in age, circumstances and needs of the children: (1) the Little Catechism, intended for children from six or seven to ten years of age; (2) First Communion Catechism, for children above the age of ten; and (3) the Week Day Catechism for children about to receive first solemn Communion. Needless to say, if used today the method would have to be revised in the light of the decrees of St. Pius X on early and frequent Communion.

A work of Catholic education of the young which has passed beyond the Italian borders is that of St. John Bosco (d. 1888),[79] and of the Salesian Congregation founded by him. The instructional method of Don Bosco aims at winning the confidence of the child by the loving kindness of the teacher and substitutes encouragement of the child for severe and humiliating punishments. It strives to make the instruction pleasant and attractive and relies much on grace and prayer. Don Bosco strove to convert a purely scholastic environment into a family environment where the child would receive the same care, affection and assistance as in Christian homes. He lived on intimate terms with the children in order to win them for Christ. Don Bosco was the exponent of the preventive as opposed to repressive system in education and of graded sodality unions for boys.

In the United States, the Rev. P. C. Yorke, a writer of the Pacific coast, published in 1898 his *Textbooks of Religion for Parochial*

[77] English translation (New York, 1868).
[78] English translation (London, 1896).
[79] Cf. J. B. Lemoyne, *The Venerable Don Bosco* (New York, 1927).

and Sunday Schools.[80] The aim of the author was to produce a graded course in Christian Doctrine corresponding to the age and capacity of children in the different grades. The foundation of Fr. Yorke's manuals is the Baltimore Catechism. The author selected carefully for each grade such questions and answers as would be suited to the capacity of the child. Sometimes the wording of the Catechism is changed in the earlier grades, but in general the substance and its presentation are retained. Each lesson consists of a connected narrative, Catechism questions and answers corresponding with the preceding part, and a hymn. Beautiful illustrations, which exemplify in a concrete manner the abstract truth of the lesson, are distributed throughout each booklet. These illustrations as well as the readings are drawn almost exclusively from Bible History, and hence the Yorke textbooks exemplify in an admirable manner the principle of correlation of the Catechism with Bible History. The child approaches the Catechism text, which is to be carefully memorized, through story, picture and poem. The Yorke textbooks were made obligatory in the Archdiocese of San Francisco in 1922 and are also used in the Archdiocese of Los Angeles and in the Diocese of Sacramento. The objectionable features of Fr. Yorke's system seem to be the following: introduction of the Catechism already into the first grade, a constant and monotonous repetition of the same matter in the various grades, an excessive emphasis on memorizing and a failure to develop the method beyond the sixth grade.

Another American educator and catechist of exceptional merit is Rev. Thomas Edward Shields (1862–1921).[81] His catechetical method and his texts grew out of a reaction against three abuses and erroneous conceptions of his day: (1) teaching religion by a slavish memorizing of the abstract theological formulas of the

[80] Revised editions, San Francisco, 1927–1928. Cf. also P. C. Yorke, *The Teaching of Religion* (San Francisco, 1918), a pamphlet. The booklet on the Mass was published in San Francisco in 1922 (Textbook Publishing Co.).

[81] His principal works are the following: *The Education of Our Girls* (New York, 1907); *The Dullard* (Washington, 1909); *Teachers' Manual of Primary Methods*, 2nd ed.; Washington, 1912); *Philosophy of Education* (Washington, 1917; also articles and notes on education in *The Catholic University Bulletin* (1907–1910), *The Catholic Educational Review* (1911–1921), and an article in the *The Catholic Educational Association Bulletin* (1908).

Catechism, which turn out to be non-functional memory loads impeding rather than promoting mental development, (2) the view that a Catholic school is in every respect the same as a public school except for the daily half-hour's instruction in religion, (3) the tendency to create Catholic readers by merely inserting a few pious pictures into secular readers.[82] Against these false methods Shields enunciated his well-known principle of correlation, which demands that after the analogy of organic life each new thought element be related to the previous content of the mind, not merely along structural lines, but in relation of reciprocal activity.[83]

Fr. Shields applied this principle in all his texts. He determined to write readers in which the religious element would be the "central, coördinating, and dominating element of the work of the child's first years in school. It must grow out of the book and be the very heart of it." [84] He demanded that the child use only one textbook in the first and second grades, because unity of all knowledge is the child's most urgent need in this period of development. All the vascular bundles of a tree, he says, run for a time in a single trunk before they diverge into separate branches. In the *First* and *Second Books* the Religious Lesson is introduced by means of a "Nature Study" and a "Home Scene." The central theme of each chapter is expressed in two songs and told with additional fullness by the series of pictures which illustrate the text. The Redemption is the theme of the *Third Book of Religion*; the Christian foundations of society, of the *Third Reader*; the Mass, of the *Fourth Book of Religion*; Church History, of the *Fourth Reader*.

Fr. Shields' method had a triple source. It was based, first, on meditations on childhood experience. Fr. Shields had been one of those children whom mistaken methods and the misunderstanding of parents and teachers had made a victim and dullard.[85] His teaching method reflects his own bitter life story and attempts to avoid the causes which kept him a failure. The second source of his method was his scientific study of biology. He devoted his postgraduate studies at Johns Hopkins University principally to this science. His educational outlook and philosophy are profoundly influenced by biology. Lastly, Fr. Shields as well as his intimate co-

[82] Cf. *Primary Methods*, 84–85.
[83] *Ibid.*, 95–96.
[84] *Catholic University Bulletin*, XVI (1910), 153–154.
[85] Cf. *The Dullard* (Washington, 1909).

laborer, Dr. Pace, looked to Christ as the model teacher and derived their inspiration from Christ's parables.

Fr. Shields rendered a genuine service to catechetics. He issued a just protest against the mechanical and phonograph-like memorizing of the Catechism. He pointed out that there is one brain and one mind in the child and that the laws governing the operations of the mind are fundamentally the same, whatever be the content of knowledge. He insisted that abstract religious truths be presented through attractive and concrete presentations which touch the child's imagination and arouse his enthusiasm. His technique also employs fully the various forms of self-activity.

Dr. Shields, however, had little experience as a teacher in the primary school. His religious books are found to be above the intellectual capacity of the children for whom they were intended. Besides, they cannot be fully utilized except by a teacher trained in the Shields Method. But the *Teachers' Manual of Primary Methods,* which contains the principles and details of the method, is not easily intelligible to the ordinary teacher. Hence, the Shields Method was never used extensively.

Catechetical activity in America, England and Ireland has often been characterized by an effort at securing a uniform Catechism. In the United States the few missionaries who in the early days labored in this vast country were so overburdened with work that composition of original Catechisms was out of the question. They had to be satisfied with compilations or reprints of European Catechisms. Local Catechisms which appeared occasionally were often suppressed because of their defective and inexact language. The question of a uniform textbook of Christian Doctrine was considered by the bishops not only at the First Provincial Council (1829) but also at the First (1852) and Second (1866) Plenary Councils of Baltimore. In the Third Plenary Council (1884) many bishops were in favor of a revised edition of Butler's Catechism.

The matter was finally entrusted to a committee of six bishops, and in 1885 was issued the *Catechism of Christian Doctrine, Prepared and Enjoined by Order of the Third Council of Baltimore.*[86]

[86] Cf. P. Guilday, *A History of the Councils of Baltimore* (New York, 1932), pp. 94, 176, 179, 239, 240; J. A. Burns, *The Catholic School System in the United States* (New York, 1908), p. 250; *Growth and Development of the Catholic School System in the U. S.* (New York, 1912), 125, 127–129, 137–138, 182–184, 189.

Soon various editions with new word-meanings, explanatory notes and even with different arrangements, made their appearance, so that there is now a good deal of diversity in the books that go by the name of the Baltimore Catechism. Among the popular modern English texts of the Baltimore Catechism are those by the following: Thomas L. Kinkead (1901), G. T. O'Brien (1912), John J. McVey (1913), M. V. Kelly (1924), E. M. Deck (1929), J. A. Newman (1931), and Ellamay Horan (1936).

In England the Second Provincial Council of Westminster under Cardinal Wiseman (1855) appointed a committee of four bishops and fifteen theologians to consider the question of a Catechism text. Their work, *The English Catechism*, was finished only after the Council had adjourned and was made obligatory for all dioceses of England by the following Provincial Council in 1859. In Ireland the subject of a uniform Catechism was discussed at the Plenary Council of Maynooth in 1875, and the book known as the Maynooth Catechism was published several years later. In 1892 Archbishop Walsh of Dublin appointed a committee to prepare a uniform Catechism for his archdiocese. But "on learning of the intention of Pope Pius X to issue a Catechism for general use throughout the Church, Dr. Walsh abandoned the idea of publishing the Catechism on which he and his committee had spent so much time." [87]

The Plenary Council held at Sydney in 1885 also decreed that a uniform Catechism should be used throughout Australia. At first it proposed to adopt the Maynnoth Catechism, but the fathers preferred that a new Catechism be written.

The need of a uniform Catechism for the whole Catholic world has often been discussed. Expressions from different quarters as to its desirability, advantages and need finally crystallized in the Vatican Council when a *Schema constitutionis de parvo catechismo* was presented to the fathers. It was proposed to prepare a new manual, which should be adopted uniformly throughout the whole of Christendom. The proposition was thoroughly discussed, and fullest liberty was granted for the expression of different opinions. Several of the fathers, including Bishop Dupanloup of Orléans, opposed the project. They pointed out that differences of educa-

[87] P. J. Walsh, *William J. Walsh, Archbishop of Dublin* (Dublin, 1928), p. 386.

tional standards, differences in nationalities and differences in the natural abilities of children stood opposed to such an undertaking. A single Catechism text leaves out of consideration the divergences in the age and capacity of children. Besides, a Catechism must change with the needs of time and place. It was also pointed out that the freedom of bishops throughout the world to draw up a Catechism in accordance with the needs of their diocese would be seriously curtailed. On the other hand, many serious reasons were urged in favor of such a uniform Catechism. It would be a safeguard against error, which easily creeps into a diocesan Catechism. It would secure unity of doctrine throughout the world. The much-desired uniformity of teaching, which is so necessary in our day when parents and children frequently change their abode, would also be attained. Besides, the Catechism would gain in authority in the eyes of the faithful if it were proposed to them by the supreme authority in the Church.

When it was finally decided to proceed with the project, the Council came to an abrupt adjournment. The subject of a uniform Catechism seemed apparently forgotten until Pope St. Pius X revived it in 1905 by imposing a uniform Catechism for Rome and for the Roman Province.

The need of a universal Catechism has been reiterated in our own day by Pietro Cardinal Gasparri in the following words of the introduction to his *Catholic Catechism*: "All who are occupied in spreading Christian Doctrine must echo the wish expressed both by the Council of Trent and by that of the Vatican that a Catechism should be published for use in the Universal Church with the view that 'as there is one Lord and one Faith, so too there should be some one general rule and method employed in teaching the faithful the duties of the Christian religion.' The need of some such uniform Catechism has become all the greater since people now move from one place to another so freely." [88] With this end in view the cardinal, with the help of Roman authorities and Roman theologians, published his *Catholic Catechism*. The Catechism is

[88] English edition (New York, 1932), p. xi. The Catechism has been revised for schoolroom use in the three-volume series, *Catholic Faith*, by Felix M. Kirsch and Sr. Mary Brendan (New York, 1932–). The question of the Universal Catechism at the Vatican Council is discussed by F. Kosak, *Dejiny české Katechetiky* (Olomuc, 1922), pp. 12 ff.

graded: the first part is intended for little children; the second, for children who have made their First Communion; and the third, for adults. For completeness and theological accuracy, the Catechism has taken its place among the best Catechisms of history.

Catechetics Today

No occasion perhaps showed so clearly the present status of catechetics as the International Catechetical Congress held at the city hall of the capital of the Duchy of Luxemburg in July, 1935. Before a large group of delegates from about thirty different nations, speakers from as many countries explained the methods of catechization in their native land.[89] While the congress dealt primarily with secondary schools, it frequently touched upon the primary schools also. Whatever might have been lacking in the latter regard was more than compensated for by the immense catechetical exhibit set up in the spacious halls adjoining the assembly room.[90] The exhibit was arranged in such a way that one could see at a glance the principal catechetical methods in each country, as well as the principal authors representing each particular school. It was the writer's unique privilege to visit this congress and the principal catechetical centers in Europe and thus to obtain first-hand information about catechization in the various countries. Through the generosity of the archbishop of St. Paul, it was possible to duplicate, in a measure, the International Catechetical Exhibit of Luxemburg and have it set up in the halls of the Sacred Congregation of the Council.

In general, one may say that contemporary catechetical methods strive to keep three important facts in view: the irreligion of the public and of the state schools, the religious indifference of parents and the progress attained in the profane pedagogical sciences.

In the French-speaking countries, in particular, one may note the following tendencies:

1. Several important episcopal pastorals have appeared dealing

[89] *Problèmes d'éducation religieuse* (Brussels, 1936).

[90] Most of the materials exhibited are now listed in the volume, *Où en est l'enseignement religieux?* (Paris, 1937). This volume is monumental and absolutely unique in the field of bibliographical literature on catechetics. The writer acknowledges his indebtedness to the authors of this volume for their generous assistance in introducing him to the contemporary literature on catechetics.

at length with the whole catechetical problem, pointing out certain defects in the traditional methods and suggesting new and more effective measures for stemming the tide of apostasy from the Church. The most significant statements are those of J. R. Maurice Landrieux, Bishop of Dijon, Elie Antoine Durand, Bishop of Montauban, Marcel Fleury, Bishop of Nancy and Toue, and Patrick Flynn, Bishop of Nevers.[91] In 1947 a Catechism for use in the French diocese was published under the title, *Catéchisme à l'usage des Diocèses de France*. It is well illustrated, and the questions and answers are supplemented by narrations, exercises, reflections, and projects.

.2 After World War I, because of the shortage of priests, many catechetical schools for lay teachers sprang up in various parts of Europe. The most notable of these are those of Antwerp, Brussels, Liège,[92] Paris and Dijon.[93] These prospective lay teachers of religion must complete systematic studies in dogma, moral, Scripture and methodology before assuming the responsibilities of catechizing.

3. The sulpician Method is still extensively used and finds able exponents in such educators as P. Boumard,[94] J. Bricout[95] and L. Desers.[96]

4. In 1922 Bishop J. R. M. Landrieux of Dijon, in a letter to his clergy, made a strong plea for the restoration of the "historical method,"[97] which consists in proposing the doctrinal and moral truths of the Catechism by means of concrete narratives from Bible History and from the life of Our Lord. This method, as will be shown later, has now many exponents in France and elsewhere.

5. In France there has also arisen a whole extra-curricular liter-

[91] Cf. C. Houle, *The Catechetical Movement in France as Shown in Recent Pastoral Letter, in Journal of Religious Instruction* (March, 1937), pp. 592 ff.

[92] Cf. J. Brifaut-Vinchent, *L'enseignement de la religion dans les catéchismes paroissiaux dans l'agglomération bruxelloise* (Brussels, 1935); also *Le Problème catéchistique tel qu'il se pose aujourd'hui* (Brussels, 1935); F. Gellé, *Programme pour le temps présent. Aux Catéchists* (Paris, 1930).

[93] Cf. A. Boyer, *Le catèchisme vivant* (Paris, 1935); *Diocése de Dijon, Programme et Guide* (Dijon, 1933); *Réglement et Programme* (Dijon, 1933).

[94] *Formation de l'enfant par le catéchisme* (Paris, 1930).

[95] *L'enseignement du catéchisme en France* (Paris, 1922).

[96] *Instruction et éducation au catéchisme* (Paris, s. d.).

[97] *Le premier enseignement par l'Evangile* (Marseilles, 1922).

ature for children and adolescents on Bible History and on the life of Our Lord. These booklets are prepared in such a way that they repeat the lessons taught at school. They are arranged in a very attractive style in order to appeal to the child during his leisure moments.

6. The so-called "active" method,[98] which is becoming increasingly more popular in France, strives to apply in catechization the sound principles of contemporary pedagogy and especially of the Montessori Method. It wishes to enlist all of the child's faculties in the service of religion. It strive not merely to inculcate a few doctrinal formulas but to arouse the child's attention and interest and to stimulate his self-activity. It aims to make the child reflect upon his religion and begin forthwith to live it. It wishes the child to become more spontaneous, more free, and consequently more active. It wants the child to love his religion so that he might also live it. The method strives to create a religious environment which would replace the religious indifference of the home. In striving to make religion vital in the child's life, it lays special stress on liturgical practice and observance.

Catechetical activity in Spain presents a strange variety. The method of Canon Andre Manjón suggests strongly that of Fr. Shields. Religion is to be intimately correlated with the secular branches and with all of the child's activities. In fact, religion is to grow out of the secular branches, which must all contribute to the religious formation of the child. Like Fr. Shields, Manjón founded training schools for the formation of teachers who would be qualified to apply his method.[99] Another catechist, Fr. Damien Bilbao Ugarriza, initiated a vast Confraternity activity. Feeling keenly the religious ignorance of his country and realizing that lay teachers have neither the time nor the patience to submit to extensive training, Ugarriza prepared the lessons in such a way that they need only be read by the Catechist.[100] A method of instructing the children and of using the Catechism, strongly resembling the

[98] Cf. M. Fargues, *Les méthodes actives dans l'enseignement religieux* (Juvisy, 1934); Antonio J. Richard, *Abbé Quinet's Work and Active Method in Teaching Catechism,"* in *Journal of Religious Instruction* (June, 1937), pp. 877 ff.; F. Derkenne, *la vie et la joie au catéchisme* (paris, 1935).

[99] Cf. *Hojas catequisticas pedagógicas*, 5 vols. (3rd ed.; Granada, 1920–1931).

[100] *Pedagogia catequistica en acción* (Madrid, 1930).

Sower Method of England, is propounded by Fr. Tusquets,[101] while Fr. Llorente advocates the "active" method as embodying the best results of modern pedagogy.[102]

In Italy we find the same emphasis on the "self-expression" methods as in the French- and German-speaking countries. The catechists strive to make religion a transformative and vital factor in the child's life. The outstanding exponents of this method are L. Vigna,[103] G. Modugno,[104] Madame Montessori,[105] the Agazzi Sisters,[106] M. Casotti,[107] A. Franzoni[108] and M. Galli.[109] The work of the Agazzi Sisters is worthy of special note. The Agazzi Method strives to reproduce as far as possible the spirit and atmosphere of the family and employs very simple means in carrying out this plan. It strives to make children live their religion in a manner conformable to their nature and age. It aims at creating an atmosphere of play, liberty, spontaneity and self-expression. Handiwork, projects and visual aids are also extensively used. In the upper grades and in the secondary schools special emphasis is placed on the correlation of religion with literature, history, science and the other secular branches.

In parochial instruction the Catechism of St. Pius X is used in most Italian dioceses, although occasionally there may be a different arrangement of matter, explanations, and illustrations. Since the Catechism of St. Pius X is also used in the curricular textbooks of the Italian schools, an admirable unity is thus attained in Italian catechization as a whole. Excellent commentaries on the Catechism have been prepared by G. Dianda,[110] P. Boggio[111] and G. Perardi.[112]

[101] *Plan ciclico* (Barcelona, 1934).

[102] *Programma ciclico de instrucción religiosa* (Valladolid, 1935); *Tratado elemental de pedagogia catequistica* (3rd ed.; Valladolid, 1934).

[103] *Ai Maestri* (Milan, 1930); *Lezioni popolari di pedagogia catechista* (Turin, 1924).

[104] *Religione e Vita* (Brescia, 1935).

[105] Cf. M. Casotti, *Il metodo Montessori e il metodo Agazzi* (Bresica, 1931).

[106] *Guida per le educatrici dell' infanzia* (Brescia, 1932).

[107] *Scuola Attiva* (Brescia, 1937).

[108] *Metodo Agazzi* (Rome, 1931).

[109] *L'istruzione e l'educazione religiosa del fancuilla* (Milan, 1921).

[110] *Il catechismo maggiore di Sua Santita Pio X spiegato al popolo* (Turin, 1933).

[111] *Magister parvulorum ossia vademecum del catechista* (Turin, 1922).

[112] *La dottrina cristiana* (Turin, 1935); *Nuovo Manuale del catechista* (Turin, 1934).

During the latter part of the nineteenth century, catechization in Germany laid great stress on the intellectual and apologetical elements. Special emphasis was placed on the minute analysis of the abstract and theological formulas of the Catechism. But a change began to take place towards the close of the century, when the so-called Munich Method was gradually coming into vogue. This method begins with concrete elements which appeal to the senses, and concludes the lesson – instead of beginning it – with the catechismal formula. The forces and tendencies set in motion by this new departure became articulate and unified at the Catechetical Congress of Vienna in 1912.

The Catechetical Congress held at Munich in 1928 took further account of the new currents in contemporary pedagogical literature and brought into even greater prominence the so-called *Werkschule* or *Arbeitschule*. The new orientation placed special emphasis on the child's loving and living his religion. The child should begin by assimilating the religious truth with all his faculties and put it forthwith into practice. This intensification of religious life is to be brought about in many ways: by visual aids, by projects and handiwork, by teaching the religious truth in so lively and vivid a manner that the child would actually relive it, by exemplifying the truth in our own conduct. The religious truths should be engrafted on the child's apperceptive masses – on certain facts of nature and of family life, on liturgical services, on the great religious characters of the present and of the past and on the catechist's own strong spiritual life. The catechist must propose efficacious motives adapted to the child's age, disposition, circumstances and needs. Great stress must be placed on the child's self-activity, reflection and application. The catechist must also develop in the child a strong love for the religious traditions of his country and of his birthplace; the child should become well acquainted with the history of his parish, church, locality and country.[113]

As far as the distribution of the subject-matter according to the different school grades is concerned, many of the German dioceses

[113] Cf. H. Schüssler, *Arbeitsschulmethode und katholischer Religionsunterricht* (Frankfurt, 1922); F. Weigl, *Heimat und Volkstum in religionspädagogischer Auswertung* (Paderborn, 1934); J. Krones, *Die neuzeitlichen Anschauungsmittel und ihr didaktischer Wert für den Religionsunterricht* (Rottenburg, 1932).

follow the *Fuldalehrplan*,[114] drawn up by the Bishop's Conference in 1925 and revised in 1932. In the *Grundschule* (6–10 years) religious instruction is directed towards preparing the child for Confession and First Communion, and hence teaching during these years is largely Eucharistic. The catechist explains the Incarnation and the Redemption, the child's relation to God and duties arising therefrom, and initiates the child into parish life. In the four years of the *Volksschule* (10–14 years) catechetical instruction strives to lay a solid foundation for the child's later Christian and Catholic life. Special reference is made to the child's problems and difficulties in later years and to the necessity of being grounded in practices of mortification and self-denial. The instruction branches by which the *Lehrplan* endeavors to attain this end are the following: Bible and Church History, the Catechism, the Liturgy, prayers and hymns, and object lessons.

A Catechism which enjoyed great popularity in Germany between 1848 and 1915 was that of Deharbe.[115] This Catechism, which was a reaction against contemporary rationalism, is clear, precise and accurate in its expression. It served a very important purpose especially in its own day. However, it is rather abstract and makes an excessive demand on memorizing. In 1915 the German Bishops commissioned Th. Moennichs to revise it. Fr. Moennichs composed, with the aid of specialists, a work which has been adopted as a common Catechism in Germany. It is known as the *Einheitskatechismus*.[116] The Catechism is in the form of questions and answers, preserves the order of Deharbe's Catechism, and adds an explanatory note to the text. Within recent years an attempt has been made to group the entire contents of the Catechism around a central idea, with a view to improve the *Einheitskatechismus*.

[114] *Lehrplan für den katholischen Religionsunterricht in der Volksschule, herausgegeben im Auftrage der Fuldaer Bischofskonferenz*" (Paderborn, 1925). Cf. J. Gründer, *Der Geist des Fuldaerlehrplans* (Paderborn, 1927).

[115] Th. N. Busch, *Der Weg der deutschen katholischen Katechismus von Deharbe bis zum Einheitskatechismus* (Freiburg, 1936).

[116] Cf. E. Herold, "A Teacher's Treasure," in *Journal of Religious Instruction* (March, 1938), pp. 587 ff.; Th. Moennichs, *Hilfsbuch zum Einheitskatechismus* (Munich, 1927); O. Hilker, *Handbuch zum Einheitskatechismus* (Paderborn, 1929); J. Gruender, *Handbuch zum deutschen Einheitskatechismus* (Paderborn, 1929); J. Bernbeck, *Katechesen für die Oberstufe nach dem deutschen Einheitskatechismus* (Munich, 1929).

P. Moog [117] wishes to center everything around the doctrine of the Mystical Body; P. Schmitz [118] seeks a Catechism that would be theocentric and Christocentric, and A. Stringl [119] aims to group all the matters around the notion of faith – sources of faith, object of faith, life of faith.

In this catechetical renaissance in Germany no small part has been played by the Liturgical Movement, sponsored especially by the Benedictines of Beuron, Maria Laach and Grussau, and by Fr. Pius Parsch of Klosterneuburg, Austria. The aim of these scholars is to asquaint not only the élite but also average laymen with the rich treasures of the Liturgy.

In 1938 the German hierarchy commissioned the foremost catechetical experts of the country to prepare a new catechism which was published in Freiburg in 1955 under the title, *Katholischer Katechismus für dié Bistümer Deutschlands.* Not only is the catechism painstakingly prepared but it is said to be the first catechism to take into consideration the kerygmatic requirements of the modern catechetical movement.

In Flanders and Holland catechetical methods seem to bear new characteristics. (1) The Catechisms are gradually abandoning the mere question-and-answer procedure, aiming rather at a continuous connected narrative divided into sections which are followed by a few brief questions.[120] (2) The so-called "active" methods are likewise beginning to prevail in The Netherlands. Catechists are striving to make catechization a school of complete religious training. They aim not only to inculcate a few abstract formulas but also to make the child live the truth and incorporate it permanently into his life.[121] Two other, catechetical methods enjoy great popularity in The Netherlands. The first, the Munich Method, was introduced into Flanders and Holland by A. Vingerhotes' translation of A. Weber's work on this subject.[122] The method is being gradually revised in the light of the best principles of modern pedagogy. The

[117] *Katechetische Blätter* (1934), pp. 345 ff.

[118] *Katechismus der katholischen Religion* (Paderborn, 1934).

[119] *Katechismus der katholischen Religion* (Wiesbaden, 1932).

[120] Cf. M. Vermolen and F. Cyprianus, *Toelichting op de erste katechismus* (Boisle-Duc, 1934). The same arrangement was advocated in Austria by W. Pichler, *Katechismus der katholischen Religion* (Vienna, 1928).

[121] Cf. A. Van der Mueren, *Op den weg der wyjsheid, Op den weg der liefde,* and *Bij de ware levensbronnen* (Louvain, 1930–1934).

[122] *De münchener methode van het catechismusonderricht* (Tilburg, 1907).

other method is Abbé Poppe's Eucharistic Method, which centers all instruction and training in the Eucharist. Many teachers have adopted this method. One of the Flemish catechists, M. Defoort,[123] adapted it especially for the training of the heart and will. The Sisters of St. Joseph Calasanz of Vorselaar[124] and A. Vandevelde[125] developed the intellectual content of the method.

Catechetics in the Slavic countries before the present Communistic enslavement had been influenced to some extent by the methods prevailing in Germany and France. In Czechoslovakia the well-known authority on catechetics, Dr. V. Kubiček, outlines a method the steps of which are fundamentally those of the Munich Method but supplemented by the latest findings in the domain of pedagogy.[126] Czechoslovakian catechetics lay considerable stress on the visual elements.[127] Another catechetical scholar of this country, Josef Hronek, gives us a history of catechization and of education in ancient and modern Bohemia, outlines the regulations of the Czechoslovakian Government in regard to the teaching of religion in the state schools and then gives timely instructions to catechists engaged in teaching religion in the public schools. He advocates a close correlation of Bible History, the Catechism, Church History, Liturgy and Prayer, and indicates the methods to be followed in presenting this subject matter.[128] Czechoslovakian catechetical literature is especially rich in syste-

[123] *Uitgewerkt programma van actieve eucharistische opvoeding* (Thourout, 1930).

[124] *Liefde zaaien, daden maaien* (Averbode, 1935); *Uitgewerkte Lessen voor 4e en 5e studiejaar* (Averbode, 1934). Cf. M. Van Raes, "Catechetical System of the Sisters of the Christian Schools of St. Joseph Calasanz," in *Journal of Religious Instruction* (October, 1937), p. 107.

[125] *Opvoedend catechismusonderricht* (Thourout, 1935).

[126] *Katechetika* (Olomouc, 1937). Cf. also his works on *Katolicka Prvouka* (Olomouc, 1935) and *Biblicke Dějiny* (Olomouc, 1936). For the history of catechetics in Bohemia, cf. F. Kosak, *Dějiny české Katechetiky* (Olomouc, 1922).

[127] Cf. F. Tomasek and Jan Jan *Kresby ke Katechizmu* (Zlin, 1936); A Zamazal, *Kresleni v Hodine nabozenske* (v Polske Ostrave, 1909).

[128] Cf. J. Hronek, *Národni Skola a Katecheta* (Praha, 1931), *Vyucovani Náboženstvi na Narodnich Skolach* (Praha, 1935), *Cesta k Bohu* (Praha, 1933), *Metodika* (Praha, 1934), *Vybor Dějin Biblickych* (Praha, 1931), *Katecheticky Slovaniček* (Praha, 1935), *zivot podle Viry* (Praha, 1934), *Dějiny katolicke Cirkve* (Praha, 1935), *Prehled katolicke theologie česke* (Praha, 1934–1935).

matic treatises on the Liturgy.[129] Manuals for the higher grades have been prepared by J. Kaspar.[130] Catechetical problems and questions are discussed in a scholarly manner in the monthly entitled *Vychovatelske Listy*, published in Olomouc.

The graded program of religious instruction published by the catechetical association of Ljubljana and Maribor [131] give us an interesting insight in catechetical activities in Yugoslavia. The theory of catechization is explained in two interesting brochures, one by Anton Krzic,[132] the other by J. K. Vreze.[133] Systematic explanations on the Liturgy are likewise numerous in this country.[134] The extensive commentary on the large Catechism by A. Veternik,[135] though published in 1902, still enjoys wide popularity. A series of manuals on the Catechism,[136] Bible History,[137] and Church History [138] have been prepared for both the elementary and secondary schools.

The catechism commentaries of J. Szukalski [139] occupy a very prominent place in the catechetical literature of Poland. Equally valuable, also, are his explanations of Bible History.[140] A compilation of interesting examples and stories illustrative of catechism questions and answers have been prepared by J. Maklowicz [141] and J. Lapot.[142] Other Polish catechists who have prepared children's texts on the various phasese of catechization are Z. Bielawski,[143]

[129] Cf. B. Augustin, *Věrouka Liturgika* (Praha, 1936); X. Dvorak, *Liturgika katolicka* (Praha, 1922); A. Podlaha, *Katolicka Liturgika* (Praha, 1930); P. M. Schaller, *Liturgie* (Praha, 1933).

[130] *Učebnice Katolickeho Naboženstvi*, 2 vols. (Praha, 1922).

[131] *Podrobni učni in vzgojni načrt* (Ljubljana, 1932).

[132] *Kratka katehetika* (Ljubljana, 1917).

[133] *Methodika katoliskega verouka* (Maribor, 1925).

[134] Cf. A. Stroj, *Liturgika* (Ljubljana, 1922); F. Vseničnik, *Katoliska Liturgika* (Ljubljana, 1933); Jaklič-Vrečar, *Liturgika* (Ljubljana, 1935).

[135] *Razlaga velikega Katekizma ali krsčanskega nauka*, 4 vols. (Ljubljana, 1902).

[136] *Katoliska Verouk*, 3 vols. Ljubljana, 1927–1931).

[137] *Zgodbe svetega Pisma*, 4 vols. (Ljubljana, 1916–1932).

[138] *Zgodovina katoliske Cerkve*, 2 vols. (Ljubljana, 1922; Maribor, 1922).

[139] *Katechezy*, 3 vols. (Inowroclaw, 1934).

[140] *Podrecznik Metodyczny do nauki Historji Biblynej* (Poznan, 1928).

[141] *Wybór Przykladow Ojczystych* (Miejsce-Piastowe, 1929).

[142] *Zbiór Przykladow* (Kielce, 1935).

[143] *Nauka Religji* (Lwow, 1935); *Dzieje Biblijne* (Lwow, 1936); *Katechezy Biblijne* (Lwow, 1932).

W. Gadowski,[144] T. Kowalewski,[145] T. Gunia,[146] A. Czastka,[147] R. Archutowski,[148] and Gerstmann-Ratuszyn.[149] Dr. W. Kailnowski [150] has elaborated several volumes for the higher classes.

In England the Rev. F. H. Drinkwater [151] initiated the so-called *Sower* Scheme, which is a synthetic and concentric method of teaching religion. The *Sower* Scheme divides religious instruction in schools into three main periods, each stage being a complete survey of Catholic doctrine and each having its appropriate contents, methods and discipline. The Catechism is used as a textzook only in the second or third period. The project of a homemade catechism, devised by A. M. Scarre, is introduced in the second period. The *Sower* Scheme lays great stress on the training of the will and heart.

In Ireland we find a hearkening to the catechetical glories of the country's past, to those heroic lay catechists who in the midst of persecution and in the absence of priests safeguarded and transmitted to their offspring the treasures of the Catholic faith.[152] The souvenirs of the past will undoubtedly give rise to a new and equally glorious catechetical movement in Ireland in the near future.

In Australia catechetical activity is intimately associated with the name of the Rev. J. T. McMahon. In his masterly work, *Some Methods of Teaching Religion,*[153] Fr. McMahon subjects to a

[144] *Mala Biblyka* (Lwow, 1929); *Dzieje Biblijne* (Lwow, 1930); *Szkice Katechez* (W. Miejscu-Piastowem, 1930); *Zarys Historji Kosciola Katholickiego,* 2 vols. (Lwow, 1927).

[145] *Historja Swieta* (w Plocku, 1926); *Liturgika* (w Plocku, 1920); *Nauka Wiary* (w Plocku, 1930).

[146] *Zasady Wiary katolickiej,* 3 vols. (Lwow, 1925–1928).

[147] *Wiara w Boga i czyn z wiary,* 2 vols (Lwow, 1926–1928).

[148] *Historja Kosciola katolickiego,* 2 vols. (Warsaw, 1934–1936).

[149] *Czytania Biblijne i Katechizmowe,* 2 vols. (Lwow, 1931–1932).

[150] Cf., for example, *Dogmatyka* (Poznan, 1930); *Etyka* (Poznan, 1928).

[151] Cf. *The Givers* (London, 1926); *Religion in School Again* (London, 1935). Cf. also *Scheme of Religious Instruction, Approved for Use in the Elementary Schools of the Diocese of Birmingham* (London, 1929); *The Sower. A Quarterly Journal of Religious Instruction* (Lower Gornal, Dudley, England).

[152] Cf. M. Brennan, *The Confraternity of Christian Doctrine in Ireland: 1775–1835* (Dublin, 1934); T. Corcoran, *Some Lists of Catholic Lay Teachers and their Illegal Schools in the Later Penal Days* (Dublin, 1932).

[153] Published in London, 1928.

searching criticism some of the catechetical methods in use to-day and then emphatically pronounces in favor of the project method. Fr. McMahon has introduced into Australia the so-called "Religious Correspondence Courses," by which he seeks to reach the children of isolated farmers and colonists scattered throughout the vast sections of his country.[154] Catholics in large cities are asked to take charge of the mailing of these correspondence courses and to send to these underprivileged children not only the lessons but also books and periodicals. They are even urged to visit their charges, if possible, and to take a personal interest in them. In 1936 the Australian bishops organized a National Catholic Correspondence Course, so that today some 10,000 families and 20,000 children are being reached by this agency. During the summer vacation the children are gathered in camps and given a fuller supplementary instruction.

Madame Marie Montessori (1870–1952) the great Italian educator, insists that all true education comes from within. It is the expansion of a vital force within the individual child. We must not anticipate, mar or stifle this mysterious power but await its manifestation. The child must find in his surroundings an equipment set up in direct relation to his internal growth. The school should be fitted in such a way that each child has the opportunity to live a child's life. In religion the ideal would be a "children's church." The teacher must devote a good deal of her time to the preparation and care of this environment and to the initiation of the child into it. The development of the senses and muscles as valuable instruments of the mind must receive special attention. Each child must be directed according to his age, ability and needs. In the teaching of religion, Dr. Montessori insists that children should learn religion by being allowed to do the actions of religion. Learning by doing, she says, is the best kind of religion. These "happy" activities of religion, the various projects and handiwork, should later be explained by apposite stories as occasion demands, and finally summarized in the clear cut statements of the Catechism. Her ideas on religious instruction are found in her work, *The Secret of Childhood* (1939). Details on the life and work of Dr. Montessori are given in the 1957 edition of the *Encyclopedia Americana* (vol. XIV).

[154] Cf. *The Bushie's Scheme at Work in Western Australia* (Perth, 1933); *The Perth Plan for Teaching Religion by Correspondence* (Dublin, 1928).

In the United States several series of religion textbooks appeared with in recent years. Among the best-known were Mother Bolton's *A Little Child's First Communion* [155] and the *Spiritual Way,*[156] *The Highway to Heaven Series,*[157] the *Christ-Life Series,*[158] and the series of Rev. A. Schorsch and of his sister, Sister Dolores M. Schorsch.[159] These series were explained by their respective authors in the *Journal of Religious Instruction.*[160] Three important series are available in the high school division, namely, those of R. J. Campion,[161] F. Casilly,[162] and J. Laux.[163] In the college department the texts of J. M. Cooper [164] remain unexcelled; they meet the problems of the average American Catholic student and make religion a vital affair in his life.

A formal course in catechetics is taught in most of the eighty-seven major seminaries of the United States. A great number of seminarians are engaged in catechization during the school year as well as during the summer vacation.[165] Several of the Catholic universities – such as the Catholic University of America, De Paul University, St. Louis University, Marquette and Detroit Universities – offer catechetical courses for the fuller education of teachers of religion. Diocesan teachers' colleges at St. Paul, Green Bay, La Crosse, Cleveland, Toledo and Dubuque offer not only courses in catechetics but various religion courses for the training of Sis-

[155] St. Anthony's Guild, Paterson, 1935.

[156] World Book, New York, 1929.

[157] Bruce, Milwaukee, 1931–1936.

[158] Macmillan, New York, 1935.

[159] Chicago School Board, 1935.

[160] Cf. A. P. Schorsch and Sister Mary Dolores Schorsch, *The Laws of Learning and the De Paul Course in Religion,* Jan., p. 386, Feb., p. 487, Mar. p. 574, April, 1936, p. 674; V. Michel, *Some Pedagogical Features of the 'Christ Life Series in Religion,'* Mar., 1936, p. 583; E. A. Fitzpatrick, *The Highway to Heaven Series,* Feb., p. 525, Mar., p. 606, Apr., 1937, p. 720; Mother Margaret Bolton, *Teaching Christ's Principles to Little Ones,* Apr., 1938, p. 681.

[161] *Religion,* 3 vols. (New York, 1928–1932).

[162] *Religion, Doctrine and Practice,* 3 vols. (Chicago, 1934).

[163] *A Course of Religion,* 4 vols. (New York, 1934).

[164] *Religion Outlines for Colleges* (Washington, 1928–1935).

[165] Cf. "The Teaching of Catechetics in Seminaries," in *Proceedings of National Catechetical Congress at Rochester* (Paterson, 1935), pp. 173 ff.; A *Questionnaire on a Seminary Course in Catechetics,"* in *Proceedings of National Catechetical Congress at New York* (Paterson, 1936), pp. 234 ff.

ters as religion teachers.[166] A genuine service to catechization is rendered by such excellent reviews as the *Journal of Religious Instruction* of Chicago, *The Catholic School Journal* of Milwaukee, and *The Catholic Educational Review* of Washington. As in Australia, children living in very remote sections of the United States are not forgotten; they are reached effectively by religious correspondence courses mailed to them regularly by Sisters, seminarians and laymen.

The chief impetus to all catechetical activity in the United States is now coming from the Confraternity of Christian Doctrine, organized in almost all the dioceses of the United States. While the activities fostered at present by the Confraternity have always been carried on in one form or another by the Church in this country, the Confraternity was not formally established in the United States until 1903, when the first unit was founded in New York City. After the publication in 1918 of the New Code of Canon Law, which ordains that the Confraternity be established in every parish, the American bishops proceeded to organize the Confraternity in their respective dioceses.[167]

The St. Paul Archdiocese has been among the pioneers of the vacation school movement. As early as 1925 two groups of students from the St. Paul Seminary launched – under the direction of the respective pastors – vacation schools in the northern and western parts of the country. It was in that same year of 1925 that Arthur H. Durand, now pastor of St. John's Church, New Canada, Minnesota, wrote a pamphlet, unique perhaps in this genre of literature and as timely today as it was then: *The Seminarian as a Summer Vacation Catechist.*

The Confraternity was formally established in the St. Paul Archdiocese on August 10, 1933, with headquarters in the Chancery Office. On March 22, 1937, the Archdiocese purchased the old Rugg Mansion to serve as the Confraternity Center at 251 Summit Avenue, St. Paul. In the month of April in 1939 a provincial catechetical congress was held in St. Paul. In August, 1940, the St. Paul Confraternity was incorporated under the laws of Minnesota, and

[166] See "What Catholic Universities Are Doing for the Training of Teachers in Religion," in *Bulletin of Catholic Educational Association* (Columbus, 1938).

[167] For a world view of catechetics, see *Lumen Vitae, International Review of Religious Education*, Apr.-June, 1956.

the certificate of incorporation was filed with the Secretary of State on September 5, 1940. In 1942 the St. Paul Confraternity published a series of religion text books for grades one to twelve. These booklets are now used as official manuals in many archdioceses and dioceses in the country.

Before closing this chapter a word should be said about the new, "kerygmatic", orientation of theology and of its consequent implications for catechetics and catechization. The terms, "kerygmatic" is related to three Greek words: "keryx," "herald;" "kerysso," "to proclaim," and "kerygma," "a publicly announced message." The kerygmatic approach to theology is the all-pervasive functional orientation of theology towards a vital and effective proclamation and teaching by the herald of the good news of our salvation in Christ and towards a living application and appreciation of it in our daily lives. It strives to understand Christian doctrine in relation to Christian living, proclaims it as the "glad tidings" of our salvation, and calls men to an altogether new life. It strives to gives the ability to pray, meditate, appreciate and live Christian doctrine. This kerygmatic renewal is not to be restricted to religious instruction in the classroom but is to permeate all agencies and forms by which the "gospel" or the good news of our salvation is proclaimed to the word.[168]

[168] Cf. Joseph A. Jungmann, *Die Frohbotschaft und unsere Glaubensverkündigung* (Regensburg, 1936); *Theology and Kerygmatic Teacing*, in *Lumen Vitae*, 1950, pp. 258–263; *Katechetik* (Frieburg, 1955); They Call it *Kerygmatic Theology*, in *The Priest*, 1956. Johannes Hofinger, *The Art of Teaching Christian Doctrine* (Notre Dame, 1957).

CHAPTER II

BIBLE AND CHURCH HISTORY

Bible History[1]

1. By "Bible History" we do not mean the whole Bible or a summary of the contents of all the sacred books. Rather, by "Bible History" we understand a compendium of biblical narratives and facts the choice of which is determined by the special purpose which a writer may have in view. The author of a Bible History may choose, among others, the following groups of stories:

a. Those necessary for a proper understanding of the Liturgical Year. Thus, the *Opera della Regalità di N. S. G. Cristo* of Milan has begun the publication of a series entitled *Bibbia e Liturgia*, the purpose of which is to acquaint the laity with those scriptural passages which are used in the Breviary and in the Mass during the liturgical year.

b. Those read at Mass on feast days and on Sundays.[2]

c. Those which depict the beauty of virtue as exemplified in the lives of holy men. In such a bible history, Abel, for example, will stand forth as a pattern of worship; Isaac, of obedience; Joseph, of purity; David, of humility and contrition; Job, of patience; and Tobias, of works of mercy.

d. Those which set forth the heinousness of sin and its punish-

[1] Cf. H. Schmitz, *Die religiöse Unterweisung der Jugend* (Cologne, 1920), 65 sqq., p. 103; H. Feilzer, *Kehreins besondere Unterrichtslehre oder Methodik der einzelnen Unterrichtsfächer* (Paderborn, 1919), pp. 18 ff.; Wolff-Habrich, *Der Volksschulunterricht* (Freiburg im B., 1917), pp. 1 ff.

[2] Cf. M. Gahery, *La plus belle histoire* (Caen, 1925); Ch. Gaume, *Épîtres et évangiles des dimanches et des fêtes* (Lyon, 1934); C. L. Guillemet, *Evangiles des dimanches et des fêtes principales* (Paris, 1932); Abbé Janvier, *Épîtres et évangiles des dimanches, des fêtes et de toutes les feriés de l'année*

ment. In this case, the author may illustrate anger and envy by the conduct of Cain, the punishment of sin by the deluge, pride by the Tower of Babel, hardness of heart by the attitude of Pharao, irreverence by the acts of the sons of Heli, and disobedience by his life of Absalom.[3]

e. Those which give a synthesis of our redemption in Christ. In this case, the stories of the Old Testament show the gradual fulfillment of the promise of a Redeemer made in the garden of Paradise – all stories point, in some way, to the future Messiah.[4]

f. Those which serve as a *point de départ* for the dogmatic and moral truths of the Catechism. We shall return to this group of stories shortly.

The Church's ministers have always made extensive use of the Scriptures in their catechetical activities. We must remember, of course, that Christ commanded the Apostles and their successors to preach and teach – not to write. Christ's Gospel was to be spread by divinely appointed ambassadors testifying to objective facts. Many New Testament writings were occasional letters, called forth by special problems and situations in the early Church and addressed to widely scattered communities. Being written on papyrus, they could not easily be rolled and unrolled, and sent from one place to another. The books of the entire Bible were not collected into one volume until about the fourth century. Prior to the use of paper and the invention of printing, Bibles were transcribed by hand and copied on expensive parchment. To possess a Bible during the first fifteen centuries of our era was to possess a fortune. Bibles during this period were so precious and rare that often they had to be chained lest they be stolen.

And yet the Church's teaching during all this time was impregnated with Scripture. The apostolic catechesis, as we already noted, consisted primarily of a narration of the history of salvation as contained in the sacred records. Scripture readings constituted an

(Tours, 1929); J. Goffine, *Explanation of the Epistles and Gospels for the Sundays, Holy Days, and Festivals of the Ecclesiastical Year* (Milwaukee, 1880).

[3] A. Urban, *Teacher's Handbook to Bible History* (New York, 1905).

[4] Cf. Sister Agnesine, *Before Christ Came* (Milwaukee, 1934); Abbé Martin de Noirlieu, *Bible de l'enfance* (Liège, 1928); Abbé Michel, *Histoire Sainte* (Namur, 1920); Pavanelli e Vigna, *Il Salvatore promesso* (Turin, 1924); B. C. Kloostermans, *Gods Volk* (Bois-le-Duc, 1931); J. Coppens, *Pour mieux comprende et mieux enseigner l'Histoire Sainte de l'Ancien Testament* (Paris, 1936).

important part of the instruction designed for catechumens. The patristic writings – whether they were doctrinal, apologetic, homiletic, or catechetical – abounded in references to and quotations from the Bible. The historical method of St. Augustine, which attributes such an important role to Biblical narratives, influenced almost every catechist up to the Reformation.[5] "Picture Bibles" and "Bibles of the Poor" were used extensively in the Middle Ages. Statues, symbols, stained glass windows and paintings conveyed many a Biblical theme to the eyes and mind of the uneducated. In the *Summa Theologica* St. Thomas manifests an acquaintance with Scripture which is nothing short of astounding. The Reformation period pushed Bible History somewhat in the background since the religious controversies of the day demanded precise and concise theological formulas such as we find in the Canisian Catechisms. In the beginning of the nineteenth century, however, Bible History textbooks came into vogue with such catechists as Overberg (d. 1826), Gruber (d. 1835), and Hirscher (d. 1965), who clearly saw the importance of the historical element in catechization.

2. *Bible History and the Catechism.* In 1922, Bishop J. R. Maurice Landrieux of Dijon, Francee, in a pastoral letter to his priests, made a strong plea for the restoration of the so-called "historical method" in catechization.[6] This method consists in presenting the doctrinal and moral truths of the Catechism in the lower grades by means of concrete stories from the Bible and from the life of Our Lord; the vivid and impressive historical narratives serve as the foundation for the development of the abstract notions of the Catechism. The suggestion of the bishop of Dijon was hailed with genuine sympathy in many educational centers. It was welcomed as affording a relief from the burdensome process of catechismal memorizing, which was no longer proving adequate to the needs of the time. The historical method has been developed and perfected by such catechists as E. Charles,[7] H. Dupont,[8] J. Mury [9] and

[5] Cf. J. V. Tahon, *The First Instruction of Children and Beginners* (London, 1930).

[6] *Le prémier enseignement par l'Évangile* (Marseilles, 1922). Cf. H. Houle, "The Catechetical Movement in France as Shown in Recent Pastoral Letters" in *Journal of Religious Instruction* (March, 1937), pp. 592 ff.

[7] *Le Catéchisme par l'Évangile*: I. "Le livre des tout-petitis," II. "Le livre de la mère et dames catéchistes," III. "Le livre du prêtre" (Marseilles, 1933).

[8] *Pour apprendre la religion aux petits* (Avignon, 1930).

[9] *Le catéchisme dans l'Évangile* (Paris, 1924).

C. Quinet.[10] The same method of correlating the principal questions of the Catechism with biblical narratives during the early years of the child's training is found in the so-called *Religionsbüchlein* [11] which have become very popular in Germany, Austria, Czechoslovakia and other countries.

a. The use of the historical method, especially in the lower grades, rests on the following pedagogical and psychological principles:

(1) *In the acquisition of knowledge the human mind proceeds from the sensible and concrete to the intellectual and abstract.* Bible History and the Catechism comprise the same subjects, namely, divine revelations; but whereas the former contains them in concrete and historical narratives, the latter expresses them in the form of abstract, doctrinal statements. Hence, Bible History is the root out of which the Catechism should grow; it should, consequently, prepare the way for the latter.

(2) *The matter should be adapted to the intellectual capacity of the child.* The intellectual powers of the children in the lower grades are little developed. The children understand only what they can see and touch. Abstract religious truths and formulas are not the appropriate food for the mind and will of the child at this age. In fact, because the catechismal formulas are so difficult of comprehension, there is danger that the child may become antagonistic to all religious instruction. Bible History, on the other hand, if propounded by a competent teacher, begets interest and joy. All educators are agreed that the story must occupy a prominent place in religious instruction,[12] and surely there are no more suitable and excellent stories than those furnished by the Bible. Their simple and vivid manner, their plain words and short sentences, their childlike tone, render Bible stories exceptionally suitable to

[10] *Pour mes tout-petits. Vingt leçons de catéchisme évangelique par la méthode active* (Paris, 1935).

[11] Cf. *Katholisches Religionsbüchlein für die Grundschule,* published by the bishops of Bavaria (Donauwörth, 1933); F. Ernst, *Katholisches Religionsbüchlein für das Bistum Rottenburg* (Rottenburg, 1930); C. Kunz, *Das Büchlein vom lieben Gott* (Munich, 1935); W. Pichler, *Ein frommes Bilderbüchlein für die Kleinen* (Vienna, 1935); *Katholisches Religionsbüchlein* (Vienna, 1935).

[12] Cf. Josef Fatinger, *Der Katchet erzählt* (Ried in Innkreis, 1934); J. N. Siebenand, "The Story Method of Joseph Fattinger," in *Journal of Religious Instruction* (November, 1937), p. 226.

children. These stories appeal to the senses and imagination of the child, and through them reach the mind and heart.

Some educators object that the use of the historical method in the lower grades violates the principle of adaptation. They advance the following reasons; the Bible is replete with Oriental terminology; the children cannot picture the natural and geographical conditions presupposed in the Biblical facts; the habits and customs of the Holy Land are unintelligible to the child Hence, they say, Bible History likewise becomes a matter of mere mechanical memory. These objections, however, hardly carry any force. Most children see pictures of Christ, of Bethlehem, of Palestine, on the walls of their home. In church they likewise see pictures and statues referring to Biblical events, and they hear the priest discussing Biblical questions in his sermon. The Bible History lesson in school can be given with the help of appropriate pictures. Sometimes the very strangeness and wonderfulness of Bible History, far from being an obstacle, admirably satisfies that natural inquisitiveness so characteristic of the child in this stage.

(3) *In catechization the teacher should supply those concrete details which the Catechism in its brevity cannot offer.* Bible History is a sort of a pictorial commentary on the Catechism. The Catechism gives us abstract definitions of God's attributes, but Bible History illustrates God's omnipotence by the story of creation, His holiness by the account of the deluge, His providence by the history of Joseph, His love by the Passion and Death of Christ. The Catechism speaks of the Incarnation and Redemption, but Bible History gives us a full and detailed account of Christ's birth, sufferings, and death. The Catechism speaks of Christ's divine power, but Bible History gives us a vivid description of the effects of that power in Christ's miracles over nature, men and the spirit world. The Catechism tells us of Christ's love and mercy towards us, but who could excel those exquisitely tender colors in which the Friend and Consoler of mankind is depicted in the parables – especially in those of the Good Shepherd, the Prodigal Son, the Good Samaritan, etc.? Bible History, then, presents to us those scriptural passages from which the catechismal answers have been deduced as brief abstract summaries.

(4) *The religious truth should become the permanent possession of the child's mind.* The doctrinal truths of the Catechism are

in themselves cold abstractions and mere outlines. They are apt to leave the child indifferent and uninterested. But let the truth in question be embodied in a concrete and striking incident, let it be reflected in the conduct of a personage of flesh and blood, and it will leave an indelible impress on the child's mind. Above all, the fact that Christ, who is God, has proclaimed a particular doctrine is sufficient argument for the child and forthwith produces intellectual obedience and conviction.

(5) *Religious instruction should transform and sanctify the child's conduct and form his heart according to Christian ideals.* In the attainment of this most important end of catechization Bible History is also of the highest importance. The child's heart in this period is not yet hardened by personal sin but is uncommonly plastic. The impressions made upon it are more or less permanent. The Bible has a power and an unction superior to those of any other religion book. God's grace is bound up with it in a unique way. Bible History depicts sin in all its ugliness; it brings out strong examples of virtue in all their loveliness (Joseph, John); it portrays the incomparable example of the Son of God, the Incarnate Exemplar and Model of all virtues. Bible stories, then, cannot but edify the children, transform their hearts and ennoble their affections.[13]

(6) *The concrete facts and details of Bible History should be summed up in the words of the Catechism.* Since Bible History has so many advantages, would it not be advisable to teach religion entirely by means of this branch, and do away with the Catechism?[14]

[13] *L'Homme né de la guerre* (Paris, 1924), pp. 12–13. The author in reflecting upon his early religious training, deplores the absence of the historical and biblical element in the following terms: "Une ou deux heures d'instruction, la semaine, qui nous ennuyaient tous, je m'en souviens, étranagement. Notre bon aumônier n'essayait pas d'entrer en concurrence, par cet attrait vivant qui capte les jeunes esprits, avec nos professeurs d'humanités ou de science. En regard des vies de Plutarque, nous offrait-il la vie des Saints, la vie même du Divin Maître? Mais non. Dans l'histoire des nations, rendait-il à l'histoire du peuple élu, à celle des apôtres, des papes, de l'Eglise, la première place qui est la leur? Mais non. Il nous parlait abstraction. Alors que la philosophie, réservée aux esprits plus mûrs, est reportée a la fin des études, il nous faisait entrevoir dès treize ans les hauts sommets de la théologie. Il dissertait, savamment je le crois, sur le péché originel, sur les vertus théologales, sur la grace. Ah! s'il nous avait lu les Actes de Sainte Cécile, le récit de la Passion dans Anne-Catherine Emmerich, ou même les 'Fioretti' legendaires."

[14] Cf., for example, J. J. Nash, *Explanation and Application of Bible History* (New York, 1902).

Was not the biblico-historical method of St. Augustine used for several centuries, and is it not still the most desirable method? Proposals such as these would be promptly rejected by modern catechists for the following reasons: [15]

(a) The historical method did not enjoy a monopoly in the early Church. The Apostles and evangelists made frequent reference to the scriptures when arguing with or writing for the Jews. St. Matthew's Gospel, which was written to prove that Christ was the promised Messias; the Epistles to the Romans and Galatians, which were directed against the claims of the Judaizers; the Epistle to the Hebrews, which was dispatched to Christian Jews who because of persecutions were on the point of apostatizing – all these make frequent allusion to the Old Testament. But that St. Paul, for example, could use another method when circumstances demanded it is evident from his speech on the Areopagus.[16]

(b) The history of dogmatic theology points to the existence of definite abstract formulas in the early Church which were inculcated in the minds of the faithful. The definition of the "consubstantiality" of the Son with the Father, made by the Council of Nicæa in 325, shows how sensitive the Church was to precision of terms. No other course, in fact, was possible. Revelation is God's immutable message and demands a statement which is itself immutable, definite, and precise.

(c) The numerous concrete statements found in the Bible and in apostolic traditions were soon summed up in concise statements, which served as credentials for the Christians and as norms for teaching, preaching and testing of new doctrines, and for the reception of converts into the Church.

(d) The Catechism came providentially into use during the Protestant Reformation when the Catholic faith faced its supreme peril.

(e) The prevalence of error and indifferentism in our day demands a clear-cut presentation of Christian doctrine. An official Catechism procures unity and orthodoxy of doctrine.

(f) An official Catechism is a bond of union between children, parents, and the preacher in the pulpit.

[15] Cf. Most Rev. John T. McNicholas, O.P., "The Content of Religious Instruction," in *Proceedings of the National Catechetical Congress in Rochester* (1935), pp. 18 ff.

[16] Acts 17.

b. *Correlation of specific Catechism lessons and Bible History stories.* The following are a few of the Bible History stories which, especially if rendered vivid by means of pictures and slides, can be profitably correlated with the Catechism lessons.[17]

CREED

Article 1 ....Six days of Creation (Gen. 1)
First parents and their fall (Gen. 3)
Articles 2–3 ......Annunciation of Our Lord's birth (Luke 1)
Article 3 ....Nativity of Our Lord and the adoration of the shepherds (Luke 2)
Article 4 ....Scourging, crowning with thorns, seven last words (Matt. 27)
Article 5 ....Resurrection (Matt. 28)
Jesus appears to the disciples at Emmaus (Luke 24)
Jesus appears to the Apostles and St. Thomas (John 20)
Article 6 ....Ascension (Acts 1)
Article 7 ....Our Lord's account of the last judgment (Matt. 24)
Article 8 ....Descent of the Holy Spirit (Acts 2)
Official of Queen Candace becomes a Christian (Acts 8)
Article 9 ....Promise and conferring of primacy (Matt. 16; John 21)
Jesus establishes priestly office (I Cor. 11)
Jesus establishes teaching office (Matt. 28)
St. Peter in prison (Acts 12)
Article 10 ....Power to forgive sins (John 20)
Prodigal son (Luke 15)
Article 11 ....Raising of young man at Naim (Luke 7)
General resurrection (I Thess. 4)

[17] Cf. Knecht-Glancey, *A Practical Commentary on Holy Scripture* (3rd Eng. edition; St. Louis, 1910); pp. 809 ff.; Joseph Guyot, *Scriptural References for the Baltimore Catechism* (New York, 1941); Eugene Charles, *The Catechism Through the Gospel* (London, 1931); *Lumen Vitae, International Review of Religious Instruction*, Apr.–June, 1948, p. 393, and entire issue of Jan.–Mar., 1955; Frances J. Connell, *Dogmatic and Scriptural Foundation for Catechists* (Paterson, 1955).

Article 12 . . . . Dives and Lazarus (Luke 16)

SACRAMENTS

Baptism . . . . The baptism of Jesus (Matt. 3)
The commandment to baptize (Matt. 28; Mark 16)
Discourse with Nicodemus (John 3)

Confirmation . . . . . St. Peter and St. John confirming in Samaria (Acts 8)

Holy Eucharist . . Promise of the Holy Eucharist (John 6); institution of the Holy Eucharist (Matt. 26; Mark 14; Luke 22)

Penance . . . . Institution of the Sacrament of Penance (John 20)
Sorrow of St. Peter (Matt. 26)
Penitent Magdalen (Luke 7)
Ten lepers (Luke 17)

Extreme Unction . Anointing of sick by disciples (Mark 6)
Testimony of St. James (Jas. 5)

Holy Orders . . . . . Jesus establishes priestly office (I Cor. 11)
Power to forgive sins (John 20)

Matrimony . . . . . . Institution of marriage (Gen. 2)
Our Lord at Cana (John 2)

COMMANDMENTS

First . . . . Moses on Mount Sinai (Exod. 19)
Idolatry of Jews in desert (Exod. 32)
Sacrilege of Baltasar (Dan. 5)

Second . . . . Blasphemer stoned to death (Lev. 24)
Esau's oath (Gen. 25)
St. Peter's perjury (Matt. 26)
Herod's oath (Matt. 14)
Jepthe's rash vow (Judges 11)

Third . . . . Jew collecting firewood on Sabbath stoned (Num. 15)
Apostles picking corn on Sabbath (Luke 6)
Jesus does work of mercy on Sabbath (Luke 6)

Fourth . . . . Joseph gives due honor to his father (Gen. 46)
Younger Tobias and his father (Book of Tobias)
End of the bad son Absalom (II Kings 18)

	Ruth and Naomi (Book of Ruth)
	Jesus an example of obedience (Luke 2)
Fifth	Cain kills Abel (Gen. 4)
Sixth	Punishment of impurity by deluge (Gen. 6, 7)
	Sodom and Gomorrha (Gen. 19)
Seventh	Achab robs Naboth's vineyard (III Kings 21)
	Gabelus restores loaned money to Tobias (Tob. 4, 9)
Eighth	Putiphar's wife slanders Joseph (Gen. 39)
	Lie of Ananias and Saphira (Acts 5)
	False witnesses against Our Lord (Matt. 26)
Ninth	David a sinner through evil desires (II Kings 11)
	Woman taken in adultery (Mark 8)
Tenth	Deside of Heliodorus to commit robbery (II Mach. 3)

CAPITAL SINS

Pride	Pharisee in temple (Luke 18)
Covetousness	Judas (Luke 22)
Lust	Prodigal Son (Luke 15)
Anger	Esau (Gen. 27)
Gluttony	Rich man (Luke 16)
Envy	Joseph's brothers (Gen. 37)
Sloth	Slothful servant (Matt. 25)

LORD'S PRAYER

First Petition	St. Peter heals lame man in name of Jeus (Acts 3)
Second Petition	Older Tobias predicts coming of God's kingdom (Book of Tobias)
Third Petition	Jesus in agony: "Not My will . . ." (Luke 22)
Fourth Petition	Raven brings loaf of bread to Elias (III Kings 17)
Fifth Petition	St. Stephen prays for the Jews (Acts 7)
Sixth Petition	Jesus tempted by the devil (Luke 4)
Seventh Petition	Daniel miraculously preserved from harm (Dan. 6)

3. *Methods of teaching Bible History.* a. The method outlined below is that of such eminent catechists as Knecht,[18] Urban,[19] Raab,[20] Faszbinder,[21] Feilzer,[22] and others. It consists of the following five stages.

(1) *Preparation.* The Scriptural fact or event which is to be the topic of the catechization is mentioned briefly and clearly in a continuous discourse. In this perspective of the subject, concrete rather than abstract terms, verbs rather than nouns, are recommended to the teacher. The child will not become interested and attentive unless he knows beforehand what subject will be treated. We quote the following words of "Preparation" from Urban's lesson on "Cain and Abel":

"Sin and its fatal consequences have passed from Adam upon all his descendants. This showed itself in the wicked Cain, one of the sons of Adam, who slew his brother, Abel. About this I shall now tell you." [23]

(2) *Narration.* That the pupil may get a bird's-eye view of the fact or event, the entire story — and not merely parts of it — is narrated. The narration is not broken by questions and interruptions, lest it lose its force and strength. While the story is told without the help of a book, the narrative of the book is carefully observed, so as not to offend against the truth and not to confuse the children who some day may themselves read the story. Since children are by nature bright and gay, the recital should be vivid, lively and accompanied by appropriate gestures, variation of the voice and pauses. The children ought to be made to see with their eyes and hear with their ears the facts and events and conversations that are being narrated. At the same time the story must be told slowly so that the children can follow the thought. In all this the catechist also strives to make the religious instruction dignified.

Dr. Urban's "Narration" in the story mentioned above covers the following four points: (a) the sacrifice of Cain and Abel, (b)

[18] *A Practical Commentary on Holy Scripture* (3rd Eng. ed.; St. Louis, 1910), introduction, p. xviii.

[19] *Teacher's Handbook to Bible History* (New York City, 1905).

[20] *Der Weg Gottes*, 2 vols. (Donauwörth, 1923).

[21] N. and H. Faszbinder, *Methodisches Handbuch zur mittleren Ausgabe der katholischen Schulbibel von Ecker* (Trier, 1922), pp. 7 ff.

[22] *Op. cit.*, pp. 21 ff.

[23] *Op. cit.*, p. 13.

God's fruitless admonition to Cain and Cain's slaying of his brother, (c) the sentence upon Cain, (d) Cain's despair.

(3) *Repetition and Explanation.* The catechist tells the story over again, but now in parts. He lets the pupil repeat each section after him. This repetition with the children will show how much the children have grasped and how much stands in need of further explanation. Dr. Urban explains such terms and expressions as the following: "firstling," "keeper," "fugitive," "vagabond," "the Lord had respect to Abel," etc. All explanations are short; the Christian Doctrine class is not to be converted into a course on etymology or archeology. The explanations must not be given before or during the Narration, because the force of the story would be weakened and the attention of the children diverted to minor details. After the various sections of the story have been repeated and explained, the catechist shows a picture embodying the story and explains it.[24]

(4) *Exposition or Commentary.* The children have now learned the course of events and understand the immediate meaning of the phrases in which the story is told. But every Bible story, besides being the narration of some fact, also discloses to us God's nature and attributes or puts before our eyes certain truths of faith and morals. The catechist now brings out these religious truths clearly for the children. He also points out the typical character of persons, institutions and events in the Old Testament. He brings out religious and moral truths especially by the help of questions and

[24] The "Story Picture Method" of a Dominican Sister in Chicago, exemplified in her two volumes entitled *A Child's True Story of Jesus, Books I and II* (Chicago, 1928), makes the picture the central point in the instruction. *Book I*, intended for the first grade, consists of blank pages at the bottom of which is printed a "legend." After the story has been heard and understood the child selects the appropriate picture from an envelope in the back of the book and pastes it above the "legend" which tells the story. In the book for the second grade a group of sentences on gummed paper forming the story is enclosed in the envelope together with the pictures. "Legend" and title are placed in the book as guides to the child. After the teacher has told the story and aroused interest, a picture illustrating the lesson is shown. Children retell the story using the small picture for illustration. They then detach the lesson printed on gummed paper. After separating the sentence each child arranges his own lesson on his desk. When the arrangement is satisfactory, the lesson and pictures are pasted in the book. Cf. *Religion Hour*, by the same author (Chicago, 1928). This method recommends itself because of its application of the *Arbeitsprinzip.*

enunciates them, as far as possible, *in the language of the Catechism.* Finally, the lessons drawn from the Bible story are learned by simultaneous recitation and repetition.

Dr. Urban deduces the following doctrinal truths from the short Bible story about Cain and Abel. The teacher will notice, however, that the terminology is rather advanced and that the commentary will have to be simplified considerably for the lower grades.

(a) *Attributes of God. His Omniscience.* Although there was no witness to give testimony against Cain for the crime he had committed, though this foul deed had been carried out in the greatest secrecy, yet God knew all about it. What do we call that attribute of God by which He knows all things, even the most hidden, the most secret? What do you mean by saying God is *omniscient? His Infinite Holiness.* The infamous act of Cain so greatly displeased God because He hates and detests all that is evil. What do you mean by saying God is holy? *His infinite Justice.* God promises to reward Cain if he will do good and punishes him for his crime. What do we call that attribute of God by which He rewards the good and punishes the wicked? What do you mean by saying God is just?

(b) *Cain's Sins.* Cain envied his brother because God showed His acceptance of his sacrifice. Among what sins is envy classed? Which are the seven capital or deadly sins? Show what other sins resulted from Cain's envy (hatred, anger, lying, deceit and, lastly, wilful murder.)

(c) *The Sins that Cry to Heaven for Vengeance.* The blood of innocent Abel cried to heaven for vengeance upon his slayer. Willful murder, then, is one of the sins that cries to heaven for vengeance. Which are the other three sins that cry to heaven for vengeance?

(d) *Abel a Figure or Type of Christ.* Abel offers a sacrifice which is agreeable to God; Christ offers a sacrifice which is infinitely more agreeable to God. Abel was a shepherd; Christ is the Good Shepherd. The innocent Abel is put to death by Cain, his brother; Our Saviour – innocence itself – is put to death by the Jews, His brethren. The blood of Abel cries to heaven for vengeance; the blood of Christ cries for mercy in our behalf. Cain, the murderer of Abel, is condemned to wander a vagabond on the face of the earth; the Jews, the murderers of Our Saviour, are condemned to wander over the fact of the earth without priest, without king, without sacrifice.

(5) *Moral Application.* The first concern of the catechist must be to form the character and supernaturalize the conduct of the children. In the application the truths elicited in the commentary are brought home to the individual child and held up to him as a rule of conduct and of life. The application is deduced naturally from the story and is not forced. It must be directed to one point, because he who attempts too much usually accomplishes very little. It must not be too long or turned into a sermon; otherwise, the children will miss the main point. It must be suited to the age and inclinations of the child, as well as to the circumstances in which he lives. Let us listen to the moral application which Dr. Urban deduces from the story of "Cain and Abel": "God knew Cain's innermost thoughts and saw his infamous act, although committed in the utmost secret. Our Lord also knows our most secret thoughts words, and deeds. Therefore, beware of thinking wrong thoughts or committing evil deeds." If possible, the moral application ought to be carried out immediately, while the child is in the proper mood and disposition; for instance, an act of adoration of the Holy Eucharist, act of faith, contrition, etc. Finally, the resolution may be expressed in a proverb or pithy saying, or in a Scriptural or liturgical text, or in a verse of some popular hymn, or in the form of a popular or liturgical prayer.

Whate'er by my thought, or act I do
My heavenly Father knows it too.

b. According to the method outlined above, the essentials of Bible History are given in the words of the Catechism. In the first grade, however, the Catechism text itself is not used, but concert repetition takes the place of the book. In this connection the *Catechist's Manual* of the Christian Brothers says "With little children, the method should be entirely oral. A book is not at all necessary for them. The teacher, of course, has a book, not to use in class, but to select matter from, to prepare his lessons from, and to supply the formulas which he is going to teach. Whether he narrates or explains, or whether he strives to fix a text in the child's memory, he should do so orally. This mode of procedure is not only the easiest and pleasantest; it is also the quickest and most profitable." [25] In

[25] Philadelphia, 1912, p. 115.

the second and third grades, however, the children may be given a Catechism in order to enable them to learn more easily the answers to the questions asked in connection with Bible History. Many of the recent Bible Histories insert the Catechism questions and answers at the end of the lesson.

The teacher desirous of placing an appropriate textbook in the hands of children in the lower grades will find an excellent manual in Fr. A. Heeg's *Jesus and I.*[26] Rarely does one find a booklet so well adapted to the intellectual capacity of those for whom it is intended. The booklet presents the essentials of faith in a series of scriptural scenes. The lessons are in the form of a simple narrative, are illustrated by artistic pictures and are summarized in a few simple questions at the end. Large charts render the lessons doubly impressive, and a *Teacher's Manual* offers additional suggestions to the teacher who wishes to use this series. The booklet of Fr. L. A. Gales, entitled *Good News for God's Children,*[27] is likewise admirably adapted to the minds of the little ones and is beautifully illustrated by colored pictures. The stories are represented as being told directly by God the Father and by His Son, Jesus Christ.

The *Bible Story* of G. Johnson, J. D. Hannon and Sister Dominica,[28] is intended for children of the fourth grade. It strives to give the children a basic knowledge of the Old and New Testaments and is entended to continue the training begun in the home. It describes the important Scriptural events in the form of a continuous narrative. It adopts the biographical method and adheres closely to the phraseology of the Bible. The Old Testament section describes the preparation of humanity for the coming of the Redeemer of the world, while the New Testament shows forth the goodness, majesty and power of Christ. Forty-eight pictures in four-color printing illustrate the text. Questions summarizing the contents of each chapter, suggestions for various projects and activities, and a glossary are found at the end of the book. The *Teacher's Manual*[29] contains many useful suggestions; each lesson contains an explanation of difficult words, explanation of the pictures, reading of the text questions and suggestions for various activities.

[26] Chicago, 1934.
[27] St. Paul, 1930.
[28] New York, 1931.
[29] New York, 1933.

The same authors, have prepared a textbook for the fifth and sixth grades, entitled *Bible History*.[30] This volume strives to give the children a knowledge of the more important historical facts contained in the Bible. The Old Testament facts are narrated in chronological order, and special reference is made to the social, economic and political setting of these events. The New Testament is centered in Christ, who is represented as the fulfillment of all prophecies and as the culmination of all preceding events. The subject matter is presented in the form of eight large units corresponding to the great epochs in the history of Redemption. A preview – preparing the pupil for the central idea in the unit and linking this idea with the main theme of the preceding lesson – is prefixed to each unit. Each lesson is followed by "Things to Know and to Do," and each unit is followed by a "Self-Test" reviewing the contents of the unit. The lessons in the *Teacher's Manual*[31] comprise a preparation, explanation, application, resolution, correlations with the Catechism and the Liturgy, and topics for discussion or for written composition. In this connection it might be noted that the lessons in the *Guide Books* of the Schorsch or De Paul Series follow much the same steps – exploration, presentation, assimilation, guidance in the formation of virtuous habits, new words, pictures, and correlated poems and hymns.

Likewise intended for the higher grades is Brother Eugene's *Compendium of Bible and Church History*.[32] The book is divided into three parts. The Old Testament centers in the great men and women of the old dispensation; the New Testament revolves around Christ; the final section is a brief history of the Church. Each chapter is a continuous narrative and is followed by questions, study devices, problems, suggested projects, readings, compositions, and correlations with the Liturgy and with profane history.

c. In the *Fulda Lehrplan*, which was drafted by the German bishops in 1925 and revised in 1932, Bible History is taught in concentric circles. The Old Testament is taught in the fifth year of the *Volksschule* (grammar school). The Bible stories follow in chronological order so that the children may see how mankind had been prepared for the coming of Christ and that Christ is the

[30] New York, 1931.
[31] New York, 1934.
[32] New York, 1927.

central figure of history. The New Testament up to the Resurrection of Our Lord is taught in the sixth year. The establishment of the Church is explained during the first semester of the seventh year. The entire Old Testament is reviewed during th second semester of the seventh year, while the entire eighth year is given to a review of the New Testament and the history of the Church.[33] In this way the entire Bible History is studied once in the *Grundschule* and twice in the *Volksschule* – each time, however, from a different angle. This repetition makes for a deep understanding and appreciation of sacred history.

d. Catechists in the French-speaking countries have devised a novel and interesting method of reviewing the school lessons in Bible History and of intensifying the study of Holy Writ. They have composed attractive, popular "home" editions of Bible History, which the child may peruse during the vacation, during the long winter evenings and during inclement weather. Some of these Bible stories are intended for coloring [34] or project work; [35] some are richly supplied with beautiful pictures; [36] some are in the form of a continuous narrative;[37] some are in the form of a dialogue; [38] some are a mere adaptation of the Biblical text; some, finally, are supplied with a commentary.[40] All of them, however, are designed to put before the child's eyes the attractive and fascinating figure of the Saviour and Son of God.

e. Old Testament Bible History may be studied solely as a preparation of the Jewish people for the coming of the Messias. In that case the future Redeemer becomes the central thought of all the lessons. The promise of the Saviour in the garden of Paradise is traced through Abraham, Isaac, Joseph, and the other great personages, figures, and types of the Old Testament until its fulfill-

[33] Cf. *Lehrplan fur den katholischen Religionsunterricht in der Volkschule, herausgegeben im Auftrage der Fuldaer Bischofskonferenz* (Paderborn 1925); J. Gründer, *Der Geist des Fuldaer Lehrplans, die Willensbildung und der Arbeitsschulgedanke im kath. Religionsunterricht* (Paderborn, 1927).

[34] M. Deck, *Evangile à colorier* (Toulouse, 1933).

[35] *Évangile en images* (Tourcoing, s. d.)

[36] E. Charles, *L'Evangile de Maman* (Brussels, 1933); M. Fargues, *Images d'Évangile expliquées* (Tourcoing, 1934).

[37] M. Compaing de la Tour Girard, *L'Évangile de mes tout-petits* (Paris, 1925.

[38] M. Marteau de Langle De Cary, *Du paradis terrestre à Noël* (Paris, 1934); *LÉvangile dans la vie des petits enfants* (Paris, 1933).

[39] J. Van Reusch, *Mon premier livre. Histoire Sainte* (Namur, 1934).

[40] Compaing de la Tour Girard, *op. cit.*

ment in the birth of Christ. A book of rare merit in this regard is the volume entitled *Before Christ Came,* by a Sister of Notre Dame.[41] Each lesson is followed by a series of questions reviewing the essential points of the chapter, by suggestions for various activities and projects, by simple moral problems to be solved by the pupil, by "Good Things to Read," and finally by a few Catechism questions which grow out of the lesson. The booklet undoubtedly combines the best traditions and methods of Bible History.

f. A student of the Old Testament or a composer of Old Testament Bible History is frequently confronted with the following problem: what attitude should one assume towards the accounts of crimes, sins and vices which occur so often on the pages of the Old Testament – narratives which are not only disedifying but which disturb the imagination of both child and adult? How are we to convince others that these sections, too, are the word of God, inspired by the Holy Spirit? Some have attempted to solve the problem by publishing "expurgated" editions of the Old Testament to be used by pupils in the religion class. But this is hardly a solution, since sooner or later the student will chance upon the entire Old Testament, will discover these passages, and may be the more troubled by them. While we do not advocate the indiscriminate reading of the Old Testament by the young, we think that every catechist should keep in mind the following principles:

(1) The Old Testament was written for a people which had just emerged from slavery and from contact with Egyptian immorality, and hence its statements are often very frank and blunt.

(2) The Old Testament is a history of the domination of original sin over the human race, and actual sin is an external manifestation of an internal law to which man became subject at the Fall.

(3) The Old Testament is also the history of man's yearning for the Redeemer. If the personages of the Old Testament were represented as morally perfect, the coming of One Who would liberate us from sin would be meaningless.

Church History

Church History is a continuation of the biblical account of God's kingdom on earth. It is the story of Christ continuing His redeem-

[41] 2nd edition; Milwaukee, 1935.

ing work in the Church.[42] The Scriptures describe the social transformation which would be wrought through the Church, and Church History shows the gradual accomplishment of these anticipated changes. The record of the Church's development and spread throughout the whole word is, therefore, a complement of Bible History. Without it the latter would be an isolated account, an unfulfilled prophecy. The Third Council of Baltimore rightly addresses the following exhortation to Catholic parents: "Train your children to a love of history and biography. Inspire them with the ambition of becoming so well acquainted with the history and doctrines of the Church as to be able to give an intelligent answer to every honest inquirer."

Church History has a manifold catechetical value. Its value is, first of all, *apologetical*. Church History brings us face to face with the fact that the powers of evil have not prevailed against the Church built on a rock. It proves the abiding presence of the Holy Spirit in the Church and shows the truth of Christ's words, "I am with you all days, even to the consummation of the world," [43] and "the gates of hell shall not prevail against it." [44] Our Lord Himself referred to His works in proof of His words when He said, "Though you will not believe Me, believe the works." [45]

Church History has an *informational* value. How much more intelligible the ritual of Baptism, Lent and the Holy Week services become to us after we read the history of the catechumenate! The origin of certain religious orders, practices, feasts, laws and fasts become intelligible only in the light of Church History, which thus inspires us to lead more fervent Catholic lives and fills us with a great veneration and love for the Church.

Church History is an *educational* and *edifying* study. The beautiful example of the saints, the zeal of bishops, priests, missionaries and apostolic laymen, the Church's extensive work of charity, all arouse and spur us to a life of virtue.

In the lower grades Church History is usually taught in a nonsystematic manner. The teacher refers to Church History in order to illustrate or confirm a truth explained in the Catechism, and to

[42] Cf. Joseph Hronek, *Vyučovani Naboženstvi* (Praha, 1937), p. 75.
[43] Matt. 28:20.
[44] Matt. 16:18.
[45] John 10:38.

strengthen the faith and increase the devotion of the children.[46] Thus, before certain feasts of the saints the teacher briefly narrates their lives and points out some trait of their character. On certain feasts of the year the teacher reads appropriate and explanatory passages from Church History; for instance, the account of the delivery of Vienna from the Turks is read on the Feast of the Holy Name of Mary; the history of St. Helena on the Feast of the Discovery of the Holy Cross; the apparitions at Lourdes are recounted on the Feast of the Immaculate Conception.[47] These selections should be graphically told and not merely touched upon. Wherever available, visual helps such as pictures of persons and events, geographical charts, etc., will make the narrative doubly interesting.

Such stories as fill the children with enthusiasm for religion and for the Church should be given preference. Heresies, as the unpleasant happenings of the family, deserve less attention; for faith is nourished by truth and love – and not by error, doubt and hatred. The supernatural character of the Church and of the saints ought to receive special emphasis in catechization. The works of the Church and the lives and sayings of saints should be clearly distinguished from purely profane events and from the lives and sayings of ordinary men. Finally, it is not advisable to insist on a multiplicity of names and dry dates, on the chronological succession and synchronic enumeration of facts. It is usually sufficient to give the approximate dates. It is not the memory but the heart and mind that are being trained.

Biography is recognized today as a highly satisfactory method of teaching history in the lower grades. Biography makes things more real and more concrete. Events become living when they cluster around a being of flesh and blood. Boys and girls are influenced more by deeds than by ideas; they are moved more by example than by the cold commandment. Thus, J. H. Ostdiek says: "All truths, traits, and principles become attractive entities and even dynamic powers when discovered in the lives of those we have come to know and admire. Witness how the athletic heroes and moving picture stars who have become enshrined as ideals in

[46] Cf., for example, D. Chisholm, *The Catechism in Examples* 5 vols., (3rd ed.; London, 1921–1922).

[47] Cf. K. A. H. Kellner, *Heortology, a History of Christian Festivals* (London, 1908).

the hearts of our people influence our social practices, our conversations, our mannerisms, and our styles. Notice how the throngs crowd into the stadiums and into the theaters to see their colorful favorites in action. So strong is the power of ideals, even though they may be unworthy, that the worldly wise are building up their amusement enterprises almost exclusively around publicized personalities. I wonder if the children of this world are not wiser in their generation than the children of light. Perhaps we should steal their fire by organizing our programs in religion around the lovable Christ and His winsome Saints rather than around dry doctrines and stern commandments." [48]

The child is by nature an imitator. Whatever he learns in his early years – whether it be walking, playing, working, writing or reading – is the result of imitation of his elders. Sin, too, is the result of imitation. When a child curses, swears or steals, he is frequently repeating what he heard or saw others do. This natural imitative tendency can be exploited for good as well as for evil. The child can be powerfully influenced by the lives of heroic and godlike men. "The catechist," says Bishop Dupanloup, "ought to accustom the children to know the Saints and, if I may say so, to live with them; every Sunday he ought to tell them something out of the grand lives of any of the Saints whose day falls in the week, or tell them something interesting out of the History of the Church." [49] Conformably with these principles, many parochial schools devote several minutes each day to the reading of the Lives of the Saints.

A systematic schoolbook of Church History should contain interesting selections rather than a strictly chronological and continuous narration of the whole of history.[50] It should emphasize the character of the Church as a sanctifier of humanity, as a Mystical Body and as a great missionary agency. It should stress the sanctification of the lives and ways of men by the grace of God. It should show how "Christ in His Church advances down the ages unto the fulfillment of His mission. The Gospel is preached to every creature, and the result is that sanctity flourishes in every age. Because of

[48] "Vitalizing Religious Instruction" in *Proceedings of National Catechetical Congress at St. Louis* (Paterson, 1938), pp. 304, 313.

[49] *The Ministry of Catechizing* (New York, 1868), p. 480.

[50] Cf. K. Buhlmayer, *Ausgeführte Katechesen über katholische Kirchengeschichte* (Munich, 1925).

sanctity, the world has been made richer, socially and intellectually, while Christian art and literature and music have bestowed treasures of beauty upon the human race. 'I am come that they may have life and may have it more abundantly.' "[51] Church History should describe the Church's influence on the home, on the lot of women, the child, and the slave, on art, on civil liberty and on social justice. The transformative activity of the Church will be brought into clearer relief if compared with paganism and heathen practices. By showing what Christianity has contributed to the eternal as well as to the temporal welfare of man, Church History will foster in the children loyalty, sympathy and gratitude towards the Church.

[51] G. Johnson et al., *op. cit.*, preface, p. vi.

CHAPTER III

THE LITURGY

The Liturgy may be defined as the official worship of the Church. An adequate worship of God is impossible apart from Jesus Christ, who by the hypostatic union was anointed eternal High Priest of the Father. On Calvary Christ rendered a perfect worship of God.[1] By His loving obedience which expressed itself through sufferings and death, Christ gave the Father an honor infinitely greater than any that can be offered by mankind. Since Christ was God-Man, His actions had a theandric value. Because He was God, His voice penetrated to the throne of the Almighty; because He was Man, He could speak and act in behalf of those of whom He was the Head. The same worship that Christ offered to God on Calvary is offered now on the Christian altars, thanks to the ministers of the Church who were invested with the priesthood of Christ at the Last Supper.

The Mass is the center of the Liturgy and of our Christian life. It is the source and consummation of all the Sacraments, for it renews the passion and sacrifice of Christ in virtue of which the Sacraments operate.[2] In the Mass it is God who offers, God who is offered, God who receives the offering. Yet, Christ is not present in the Sacrifice of the Mass as an isolated individual; He is there as Head of His Mystical Body. The Liturgy then is the mystical body of the Church intimately united to its Head in expressing its profoundest homage to the One and Triune God. In this corporate

[1] St. Thomas, *Summa Theologica*, III, Q. lxii, art. 5: "Per suam passionem Christus initiavit ritum Christianæ religionis"; Q. lxiii, art. 3: "Totus autem ritus christianæ religionis derivatur a sacerdotio Christi."

[2] St. Thomas, *Summa Theologica*, III, Q. lxv, art. 3, Q. lxxiii, art. 3.

prayer and worship Christ our Head gathers up our imperfect adoration and feeble petitions and unites them with His own perfect homage and all-powerful appeal.[3] In and by and through our Chief we render perfect worship to God.

The Liturgy, understood in this sense, is an integral part of religion. Considered as a virtue, religion ranks immediately after the three theological virtues. It inclines the will to render due worship to God on account of His infinite excellence. Now the highest form of religious worship is the official corporate prayer of the Church, the Liturgy.[4]

In instituting this worship the Church adapted herself, as far as possible, to the psychological laws and needs of human nature. Her prayers and chants, her symbolism and ceremonies, her celebration of the feasts of Our Lord and of the saints, are all based upon and exemplify important principles of educational psychology recognized today. Hence, to disregard the Liturgy as an element of catechization would be to neglect an important factor in the training of the mind and heart. We shall explain now some of the psychological laws on which the Liturgy is based.

[3] Cf. the Encyclicals of Pius XII, *Mystici Corporis Christi* (June 29, 2943) and *Mediator Dei* (Nov. 20, 1947). Cf. the following articles in *Orate Fratres;* O. Jacobs, "Definition of Liturgy," IX, 449–454; W. Busch, "Substance of the Liturgy," V,50–54; B. Stegmann, "Soul of Liturgical Life," II, 71–75, and "What Is the Liturgy?" II, 45–51. Cr. also I. Schuster, *The Sacramentary* (New York, 1924), I. 3; H. Schmitb, *Die religiöse Unterweisung der Jugend* (Cologne, 1920), pp. 136 ff.; L. Beauduin, *Liturgy the Life of the Church* (Collegeville, 1929); L. Bopp, *Liturgical Education* (Milwaukee, 1937); A. Caronti, *The Spirit of the Liturgy*, (Collegeville, 1926); A. De Serant, *The Life of the Soul in the Liturgy* (London, 1934); R. Guardini, *The Spirit of the Liturgy* (New York, 1931); J. Kramp, *Eucharistic Education* (St. Paul, 1929); V. Michel, *The Liturgy of the Church* (New York, 1937); *Lumen Vitæ, International Review of Religious Education*, Jan.–Mar., 1952, and entire issue of Apr.–Sept., 1955; Denys Rutledge, *Catechism Through the Liturgy*, 4 vols. (London, 1949). L. Bouyer, *Liturgical Piety* (Notre Dame, 1955), Mary Perkins, *The Sacramental Way* (N.Y., 1948), G. Ellard, *Men at Work at Worship* (N.Y., 1940), Olivier Rousseau, *The Progress of the Liturgy* (Westminster, Md. 1951, Joseph Jungmann, *Liturgical Worship* (N.Y. 1941).

[4] Cf. A. Croegaert, "La Liturgie et le Cours de religion" in *Semaines Liturgiques* (Louvain, 1925), pp. 32–33; G. Lefèbvre, *Catholic Liturgy* (New York, 1924), pp. 214 ff.; and these articles in *Orate Fratres*: Sister Estelle, "Liturgy and Religious Instruction in the Grades", V, 64–69; "Through Christ Our Lord" (on the *Christ-Life Series in Religion*), VII, 307–312; A Durand, "Liturgy and the Teaching of Religion," I, 172–176; B. Confrey, "Training Children to Live the Liturgy," V, 543–547.

The External Expression of Liturgical Worship and Psychological Laws

1. *The Liturgy and Apperceptive Masses.* Christ, the Founder of the Church, always strove to engraft His heavenly doctrine upon the apperceptive masses or acquired knowledge of His listeners. In His parables He seized upon the mental content of His hearers and upon the material things within their experience and used them as stepping stones to supernatural verities and realities. In ordering her ritual the Church followed much the same process. She often incorporated into the Liturgy ceremonies and rites that were a part of the life of the people whom she converted. "Even in the times of the Catacombs," says Msgr. Glorieux, "but more especially after the first social triumph of the Church, a whole luxuriant Liturgy grew up around the Consecration and Communion, borrowing from every tongue, adopting the most majestic, the most imposing forms, striving to fit itself for its exalted task." [5] For the pagan festival in honor of the "Unconquered Sun" held on December 25 (the period of the winter solstice), the Church substituted the Christian festival in honor of the divine "Sun of justice." She supplanted the Lupercalia, pagan festivals in which the carrying of light was a leading feature, by the Candlemas procession wherein the lighted candle represents the true Light of the world. In this way she teaches her children to rise, through the objects and materials incorporated into their experience, to the invisible and spiritual realities of the supernatural world.

2. *The Liturgy and Bodily Attitudes and Movements.* Liturgical worship calls for certain definite bodily gestures, attitudes and movements. The sign of the cross, genuflections, bowing, striking the breast, down-cast eyes, face turned towards the ground, hands extended or folded in prayer, standing at attention, kneeling — these are some of the bodily attitudes assumed successively by a participant in liturgical worship. And the Church has acted wisely in making these bodily movements a part of her religious service, for they are based on the following psychological laws.

a. God is the Creator of man's body as well as of his soul, and therefore man must worship God through both; man must acknowl-

[5] "La Musique d'Église" in *Congress of Sacred Music* (Tourcoing, 1919), p. 59.

edge the dependence upon God of both his soul and body. The soul recognizes God's dominion over it by interior acts of adoration, praise and thanking. The body shares in the soul's acknowledgment of dependence upon God by means of physical attitudes and movements such as genuflecting, bowing, etc. To deprive God of worship expressed by the body is to deny Him worship which is justly due to Him. To insist only on interior worship, as the Protestants do, and to disregard the correlated bodily attiudes is to run counter to all psychological and natural laws.

b. Man's body and soul are substantially united; they form one indivisible whole. Man acts as a unit, and hence he should take part in sacred worship in both a spiritual and bodily manner. No other procedure, in fact, is possible. "The Church," says Dom Lefèbvre, "is a society composed of men, and since man consists of body and soul and is moreover a social being, therefore her worship must be exterior as well as interior and must be shared by all in common." [6] Because of his dual nature, man must render to God a spiritual as well as a corporal worship.

c. Because of this substantial union of soul and body there is a constant reciprocal and causal interaction between these two component elements of our nature. Every internal idea or thought produces a bodily state, and vice versa. From this psychological law two consequences immediately follow.

(1) Certain bodily attitudes during liturgical worship evoke specific mental states. Kneeling with folded hands and closed eyes is a bodily attitude that will evoke the mental attitude of reverence and adoration. Extension of the hands upright or in the form of a cross will evoke the mental state of earnest supplication. The bent body and striking of the breast during an act of contrition arouse in us a deep sense of sorrow and humility. To eliminate the bodily movement would be to suppress the corresponding religious idea itself. What, for example, would become of our faith in the Eucharist if we ceased to genuflect, genuflected only occasionally, or genuflected only carelessly before the Blessed Sacrament? What would become of the priest's devotion to the Mass if he ceased to observe the rubrics – those laws which, while providing for the

[6] *Op. cit.*, p. 13. Cf. Tanquerey, *De Religione* (22nd ed.; Paris 1927), pp. 106 ff.

due external and bodily celebration of the Mass, safeguard the priests's internal devotion towards the Eucharistic Sacrifice?

(2) Again, while it is true that one may say his prayers in an easy chair or lying in bed, yet these bodily attitudes will hardly be conducive to attentive and reverent lifting up of the mind towards God.

d. An idea – especially a religious idea – expressed externally and in action, becomes stronger and more vivid. By calling into play our bodily as well as our spiritual powers, the idea becomes more completely our possession. It becomes a part of us, and if exteriorized with sufficient frequency will develop into a permanent habit and a dominant force. These are the days of the "active" methods, of the *Werkschule* and *Arbeitschule,* of handiwork and projects in catechization. They are all reducible to the simple principle: learn by doing. The Church's liturgical worship, which has made adequate provision for the appropriate bodily expression of our religious beliefs, has long anticipated these demands of modern psychology and catechists.

3. *The Liturgy and Sense Activity.* Liturgical worship has a manifold sense-appeal. Lights, color, incense, vestments, architecture, sculpture, statues, symbols and floral decorations, the ceremonial, melodies of sacred music, hymns and chant – all these appeal to one or another of the senses, and through the senses serve the cause of religion. "The ecclesiastical architecture, especially the prayerful Gothic, persistently lifts the eyes to the overhanging vault, where the nerves of the fluted columns converge. The cross, the lance, the nails have been carved into the architecture of the world. And, lest the light of heaven should shine without bringing with it the story of man's redemption, the windows have been filled with stained glass figures of things divine. The riot of color on marble and canvas fills the interior with whisperings angelic. The soothing tones of the organ at Mass, Vespers or Benediction awake distant longings for something better. The flickering tapers around the altar complete a picture 'no artist can paint.' For others the poetic verse in which the lives of the Saints and the doctrines and glories of the Church are sung in every language, would at first entertain and then instruct." [7]

[7] E. J. Mannix, "Types of Converts," in John A. O'Brien's *White Harvest* (New York, 1927), pp. 125–126.

This sense-appeal of the Liturgy is based on important psychological laws.

a. In the first place, sense-impression is the origin of all knowledge. Nothing can enter the mind unless it first passes through the portals of one of the senses. In her Liturgy, the Church has long anticipated the principle of the Scholastics, of Comenius, and of Pestalozzi: *Nihil est in intellectu quod non prius fuerit in sensu.*[8] The ceremonies and ritual of the Church, the administration of the Sacraments, the adornments of the churches, are visible sense-forms through which the Church wishes us to discern the invisible things of God.

b. The child is at first pleased and charmed by these sense-forms of the Liturgy. These external elements of worship captivate his attention and fill him with delight. For a while these impressions will continue as mere pleasurable sense-stimulations and as such will not be devoid of all educational value. They will cultivate in the child an artistic and æsthetic sense and train him to distinguish what is beautiful from what is ugly.

c. But sooner or later this initial experience will be followed by an attitude of inquisitiveness or curiosity. The child will seek to know the meaning and significance of all these things and the reason why he is taking part in them. This period is extremely important in the liturgical training of the child and, if not properly met, may prove harmful to both the liturgical observance and religious life of the child. For these sense-stimulations will gradually lose their first appeal and become tiresome. This result will frequently come about sooner than we anticipate, because the child is receiving a multitude of other sense-impressions — some of them

[8] The Council of Trent, Sess. XXII, Cap. 5, says: "As it is the nature of man that he cannot, without external helps, easily rise to the contemplation of divine things, the Church, as a loving Mother, has instituted some rites, *e.g.*, that some things are spoken in a subdued, others in a loud voice. She also makes use of ceremonies — many of them being handed down from the Apostles — by which the majesty of this great sacrifice should more clearly appear and the minds of the faithful should, by these visible signs of religion and piety, be excited to behold the higher things hidden in this sacrifice." Sixtus V declared in his Bull *Immensa* that "the sacred rites and ceremonies which the Church, taught by Apostolic tradition, employs in the administration of Sacraments, in the Divine Office, and in all which appertains to the worship of God or of the Saints, are a powerful means of instruction for the Christian people in the true faith; by them souls may easily be led to meditate on sublime truths, and thus will find their devotion enkindled."

of a much higher quality – but devoid of all religious implication. It is at this point that the teacher must point out to the child the deeper meaning of these liturgical sense-forms.

d. The catechist must explain, in the first place, that by means of these external, visible and sensible representations the Church aids millions of her children – of every race, tongue and culture – to grasp the great and sublime truths which are beyond the reach of sense. The Christmas crib makes intelligible even to children the great dogmas of the Incarnation and of the Eucharist. Paintings and stained glass windows tell us in their own attractive way of the mysteries of the Redemption, Resurrection and Pentecost, or they narrate to us some event from the life of Our Lord, of Our Lady, or of some saint. The color of the vestments suggests to us the character of the feast, and the ceremonies of the Mass depict for us in a striking way the renewal of the Sacrifice of Calvary. A child who has been trained to detect the inner import of these outward forms will find the meaning of the Liturgy ever richer and deeper.

e. The important principle of correlation and association enters in at this point. Our Lord Himself associated His heavenly truths with something well-known in the experience of His hearers – with something apt to serve later as a reminder of a divine truth. Thus, the husbandmen could not look at the vine and the branches, nor the shepherd at his sheep, nor the fisherman at his nets, nor the farmer at his crops, without recalling the truth which Christ associated with these objects in His parables. The same is true of the Liturgy. Here divine truths are associated with images and impressions drawn from every region of sense-experience. By being correlated with lofty ideas these sense impressions are purified and ennobled. Whenever these sense-experiences occur in daily life, they will bring to consciousness the ideas supplied by the Liturgy, and through these ideas the Liturgy will exercise a constant and vital influence on the child's conduct.

f. The purpose of the sensible forms of the Liturgy is not merely to elevate sense-impressions, to lay the foundations for æsthetic culture, or to teach abstract dogmatic truths. In the economy of the supernatural life the outward forms have a deeper and higher purpose. By divine right they are not only the vehicles of divine truths but also the channels of the life of the Mystical Body, of the

Christ-Life.[9] Ever since the Divine Word, the Second Person of the Blessed Trinity, assumed human nature in order that the sons of men might become sons of God by participating in the life of their Head, all the means of our sanctification have been enshrined in sensible forms. Water, oil, the sign of the cross, the imposition of hands — these external signs used in the administration of the Sacraments — do not merely represent in a perceptible form the spiritual effects wrought in the soul; they *are* the visible forms in which the Christ-Life is incarnated, in which it pulsates and through which it flows. And when we come to the bread and wine of the Eucharist, we come to elements which contain the very source of the Christ-Life. Hence, in all our study of the Liturgy we must not stop until we have reached the Christ-Life in its very fountainhead — until we have thoroughly realized our living union with Christ the Head of the Mystical Body, with whom we offer and with whom we are offered in a Sacrifice fully acceptable to the Triune God.

Once we realize and fully appreciate this central reality of the Liturgy, our conduct will be transformed and supernaturalized. For if we are living members of Christ and temples of the Blessed Trinity, we can no longer use our bodies as instruments of sin. If in and through Christ we are members of one another — a truth which is forcibly expressed by corporate liturgical worship — we can no longer commit sins of lying, calumny, detraction and injustice. For Christ and His Mystical Body are one, and Christ is not divided against Himself. There can be no schism within the Mystical Body. In fact, only when the exponents of the doctrine of the Mystical Body and of the Liturgical Movement have duly emphasized and fully exemplified in their own lives the moral implications of these beautiful truths, only then will these doctrines become active and potent forces for social reconstruction. For those who, because of their intellectual and theological prefer-

[9] Cf. V. Michel, Adequate Preparation for Teaching the Mass in *Journal of Religious Instruction*, VIII, 594, VIII, 765, *Life in Christ* (mimeoprint, Collegeville), *The Christian in the World* (mimeoprint, Collegeville), *The Liturgy of the Church* (New York, 1937); P. Parsch, *The Liturgy of the Mass* (St. Louis, 1938); W. Busch, *The Mass Drama* (Collegeville, 1930); F. Boeser, *The Mass Liturgy* (Milwaukee, 1935); B. B. Miller, *The Eucharistic Sacrifice* (New York, 1930).

ences, should be most charitable must not in their daily life be most uncharitable.

Many a soul has been moved and ultimately brought into the Church by the Liturgy. Writing of the Catholic Church before his conversion, Cardinal Newman says, "I looked at her – at her rites, here ceremonial, and her precepts – and I said: 'This is religion'"[10] Herman Cohen, a pianist of great renown, is called to replace the director of a group of artists in the Church of Sainte-Valère in Paris. While the priest raises the monstrance at Benediction, he experiences extraordinary emotions at once of remorse for the past and attraction towards the Catholic Faith. Later on, in Ems, Germany, during the elevation at Mass, his eyes suddenly fill with tears, and he receives the gift of faith.[11] Robert Bracey, full of contempt for the papacy and ritualism, enters in his sixteenth year the oratory of Edgbaston to assist at High Mass. Contact with the sensible forms of grace suddenly transforms his soul, and he leaves the church convinced of the truth of the Catholic religion.[12] "I am haunted by Catholicism," Huysmans makes Durtal repeat to himself, "intoxicated by its atmosphere of incense and wax. I prowl about it, moved even to tears by its prayers, touched even to the marrow by its psalms and chants."[13] The well-known Danish convert and writer, Johannes Jorgenson, likewise confesses that "the whole of the liturgical, ceremonial, and decorative side of Catholicism attracted me."[14] Paul Claudel, an unbeliever from his eighteenth year, enters the cathedral of Notre Dame in Paris to assist at the Christmas offices. With a feeling of superior dilettanteism, he hopes to find an appropriate literary inspiration in the decadent ceremonies of the Church. As he listens to the solemn strains of the *Magnificat*, grace suddenly illuminates his soul, and the gladsome chant of the *Adeste Fideles* confirms him in his sudden conversion.[15]

The Liturgical Year

Conscious of man's tendency to forgetfulness and neglect, realizing that intellectual knowledge is dependent upon concomitant

[10] *Apologia pro Vita Sua* (London, 1886), p. 340.
[11] C. Sylvain, *Vie du R. P. Hermann* (4th ed.; Paris, 1909), pp. 4 ff.
[12] *Roads to Rome* (London, 1901), pp. 10 ff.
[13] *En Route* tr. by C. Kegan Paul (London, 1922), p. 15.
[14] *An Autobiography,* tr. by I. Lund (New York), p. 297.
[15] Cf. Th. Mainage, *Les Témoins du Renouveau Catholique* (5th ed.; Paris, 1919), pp. 61 ff.

sensible activity, the Church desires to enact before our eyes yearly and in a concrete manner the principal events of Christ's life. She wishes to set before us the galaxy of saints in whom God has been truly wonderful (*mirabilis Deus in sanctis suis*), to whom Christ has, in very deed, been the Way, the Truth, and the Life. This annual celebration of the mysteries of man's salvation and of the memory of the saints constitutes the liturgical year. The feasts succeeding one another in the course of the year impart a special background and character to the Mass and to the Divine Office. In each mystery the Church shows us the graces to be obtained, the virtues to be acquired, the mortifications and self-denials to be undertaken in union with Christ the Head of the Mystical Body. "What is this admirable, liturgical year?" asks Bishop Dupanloup. "You know well, and I am not afraid to repeat it, that it is one of the most beautiful institutions of the Church. There is nothing more beautiful, nothing more captivating. It is all a poem, a sublime poem, the great Christian poem, that which God Himself conceived in His thoughts and executed by His power. The whole of Christianity is there – all the mysteries, all the divine actions, all gospel teaching, everything that enlightens souls and sanctifies them – and all this grouped around the Sacrifice, the center and the soul of all Catholic worship; all shown and celebrated in the hymns, the psalms and the canticles, and in the teachings which accompany every festival by the mouth of the priest; without any doubt, it is one of the grandest inspirations of the Spirit of God, and perhaps has a more powerful influence over souls than one can even imagine." [16]

There is no doubt, then, that the more fully children understand, according to their ability, the significance of the liturgical year, the more will the knowledge as well as the practice of religion be a joy for them. In fact, if the faithful were properly instructed con-

[16] *The Ministry of Catechizing* (New York), pp. 69–70. Cf. also C. C. Martindale, *The Mind of the Missal* (New York, 1929), *The Words of the Missal* (New York, 1932), *The Prayers of the Missal* (New York, 1937); V. Michel, *The Liturgy of the Church* (New York, 1937), *My Sacrifice and Yours* (Collegeville, 1927); O. Haering, *Living with the Church* (New York, 1930); E. Loehr, *The Year of Our Lord* (New York, 1937); P. Parsch, *Das Jahr des Heiles*, 3 vols. (Klosterneuburg, 1932), Florence E. Berger, *Cooking for Christ, The Liturgical Year in the Kitchen* (Des Moines, 1949), Bernard Strasser, *With Christ through the Year* (Milwaukee, 1947), Jean Cardinal Villeneuve, *An Introduction to the Liturgical Year* (N.Y., 1946), Martin B. Hellriegel, *Vine and Branches* (St. Louis, 1948).

cerning the nature of the different feasts, if they celebrated the feasts in the spirit of the Church, they would obtain an increase of knowledge and piety, and their lives would consequently be transformed. In the encyclical *Quas Primas,* Pius XI says: "People are instructed in the truths of faith and brought up to appreciate the inner joys of religion far more effectually by the annual celebration of the sacred mysteries than by an official announcement of the teaching of the Church." [17] The liturgical feasts are arranged with a view to make the mysteries penetrate deeply into the mind and heart and to move the soul to a virtuous life. In the introduction to his invaluable *Catéchisme des Fêtes,* Bossuet writes: "One of the principal ends which the Church sets before herself in the institution of feasts is the instruction of the faithful. The solemnities occur at different times in order that we may thereby learn what God has deigned to do for our salvation, and what we must do to lay hold of it." [18]

The liturgical year keeps Christ living in our minds and hearts. We are too inclined to consider Christ's Nativity, Resurrection, and Ascension as mere historical events. We forget that Christ is continually being born anew in the hearts of men through sanctifying grace. We forget that every day is a day of our Risen, Glorious and Ascended Chief, of whose Mystical Body we are the members. We forget that the Holy Spirit is continually descending invisibly and indwelling in our souls. In the liturgical year the past is renewed, and we all contemplate once more Christ and His sacred mysteries. A glance at the Collects of the different feasts will readily assure us of this fact:

"Deus, qui hanc sacratissimam noctem veri luminis fecisti illustratione clarescere . . ."	"O God, who has made *this most holy night* to shine forth with the brightness of the true light . . ." [19]

[17] December 11, 1925. In *La Croix* of August 5, 1911, G. Kurth writes: "Selon moi, l'une des plus grandes causes de l'ignorance religieuse, sinon la plus grande, est l'ignorance liturgique. Rendre aux fideles l'intelligence et par suite l'amour des mystères qui se celebrant à l'autel, *remettre dans leurs mains le missal* qu'ont replacé tant de livres de devotion vulgaires et médiocres, c'est la vraie manière d'enseigner la religion, d'attacher au temple ceux qui le visitent encore et d'y ramener plus tard ceux qui l'ont désérté," quoted in *Semaines Liturgiques* (1924), p. 11. Cf. also K. Mosterts, *Junglingsseelsorge* (2nd ed.; Freiburg im. B., 1923), pp. 161 ff.

[18] *Œuvres de Bossuet* (ed. F. Lachat, Paris, 1885), V, 139.

[19] Collect of the First Mass of Christmas.

"Deus, qui hodierna die Unigenitum tuum gentibus stella duce revelasti . . ."	"O God, who on *this day* by the guidance of a star didst reveal Thine only-begotten Son to the Gentiles . . ." [20]
"Deus, qui hodierna die per Unigenitum tuum æternitatis nobis aditum devicta morte reserasti . . ."	"O God, who *this day* didst reopen to us the approach to eternity by Thine only-begotten Son, victorious over death . . . " [21]
"Hodierna die Unigenitum tuum Redemptorem nostrum ad cœlos ascendisse credimus . . ."	"We believe Thine only-begotten Son, our Redeemer, to have ascended *this day* into heaven . . ." [22]
"Deus, qui hodierna die corda fidelium Sancti Spiritus illustratione docuisti . . ."	"O God, who on *this day* didst instruct the hearts of the faithful by the light of the Holy Spirit . . ." [23]

Separated from the Liturgy, the Holy Eucharist, especially for the humble and the little ones, would be distant, abstract and impersonal. In the Liturgy Christ steps forth from the immobility and silence of His sacramental state. Each day it is a new mystery, a new Jesus, that the Missal presents to us. Thanks to their Missal, the faithful find the Master at the border of the well, on the mountain, in the busy highway, on the shore of the lake at Bethany – in short, in all the states of His terrestrial life. In this way the Mass becomes almost as intimate a companionship with Christ as that enjoyed by the disciples themselves.

The liturgical feasts and seasons produce in us the effects of the mysteries which they represent. Some special fruit is to be derived from the observation of every current festival of the ecclesiastical year. The mind of the Church in this regard is clearly manifested in the following prayer:

"Deus, qui nos resurrectionis Dominicæ annua solemnitate	"O God, who didst give us joy by the yearly solemnity of Our

[20] Collect of the Epiphany, January 6.
[21] Collect of Easter Sunday; cf. also the Introit.
[22] Collect of the Feast of the Ascension.
[23] Collect of the Feast of Pentecost.

lætificas: concede propitius; ut per temporalia festa quæ agimus, pervenire ad gaudia æterna mereamur."	Lord's resurrection, mercifully grant that by celebrating these feasts in time we may deserve to attain eternal joys." [24]

Christ merited for us from the first moment of His Incarnation up to His death on the Cross. Christ redeemed us by His whole life but principally by His passion and death. Each moment of His life and every action of His had a redemptive touch. At each stage of His life – whether it be the infancy, or the hidden life, or the public life, or His passion and death – Christ merited special graces for us. Through the various feasts of the liturgical year in which Christ Our Head reënacts the mysteries of His earthly existence, we His members participate in the graces which He merited for us during His thirty-three years upon earth.

Besides recalling to us the principal events of Christ's life, the Church wishes through her liturgical year to keep before our eyes those in whom the life, teaching and example of the Supreme Model have been reflected in a truly wonderful manner. The purpose of the *Sanctorale* is beautifully indicated in the following two prayers.

"Concede, ut ejus auxilio, et imitatione certantes in terris, coronari cum ipso mereamur in cœlis."	"Vouchsafe unto us that, after battling upon this earth even as he battled, helped by his prayers, it may one day be ours to be crowned with him in heaven." [25]
"Fac nos, Domine Deus, supereminentem Jesu Christi scientiam, spiritu Pauli Apostoli ediscere."	"Make us, O Lord God, in the spirit of St. Paul the Apostle, thoroughly to learn the knowledge of Jesus Christ, a knowledge surpassing all understanding." [26]

The child tends by natural impulse to imitate the examples set before him. The first word he utters, the first lesson he reads and the first picture he draws are all the result of imitation of mother or teacher. Later on his inspirations are drawn from examples of the past as set forth in history, biography or literature. The Church

[24] Collect of the Wednesday of Easter Week.
[25] Collect of the Mass of St. Ignatius Loyola, July 31.
[26] Collect of the Mass of St. Anthony Maria Zaccaria, July 5.

understands the meaning of imitation in the educative process, especially in the teaching of religion. In her festivals she proposes as models of imitation those who have exemplified in a high degree the teaching and precepts of Christ. She encourages us to walk in the footsteps of men who had to struggle against the very difficulties and temptations which we encounter — men who gave up everything, even life itself, in order to win Christ and save their souls. Through the saints we learn to know better Jesus who was their Model, we procure the aid of their powerful intercession, and we realize more fully the doctrine of the Communion of Saints.

The apprehension and understanding of sublime truths demands on the part of the recipient a certain amount of attention, preparation and receptivity. The liturgical year again admirably meets this requirement of educational psychology. The principle of preparation, as a matter of fact, runs throughout the whole course of God's dealing with mankind. The Old Testament is a preparation for the New Dispensation. The coming of the Messias is foretold by the prophets and foreshadowed by type and sacrifice. In Christ's teaching the way for a new doctrine is prepared either by Christ's own life of unique holiness, by a miracle or by a parable. The Church, too, always insists upon a careful preparation before entering upon the contemplation of the sublime mysteries of religion. Her chief festivals are preceded by novenas or by vigils of prayers and fasting. During the four weeks of Advent she prepares the faithful for the celebration of Christmas, and during the seven weeks of Lent she prepares them for the celebration of the Christian Pasch. In this way the Church develops in us a sense of sin and a spirit of humility and makes us receptive to the workings of divine grace.

Great care, therefore, must be taken that the liturgical year becomes a Catechism of the children and the people. For once the children have left the Catholic school, the Church has no way of reaching them, generally speaking, except through the Liturgy. If the children have grown up ignorant of the Liturgy, there is little probability that they will persevere in coming to church. They will weary of the Liturgy because they have never been initiated into its inner meaning. In order that the Liturgy may in later life be a constant reminder to the children of the principal points of Catholic teaching, the teacher must in his catechetical instructions correlate Christian Doctrine with the Liturgy whenever a convenient occasion presents itself. We offer the following examples of correlation as mere suggestions.

Faith	Baptismal ritual
	Nicene Creed
Hope	Season of Advent
	Season after Pentecost
The Blessed Trinity	Trinity Sunday
	Votive Mass of the Blessed Trinity
	Preface of Trinity Sunday
	The Mass (cf. below)
	Baptismal formula
	Absolution formula, etc.
	Athanasian Creed
	Conclusion of hymns
	The *Gloria Patri*
Angels	Feast of the Guardian Angels
	Feasts of SS. Michael, Gabriel, Raphael
	Votive Mass of the Angels
	Prefaces
Creation	Holy Saturday
Original Sin	Holy Saturday
	Baptismal Ritual
Immaculate Conception	Feast of the Immaculate Conception (Collects)
Promise of a Redeemer	Advent liturgy
Incarnation	Feast of the Annunciation
	Feast of St. Gabriel
Birth of Christ	Christmas liturgy
	Epiphany liturgy
Nature of Christ	Nicene Creed
Baptism of Christ	Commemoration of the Baptism of Our Lord Jesus Christ
Passion of Christ	Lent and Passiontide
Death of Christ	Good Friday
Resurrection	Paschal liturgy
Ascension	Ascension liturgy

Descent of the Holy Spirit	Pentecost liturgy
Blessed Virgin Mary	Marian character of Advent; feasts
Primacy of St. Peter	Feast of SS. Peter and Paul
	Memento of the pope in the *Te Igitur*
Priestly Office	Holy Thursday
Teaching Office	Easter Friday
Communion of Saints	Feast of All Saints
Purgatory	Feast of All Souls
Judgment	Twenty-fourth Sunday after Pentecost
	First Sunday of Advent
Death	Ash Wednesday
	Requiem Masses
Baptism	Lent
	Holy Saturday
	Paschal liturgy
	Baptismal ritual
Confirmation	Rites and ceremonies of Confirmation
	Blessing of the oils on Holy Thursday
	Pentecost
Eucharist	Holy Thursday
	Corpus Christi
	Benediction and Forty Hours' adoration
Mass	The altar
	Mass prayers
Penance	Lent
	Absolution formula
	Confiteor of Mass
Extreme Unction	Ritual
	Blessing of the oils on Holy Thursday
Holy Orders	Holy Thursday
	Ordination prayers and ceremonies

Matrimony	*Missa pro Sponso et Sponsa*
Reverence for God's Name	Feast of the Holy Name
Obedience to Authority	Feast of the Holy Family
Saints	The *Sanctorale*

The Mass

The liturgical year – the annual celebration of the mysteries of man's salvation and of the feasts of the saints – constitutes the setting and background, as it were, of the daily Mass. The relation between the virtue of religion and the Mass is, as we have already said, very intimate. The virtue of religion inclines the will to render the Triune God due worship because of His infinite excellence. The Catechism tells us that God made us "to know Him, love Him, serve and worship Him." The One and Triune God must be the center of all our devotions and worship here below, as in the next life He will be the principal object of the Beatific Vision. What better way of discharging our duty of adoration towards God than through the Mass? A sacrificial act and worship of *latria* surpassing all others, the Mass has for its object the One and Triune God – *Suscipe, sancta Trinitas, Placeat tibi, sancta Trinitas.* Let us indicate a few of the numerous references to the Blessed Trinity in the Mass, at the same time pointing out the possibility of correlating the Mass with the Catechism:

THE SIGN OF THE CROSS

"In the name of the *Father,* and of the *Son,* and of the *Holy Spirit.*"

THE GLORIA PATRI

"Glory be to the *Father,* and to the *Son,* and to the *Holy Spirit.*"

THE KYRIE

"*Kyrie* eleison, *Christe* eleison, *Kyrie* eleison . . ."

THE GLORIA IN EXCELSIS

"O Lord God, *Father* Almighty . . . O Lord Jesus Christ, the only-begotten *Son* . . . together with the *Holy Spirit* . . ."

THE COLLECTS

The Collects are addressed to the *Father,* through Our Lord *Jesus Christ,* Who reigns with the *Holy Spirit.*

THE CREDO

"God the *Father Almighty* . . . Lord Jesus Christ, the only-begotten *Son of God* . . . and in the *Holy Spirit* . . ."

THE OFFERTORY

"Receive, O Holy *Father* . . . Who vouchsafed to become partaker of our humanity, Jesus Christ, Thy *Son* . . . Come, Thou *Sanctifier.*"

PRAYER TO THE TRINITY

"Receive, *O Holy Trinity* . . ."

THE SANCTUS

"Holy, holy, holy . . ."

THE CANON

"Wherefore, O most merciful *Father* . . . through Jesus Christ, Thy *Son,* in the unity of the *Holy Spirit* . . . Be pleasing to Thee, *O Holy Trinity."*

THE FINAL BLESSING

"May Almighty God bless you, the *Father,* the *Son,* and the *Holy Spirit."*

The Mass must not be considered as something carried on apart and without any reference to the individual. The members of Christ's Mystical Body are indissolubly associated with the Head in His act of supreme homage. The "we" formulas of the Mass clearly establish this fact. "Brethren, pray that my sacrifice and yours may be well pleasing to God"; "Be mindful, O Lord, of Thy servants . . . for whom we offer, or who offer up to Thee, this sacrifice of praise"; "We beseech Thee, O Lord, graciously to receive this oblation which we, Thy servants, and with us Thy whole family, offer up to Thee." In union with our Head we adore God, offer to Him our satisfaction for sin, and so work out our salvation:

"Concede nobis, quæsumus, Domine, hæc digne frequentare mysteria; quia, quoties hujus hostiæ commemoratio celebratur, opus nostræ redemptionis exercetur."

"Make us, we beseech Thee, O Lord, to assist worthily and assiduously at these sacred mysteries; for, as often as this saving Victim is offered up, so often is Our Redeemer's work made to avail in our behalf." [27]

Not only do Christ's members offer with Him, but the whole Mystical Body is victim with its Head. "Christ, Head and members, offers; Christ, Head and members, offers Himself. If He cannot disjoin or tear off His members for oblation, He must retain them

[27] Secret, Ninth Sunday after Pentecost.

for oblation of Himself." [28] If Christ alone were Victim, why should we pray in the Liturgy that "we find favor," that "our sacrifice be pleasing" and carried up to God by angelic hands? An acquaintance with these sublime truths cannot but beget a desire for greater and better knowledge of the Mass, of its prayers, rites and ceremonies. Only when Catholics will have realized that the Mass is an action in which they are vitally concerned will they cease to be bored by the divine services and assist at them with eagerness and joy.

A worthy assistance at Mass presupposes in turn an acquaintance with the Missal. It may perhaps be no exaggeration to say that, because the Missal remained to them a sealed book, many young people, after having spent six or seven years in a Catholic school where every day begins with the Holy Sacrifice, assist at Mass with a languishing faith and only because constrained by the laws of the Church. "The Missal," writes Fr. Drinkwater, "is religion pure and undefiled – essential Catholicism. It is the greatest book in the world – greater, in a way, than the Bible, which is its source, because it is the Bible read with wondering new eyes by the Church, read in the all-revealing light streaming from the Calvary-Eucharist altar. It is the book of words that has gathered itself round the action of the Mass – poetry, theology, history, all Catholic humanity's hopes and fears and highest longings and most secret thoughts, fused together into the one serene emotion – which is the response of the human heart when it contemplates God's truth." [29]

[28] Grimaud-Newcomb, *'My' Mass* (New York, 1928), p. 41. Cf. also: G. Johnson, "The Liturgy as a Form of Educational Experience" in *Cath. Educ. Rev.* (Nov., 1926), p. 532; J. Baierl, *The Holy Sacrifice of the Mass* (Rochester); F. Boeser, *The Mass Liturgy* (Milwaukee, 1935); W. Busch, *The Mass Drama* (Collegeville, 1930); J. De Puniet, *The Mass* (New York, 1932); A. Fortescue, *The Mass* (New York, 1937); N. Gihr, *The Holy Sacrifice of the Mass* (St. Louis, 1934); W. Herbst, *Holy Mass* (New York, 1934); J. Kearney, *The Meaning of the Mass* (New York, 1936); J. Kramp, *Liturgical Sacrifice of the New Law* (St. Louis, 1926); N. Maas, *The Treasure of the Liturgy* (Milwaukee, 1931); M. Montessori, *The Mass Explained to Children* (New York, 1934); P. Parsch, *The Liturgy of the Mass* (St. Louis, 1936); Sister M. Brendan Leger, *Children's Understanding of the Mass* (Washington, 1948), Joseph A. Jungmann, *The Mass of the Roman Rite* (N.Y., 1955), Dom Benedict Stewart, *The development of Christian Worship* (London, 1953), G. Ellard, *The Mass of the Future* (Milwaukee, 1948), T. Klauser, *A Brief History of the Liturgy* (Collegeville, 1953), John L. Murphy, *The Mass and Liturgical Reform* (Milwaukee, 1956).

[29] *The Givers* (New York, 1926), p. 13.

The liturgical method is profoundly scriptural.[30] In Christian antiquity, as St. John Chrysostom so eloquently testifies,[31] religious instruction was basically Scriptural. Many patristic writings were an adaptation of the Bible with a view to catechization. The reason for this procedure is easily intelligible. The Bible is the Book of God, a record of His communications to men throughout the ages, the witness of His mercies, the code of His sovereign wishes. The Bible is also the Book of Christ, who is yesterday, today, and the same forever, whose redeeming work is narrated from the *proto-evangelium* to the visions of the Apocalypse. "To ignore the Scriptures," wrote St. Jerome, "is to ignore Christ."

This traditional method can be restored in two ways: first, by spreading popular editions of the Gospels and Epistles among the faithful; secondly, by a more extensive use of the Missal. The first procedure is being followed by the Confraternity discussion clubs. Manuals covering the whole New Testament and part of the Old, and written in a language intelligible to the average reader, are successfully introducing laymen to the rich treasures of the Scriptures. By correlating each lesson with the Liturgy, they gradually introduce the discussion club members to the second method, namely, the use of the Missal. By an intelligent use of the Missal the faithful are acquainted further with the mysterious language of God. In the Missal they find Christ's life reproduced by the liturgical cycle, foretold in the psalms and prophecies, narrated in the Gospels, commented on in the Epistles and homilies, exemplified in the lives of the saints and made efficacious by active participation in the holy mysteries. In a word, the Liturgy is Sacred Scripture popularized, condensed, illustrated and rendered accessible to all.

The catechetical method of Christian antiquity, as is evident from the old Roman ceremonial books and the writings of the Fathers, was essentially a "prayer method." Religious truths were not communicated to the faithful in dry, abstract formulas. Religious instruction took the form of adoration, praise, thanksgiving and prayer; it was thus sacred and sanctifying; it was fused with the hymns, antiphons, doxologies, homilies and chants, all of which throbbed with faith and love. As soon as a new definition was pronounced or a new precision of doctrine made, it was immediately

[30] Cf. F. Cabrol, *Liturgical Prayer* (New York, 1922), pp. 1 ff.
[31] Cf. *Semaines Liturgiques* (1924) pp. 13 ff.

transformed into a liturgical hymn, chanted at the altar, and integrated into the celebration of the holy mysteries. The faithful prayed their faith. Their worship, their adorations and their praises were an index of their creed: *Lex orandi, lex credendi.* The church, the sanctuary, the altar, were the center of religious life, the hearth whence religion radiated. The truths gradually penetrated the receptive soul and filled it with celestial blessings.

The intelligent participation of the faithful in the Liturgy will necessarily imply a restoration of the "prayer method." True, a methodical exposition of Christian Doctrine is necessary in the face of heresy. But abstract formulas will not of themselves develop Christians with a strong faith and profound, solid piety. The dry formulas often remain inoperative and dead in the soul. The Liturgy, on the other hand, is our faith felt, lived, sung, confessed, prayed and revived through contact with the faith of our brethren and of the whole Church. The doctrinal and collective prayer of the Church is an indispensable complement of the Catechism. The relation of the latter to the Liturgy is the same as that of the grammar to spoken language. The Catechism tells us, for example, that the Second Person of the Blessed Trinity becames incarnate. In order to become effective in our lives, this catechismal formula must be felt and assimilated. It is made vital through the liturgy of Advent, Christmas, and Epiphany.[32]

Suggestions

Where liturgical instruction cannot be given systematically, it should at least be given by way of illustration, application or correlation with the Catechism. The children should be taught to assist and participate intelligently in the Mass and should be made acquainted, if at all possible, with the use of the Missal. At the approach of a liturgical season or feast the catechist should explain

[32] A. Croegaert, "La Liturgie et le Cours de Religion," in *Semaines Liturgiques* (1924), p. 34, writes: "Les rites liturgiques sont plus que de vains symboles: ils expriment le dogme, car l'Église adore et prie comme elle croit, Sa Liturgie est donc son dogme prié, son dogme chanté, son dogme confessé dans l'assemblée vivante des frères, groupés matériellement autour du même autel, unis dans la célébration concrète de la même Fraction du pain, des mêmes offices, sous la presidence du mêmes Pasteur. La prière liturgique, c'est la religion parlée et vécue c'est le dogma appliqué et exprimé dans une langue toute chargée d'énergies surnaturelles et à laquelle l'appoint de tous les arts donne son maximum de pénétration dans les âmes."

to the children the meaning of the feast or of the season. The explanation of the Gospel of the day is very instructive because the central dogma of the feast is often enunciated in it. Whenever possible the teaching of Bible History and of the Catechism should follow the ecclesiastical year. Facts from the Bible and Church History which are the cause of some particular feast or ceremonies should be clearly explained. In arranging religious devotions the catechist should also consider the ecclesiastical year and pray with the Church. The catechist should explain the ceremonies connected with certain feasts – for example, Candlemas and Corpus Christi processions, Holy Week ceremonies, etc.

The catechist should acquaint the children with the contents and belongings of the church, the sacristy, baptismal font, pulpit, confessionals, altar, vestments, vessels, liturgical books, etc. This instruction should be given primarily by showing the things themselves.[83] When this cannot be done, recourse to pictures and drawings is the next best thing. The meaning of sacramentals in frequent use (such as holy water, rosaries, medals, St. Blaise's blessing) should be made clear to the child. Among the Mass ceremonies only those which recur often should be explained. The catechist should instruct the children about the actions which they themselves are to perform; he or she should make them realize the spirit which should inform those actions. The catechist should also teach the children the actions which accompany the reception of the Sacraments, especially the Sacraments of Penance, the Holy Eucharist, Confirmation, and Extreme Unction.[84]

The Church intends the Liturgy to be the book of the unlearned It would be a mistake to think that liturgical explanations are tc be reserved for adults and the educated and that children cannot grasp the significance and inner meaning of liturgical symbols and ceremonies. A catechist who is well trained in the Liturgy will find in it excellent illustrations of the profoundest mysteries taught in the Catechism. The children are naturally inquisitive and desire an explanation of every object that they behold. The virtue of faith infused into the child's soul at Baptism creates a certain co-natural-

[83] Cf. *Semaines Liturgiques* (1924), pp. 7 ff., 76; (1925), p. 107.

[84] Useful books to consult in this regard are M. S. McMahon's *Liturgical Catechism* (Dublin, 1926) and F. J. Sullivan's *The Visible Church* (New York, 1921).

ness between the child's soul and the supernatural. Availing himself of the child's receptive disposition, the catechist can easily arouse interest in the sacred things which the child has seen so often but without grasping their meaning.[35] That the official prayer of the Church is intended to have a catechetical value is clearly stated in the Collect of the Saturday after Passion Sunday:

"Proficiat, quæsumus, Domine, plebs tibi dicata, piæ devotionis affectu; ut sacris actionibus erudita, quanto majestati tuæ fit gratior, tanto donis potioribus augeatur."	"We beseech Thee, O Lord, may the people prosper who are devoted to Thee by the affection of pious devotion: that, instructed by holy actions, they may be blessed with better gifts, as they are made more pleasing in the sight of Thy Majesty."

We shall conclude this chapter on the Liturgy by quoting from the allocutions of His Holiness, Pius XII, delivered to the delegates of the Assisi Liturgical Conference in 1956: "It would be difficult to find a truth of the Christian faith which is not somehow expressed in the liturgy, whether it is in the readings from the Old and the New Testaments in the Mass and the Divine Office, or the riches which mind and heart discover in the psalms. The solemn liturgical ceremonies are, besides, a profession of faith in action."

But the Supreme Pontiff adds a word of caution: "The liturgy is not however, the whole Church; it does not exhaust the scope of her activities. . . . When we say that the liturgy does not exhaust the scope of the Church, we are thinking above all of its tasks of teaching and pastoral care. . . . Our Encyclical, Mediator Dei, had already corrected certain erroneous assertions which were tending to direct religious teachings and pastoral activity along an exclusively liturgical path" (AAS, Oct. 29, 1956).

[35] Cf. H. Schmitz, *Die religiöse Unterweisung der Jugend* (Cologne, 1920), pp. 136 ff.; Wolff-Habrich, *Der Volksschulunterricht* (Freiburg im B., 1917), pp. 62 ff.; Feilzer, *Kehreins besondere Unterrichtslehre oder Methodik der einzelnen Unterrichtsfächer* (Paderborn, 1919), pp. 44 ff.

CHAPTER IV

SACRED HYMNS AND MUSIC

The Psalms

Since the League of the Divine Office is rapidly gaining in popularity, it is fitting that we consider, in the first place, the religious and educational value of the Psalms. The word "psalm" is derived from the Greek term *psalmos* (*psallein*), and denotes "a sacred song to be sung to the accompaniment of a stringed instrument." [1] The two clauses of the Psalm verses are frequently parallel, the second either echoing the thought of the first or pointing out its opposite. The central thoughts of the Psalms are God, the Messias and man.[2] The Psalms describe the creative power, the omnipotence, omniscience, holiness and fidelity of God. They predict the coming of His Messias and describe His empire, His victories and the universality of His Church. At the same time they echo man's appeal to God in the midst of his trials, sorrows and persecutions by the enemy. We are told that God does not abandon those who come to Him with a contrite heart and who have confidence in Him. Hence, we find the psalmist calling upon all creation to come to his assistance and aid him in singing the praises of the Lord.

Intimately related to the Psalms are a certain number of Biblical songs known as the Canticles. Since the fourth century the Canticles have enjoyed the same honorable place in the Liturgy as the Psalms. They are recited in different parts of the Divine Office or read as lessons in the Mass. The Canticles most frequently used in

[1] M. Britt, *A Dictionary of the Psalter* (New York, 1928), p. 220.

[2] Cf. T. E. Bird, *A Commentary on the Psalms* (London, 1926), I, 50 ff.; P. Boylan, *The Psalms* (Dublin, 1920), I, lxi ff.; A. E. Kirkpatrick, *The Book of Psalms* (Cambridge, 1921), introduction, p. ix.

the Liturgy are the following: the Canticle of the Three Children in the Furnace; [3] the *Benedicite*; [4] the *Magnificat*; [5] the *Benedictus*; [6] and the *Nunc Dimittis*.[7] It might be noted in passing that the lofty sentiments of the biblical Canticle *Benedictus* inspired St. Francis to compose his famous *Canticle of the Sun.*

The Fathers of the Church and the theologians testify in an eloquent manner to the countless blessings and consolations which men have always derived from these sacred hymns. "Psalmody," says St. Basil, "is tranquillity of mind, the arbiter of peace, the curb of tumultuous thoughts, the assuager of anger, the bond of friendship, the reconciler of enemies; for what man can retain in his heart enmity towards a brother or sister whose voice commingles with his own in giving praise to God?" [8]

"In the Book of Psalms," says St. Ambrose, "there is medicine of salvation for the human race: the Psalm is the benediction of the people, the praise of God, the voice of the Church, the confession of faith, the full devotion of authority, the joy of freedom, the cry of rapture; it mitigates anger, it banishes care, it alleviates sorrow, it hails the birth of day, it attends also its decline, it sanctifies the stillness of night. The Apostle commands women to keep silence in the church, but they chant the Psalm with praise. This is sweet to every age and becoming to both sexes; this old men sing and forget their infirmities; this young men sing and commit no intemperance; youths sing the Psalm without danger to their innocence, and maidens without disparagement to their modesty. Children love it, and it even fills infants with admiration. Kings and emperors sing it with their people, because the Psalm is profitable to all." [9]

"Who can enumerate all the virtues of the Psalms?" asks Hugo of St. Victor. "Who can number those ignited compunctions of holy affections with which the mind that uses them is kindled in prayer, when the most grateful sacrifice to God is offered upon the altar of the heart." [10]

[3] Dan. 3:26.
[4] Dan. 3:57.
[5] Luke 1:46.
[6] Luke 1:68.
[7] Luke 2:29.
[8] *Homilia in Psalmum Primum,* in *P. G.,* XXIX, 211.
[9] *In Psalmum primum enarratio,* in *P. L.,* XIV, 924.
[10] *De Modo Orandi,* in *P. L.,* CLXXVI, 985.

The Psalms have been incorporated into the Liturgy, especially into the Divine Office and into the Mass. Hence, he who would enter thoroughly into the spirit of the Liturgy must be well acquainted with these sacred verses. In them he will find an unearthly wisdom satisfying every aspiration of the human heart. In them he will discover sentiments which will reflect every state of the soul. Every one of his experiences will in turn throw a new light on these sentences of perennial interest and reveal a new meaning in them. "When I remember the tears I shed," says St. Augustine, "at the Psalmody of the Church in the beginning of my recovered faith, and how at this time I am moved not with the singing but with the things sung, when they are sung with a clear voice and modulation most suitable, I acknowledge the great use of this institution." [11]

Sacred Hymns [12]

Although the faithful ordinarily modelled their prayers on the Psalms, occasionally they were themselves favored with in inspiration and expressed in a sacred hymn the devotion and aspirations which filled their souls. These songs rose naturally to the lips of those Christians who understood thoroughly the deep significance of the feasts and offices of the Church. In the early days of the Church these compositions were very numerous. With the Psalms, lessons, and prayers, they constituted the primitive Liturgy. Traces of some of them are to be found in St. Paul's epistles and in other books of the New Testament. Because of the disfavor brought upon hymns by the heretics, the greater number of the religious songs of the first three centuries have been lost.

The use of hymns in the sense of metrical compositions dates from the fourth century, from the days of two Doctors of the Church, SS. Hilary and Ambrose. The efforts of St. Hilary seemed to have been attended with little success, and most of his hymns have perished. The hymns of St. Ambrose became very popular, and from Milan they rapidly spread throughout the West. Many poets imitated the style and meter of St. Ambrose, and their hymns were given the general name Ambrosian.[13] Among the Christian

[11] *Confessions*, IX.

[12] Cf. "Hymnody and Hymnology," in *Catholic Encyclopedia*, VII, 596; M. Britt, *The Hymns of the Breviary and of the Missal* (New York, 1924), pp. 21 ff.

poets who wrote during the period between Ambrose and Charlemagne, and who in meter and outward form imitated the hymns of St. Ambrose, the following are deserving of special mention: Sedulius, who gave us the beautiful Christmas hymn, *A solis ortus cardine*; Fortunatus, the author of the *Vexilla Regis* and *Pange lingua*; Archbishop Rabanus Maurus of Mainz, the probable author of the *Veni Creater Spiritus.*

The period of the greatest activity in the composition of hymns was that extending from the ninth to the sixteenth century. The favorite topics of this period were the Redemption, the Holy Name, the Last Things of man, Our Lady, and the saints. Chief among the great composers of this period are St. Thomas, the poet of the Holy Eucharist; Jacopone da Todi, the probable author of the *Stabat Mater*; Thomas of Celano, the probable author of the *Dies Iræ.* With the close of the Middle Ages, with the decline of Latin as a living language and with the advance of the Renaissance, the art of Latin hymn-writing gradually disappeared.

It seems quite certain that hymns were introduced into the Liturgy by St. Benedict. Rabanus Maurus tells us that hymns were generally used in his time. The churches of Rome admitted hymns into the liturgical services in the twelfth century. This does not mean, however, that hymns were not sung throughout the West before their being made officially a part of the liturgical service. Since the days of St. Ambrose, the singing of Latin hymns enjoyed the same place in the Church as is now occupied by hymns in modern languages.

Of what strong religious emotions and even of conversions have not the Church's canticles and hymns been the source! Who is there that at one time or another has not felt the tender confidence of the *De Profundis*, the terrific warning of the *Dies Iræ*, the inutterable sadness of the *Tenebræ*, the solemnity of the *Magnificat*, the gladsome note of the *Adeste Fidelis*, the enthusiasm of the *Salve Regina*, the penetrating sorrow of the *Miserere* and of the *Stabat Mater*, the splendid warmth of the *Lauda Sion*, the profound faith of the *Adoro Te*, the majestic omnipotence of the *Te Deum*? It is said that more translations have been made of the *Dies Iræ* than of any other poem in the Latin language. Fragments of it fluttered on the dying lips of Sir Walter Scott; Dr. Johnson

[13] Cf. "Ambrosian Hymnography," in *Catholic Encyclopedia*, I, 392.

seldom read its tenth stanza without shedding tears.[14] Goethe makes Marguerite in *Faust* faint with horror and dismay as she hears it sung in the cathedral, and from that moment of salutary pain she becomes another woman. It was while listening to the solemn strains of the *Magnificat* and the gladsome chant of the *Adeste Fidelis* that Paul Claudel received the gift of faith.[15] The tones of the *Gloria in excelsis Deo,* so expressive of divine admiration, suddenly overpowered Johannes Jorgensen in the basilica of St. Boniface in Munich and made him understand that Christ was the Truth, the Way and the Life.

Sacred Music

1. *Liturgical Music.* The Liturgy, as we have said above, expresses the highest and most sublime truths, not only in a concrete, but also in an artistic manner. The music which it demands must be such as will interpret the thoughts and sentiments of Christ and of His Mystical Body in their united action. It must be a suitable means for conveying to God's throne the petitions of the faithful. According to the *Motu Proprio* of St. Pius X, chant is an integral part of divine worship, and those who sing it have a true liturgical office. Though not an essential, it is nevertheless more than a mere accessory, for it "contributes to the decorum and the splendor of ecclesiastical ceremonies," and "participates in the general scope of the Liturgy, which is the glory of God and the sanctification of the faithful."

The chant of the Church, according to Benedict XIV, is plain chant. The latter contains in itself the musical traditions of both the synagogue and the Church. It is essentially diatonic, that is, its melodies are formed out of the tones of the diatonic scale without any preconceived relation to harmonic accompaniment.[16] The melodies are sung in unison, without any fixed time-measurement, but according to the rhythm of the spoken language. It is called Gregorian chant, because the honor of having collected and published these melodies belongs to St. Gregory the Great. From Rome the Gregorian *Antiphonary* gradually spread throughout

[14] For an appreciation of the *Dies Iræ,* cf. J. K. Huysmans, *En Route* (London, 1896), pp. 7–8.

[15] Th. Mainage, *Les Témoins du Renouveau catholique* (5th ed.; Paris, 1919), pp. 61 ff.

[16] *Vita Vera* (3rd ed.; Paris, 1919), pp. 89 ff.

the world. St. Augustine and his forty-nine monks are said to have delighted the natives of Britain by their Gregorian chant. St. Boniface used it to soften the savage manners of the early German people. Charlemagne favored its expansion throughout the Frankish Empire and, in union with the Roman pontiffs, made use of it as one of the most powerful instruments for civilizing his vast empire. Well has it been said that the Church through the sublime music and poetry of her Liturgy has contributed as powerfully to the conversion of nations as by her preaching itself.[17]

"Sacred music," said St. Pius X, "should possess in the highest degree the qualities proper to the Liturgy, and precisely sanctity and goodness of form, from which its other character of universality spontaneously springs. These qualities, he continues, are to be found in the highest degree in the Gregorian chant, which is, consequently, the chant proper to the Roman Church. Secondly, these same qualities are also possessed in an excellent degree by the classic polyphony, especially of the Roman School, which reached its greatest perfection in the fifteenth century owing to the works of Perluigi da Palestrina (d. Rome, 1594). By adhering to the ecclesiastical scale and avoiding chromatic progressions, by clinging to purely religious thought, Palestrina produced works which have remained to this day models of church music. Lastly, since the Church favors the progress of arts, since she has admitted into her service of worship everything good and beautiful discovered by genius in the course of ages, modern compositions noteworthy for their sobriety, excellence, gravity and their conformity with liturgical functions, may also be admitted into the church. However, care must be taken that the modern musical compositions contain nothing profane, that they be free from reminiscences of motifs adapted to the theatre and that they be not fashioned even in their external forms after the manner of profane pieces.[18] In short, while some modern music is authorized, and while Pales-

[17] Cf. "Plain Chant," in *Catholic Encyclopedia*, XII, 144.

[18] In Huysmans' *En Route* (London, 1896), p. 265, Durtal gives expression to the following reflections on church music in Paris: "What we hear now at Paris, in the churches, is wholly incredible . . . There they howl the 'Tantum Ergo' to the Austrian National air; or what is still worse, muffle it up with operatic choruses, or refrains from canteens. The very text is divided into couplets which are ornamented like a drinking song with a little burthen." Cf. also *Orate Fratres* (February, 1929), p. 125.

trinian music is recommended, Gregorian chant is absolutely imposed.

In an Apostolic Constitution prepared on the twenty-fifth anniversary of the *Motu Proprio* of St. Pius X, Pope Pius XI strives to further the aspirations of his predecessor.[19] He urges the people to take an active part in divine worship and to learn the chant so well that they may join in the singing during services, as formerly was the custom everywhere. He suggests that churches, schools, associations and unions could contribute greatly to this work. It is absolutely essential, His Holiness says, that the faithful be not strangers or dumb spectators, but, seized by the beauty of the Liturgy, they should take part in the ceremony, mingling their voices alternatively with that of the priest. On December 25, 1955, His Holiness, Pius XII, in his Encyclical, *Musicae Sacrae,* repeated the prescription of his predecessors and indicates means and methods of putting these into practice; the Encyclical fiives a short history of hymn-singing and sacred music, explains the meaning and purpose of art, and points out the purpose and function of liturgical as well as non-liturgical music.

2. *Non-Liturgical Music.* During private Masses and functions that are not strictly liturgical, hymns in the vernacular may be sung, provided that the words and music have received the proper authorization.[20] No style of music may be rendered at non-liturgical functions which has been declared as unfit for liturgical services. For, if music is unfit for liturgical functions, it is unfit for use in church on any occasion. Sobriety, gravity and nobility must always characterize music rendered in holy places. It is especially important to keep all cheap hymns from children. If street songs are rendered in the house of God with no change except in the words, they will have a detrimental influence on the child's taste. If the hymns are commonplace, wearisome and devoid of all inspiration, they will stifle religious devotion instead of fostering it and eventually create a distaste for the Church's music.

Religious and Educational Value of Sacred Chant and Music

1.That sacred hymns and music are a powerful means of training the mind and heart can scarcely be denied. The different tones of

[19] *Constitutio Apostolica de Liturgia deque cantu Gregoriano et musica sacra cotidie magis provhendis, in Acta Apostolicæ Sedis* (February, 1929), pp. 33 ff.

[20] Cf. P. Hume, *Catholic Church Music* (N.Y., 1956).

the voice and of music evoke in man corresponding emotions.[21] There is a mysterious relation between music and melody and the deepest human aspirations. Sacred song excites in us a loathing of the sinful things of earth. "Music," says Cassiodorus, "dispels sorrow, soothes anger, softens cruelty, excites to activity, sanctifies the quiet of vigils, recalls men from shameful love to chastity, by the sweetest rapture expels the diseases of the mind, and soothes, through the medium of the corporeal senses, the incorporeal soul."[22] Music fills the soul with joy and consolation. Homer's hero found relief from the pains of a diseased heart by sitting beneath a lofty rock on the seashore and giving himself to singing. Saul's tumultuous passions were appeased, his gloom and suspicion and envy were dispelled, by the music of David's harp.

2. Music also awakens in us a longing for heavenly things. "Nothing," says St. John Chrysostom, "so exalts the mind, and gives it as it were wings, so delivers it from the earth, and loosens it from the bonds of the body, so inspires it with the love of wisdom, and fills it with such disdain for the things of this life, as melody of the verses and the sweetness of holy song." [23] St. Augustine tells us how tenderly he was moved when listening to the sacred melodies: "How I wept in hearing Thy hymns and canticles, touched to the quick by the voices of Thy well-beloved Church! The voices flowed into my ears and Thy truth distilled into my heart, whence the affections of my devotion overflowed, and tears ran down, and happy was I therein." [24] "Many a time," writes Charles Warren Stoddard, "did I listen to the music that was wafted from that beautiful church over the way. It was music unlike any I have ever heard – music that soothed and comforted me, yet at the same time filled me with an undefinable yearning." [25]

3. Gregorian chant, in particular, is admirably adapted to express the thoughts and sentiments of the soul. Its varied tonality, its

[21] Sr. M. Borgia, "The Educational Value of Music" in *Catholic Educational Review*, VI, 309, remarks, "The voices of animals, the running streams, the angry storm, the whistling wind, the waterfall, the song of birds, all offered suggestions which his (man's) power of imitation developed into those forms needed for expression, and which generation after generation perfected and elaborated into the great musical structures of our day."

[22] *Variarum*, Lib. II, Ep. xl, in *P. L.*, LXIX, 570.

[23] *Expositio in Ps. XLI*, in *P. G.*, LX, 156.

[24] *Confessions*, IX.

[25] Quoted in J. A. O'Brien, ed., *White Harvest* (New York, 1927), p. 126.

simple and majestic rhythm, its long and diversified neums, constitute a sort of a prolonged affective meditation which illuminates the divine truth and enkindles piety.[26] The liturgical chant of the Church diffuses charity and concord and forms a bond of union between the faithful; for union of voices produces a union of hearts. And when the same melodies are chanted in the Universal Church there is formed an external brotherhood of men expressive of that corporate worship and internal unity which arise from our common membership in the Mystical Body of Christ. How inspiring it must have been to have heard the Psalms sung duly in majestic Gregorian strains under the vaults of those beautiful medieval cathedrals! The spirit of the Psalms and of Gregorian chant permeated medieval society and became the spirit of the times.

No one has described so exquisitely the beauties and qualities of plain chant as J. Huysmans in his volume *En Route*. The melodies of plain chant, in his view, are in striking agreement with different styles of architecture. "It [plain chant] also bends from time to time like the sombre Romanesque arcades, and rises, shadowy and pensive, like complete vaulting. The *De Profundis*, for instance, curves in on itself like those great groins which forms the smoky skeleton of the bays; it is like them slow and dark, extends itself only in obscurity and moves only in the shadow of the crypts." [27] At other times the "Gregorian Chant seems to borrow from Gothic its flowery tendrils, its scattered pinnacles, its gauzy rolls, its tremulous lace, its trimming light and thin as the voices of children." [28] By way of a summary he adds, "Born of the Church and bred up by her in the choir schools of the Middle Ages, plain chant is the aerial and mobile paraphrase of the im-

[26] W. Verkade, *Le Tourment de Dieu* (Paris), pp. 248–249, cites the following appreciation of plain chant by one the Benedictine monks of Beuron: "Oui, ce chant, ce merveilleux chant grégorien, je la chante, déjà depuis vingt ans et je découvre chaque fois de nouvelles beautés dans ces mélodies. Il est vrai qu'il faut souvent bien du temps avant qut nos orielles gatées, s'y mettent car la mélodie y suit une tout autre ligne que dans la musique profane. Cepedant l'art de varier une idée mélodique d'y entrelacer constamment les ornements les plus divers, ne se trouve nulle part si developpé que dans le chant grégorian. . . . Le cœur du chantre tressaille de joie, quand il recontre un de ces passage de neumes onduleux (Graduel et l'Alleluia), qui n'ont pas besoin de textes. Alors, il ne peut que jubiler comme une alouette dans l'air."

[27] P. 6.

[28] *Loc. Cit.*

movable structure of the cathedrals; it is the immaterial and fluid interpretation of the canvases of the early painters; it is a winged translation, but also the strict and unbending stole of those Latin sequences, which the monks built up or hewed out in the cloisters in the far-off olden time." [29]

4. That hymns are valuable vehicles of conveying and transmitting knowledge is evident from the frequent use which heretics made of them in disseminating their errors. Let us quote a few examples.

a. The Gnostics composed hymns of exquisite charm and beauty into which, however, they instilled the poison of their erroneous teaching concerning the nature and work of Christ. The success of these hymns induced St. Ephraem to compose Syrian hymns which were to serve as an antidote to the Gnostic songs.

b. The offensive doctrine of Apollinaris that Christ lacked a rational soul was also propagated through the medium of delightful melodies.

c. The heretical Arius likewise embodied his Christological errors in pleasing hymns. At sunset on Saturdays, Sundays and feast days the Arians of Constantinople gathered in the public places of the city and all through the night sang Arian hymns. To counteract this heretical propanganda, St. John Chrysostom organized a system of nightly processional hymn-singing.

d. Luther spent several years in teaching his followers the Protestant hymns which became a powerful secondary means of promoting the Reformation. These hymns were sung in the streets, fields, workshops and churches. In fact, Protestantism is said to owe its influence over the people largely to its soul-stirring hymnody which appeals so powerfully to the religious emotions.

5. In the chapter on the history of catechization we indicated how frequently catechists resorted to singing while instructing others. St. Francis Xavier composed hymns for the use of his catechumens and set to music the "Our Father," the "Hail Mary," and the Apostles' Creed. In this way he not only banished the evil songs of the community but provided a new means of inspiration for his converts. The biographers of St. Francis tell us that his hymns were so pleasing to the members of his flock that they sang

[29] *Ibid.*, p. 7.

them day and night. St. Charles Borromeo achieved similar results in Milan by the hymns which he caused to be sung during catechization. In the life of St. Francis de Sales we read that the holy bishop took turns with his canons in the work of catechizing. After a certain time had elapsed, a devout hymn was sung — sometimes unaccompanied, sometimes with the accompaniment of an organ. Frequently the hymn was written by the saint himself, who occasionally composed religious poetry. At other times he chose one of the Psalms, and charged the musician to set it to a tune. According to Bishop Dupanloup, to propose to conduct a catechism class without singing hymns would be to attempt an impossibility.

"Those in charge of the religious instruction of boys and girls," says Pius XII in his Encyclical, *Musicae Sacrae* (Dec. 25, 1955), should not neglect the proper use of these effective aids. Those in charge of Catholic youth should make prudent use of them in the highly important work entrusted to them. Thus there will be hope of happily attaining what everyone desires, namely the disappearance of worldly songs which because of the quality of their melodies or the frequently voluptuous and lascivious words that go with them are a danger to Christians, especially the young, and their replacement by songs that give chaste and pure pleasure, that foster and increase faith and piety."

That sacred singing is a valuable aid to the catechist is evident from the following considerations.

a. It prevents weariness in the children, refreshes them and rests them after the more serious exercises. It helps to keep order and silence and prevents distraction. It serves as an outlet for an overflow of energy, subdues nervous tension and excitement, exercises the lungs and vocal organs and in general conduces to cheerfulness, good health and strength. In this way it makes assistance at the religion classes pleasant and draws children powerfully to them.

b. Singing may be employed to some extent as a substitute for the painful process of learning by rote. To learn by mere repetition the prayers, Commandments, Sacraments, and Catechism answers is often to the child a fatiguing and distasteful task. To learn them by singing can easily become a child's delight. The words will be helped by that powerful charm which music exercises over our whole being. In fact, there seems to be an affinity between memorizing and music, for the pleasure of music arises from exactness and from uniform arrangement, movement and accord.

c. Sacred hymns are powerful means of sound instruction. As Pius XII says in his Encyclical *Musicae Sacrae* (Dec. 25, 1955), "they serve as a sort of catechism." Every page of a hymn book contains truths of faith, moral precepts and motives for avoiding evil and doing good. Besides, in religious music everyone instructs and exhorts himself, without the aid of any teacher. In this way the mind responds more readily to good inspirations.

d. Sacred singing arouses the religious element in the child's being and disposes the child to profit better by the catechetical instruction. The words sung in unison warm the heart with enthusiasm, lift the soul heavenward and prepare the ground for the growth of the seed of God's truth. The correlation of an appropriate hymn with the Catechism lesson always gives unction to religious instruction. Hence, when the Nativity is spoken of, a Christmas hymn is appropriate. When God's attributes are explained, the *Te Deum* is a suitable selection.

e. Sacred chant is prayer; it is religion in practice. Almost every hymn contains a profession of faith in some truth of divine revelation. Every hymn, Psalm, or Canticle is a prayer of praise, of thanksgiving and of supplication to God. It obliges the child to make acts of faith, hope, love, contrition and good resolve.

CHAPTER V

PRAYER

Prayer is the raising of the heart and mind to God. With this thought clearly before him, the religion teacher will realize that there is a great difference between teaching a child to pray and teaching a child its prayers. In the first instance we lead the child to raise his mind and heart to God, to speak to God as one would speak intimately, lovingly and confidently to one's own father. In the second instance we place before the child definite forms which the Church has approved and which people have used through the ages to address God in a more formal manner.

Generally speaking, all Catholics have been taught formal prayers, the "Our Father," the "Hail Mary," the Creed, etc. How many have formed the habit of speaking to God from the heart in language all their own, expressing in their own words their personal needs and desires? Strange, is it not, that we know very well what to say to those we love on earth and that we have so often to resort to printed words when we wish to speak to God? True, Christ Himself has given us the most perfect prayer in the "Our Father," but often, too, a cry burst from His lips that expressed from the very depths of His Sacred Heart a great plea for the need of the moment, "Father, forgive them, for they know not what they do." [1]

Long before the children can pronounce the more difficult words of the ordinary prayers, they should be taught to speak to God, His Blessed Mother, their Guardian Angel, St. Joseph, and perhaps one or two other saints in their own words; this practice of spontaneous prayer should be kept up through life.

[1] Luke 23:34.

Let us consider in detail some practical suggestions for the teaching of prayer on the various grade levels.

Prayers for the Pre-school Child

Whenever and wherever possible, parents should be reminded that they cannot begin too early to teach the child about God. Naturally, this knowledge must be based on the child's own experiences. God loves us as father and mother love us. God watches over us and gives us all we have. We can talk to Him as we talk to others. Parents teach the little ones more by their own attitude towards God and holy things than by their words. In fact, their attitude of reverence, love and humility is impressed upon the child's mind long before words have any meaning for him. A good mother's love of God and Our Lady will shine out of her eyes as she looks at the crucifix or a sacred picture while her lips move in prayer. As one person expressed it, "I appreciated Mass ever since I remember. My mother always took me with her to Mass, and I wanted to love everything she loved."

As soon as baby lips learn to say the names of father and mother, they can also learn to say the holy names and to associate them with all that is good and beautiful. Little hands should be folded in prayer at least for a few moments, and there might be a good night kiss for Jesus and His Blessed Mother at bedtime.

The next step is the short informal prayer that the child can easily understand, such as, "God bless father and mother. God bless baby brother. God bless me and make me a good child." Or: "Dear God, I have been a naughty boy today. Please forgive me. I will not be naughty again."

The sign of the cross may be made with the help of the parents at a very early age, as part of the regular prayers. A little later, simple rhymed prayers may be added, such as: "Dear Angel, ever at my side."

Good pictures – preferably such as tell a story, like Plockhorst's "Christ Blessing the Children" – are a great aid in teaching the little ones about God and His great love for mankind. The children in that picture were talking to Christ? What were they saying?

If children learn readily, they can be taught the "Our Father" and "Hail Mary" before they reach school age. These prayers should be taught phrase by phrase, however, a little at a time.

Pictures, stories and rhymes illustrating and explaining these prayers can be easily obtained and are splendid aids in making prayer more intelligible to the child.

Primary Grades

A good many children when they first enter school or come to instruction class not only cannot make the sign of the Cross or say even the simplest prayer, but frequently know nothing whatever about God. In such cases – and they are not so rare as we ordinarily suppose – it will be necessary to begin by teaching them first about God and His love for us, His greatness, goodness and majesty. Once that idea is established, informal prayer should be introduced side by side with doctrinal truths. For example, we teach that God can do all things. We speak of the wonderful things He has done. We look around us for some of the more striking manifestations of God's love, a gay flower, a beautiful bird, a glorious rainbow; and then and there we pause to praise and thank God for His goodness and love. At first the teacher from the fullness of his heart may make the prayer himself, while the children reverently "think" along, "Dear Lord, how good you are to give us these beautiful flowers. I thank you, dear Lord." Gradually the children themselves should be encouraged to say such little prayers aloud.

Especially at opportune moments should the children be taught to raise their hearts to God quite simply and naturally. A little girl comes with beaming eyes to say that father has obtained a new and better position. Just as a pious mother at home, with the children gathered around her, would thank God for the favor, so the instructor, making up for the deficiency of the parents, might call upon all the children to help the little girl express her thanks for God's blessing.

In the meantime formal prayers are not to be neglected. The teacher should lead up to them gradually by means of stories, pictures and informal talks, so that, when he is ready to teach a certain prayer, the child's mind has already grasped the meaning. Let us take, for example, the act of contrition, which may be taken first in a simplified form and expressed in a number of different ways. By means of questions such as: "Why are you sorry?" "How do children prove that they are really sorry?" and by means of cases taken from their own experiences, the prayer is gradually formulated. Difficult words such as "heartily sorry," "detest my sins," are placed in their proper position only after the simpler terms have made the thought familiar. Then, and only then, should memorization of the prayer begin.

The prayers usually taught are: the sign of the Cross, the "Hail Mary," the "Our Father," prayer to the Guardian Angel, act of contrition, acts of faith, hope and charity, the *Angelus*, grace at meals, the Creed.

The order in which these prayers are to be taught and the time at which they are taught will depend on the preparation, age, intelligence and attitude of the children.

Through the informal prayer in particular the teacher will have opportunity to show without long explanations how prayer is used sometimes to adore and praise God, at other times to ask or thank Him for something, and again to tell Him how we feel about things, especially when we are sorry for having offended Him. When possible, prayers should be taught as a result of a natural situation, as has already been stated. Let us take another example. The teacher may say to the class, "John tells me this morning that his mother is very sick. Would you like to say a little prayer for her? Dear God, please make John's mother well again. Dear Mother Mary, help her." A formal prayer such as the "Hail Mary" may be added as soon as the children can say it. Later John reports that his mother is better. A prayer of thanks follows: "Dear God, how good you are! Thank you for making John's mother better. Thank you, dear Mother Mary."

Intermediate Grades

1. Regardless of the grade placement, when children know little or nothing about God, the procedure in teaching prayer should be much the same as in the primary grades, except that the process may go on more rapidly.

Presuming, however, that the children of this group already know the more common prayers, the teacher must assure himself of two things, that the pupils can say the prayers correctly and that they know what they are talking about.

To make sure of the first point, the teacher should request the children to write the prayers from memory, not too many at a time, however; or the task of reading and correcting them, and more particularly the revelation they may contain, might easily become overwhelming.

Skillful questions will bring to light how well children understand the prayers they are saying. Most probably repetition of some of the work for the primary grades will be necessary. It must be remembered that it is far more difficult to root out bad habits of prayer and replace them with good ones than it is to form altogether new habits. It will take much patience, instruction and repetition to change habits of mechanical repetition of prayers to those of heartfelt, sincere communion with God. Yet it must be done if we are to prepare the children to lead intelligent Catholic lives.

It is hardly possible that boys and girls who have learned the true meaning of prayer, who have tasted the nearness of God in the soul and who have poured out their joys and griefs in intimate union with Him – it is hardly possible that they should go permanently astray. On the other hand, it can be readily seen how those who have rattled off prayers mechanically for half a lifetime could easily be convinced that all of religion is mere mummery, just as their prayers have been.

By means of a repetition of the prayers commonly used in the earlier grades, the children's understanding and knowledge should be largely enriched. The "Our Father," for example, should now take on a deeper meaning by reason of their wider experience in life. "Thy kingdom come" would include now a desire to aid the missions in both a spiritual and a material sense. Similarly, "to atone for my sins," in the act of contrition, should make the child aware of his obligation to perform little penances, particularly during the penitential seasons.

2. The aim of the teacher in the intermediate grades, then, should be more to give the children a better understanding and appreciation of the prayers ordinarily said and approved by the Church than to add a multiplicity of devotions. In general children in this group should have well balanced ideas of the following:

a. What prayer is and how it should be used.

b. The difference between formal and informal prayer and the special value of each.

c. An understanding of the more commonly used formal prayers, including the Rosary, the Stations of the Cross and the litanies.

4. Some knowledge of the value of the Mass and the best way of

participating in the Mass. A simple book of Mass prayers possessed by every child would be of great assistance for occasional group instruction in the Mass; by now, the children should also be able to recognize the distinction between the outstanding prayers and devotions approved by the Church and so-called "pet devotions."

Upper Grades

1. Again the teacher must assure himself, as in the earlier grades, that the pupils can say the ordinary prayers correctly and that they know what the prayers mean. If their knowledge of these essentials is deficient, it is far better to give them a good general foundation and send them away with a thorough understanding of a limited number of formal prayers than to try to accomplish too much without a good foundation.

2. In addition to the requirements already stated for younger groups, the children of the upper grades should be more particularly instructed in the following:

a. A more intimate knowledge of the ordinary prayers, particularly of the Creed. This knowledge is to be acquired largely in correlation with the doctrinal instruction.

b. The use of the Missal and with it an understanding of the liturgical year.

c. The use of the Psalms or parts of Psalms as a desirable form of prayer for various occasions.

d. An introduction to the practice of meditation in the shortest and simplest form.

e. An introduction to spiritual reading as a part of one's spiritual life, and in particular an appreciation of the New Testament. Many of the texts, read slowly and thoughtfully, would be a nucleus for the simple form of meditation suggested above.

Senior High School

1. Provided that the senior high school students have the necessary foundation, special stress should be laid with this group on the intimate relationship between their spiritual life and their conduct, between their life of prayer and their life of activity. In other words, the teacher should employ every possible means to cultivate in the pupils a childlike simplicity and absolute sincerity in their

intercourse with God. Nowhere is this attitude better reflected than in the story of the Pharisee and the publican, hand in hand with which Richard Crashaw's "Two Went into the Temple to Pray" could also be studied. In this connection the petitions of the Lord's Prayer – "Our Father," "Forgive us our trespasses," etc. – will help the pupils to a clearer insight into their relationship with their fellowmen. There must be no discrepancy between their words and their deeds. Also, there should now be a better understanding of the differences between genuine prayerfulness and mere sentimentality. Their prayer, as their Catholicity, should become more and more virile as they increase in knowledge and age.

2. Other points to be taken into consideration at this stage are:

a. The great necessity of prayer, especially at the time of temptation.

b. The need of perseverance in prayer, especially when one is tempted to say: "I cannot pray."

c. The cultivation of a great personal friendship for Christ, particularly through a life of prayer.

d. The realization that prayer does not necessarily need to be expressed in so many words, but that all our actions can be made a prayer by one good intention.

e. An explanation of the prayer of praise and adoration as the highest and most acceptable form of prayer. Use of the *Gloria Patri, Gloria in Excelsis Deo, Te Deum,* etc., with the intention in mind.

f. A more complete understanding of the Liturgy, particularly the use of the Missal as the best means of keeping up one's Christian life in accordance with the spirit of the Church.

g. The practice of simple meditation more as a thoughtful reading and pondering of scriptural selections than as any particular form of mental activity.

h. Informal discussions on prayer in the Christian home and an attempt to inculcate high Christian ideals into the minds of the students as future home-makers.

At this juncture the first part of the chapter dealing with prayers for the pre-school child may be discussed with the student.

3. In conclusion, let us recall once more that in every case the teacher must begin with his class at the spiritual level at which he finds it and start to build from that level. A high school group that has had little or no instruction in prayers, for example, will gain

more by a simple explanation of the "Our Father" and by learning to pray with humility, sincerity, perseverance and confidence, than by an attempt to impose the prayers of the Missal upon them before they are ready to appreciate such prayers. Above all, let the instructor keep firmly in mind his duty not only to teach the children their prayers but also and principally to teach them *how to pray*.

CHAPTER VI

RELIGION AND THE SECULAR BRANCHES

A discussion concerning the place of religion in a Catholic curriculum necessarily bears upon the very essence of our Catholic school system. While our educators are generally ready to proclaim Catholic education as superior to every other, they are frequently not quite clear as to its precise nature. All admit that a Catholic school should have a religious spirit, but they are not agreed as to the source or sources of such a spirit. Some attribute this refining and religious atmosphere to the ornamentation of the schoolroom – the crucifix and holy pictures on the wall – to the use of holy water and to the religious garb of the teacher. Others ascribe it to the recitation of prayers and to the singing of hymns. Others assign it to the extracurricular forms of Catholic influence, such as services, sermons, sodalities and leagues for social action. All these, let us say at once, although good and necessary in themselves, are only manifestations of the Catholic spirit. They do not enter vitally into teaching or into the thought-processes of the child. The religious atmosphere must not only surround the child; it must be breathed by him in his classwork.

The authoritative statements of several popes will point out to us the solution of this delicate problem. In an Apostolic Brief addressed to the bishops of Ireland, Pius IX affirms that our divine religion must be the very soul of the entire academic education. "It will be the task of the bishops," he says, "to exert the most watchful care in providing that our divine religion will be the soul of the entire academic education. Therefore, let the holy fear and reverence of God be cherished and developed, the deposit of faith kept intact; let all branches of learning expand in the closest alliance with religion, all types of study be enlightened by the bright rays of Catholic truth, and the educative force of sound teaching be rigorously maintained." [1]

A similar admonition is addressed by Leo XIII to the Bishops of Austria, Germany and Switzerland. "It is, therefore, necessary not merely that young men should be taught religion at fixed hours, but that all the other subjects of their educational course should breathe in fullest measure the spirit of Christian piety. If that is lacking, if that hallowed life-breath does not thoroughly penetrate and stimulate the minds of both teachers and pupils, but little advantage will be derived from any branch of study; often the resultant losses will be considerable. The acquisition of many branches of knowledge must have as its allied function the thorough development of mental power. But let religion thoroughly inform and dominate every subject of instruction, whatever it be." [2]

Since God is inseparable from the universe as a whole, He is likewise inseparable from any part of it which, for the sake of convenience, we study in the so-called secular branches. "All knowledge," says Cardinal Newman, "forms one whole, because its subject-matter is one; for the universe in its length and breadth is so intimately knit together that we cannot separate off portion from portion, and operation from operation, except by a mental abstraction; and then again as to its Creator, though He of course in His Being is infinitely separate from it, and theology has its departments towards which human knowledge has no relations, yet He has so implicated Himself with it, and taken it into His very bosom, by His presence in it, His providence over it, His impressions upon it, and His influences through it, that we cannot truly or fully contemplate it without in some main aspects contemplating Him." [3] Secular branches, then, which are taught without any reference to God the Creator lack the proper orientation and expansion. If religion is not the animating spirit of the entire system of truth that is being implanted in the developing mind, religion itself will suffer; it will remain unsupported, whereas the secular branches support one another to a considerable extent. And if by chance

[1] *Optime Noscitis,* Mar. 20, 1854.

[2] *Militans Ecclesia,* Aug. 1, 1897.

[3] *Idea of a University* (London, 1896), pp. 50–51

it is introduced into lessons which have been so organized as to leave no room for it, it will appear as an intruder and usurper.

The ideal set before us by the popes, let it be carefully noted, cannot be fully attained unless all the students of an institution are Catholic, unless the textbooks used are written by authors of Catholic conviction, and unless, and above all, the teachers themselves are not only Catholic but trained under a genuinely Catholic system of education. Any other arrangements are apt to lead to compromises and foster unconsciously a refined indifferentism.

This intimate correlation of religion with the secular branches is not without foundation in the parable method of Our Lord. As Author of nature and Finisher of faith, He knew the true relations between objects and events in the natural order and His dealings with men in the supernatural order. He knew that His works in the natural order could and should be made to convey lessons in heavenly truth to men's minds. In His parables He spoke of sublime and supernatural truths in terms of the facts of nature and of the vital daily experience of His listeners. To the husbandmen He spoke of the vine and branches; to the Galilean farmers He spoke of the seed and the harvest, of the wheat and the cockle; and to the Judean shepherds He spoke of the sheep and sheepfold. The parable was not merely something transitory; it left a lasting, vivid impression. With every subsequent observation of the natural object, the lesson which Christ drew from it was recalled; with each repetition a firmer grasp of His truth was obtained. Through the visible things in the natural order the disciples of Our Lord came to perceive the invisible things of the supernatural order. They saw that there was no opposition but rather a beautiful harmony between God's teachings through nature and God's teaching through revelation. The things and events on which the parables were based were not peculiar to Christ's time and surroundings; they fall within the experience of men of all ages. Their value as means of introducing Christ's immutable truths is perennial.

The same principle of correlation underlies and is exemplified in the Liturgy. There every department of the domain of sense is made to serve the cause of truth and grace. The art of the builder, the painter, the sculptor and the musician is pressed into the service of religion. The Church surrounds the faithful with emblems of divine things; she proposes her teaching through images drawn from every department of sense experience. Ordinary sense-impressions are associated with divine truths, and the recurrence of the impression involves the revival of its correlated idea. The various experiences of everyday life call into action the ideas which the Liturgy has supplied, and the Liturgy thus exercises a vital influence on our lives.

Individual practice, however, often ignores the principles of sound instruction enunciated by Our Lord and by the Church. How often, after we have constructed a parochial school at an enormous cost, have we boasted that the curriculum in the Catholic school is exactly the same as that of the neighboring secular school, except for the half-hour daily religious instruction! Such a school, needless to say, would be Catholic only by extrinsic denomination. "The fatuous policy that is sometimes followed in Catholic schools," says Fr. Shields, "of copying the curriculum of the de-Christianized schools, and adding to this a half-hour religious instruction each day, can scarcely fail to destroy effectively the roots of Catholic faith in the lives of children entrusted to these schools by confiding parents." [4] If the half-hour of Catechism were the only difference between a Catholic and non-Catholic institution, why not send our children directly to the latter and arrange for Catechism lessons, at a smaller sacrifice than the one which our good laity is shouldering at present? Why not, on the same principle, give unqualified approval to our students attending secular universities, provided they append a religion class to their course?

The problem of suitable Catholic "readers," which arose in Fr. Shields' day, is another such example. At that time certain publishers approached Catholic teachers and asked them to "Catholicize" the current secular readers by inserting into them a few pious stories, pictures and sacred hymns. Fr. Shields revolted against this affront to Catholic teachers. In order to banish from the schools the diluted secular text, he wrote his own "readers" in which religion was to be the "central, coördinating, and dominating element of the child's first years in school." Although classroom practice has shown that his "readers" are above the average intellectual capacity of the children for whom they were intended, Fr. Shields nevertheless rendered the Church in this country noble service in combating such erroneous doctrines concerning the nature of

[4] *Primary Methods* (Washington, 1912), p. 100.

Catholic education. He repeatedly protested against making religion a mere unassimilated "extra" or "appendage." It must "grow out of the book and be the very heart of it." Just as all the vascular bundles of a tree, he says, run for a time in a single trunk before they diverge into separate branches, so all the branches of the school curriculum should run together during the early development stages of the child's mind. Without the proper correlation religion will become an intruder and usurper, an isolated nonfunctional memory load. It will remain a mere garment to be donned on Sunday and laid aside on Monday morning.

This isolation of religion from the other subjects of the curriculum is frequently perpetuated by the methods of teaching it. Christian Doctrine is often rendered distasteful in comparison with the secular branches. Beautiful illustrations, colored pictures, projects, maps, charts – everything, in fact, that appeals to the child's senses and arouses his curiosity and interest, is enlisted in the teaching of secular subjects. Religion, on the other hand, is still taught in abstract formulations and comes to be associated in the child's mind with uninteresting memory drills and penny Catechisms. Due allowance being made for faith, grace and character-formation, religion should not be taught by methods unlike those proper to the other branches of knowledge. There is one brain and one mind in the child, and the laws governing the operations of the mind are fundamentally the same, whatever be the content of knowledge.

While the systematic correlation envisaged by Fr. Drinkwater of England and by Fr. Shields would be difficult of application beyond the primary grades, incidental correlation is always within the possibilities of the average Catholic school and Confraternity teachers. At a retreat to his priests, Cardinal Mercier of Malines once declared that "we do not teach the secular branches in a sufficiently religious manner." Whereupon some priests asked, "How can a science such as mathematics, for example, be taught in a religious manner?" Yet, it is worthy of note that the greatest mathematicians, as Descartes, Cavalieri, Newton, Liebnitz and Kepler, nourished their profound religious faith by their lofty mathematical speculations. Catholic faith has carved into the religious architecture of the world, as expressive of divine truths, the inscribed hexagon, the equilateral triangle, the octagon, circle, etc.

Apart from this, educators have always looked upon the science of mathematics as a training school in exactness, honesty, patience, justice, bridling of the imagination, intellectual self-restraint, and in giving to God and our neighbor their just due.

Religion, too, is the permanent and enduring element in the world's best literature. All genuine and noble literature has in some way been inspired by a religious ideal and has an appreciable religious content. Being a verbal portrayal of life, a record of human experience and an expression of human emotions, literature must needs take into account the unceasing and universal striving of the soul after God. The cry of the human heart seeking after God gives rare quality to many a page of literature. The Vedas, the earliest-known piece of literature, are to the Far East what the Bible is to the West. A religious spirit pervades the epic, whether its author be a pagan Virgil or a Christian Milton. The drama is said to have been born at the foot of the altar, both in pagan and in Christian times. The essay and the best fiction have not failed to give due heed to the religious concept.[5]

The correlation of religion with nature study is of paramount importance in our own times. The more science progresses and the more earnestly it is studied, the more necessary it is to draw from nature, as Christ did, the lessons of religious life. Nature study reveals the marvels of God's creation and the glory of His goodness, providence and power. It reveals to the pupil the extent and wonders of the habitation which God made for us, and shows him how God, the beneficent Author of all, has made provision for life in every part of the earth. A Catholic student whose scientific course is properly orientated and unfolded according to a well-defined Christian philosophy of the universe

> Finds tongues in trees, books in the running brooks,
> Sermons in stone, and good in everything.

To him nature speaks the language of God: "The heavens show forth the glory of God, and the firmament declareth the work of His hands." [6] "For the invisible things of Him, from the creation of the world, are clearly seen, being understood by the things that are made." [7] The beauty of nature and of the heavenly orbs fasci-

[5] Cf. Brother Leo, *Religion and the Study of Literature* (New York, 1923).
[6] Ps. 18:2.
[7] Rom. 1:20.

nates the Catholic student; their glory enraptures him, and he breaks forth singing the infinitude of God. To minds thus trained to see the harmony between God's teaching through nature and His teaching by means of revelation, a conflict between science and faith is impossible. If the opportunity for such training is neglected, there is danger that the pupil will lapse into naturalism. He will come to look upon the world as something complete in itself, without any need of a Creator, and should it happen that he retain his faith, it will always remain quite distinct and remote from his other knowledge.

Catholic education, then, does not confine itself to written revelation; it embraces and includes every manifestation of God, whether in nature, in history or in life. In Catholic education religion energizes and vitalizes the whole field of instruction; all "branches of science expand in the closest alliance with religion." [8] and "all types of study are enlightened by the bright rays of Catholic truth." [9] Under the teacher's prudent guidance, the pupils learn to reflect upon God's place in their life and in the universe, and so detect the relation of all their human knowledge to God and to religion. This correlation need not be forced and exaggerated. The teacher need not moralize on every rule of grammar and on every problem of arithmetic. It is rather implicit than explicit. The child's power of reflection is so developed that he is able to learn gradually to apply the principles of religion to his intellectual, industrial, civic and professional life.

[8] Pius IX, *op. cit.*
[9] *Ibid.*

CHAPTER VII

THE CONFRATERNITY MANUALS OF THE ST. PAUL ARCHDIOCESE

The contents of the St. Paul Confraternity Manuals is arranged according to concentric circles. The great religious truths are covered at least three times in the twelve grades, but each time in a manner adapted to the child's needs, intellectual capacity and general development. This concentric syllabus, to use the words of Rev. F. H. Drinkwater, "might be compared to climbing a high tower with three successive lookout posts giving an everwidening view of the same country; and the comparison would be improved if one supposes a pair of field glasses at each window – each pair more powerful than the one below. The climber would see the same countryside at each stage, but with greater range and greater meaning and also with more detail." [1]

The First Six Grades

Instruction in *the first three grades* centers principally around preparation for First Confession and First Holy Communion. The method and contents of the instruction for this period are outlined in the teacher's introductory manual, the *Syllabus of Religious Instruction and Education* (pp. 15–48). The basic doctrines are correlated with other catechetical materials and hence permit of a simple or detailed treatment, as the circumstances of the case may allow or require. The plan as outlined in the *Syllabus* contains detailed suggestions for both the school year and vacation schools.

Since it was found that the largest number of pupils attending

[1] *The Givers* (London, 1936), p. 178.

religion classes come from the *fourth, fifth and sixth grades,* the Confraternity manuals destined for the intermediate grades cover in a thorough manner the three parts of the Baltimore Catechism – namely, the Creed, the Sacraments and the Commandments. Some if not many of these pupils will not return to the religion class when they reach the junior and senior high schools. The ecclesiastical authorities of the St. Paul Archdiocese wanted to be assured that the child will cover at least once in his lifetime the fundamental truths of our holy religion, the *basic Catechism.* Hence the three manuals prepared for this period: *The Apostles' Creed and the Life of Christ, The Sacraments and the Mass,* and *The Commandments of God and Precepts of the Church.* Special teacher's helps for teaching the lessons in these intermediate manuals are found in the *Syllabus* (pp. 50–96).

The Junior High School

We come now to *the Junior High School – to grades 7, 8, and 9.* The child in the seventh and eighth grades stands at the threshold of life. He faces, as it were, a threefold world: the world of his own internal experiences, inclinations and habits; the religious and devotional life of his home, parish and community; and the outside world of irreligion in which he habitually moves and has his being. In each of these worlds he needs counsel, assistance and the help of divine grace. In each of these experiences he must be guided by an authoritative hand. Hence follows the reason for the three manuals assigned to the junior high school period: the manual on *The Saints Through the Ages,* which inculcates the virtues so necessary in this period by means of the exemplary lives of the saints; the manual on *In Christ Through the Parish,* which strives to give the pupil an all-round acquaintance with the life in the Church; and the manual on *Vital Problems* which discusses and evaluates the various intellectual and moral problems which are forced upon the child from the naturalistic atmosphere in which he lives.

1. *The Saints Through the Ages.* The children in this period are in a critical and formative period of life. Their characters are being rapidly molded. The habits of thought and conduct acquired at this time will carry over into manhood and womanhood. Hence much attention should be given to the development of good habits in daily life.

In the first place, the teacher should develop in the pupils a sense of personal responsibility and a spirit of *self-reliance*. The restraints of authority should be gradually relaxed so that the child's will may get a chance to work. For unless a child is as nearly independent as possible in matters of religious practice when he finishes school, he will become a life-long weakling and a prey to every leader or tempter. The children should now be told the motive of their obedience, namely, the will of God manifesting itself in the authority of parents, of teachers, of the pastor, of the bishop and of civil authority.

This period also coincides with the age of puberty. Hence, in order to prepare the child for the storms and temptations that await him, the principal aim of the moral training of this period must be to develop the habit of mortification and self-denial. *Self-mastery* is as important for a young Christian stepping out into the world as is bodily and intellectual development. The education in self-control is effected by the formation of positive virtuous habits which strengthen self-control by a struggle against the dominant passions, and by a daily examination of conscience. This training, however, must be adapted to the intellectual and spiritual capacity of the children. Above all, the practices of self-control and self-denial must be inspired, developed and perfected by and through the love of God.

It is the aim of the course on *The Saints Through the Ages* to inculcate virtues through *hero-worship* – through the example of the saints and the lives of these heroes and heroines of the Church. While pursuing this principal aim, the course does not neglect the other objectives of a Church History manual. In the fourth, fifth and sixth grades, the children investigate the great truths of our religion. In the upper grades they should see how these same truths have been exemplified in the lives of great men and women and verified in the events of history. The abstract doctrines of our faith become more intelligible when they are embodied in the concrete and striking events of history. Virtue becomes more real, it puts on flesh and blood when it shines forth in the life of a human person, in one who has to face the same problems and difficulties as we do.

2. *In Christ Through the Parish*. Instruction in this course aims at an all-round acquaintance with Catholicism. It strives to explain

whatever will in any way touch upon the religious and spiritual life of the child after he leaves school. It aims especially to introduce the child into the Church's rich liturgical and devotional life. The children must not go into life as mere nominal Catholics, as dumb spectators of the Church's life. They must go forth as practical Catholics. They must learn to participate intelligently and effectively in the Church's liturgical and devotional life and intensify in their souls the divine life of the Son of God.

The course, then, takes special care to make the liturgical year, the Mass, the Sacraments and devotions serve at once as the Catechism of the children and as essential elements in their religious life. For once the children have left the religion class, the Church has no way of reaching them, generally speaking, except through the Liturgy. If the children have grown up ignorant of the Liturgy, there is little probability that they will persevere in coming to church. They will weary of the Liturgy because they have never been initiated into its inner meaning. In order that the Liturgy may in later life be a constant reminder to the children of the principal points of Catholic teaching, the course correlates and *associates Christian Doctrine with the Liturgy* and devotions whenever a convenient occasion presents itself. It strives even more to make the children realize that the outward forms of the Liturgy are channels and vehicles of the divine life of the soul.

3. *Vital Problems.* The purpose of the course, *Vital Problems,* is to prepare the child for the world in which he must live after he graduates from the eighth grade and leaves school. For many of the children will not return to school the next fall, while others will enroll in the public high school. Whether they return to school or not, there will be countless influences which will bear upon their lives, affect their thinking, and directly or indirectly touch upon their religious and moral lives. Take, for example, the powerful influence which will be exercised upon them by the movies, the radio and television, and you will understand how necessary it is to forestall the evil effects wrought by these three great educational agencies of our day.

First of all, there are certain forces which will influence the child's *religious thinking.* He cannot fail to be affected by the fact that more than half of the American people are not affiliated with any church whatsoever, are not restricted by a strict code as are the Catholics and are living as practical atheists. In fact three out of every five people whom he will meet will belong to this group. Then again he will be confronted with the peculiarly English and American heresy – which is becoming daily more widespread because of mixed marriages, brotherhood weeks, tolerance weeks, membership in the two "Y's", etc. – that it does not matter what religion a man chooses as long as he leads a good and clean life. The child cannot but be puzzled by the multiplicity of mutually contradictory sects which coexist in almost every American community. Added to this will be certain attacks made upon the Church by such noisy propagandists as the Witnesses of Jehovah and other groups. In several instances children have been known to be disturbed by the teaching of the animal origin of man as early as the sixth grade. All this is bound to have some effect on the child's faith, especially when no solution to his difficulties is forthcoming.

Secondly, there will be many agencies influencing the child's *moral judgment.* Think of all the strange and erroneous ideas about human nature, about sex, about the nature of marriage and of the married life, about the value of human life, which the child will imbibe from the movies, from the radio, from television, from plays and billboards, from the "funnies," from the countless sex and crime sheets exhibited on every magazine rack of the country and from the unwholesome sex education in vogue in many public schools. Add to this fact that the seventh and eighth grades will in many instances coincide with the period of puberty, when the youngster becomes conscious of sex and sex faculties and feels himself drawn to the opposite sex. An exchange of ideas on these points with companions on the street corner will not be apt to elevate the child's moral values. The multiplicity of public dance halls and beer parlors, the language and conduct prevailing in many of them, the large number of young men and women frequenting them – all this is bound to have an effect on the development of the child's character. Through their parents, brothers and sisters, even the conflicts between capital and labor, and the international upheavals, are influencing the child's outlook upon life.

The question of *one's vocation in life* begins to occupy actively the child's mind in this period. What is a vocation? How can I ascertain my vocation? What are some of the vocations in life that I might choose? These are some of the questions which press upon the child's mind and demand an answer.

Senior High School

The aim of the senior high school course is to review once more the great truths of our holy religion in terms of the *Creed,* the *Sacraments, Mass and the Liturgical Year,* and the *Commandments.* Hence the three manuals bearing these titles. Since many of the pupils probably received only an imperfect religious training in the grades, and since this may be the last opportunity of giving them a formal course in religion, it is absolutely necessary to dwell on the fundamentals of the Catholic faith. The course, however, is *adapted to the pupil's more developed intellectual capacity* and takes into consideration the *intellectual currents and moral problems of the day.* Thus the booklet on the Creed considers in addition to the great dogmas of the Church such questions as religious indifference, religious indifferentism, evolution, modern sects, etc. The booklet on the Commandments treats such problems as forbidden societies, the relation of employer to employees, mercy-killing, movies, dances, salacious literature and Communism. Finally, the student is fully acquainted with the structure of the Mass and of the liturgical year.

Conclusion

In conclusion, let us point out some special features of the St. Paul Confraternity manuals:

The abstract truths of each lesson are anchored in the senses by means of apposite religious pictures. With few exceptions the pictures are reproductions of masterpieces. The children are thus forming their taste along right lines and without conscious effort, are laying the foundation of an art culture that will at a later day save them from the gross materialism of the day. Their esthetic faculty is thus developed instead of being demoralized by wretched drawings and color daubs approaching sometimes in atrocity the work of the Sunday supplement. In the booklet on the Commandments and Precepts of the Church, where it was difficult at times to procure truly illustrative pictures, the lesson is made concrete especially by means of those symbols which are of the most frequent occurrence in the Church's art.

The truths of each lesson are impressed upon the *mind* with the help of the best pedagogical devices. After a brief exposition of the truth, the doctrine is impressed on the child's mind by means of various tests and exercises such as filling in the missing word or words, matching phrases, underlining phrases, etc.

The truth is impressed upon the child's *heart and conduct* by means of the "case" method. A hypothetical case from the life of children is submitted to the child's judgment. In evaluating the case, in condemning the evil and approving the good which it contains, the child is really laying down the norm of action for his own future conduct.

Each lesson presents those elements which the Catechism in its brevity cannot offer. Yet it was recognized that after a doctrine has been thoroughly explained, the immutable divine truth should be summed up in precise formulae and made the child's *permanent possession* by a process of memorizing. Hence each lesson is correlated with the Catechism, and in the intermediate texts the questions and answers of the *Revised Baltimore Catechism* are stated in full. The memorizing of the catechismal answer is thus a finishing touch to a long catechetical process.

Finally, the catechist, especially the lay teacher, must have a sense of security. He must be certain that he is not only using the correct methods in explaining the lessons but also that he has the correct answers to the various tests, exercises, problems and "cases." Hence a *Teacher's Manual,* containing all this information, has been prepared to accompany each student's text.

PART II
THE METHODS OF CATECHIZATION

CHAPTER I

THE DIVINE PEDAGOGUE

Introduction

He who created the human soul and determined the laws according to which the mind assimilates and attains truth must of necessity be the pedagogue and educator *par excellence.* In the Old Testament the future Messias stands out pre-eminently as a great teacher and prophet: "The Lord thy God will raise up to thee a Prophet of thy nation and of thy brethren, like unto me; Him thou shalt hear." [1] The Jews were not long in acknowledging and proclaiming this quality of Christ's office: "A great prophet is risen up among us;" "This is the prophet indeed." [2] Our Lord willingly acquiesced in this testimony of Himself: "You call Me Master, and Lord, and you say well, for so I am" [3]; "One is your Master, Christ." [4] This title of the Saviour was confirmed by God in a special manner at the Transfiguration when He proclaimed His beloved Son as the Doctor and Legislator whom all should hear.[5]

The Incarnate Word had for centuries been foreshadowed — especially in the sapiential literature of the Old Testament — as "Divine Wisdom" and "Word of God." In the Gospel of St. John these titles are applied directly to Christ, and the beloved disciple salutes Him as "full of grace and truth." [6] The clouds of error and ignorance which had for ages been settling and thickening around man's intellect darkened by original sin — the deep midnight

[1] Deut. 18:15.
[2] Luke 7:16; John 7:40.
[3] John 13:13
[4] Matt. 23:10
[5] Luke 9:35.
[6] John 1:14.

which had been brooding over peoples of the earth – were finally dispelled by a healing light from the East. How frequently the evangelists emphasize the fact that Christ is verily *lumen de lumine!* According to St. Luke, the proximate purpose of the Incarnation was to "enlighten them that sit in darkness, and in the shadow of death: to direct our feet into the way of peace." [7] St. John hails the Incarnate Word as "the true light, which enlighteneth every man that cometh into this world." [8] St. Paul tells us that Christ's knowledge is far superior to that of men and angels because "In Him are hid all the treasures of wisdom and knowledge." [9] Christ with a special predeliction identifies Himself with the "light": "I am come a light into the world; that whosoever believeth in Me, may not remain in darkness"; [10] "I am the light of the world; he that followeth Me, walketh not in darkness, but shall have the light of life"; [11] "I am the way and the truth and the life." [12]

A divinely conferred office carries with it its correlative graces. As Head and Redeemer of the human race our Lord had a perfect knowledge of all the truths necessary for salvation. Whenever Christ taught these supernatural truths He at the same time aided the hearer's mind internally by illuminating it with grace. Christ derived His knowledge from neither Jewish nor Greek scholars nor from any human master. He was independent of every human school and of all human authority: "And the Jews wondered saying: How doth this man know letters, having never learned? Jesus answered them, and said: My doctrine is not Mine, but His that sent Me." [13] His was a fullness of knowledge by reason of the hypostatic union. Scripture affirms that the Son who proceeds from the Father received directly from God His authority to teach and that He transmitted the same power to the Church: "As the Father hath sent Me, I also send you"; "going therefore teach ye all nations"; [14] "he that heareth you, heareth Me; and he that despiseth you, despiseth Me; and he that despiseth Me, despiseth Him that sent Me." [15] In fact, to such an extent were the Apostles and their successors to share in Christ's divine power to teach that those

[7] Luke 1:79.
[8] John 1:9
[9] Col. 2:3.
[10] John 12:46.
[11] John 8:12.
[12] John 14:6.
[13] John 7:15, 16.
[14] John 20:21; Matt. 28:19.
[15] Luke 10:16.

who refuse to hear them will incur eternal damnation: "Go ye into the whole world, and preach the gospel to every creature. He that believeth and is baptized, shall be saved; but he that believeth not, shall be condemned." [16]

The Fathers of the Church and Catholic theology attribute to Christ all perfections which are not opposed to the end of the Incarnation. Ignorance and error, however, unlike bodily sufferings, were in no wise conducive to the purpose of the Redeemer; besides, the Divine Person, to whom all the actions of Christ's human nature are properly attributable, could not make its own such states of the mind. The human intellect is capable of a threefold perfection: experimental knowledge, which is acquired through the senses and the abstractive powers of the mind; infused knowledge, which is derived from ideas innate in the mind or placed into it directly by God; beatific vision, which is a facial intuition of God and a knowledge of all things in Him. Christ possessed the beatific and infused knowledge in their full perfection from the first moment of the creation of His soul, and successively revealed to men the treasures of wisdom hidden within Him. The perfection of Christ's human intellect demanded, however, that He not only know all things but that He also know the different ways of acquiring knowledge. In His experimental knowledge — which was successive and progressive, in accordance with the developing perfection of His cognitive faculties [17] — Christ did not learn new things but He learned in a new way truths already known to Him. There was no progress in the number of truths known but only in the manner of knowing them.

The Teacher and Educator of all mankind knew all truths and ways of knowing and actually experienced the manner in which the human mind functions in acquiring truth. His method of imparting truths to the human mind, consequently, must necessarily excite our interest and reverent curiosity. To what extent did He appeal to the Old Testament and to Bible History? Did He use the question-and-answer method? How did He present abstract supernatural truths? By what means did He strive to make these truths a permanent acquisition and motor forces in the lives of His hearers?

[16] Mark 16:15, 16.

[17] Luke 2:52.

Christ and the Old Testament – Bible History

1. The Old Testament was to the Jews of our Lord's time the Book of books, the book *par excellence.* There was no piece of literature comparable in the eyes of the Jewish people to the Hebrew Bible. It contained the history of the patriarchs, the precepts given to the Jews by Jahve and the prophecies of the seers of many centuries. From this cherished sacred work – written under divine inspiration and containing God's message to men – the Jews at all times derived counsel, consolation and assurance of redemption.

a. Christ frequently recalled the teaching of the Old Testament in order to prepare His listeners for the lesson or the truth which He was about to expound. Fully aware of their love for Holy Writ and of their familiarity with its contents, Our Lord used the sacred text as a common meeting ground, as a basis upon which to establish the new truths which He wished to communicate to them. A quotation from one of its pages was sufficient to bring to the foreground of the hearers' mind that desired mental content upon which the new idea might readily be engrafted.

b. This method of teaching the new in terms of the old finds its first apt illustration in Our Lord's claims concerning His divine mission. In proving to the Jews that He is the Anointed One of God, Christ frequently quotes apposite prophecies from the Old Testament. He establishes the identity of John the Baptist as precursor of the divine Legate by a quotation from the Old Testament: "Behold I send my Angel before Thy face, who shall prepare Thy way before Thee." [18] On another occasion, when teaching in the synagogue of Nazareth, Christ correlates His divine embassy with a prophecy from Isaias: "The Spirit of the Lord is upon Me. Wherefore He hath anointed Me to preach the gospel to the poor, He hath sent Me to heal the contrite of heart, to preach deliverance to the captives, and sight to the blind, to set at liberty them that are bruised, to preach the acceptable year of the Lord, and the day of reward." [19] And while the eyes of the multitude were fixed upon Him, Christ, as He was closing the book, added, "This day is fulfilled this scripture in your ears." [20] To impress upon the minds of His hearers the dignity of His Person, He compares Himself with

[18] Matt. 11:10. [19] Luke 4:18, 19. [20] Luke 4:21.

outstanding personages of the Old Testament: "As Jonas was in the whale's belly three days and three nights, so shall the Son of man be in the heart of the earth three days and three nights"; [21] "Behold a greater than Solomon is here." [22] On another occasion, after calling the previous mental content of the Jewish listeners to the foreground of their consciousness by the parable of the husband-man, our Lord continues, "Have you never read in the scriptures: The stone which the builders rejected, the same is become the head of the corner? By the Lord this has been done; and it is wonderful in our eyes." [23] The evangelists conclude their accounts with the assurance that the chief priests and Pharisees "knew that He spoke of them." They must, therefore, have understood that Christ professed Himself to be the divine Ambassador, the Messias, "the stone which the builders rejected." Finally, to impress upon His hearers the heavy guilt of those who refused to accept His doctrine and the punishment that would befall them, Christ recalls to their minds the fate of Sodom and Gomorrha in the days of Abraham and Lot.[24]

c. Christ's method of correlating the new with the old is illustrated even more clearly in the Sermon on the Mount. In proclaiming His Law Christ begins by recalling several commandments of the Old Law. He carries the Jews back in spirit to Mount Sinai, to the circumstances amid which the Lord appeared to Moses. The recollection of this event prepares the minds of the listeners for the new and more perfect law which He is about to communicate to them. The solemn statements exemplifying this method are well known to all:

(1.) "You have heard that it was said to them of old: Thou shalt not kill. And whosoever shall kill, shall be in danger of the judgment.

But I say to you

Whosoever is angry with his brother, shall be in danger of the judgment. And whosoever shall say to his brothers, Raca, shall be in danger of the council. And whosoever shall say, Thou fool, shall be in danger of hell fire." [25]

(2.) "You have heard that it was said to them of old: Thou shalt not commit adultery.

[21] Matt. 12:40.
[22] Matt. 12:42.
[23] Matt. 21:42.
[24] Matt. 10:15.
[25] Matt. 5:21, 22.

But I say to you

Whosoever shall look on a woman to lust after her, hath already committed adultery with her in his heart." [26]

(3.) "You have heard that it was said to them of old, thou shalt not forswear thyself, but thou shalt perform thy oaths to the Lord.

But I say to you

Not to swear at all, neither by heaven for it is the throne of God; nor by the earth, for it is His footstool; nor by Jerusalem, for it is the city of the great king; neither shalt thou swear by thy head, because thou canst not make one hair white or black." [27]

(4.) "You have heard that it hath been said: An eye for an eye, and a tooth for a tooth.

But I say to you

Not to resist evil; but if one strike thee on thy right cheek, turn to him also the other." [28]

(5.) "You have heard that it hath been said, Thou shalt love thy neighbor and hate thy enemy.

But I say to you

Love your enemies, do good to them that hate you, and pray for them that persecute and calumniate you." [29]

d. The principle of assimilative correlation, which underlies all these examples, cannot be sufficiently stressed in contemporary catechetics. For it is clear that isolated truths will turn out to be mere nonfunctional memory loads which impede rather than promote mental development. Each new thought element must be related to the previous content of the mind in a relation of reciprocal activity. Each new idea must shed its light upon every item of previously assimilated knowledge and be in turn illumined by the truths which already hold a place in the structure of the growing mind. Apperception or association – that is, the vital assimilation of new images and concepts with the old ones latent in the child's mind – is always an important part of the learning process. Accordingly, the preparation for a new lesson must always take the form of a review of knowledge already possessed.

[26] Matt. 5:27, 28.
[27] Matt. 5:33, 36.
[28] Matt. 5:38, 39.
[29] Matt. 5:43, 44.

2. Since His listeners were well acquainted with Old Testament history, it was not necessary for Our Lord to teach it in a systematic manner. He usually referred to the sacred history of the Jews merely to illustrate and confirm a truth or to strengthen the faith and devotion of His followers. The following comparisons of historical incidents with present events will readily illustrate this principle:

a. David in the temple – disciples and the Sabbath.[30]
b. Ninivites – His unrepentant generation.[31]
c. Times of Noe and Lot – watchfulness.[32]
d. Sodom and Gomorrha – rejection of Christ's doctrine.[33]
e. Solomon and Jonas – His Divinity and Resurrection.[34]
f. Brazen serpent – Redeemer.[35]
g. Manna – the Eucharist.[36]
h. Elias and Eliseus – Christ and strangers.[37]
i. The burning bush – objections of the Sadducees.[38]
j. Solomon's glory – God's Providence.[39]
k. Prophecies – Christ's Messiaship.[40]

3. Our Lord not only engrafted the New Testament upon the Old and explained the former in terms of the latter, He not only interpreted accurately individual scriptural passages, but He accomplished what the Scribes and Pharisees failed to do. He emphasized the true spirit of the Old Testament by showing that it is Christocentric and refers primarily to Himself. He instructed His disciples and Apostles concerning this correct view of the Old Testament. He explained to the two disciples of Emmaus that if He had not suffered, He would not be the Messias of whom the Scriptures spoke: "O foolish, and slow of heart to believe in all things which the prophets have spoken. Ought not Christ to have suffered these things, and so to enter into His glory? And beginning at Moses and all the prophets, He expounded to them in all the scriptures the things that were concerning Him." [41] Shortly before His Ascension He recalled to the Apostles that during His mortal sojourn He had been wont to point out to them the passages in the Pentateuch and other books of the Scriptures which had reference to the mysteries

[30] Matt. 12:1–8.
[31] Matt. 12:41.
[32] Luke 17:26–30.
[33] Matt. 10:15.
[34] Matt. 12:39–42.
[35] John 3:14, 15.
[36] John 6:31–35.
[37] Luke 4:25–30.
[38] Mark 12:26.
[39] Luke 12:27.
[40] Luke 24:25, 26.
[41] Luke 24:25, 27.

of His life, death, and glory: "These are the words which I spoke to you, while I was yet with you, that all things must needs be fulfilled, which are written in the law of Moses, and in the prophets, and in the psalms concerning Me. Then He opened their understanding, that they might understand the Scriptures." [42]

Our Lord indicated to His followers how the Old Testament leads naturally to the New Testament, how in the Old Testament the New Testament lay concealed and how in the New Testament the Old Testament was made manifest. This viewpoint might well be kept in the mind by the teacher of Bible History. He must remember that a class in Old Testament history is nevertheless a class of *Christian* doctrine. Under the teacher's prudent guidance the children must learn and realize that Christ stands at the center of the entire history and doctrine of salvation. They must learn to refer all religious truths to Christ, to find in Him all their motives for action and to consider Him as the beatific end of all human existence. They must learn to love Him who is the Way, the Truth and Life, the beginning and end of faith, the Light of the world, Jesus Christ, the same yesterday, today and forever. Jesus Christ must be the one focus in which all rays of biblical and catechetical knowledge converge and from which they derive their intelligibility and meaning.

4. The words of the disciples of Emmaus clearly show how effectively Christ interpreted the Scriptures. Their minds were illumined by faith and their hearts inflamed with love while Christ conversed with them: "Was not our heart burning within us, whilst He spoke in the way, and opened to us the Scriptures?" [43] When in His native city He was pointing out to the multitude that the prophecy of Isaias referred to Himself, "All gave testimony to Him: and they wondered at the words of grace that proceeded from His mouth." [44] His words in the Sermon on the Mount show His great esteem for the Old Testament and His efforts to inculcate into others the same high regard for Holy Writ: "Amen I say to you, till heaven and earth pass, one jot, or one tittle shall not pass of the law till all be fulfilled" [45] – "the Scriptures cannot be broken." [46] The force of the Scriptures is comparable to the testimony of a man risen from the dead; if the brothers of the rich

[42] Luke 24:44, 45.
[43] Luke 24:32.
[44] Luke 4:22.
[45] Matt. 5:18.
[46] John 10:35.

man "hear not Moses and the prophets, neither will they believe, if one rise again from the dead." [47]

Question-and-Answer Method

1. Our Lord employed principally, if not exclusively, the lecture form of catechizing and made constant use of explanation and demonstration. Since He wished to influence the will of His hearers as well as enlighten their minds, He spoke — if we may say so — from the fullness of His heart and gripped His listeners with His own divine earnestness, enthusiasm and sincerity. Secondly, since it was His mission to announce positive supernatural truths which are not discoverable by a process of reasoning and questioning but come to us only through preaching and hearing, narration was the only suitable means of instruction. Finally, the narrative or lecture-form was best adapted to the nature and disposition of His listeners who were mostly adults and who relied directly on His spoken and personal word. Hence, whenever He was about to hold a discourse in the synagogue, He first read, according to Jewish custom, a passage from Sacred Scripture, and then explained and supplemented it. "He rose up to read," says the evangelist, "and the book of Isaias the prophet was delivered to Him." [48]

2. Christ's imparting knowledge through the narration method did not mean that the listener was to remain wholly passive; on the contrary, our Lord always strove to develop His theme with the hearer's active co-operation. If it is true that the personal expression of ideas stimulates the creative instinct more than the reading of a book, we can readily understand why Christ endeavored to stir up the listener's interest and self-activity by means of formal or implicit questioning. This erotematic procedure is in evidence in the preliminary remarks with which He occasionally prefaces His explanations and parables: "How readest thou?" "What is written in the law?" [49] "What did Moses command you?" [50] An intensive use of the erotematic method is found in His discussion concerning the sonship of Christ:

"And the Pharisees being gathered together, Jesus asked them,

"Saying: What think you of Christ? whose Son is He? They say to Him: David's.

[47] Luke 16:31.
[48] Luke 4:16, 17.
[49] Luke 10:26.
[50] Mark 10:3.

"He saith to them: How then doth David in spirit call Him Lord, saying:

"*The Lord said to my Lord, Sit on My right hand, until I make Thy enemies Thy footstool?*

"If David then call Him Lord, how is He his Son?

"And no man was able to answer Him a word; neither durst any man from that day forth ask Him any more questions."[51]

When the chief priests and ancients inquired concerning His authority to teach in the temple, He in turn asked them a preliminary question concerning John's power and authority to baptize:

"And when He was come into the temple, there came to Him, as He was teaching, the chief priests and ancients of the people, saying: By what authority dost Thou these things? And who hath given Thee this authority?

"Jesus answering, said to them: I also will ask you one word, which if you shall tell Me, I will also tell you by what authority I do these things.

"The baptism of John, whence was it? from heaven, or from men? But they thought within themselves saying:

"If we shall say from heaven, He will say to us: Why then did you not believe him? But if we shall say from men, we are afraid of the multitude: for all held John as a prophet.

"And answering Jesus they said: We know not. He also said to them: Neither do I tell you by what authority I do these things."[52]

By questioning processes such as these Our Lord stimulated His listeners to serious thought and reflection and enabled them to arrive at conclusions which – because they were attained with the help of their own reasoning – became permanently effective in their lives.

3. Our Lord combined all teaching modes in a wonderful harmony. Frequently He supplemented a parable or a comparison with a question and elicited an answer which clarified His teaching and impressed the truth deeply upon the mind and heart. At the conclusion of His parable of the good Samaritan, He turned to the lawyer and addressed this question to him: "Which of these three, in thy opinion, was neighbor to him that fell among the robbers?" And having obtained the correct answer – "He that showed mercy to him" – our Lord bade him to put his own conclusion into prac-

[51] Matt. 22:41–46.

[52] Matt. 21:23–27.

tice: "Go, and do thou in like manner." After the narrative of the two sons who should have worked in the vineyard, He immediately asked, "Which of the two did the Father's will?" And upon obtaining the correct answer from the listeners to whom the comparison properly referred, He forthwith made the application: "Amen I say to you, that the publicans and the harlots shall go into the kingdom of God before you." Following the parable of the husbandmen who killed the servants and the son of the householder, He inquired, "When therefore the lord of the vineyard shall come, what will he do to these husbandmen?" The priests and Pharisees whom He addressed, by condemning the husbandmen, implicitly admitted their own sinfulness and pronounced verdict upon themselves: "He will bring those evil men to an evil end, and will let out his vineyard to other husbandmen, that shall render him the fruit in due season." [53] In all these instances the question of Our Lord — and this point is of supreme importance to the catechist — served a twofold purpose: it brought to the foreground the main point of His discourse and introduced the application to conduct.

Like His narrations the questions of Our Lord were noted for their simplicity and definiteness. Although the Pharisees, out of malice, frequently misinterpreted His words, His questions admitted of only one answer. Apart from the occasions when Our Lord wished to elicit a demand for an explanation,[54] they were adapted to the age and intellectual capacity of His listeners. On only one occasion did He ask a question to which He expected in answer a simple "yes." "Have ye understood all these things? They say to Him: Yes." [55]

4. Some of His questions were purely rhetorical and demanded no answer. These rhetorical questions, which are interspersed throughout the Gospels, are noted for their naturalness and charm. We shall quote only a few examples:

"To what shall we liken the kingdom of God, or to what parable shall we compare it? It is as a grain of mustard seed." [56]

"Whereunto shall I esteem the kingdom of God to be like? It is like to leaven." [57]

"Whereunto then shall I liken the men of this generation? and to what are they like?" [58]

[53] Luke 10:36, 37; Matt. 21:31, 40, 41.
[54] Matt. 22:45.
[55] Matt. 13:51.
[56] Mark 4:30, 31.
[57] Luke 13:20, 21.
[58] Luke 7:31.

"Why do you not know My speech? Because you cannot hear My word." [59]

"Doth he thank that servant, for doing the things which he commanded him? I think not." [60]

Our Lord desired that His Apostles ask questions. Frequently He did not make His explanation exhaustive in order to leave something to their own initiative and activity, to incite them to personal deliberation and reflection and thus to lead them to seek an explanation.[61] He was always ready to help solve their problems and difficulties, and He often furnished the necessary explanation before the questions became articulate in their minds. Although Our Lord was often obliged to formulate and explain concepts, one would seek in vain in His discourses for strict definitions, formulae and abstract catechetical questions and answers. His one aim was to impress the truth upon the mind and by means of an apposite comparison or illustration make it operative in daily life.

5. Whenever Our Lord dealt with men who had reached a certain spiritual maturity, He employed the dialogue form of instruction. This procedure permitted the listener to make observations, raise objections, ask questions and speak with a certain independence. Our Lord employed this method in dealing with the common people. He used it even more frequently in speaking to the learned Scribes and Pharisees. It was His favorite procedure with the Apostles, as the latter's eagerness, earnestness and many questions clearly show. It is the method employed in the Saviour's discourse on the promise of the heavenly bread [62] and in His conversation with the Samaritan woman.[63] The eighth chapter of St. John's Gospel shows how frequently He permitted His apologetical discourse to be interrupted. How interesting, too, is His conversation with the disciples at the first multiplication of the loaves [64] and His discourse with the disciples of Emmaus in which He introduced the stirring explanation of Sacred Scripture.[65] The importance and advantages of this dialogue method for the Apostles need no special comment. In their questions more than in their answers lay a repetition and deepening of their knowledge concerning a certain

[59] John 8:43.
[60] Luke 17:9, 10.
[61] Matt. 13:36, 15:15.
[62] John 6.
[63] John 4:1–42.
[64] Matt. 14:15–21; 16:18–12.
[65] Luke 24:27–32.

truth, for the formulation of a question presupposes a certain grasp of the object. Through the dialogue form of instruction — so carefully directed by the divine Master — the independence of the Apostles as future teachers was gradually developed.

The questions of Our Lord were of a purely pedagogical nature. He "asked questions"[66] to instruct others, not to learn something new. By His questions He compelled the listeners to acknowledge their own ignorance, incited them to personal activity and reflection and made them more desirous and receptive of the heavenly doctrines which He was about to enunciate. By the erotematic process He enabled His hearers to arrive at their own conclusion and, in consequence, co-ordinate, deepen and broaden their knowledge.

6. From these considerations we can deduce in the form of conclusions the following principles in regard to the question method in catechization. This method should be used for the following ends:

a. To counteract the child's passivity, arouse his attention and stimulate him to personal activity.

b. To test the child's knowledge in order to ascertain if he has understood and learned the subject explained. A teacher who asks no questions is like a man pouring water into a vessel without making sure whether it leaks or not.

c. To summarize at the end of a lesson the matter gone over — to gather up and connect its parts.

d. To examine the children at the beginning of a lesson about the matter studied in the last class.

e. To use rarely — except with the weak, timid, and very young children — questions which require only a "yes" or a "no" for an answer. Such questions make the child inattentive, inactive and careless. In all such instances the teacher should demand a reason for the answer.

f. In Bible History and Church History the doctrinal and moral truths should be brought out with the help of questions such as these: "What pleases you in this person?" "What displeases you in that one?" "What do you think of such a person?" "What would you have done?" "What does the story teach you about God and

[66] Luke 2:46.

Our Lord?" The children are thus compelled to think and work with the teacher. Their judgment is sharpened and their interest in the subject awakened.

g. Memorizing of the Catechism answers should not be the first step but the last step or finishing touch to a process of explanation and understanding. Memorizing is not without its importance in catechization. Divine immutable truths demand accurate and precise expression. The terse and concise formulas of the Catechism are more easily impressed upon the memory, and misunderstandings and errors are thereby more easily avoided.

The Synthetic Method

1. Although the New Testament sets forth touching examples of Christ's great love for children and of His deep appreciation of their immortal supernatural destiny, the sacred pages do not record any catechetical instruction of our Lord delivered to children. The Saviour insisted, however, that "unless you be converted, and become as little children, you shall not enter into the kingdom of heaven." [67] He declared that God's truths were not revealed to the proud Scribes and Pharisees but to the lowly and humble of heart. He thanked the heavenly Father for communicating divine truths to souls which – devoid of all useless earthly wisdom and endowed with the gifts of grace and faith – were fit recipients of the heavenly message.[68]

In directing men's minds to the invisible things of God, Christ used examples and comparisons from the visible things of nature and daily life – from facts which were intelligible to both adult and child. If in a certain instance the parable was adapted to the former and not to the latter, the principle underlying the parable – namely, that the images must be derived from the circle of the hearer's daily and immediate experiences – remains perenially valid in all catechization. The illustrations, comparisons and stories which the teacher selects must be extracted from the child's concrete experiences and be adapted to his mental capacity. Images derived from home scenes – from the child's intercourse with his parents and other members of the family – and which are experienced by the child first, should logically precede those from nature.

[67] Matt. 18:3.

[68] Matt. 11:25.

The Incarnate Word not only knew all truths and all the ways of knowing, but He Himself actually experienced in His human soul the operations of the mind in the acquisition of knowledge. On the other hand, man's mind has not evolved in the course of the centuries but is a faculty of the divinely created soul. Moreover, iti is one and the same mind which assimilates both profane and supernatural truths. Hence the catechetical principles of Our Lord cannot stand in contradiction to genuine didactic methods. When modern educators propound certain pedagogic principles as the discoveries of contemporary education psychology and insist that catechetical methods be brought into harmony with them, they seem to forget that these very perennial laws were enunciated or at least insinuated almost two thousand years ago by the great Teacher and Educator of mankind. True, the religious instructor must rely on divine grace and faith; the religious truths which he is teaching are not wholly conprehensible by reason but are ultimately accepted — with God's aid — on faith; these same truths are not to remain mere ornaments of the mind but are to issue in a transformation of the child's conduct. But grace does not destroy nature, and correct pedagogy and catechetics — far from contradicting one another — should mutually and reciprocally aid one another.

Now, what are some of the features of Christ's pedagogical method? In the first place, an uninterested mind does not readily assimilate a given truth but soon expels it after receiving it; hence, Christ strove first of all to create in His hearers an attitude of receptivity and expectancy. He endeavored to arouse their interest. He appealed to their acquired mental content; He passed before their mental eye the awful events of Mt. Sinai and the majestic forms of the Old Testament patriarchs and prophets; with these He associated His new and heavenly doctrine. He engrafted the general upon the particular, principles upon concrete facts. With a few exceptions — notably the Beatitudes — Our Lord proceeded to the abstract by means of the concrete. To enable His audience to grasp the supernatural truths, Our Lord used as starting points and as stepping stones the familiar scenes of intimate home life, the concrete processes and facts of nature or the activities peculiar to the profession to which His hearers belonged. In other instances He attained the same end, perspicuity, by means of striking contrasts.

In order to impress His doctrines permanently on the minds of His followers and in order to reach men of difficult callings and different intellectual capacities, Our Lord at times resorted to varied repetitions, explanations, comparisons and striking – sometimes hyperbolic – sayings. Above all, He desired that the supernatural truths be incorporated into our daily lives, become the motive force of our actions and fructify abundantly unto eternal life.

2. *Through Apperceptive Masses.* In propounding His sublime doctrines, Christ proceeded slowly and gradually, after the manner of a true pedagogue. He engrafted the new upon the old, the unknown upon the known. The acquired mental content was used as a stepping stone to higher truths. In the religious training of the human race the new is frequently correlated with the old, and the old is used as a means of creating interest and a receptive attitude toward the new. The Old Testament itself is a preparation for the New Dispensation. "In the Old Testament," says St. Augustine, "there is a veiling of the New Testament, and in the New there is a revealing of the Old." Although the history of the Jewish people has an interest of its own – being that of the only nation of antiquity which had the knowledge and worship of the true God – yet its great importance and significance lies in the fact that it reveals the divine preparation of Christ's kingdom among men. A few examples will readily illustrate this truth.

The divine Word – eternally hidden in the bosom of the Father – announced little by little, through the succession of Messianic prophecies, His advent upon earth. Proclaimed at first as the "seed of the woman" the future Redeemer is successively represented as a member of the family of Sem, Abraham and David. He is depicted as King, as Priest, as Son of God. His miraculous origin, His birthplace, His divine attributes and endowments, His passion, death and resurrection are narrated to us with unusual accuracy as the long line of prophets slowly passes over the world's stage. In fact, the Messias' figure permeates the whole history of Israel and enters into its very texture. From Genesis to Malachias each patriarch and prophet adds some new feature, some new detail. And thus the human race is gradually educated for the coming of the Messias. When He finally comes and when His life begins to unfold before men, they can readily recognize in Him the Promised One of the Old Testament. Christ Himself reminded the Apostles that "all things must needs be fulfilled, which are written in the law of Moses, and in the prophets, and in the psalms, concerning Me." [69]

Men were gradually prepared and educated for the coming of the Messias by the types and figures by which He was foreshadowed. As the twilight announces the approach of dawn, so the lives of the patriarchs announce the coming of Christ or prefigure one or several of His attributes. The Innocent Victim and the Good Shepherd are prefigured in Abel; the King and Priest, in Melchisedech; the wood of the cross and Calvary, in the sacrifice of Isaac; His betrayal by His brethren, in the selling of Joseph; the saving virtue of His Blood, in the Paschal lamb; His sacrifice, in the multitudinous sacrifices of the Old Law; the victim of expiation, in the scapegoat; the quickening power of His cross, in the brazen serpent; and His resurrection, in Jonas. When grouped together these images acquire new strength and clearness. They create an attitude of expectancy and interest. They point to and prepare for Him whom they represent.

Our Lord frequently seizes upon a certain mental content or develops a certain mental attitude in order to engraft upon it His heavenly doctrine. His own public ministry is not ushered in suddenly and unexpectedly but is heralded beforehand by John the Baptist. He bids the Apostles behold the birds of the air and the lilies of the fields, and, while they are observing the joyous carelessness of the former and the unexcelled beauty of the latter, He proposes His doctrine on God's providence.[70] At Jacob's well He asks the Samaritan woman for a drink of water; by revealing her sinful past He arouses the woman's curiosity and stimulates her interest. Thereupon He proposes His doctrine concerning the living water.[71] He calls a child to Himself and sets him in the midst of His inquisitive and astonished audience; then He points to the child as an example of that humility and simplicity required for entering God's kingdom.[72] On the way to Caesarea Philippi, Christ by means of apposite questions, elicits from Peter, in the presence of the other Apostles, a profession of faith in His divinity; He then makes Peter head of the Church.[73] At the Feast of Tabernacles water was drawn from the pool of Siloe, taken in solemn procession

[69] Luke 24:44.
[70] Matt. 6:26–29.
[71] John 4:4 ff.
[72] Matt. 18:3.
[73] Matt. 16:13–19.

to the Temple and there poured out upon the altar. At the same time were sung the words of the prophet Isaias, "You shall draw water with joy out of the Saviour's fountain"; at this juncture Christ cries out, "If any man thirst, let him come to Me, and drink." [74] While the Jews are gazing with admiration at the magnificent candelabra in the temple, Christ stands up and says: "I am the light of the world." [75] When the Apostles are in wonderment at the draught of fishes which through Christ's power they had miraculously taken, the Saviour promises them that He will make them "fishers of men." [76] Finally, the coming of the Holy Spirit is repeatedly announced to the Apostles many days before Pentecost.[77]

The Sacraments, too, were not without their types and foreshadowings, nor were men, in consequence, wholly unprepared for the institution of these divine channels of grace. The Sacrament of Penance was prefigured by the mercy seat above the ark of the covenant and by the cure of the palsied man. Baptism was foreshadowed in at least five different ways: by the rite of *circumcision*, by which the Jew was aggregated to the chosen people of God and cleansed from the guilt of original sin; by the *ark of Noe* which rose above the flood and saved Noe's family from the common destruction; [78] by the *passage through the Red Sea* in which the enemies, who had held the Jews captive, were completely blotted out; [79] by the *washing of Naaman* the Syrian in the Jordan – a washing which completely cleansed him from leprosy; [80] by the *Probatica pond*, whose waters were periodically moved by an angel, and where those who were submerged into the waters after the moving, were cured.[81]

Nowhere is the building up of apperceptive masses in the minds of men with a view to a future doctrine so interestingly exemplified as in connection with the Holy Eucharist. God successively prepared and educated men for the sensible signs, effects and institution of this admirable Sacrament. The sensible signs were adumbrated in the sacrifice of bread and wine which Melchisedech offered to God,[82] by the shewbreads or loaves of proposition which were renewed on every Sabbath [83] and by the "hearth cake" which

[74] John 7:37; Isa. 22:3.
[75] John 8:12.
[76] Matt. 4:19.
[77] John 14.
[78] I Pet. 3:20, 21.
[79] I Cor. 10:1, 2.
[80] IV Kings 5:14.
[81] John 5:2.
[82] Gen. 14:18.
[83] Lev. 24:5 ff.

the angel brought to Elias, in the strength of which Elias walked to the mount of God.[84] The effects of the Eucharist were prefigured by the white bread — the manna — which came down daily from heaven and strengthened the Jews on their journey through the desert to the promised land. The institution of the Holy Eucharist — the changing of created things, namely, bread and wine, into Christ's Body and Blood — was foreshadowed in many ways. Christ's power over created things was forcibly illustrated by His changing water into wine in Cana, by His stilling the tempest at sea and by His walking over the waters. His power over the human body was manifested in His miraculous cures of men's diseases and in His own Transfiguration. The proximate preparation for the promise and institution of the Eucharist was the multiplication of the loaves. This miracle manifested in a striking manner Christ's divine power, established His authority as a teacher and filled the minds of His followers with eager expectancy for His further teaching. From the material and corruptible bread, which they had seen marvelously multiplied and with which they had been fed, Christ could then easily direct their thoughts to a heavenly Bread which was to be the spiritual food of His countless followers.

3. *Through Nature and Human Experience — the Parable.* Our Lord could have, like the philosophers of ancient Greece, proclaimed His teaching in abstract propositions and exact definitions. He could have enunciated the religious truth in the form of a precise principle, and then dissected and analyzed this principle, resolved it into its component parts, explained each in succession and finally combined the parts into a whole. But ordinarily He did not do so. The Sermon on the Mount, it is true, enunciates the Beatitudes in abstract statements which it afterwards illustrates by concrete examples. But even here the concrete element thickens and increases as the discourse proceeds.

Christ usually introduces lessons of great spiritual importance by means of a figurative statement. He employs the parable — a story drawn from nature or from ordinary human experience — as a means of opening men's minds to sublime supernatural truths. Like His miracles, Our Lord's parables engendered the proper mental attitude toward His teaching. As the parable began, the hearer's attention was turned in the right direction; his attitude

[84] III Kings 19:6–8.

became one of expectancy; his desire to know was stimulated. The lively interest which the parable immediately aroused could not have been awakened by a dry statement or a precise theological formula. The hearer's interest became keener as the story proceeded and suggested a deeper meaning than appeared in the simple narration. Toward the end, the hearer drew from the story this deeper meaning or asked for an explanation. The images called up in his mind constituted an appropriate setting for the supernatural truth.

All this, as we have already indicated, is quite in conformity with what is recognized as best in contemporary pedagogy. No item of knowledge can gain admittance into the domain of the mind unless it first enters through the portals of one of the senses. A man who would lack all five senses could not possibly — save by a miracle — have any knowledge in his mind. All intellectual knowledge depends upon antecedent and concomitant sense-activity. The child as well as the adult is dependent on his senses for all knowledge and understanding. This is all the more the case when there is question of gaining knowledge of entirely spiritual and supernatural realities.

Secondly, man assimilates a given subject gradually and not in one act. He begins with apprehension, then passes on to understanding and finally proceeds to application. In the first stage the child exercises principally his senses; in the second, the intellect; in the third, his will and emotions. The teacher, in turn, must accommodate himself to this threefold process and patiently minister to the child's nature in order to make it yield the desired results. The teaching of the matter must begin by making the child see, if not with his bodily eye, at least with the eye of his imagination that which the teacher is expounding.

Our Lord fully realized that the mind of man — and especially the mind of the child — clings to sensible objects and grasps more easily whatever it can see. Understanding fully man's nature and powers, Christ adapted Himself to the intellectual aptitudes and needs of His hearers; He brought supernatural truths near to their senses by means of the parable. He narrated a fact from nature or daily life and made it the vehicle of a supernatural truth. By means of His simple illustrations truths in themselves difficult of comprehension were made intelligible to the multitudes. With the aid of the parable, doctrines sublime in their nature and far-reaching in their consequences were made utterly familiar to His listeners.

Christ's parables were based on the vital experience of His followers — that is, upon the customs, labors, thoughts and feelings of those who listened to Him. Speaking of that great chapter of parables in St. Matthew's Gospel — the chapter [85] containing the parables of the sower and of the mustard seed, of the pearl of great price and of the fishing nets — one author points out how local scenes and actions gave Our Lord the suggestion for the parables: "On the nearby hill-slope a husbandman is scattering broadcast golden grain upon the fields; the birds of the air are unconsciously winging their way above their Creator's head, bringing food to their fledglings in the gigantic Oriental yellow-green mustard bush; on the highroad a merchant's caravan winds its dusty way to Capharnaum, and the merchant himself, seated on an Arabian steed, is perhaps dreaming in hopeful desire of finding in this new market the pearl of great price that shall please his mistress of Theman; farther on, half-naked fishermen are drawing the night's catch to shore, sorting the good fish into their vessels and casting the others on the sands to perish." [86]

In His discourses Christ continually refers to objects in nature and makes them reflect His heavenly truths. The clouds, rains, winds and flood; the wheat, cockle and mustard seed; the fruits, vines and vineyards; the fig tree, the lilies and grass of the field; the sunlight, rock and mountain — all these are elevated to serve as vehicles of the highest and most magnificent verities of the supernatural order. These comparisons between supernatural realities and visible creation were easily made, for, since both are the work of the same God, they bear striking resemblances in many ways. There are two rays of light — that of supernatural revelation and that of natural truth. These two, proceeding from a single Sun, can never cross in conflict — reason can never be opposed to faith — but mutually witness to one another and to the primeval truth from which they originally spring. In the words of the sacred writers, "The invisible things of Him, from the creation of the world, are clearly seen, being understood by the things that are made," [87] and again, "The heavens show forth the glory of God,

[85] Matt. 13.

[87] Rom. 1:20.

[86] J. M. Simon, *A Scriptural Manual* (New York, 1928), II, 216.

and the firmament declareth the work of His hands."[88] Men thus trained to see the harmony between God's teaching through nature and His teaching through revelation will not easily lapse into materialism – a danger which is very real today when one considers the orientation, temper and viewpoint of contemporary natural science. Such men will not look upon the world as something complete in itself, with no need of a Creator to explain its origin and the ceaseless operation of its laws. Their faith will not be a form of belief quite remote and distinct from their other knowledge. They will clearly understand whence the world came, what it is and whither it is going.

The parables were drawn, secondly, from human experiences and from the range of men's interests. The parables derived from the various domains of contemporary Jewish life may be roughly divided into the following groups:

a. Parables based on *family and home scenes*: the children and the dogs, the two sons, the vigilant servants, the friend at midnight, the prodigal son.

b. Parables based on *agricultural life*: the sower, the seed cast into the ground, the tares or cockle, the great harvest and the few laborers, the laborers in the vineyard.

c. Parables based on *social life*: the bridegroom and the wedding guests, the marriage of the king's son, the great supper, the poor guests, the last place at the feast, the ten virgins.

d. Parables based on *economic life*: the hidden treasure, the pearl of great price, the rich fool, the five talents, the pounds, the unjust steward, the unmerciful servant.

e. Parables based on the *religious life*: uprooted plants and blind leaders of the blind, the kingdom of heaven and of Satan, the Pharisee and the publican.

These parables were at all times perfectly adapted to Our Lord's audience. If He noticed among His listeners men of different professions and of different capacities, He uttered – as for example, in the thirteenth chapter of St. Matthew's Gospel – one parable after another, touching with one the apperceptive masses of one group of persons, with another a second group, and so on, until His lesson had been inculcated in the minds of all His hearers. To the farmers of Galilee He spoke of the sower, of the wheat and the cockle, of the

[88] Ps. 18:2.

seed cast into the ground; to the Judean shepherds He spoke of the sheep and sheepfold; to women He spoke of the leaven; to the merchants He spoke of pearls and treasures; to the fishers He spoke of fish and fishing nets; to the husbandmen He spoke of vines and vineyards; and to the householder, of laborers, servants and stewards. In each instance Christ associated the truth with something which was vital in the experience of His hearer and which later would serve as a continual reminder of a supernatural truth. Thus the husbandman could not look at the vine and branches, nor the shepherd at his sheep, nor the fisherman at his nets, nor the farmer at his crops, without recalling the truth which Christ in His parables associated with the objects. With each subsequent observation the object recalled that lesson and engraved it more deeply upon the mind. The things and events on which Christ based His parables were not peculiar to Palestine but fall within the universal and perennial experience of man. Hence the value of parables and similar stories — as vehicles of Christ's sublime and immutable truths — was not transitory but lasting.

In conclusion, let us note the essential difference between Christ's catechetical method and a method frequently used in our classroom. The latter procedure may be described as follows: the Catechism text is read; then one word after another is briefly explained; and then the text is repeated over and over until the children become fully familiarized with the terms. The whole chapter, which is handled and explained in this way, must be memorized at home. In the next lesson it is repeated word for word. If the child fails to answer immediately, he is prompted by the first word. Such a method will in most instances fill the children with disgust for religion. It lays too much emphasis on the dead letter. Sentences so painfully hammered into children will soon be forgotten. The unassimilated abstract formulas, instead of promoting religious life, will become nonfunctional memory loads and dead accumulations and will soon be expelled from the mind.

4. *Contrasts.* Our Lord frequently strives at perspicuity by means of striking contrasts. A contrast is the placing side by side of two objects, whether of the same or another kind, to show the difference and dissimilarity or contrariety of their natures or qualities. Just as light and shade throw each other into relief, so, too, contraries are better grasped when they are placed side by side. The beauty of

virtue and the attributes of evil stand in bolder relief when contrasted one with the other. These comparisons are all the more striking when enshrined in images derived from nature or from daily life. In the Gospels truth and error, the evil and the good are depicted under the following antitheses: the narrow path and the broad way,[89] the good and evil tree,[90] the wheat and the cockle,[91] the new and old garments,[92] the new and old wine-skins,[93] the new and old wines,[94] the children and the dogs,[95] the repentant son and the insincere son,[96] the kind master and the unmerciful servant,[97] the proud Pharisee and the humble publican,[98] the good Samaritan and the heartless priest and levite,[99] the wise and foolish virgins,[100] the industrious and the slothful servants,[101] the rich glutton and the beggar Lazarus,[102] Magdalen and Simon,[103] the good shepherd and the selfish hirelings,[104] the first and the last,[105] the exalted and the humbled,[106] the called and the chosen.[107]

5. *Through the Concrete and Miraculous.* The multitudes with which Our Lord came into contact were made up of persons of varied capabilities. In instructing them Christ always adapted Himself to their intellectual capacity. In dealing with the simple and untutored He employed familiar and commonplace objects as means of imparting profound and sublime truths. Besides the parable, Our Lord used another concrete pedagogical means which not only appealed to the senses – especially the senses of sight and hearing – but which supplied immediate evidence, reached efficaciously the understanding, and stimulated religious faith, namely, the miracle. The miracle was especially effective in dealing with men who not only adhered to things of sense but who were solidly entrenched in their prejudices and obstinate against the divine advances, men who were unwilling to give the time and attention required by the oral preaching of supernatural truths. Although the faith of such hardhearted men was less meritorious, yet it was

[89] Matt. 7:13, 14.
[90] Matt. 7:16–20.
[91] Matt. 13:24–30, 37–43.
[92] Matt. 9:16.
[93] Matt. 9:17.
[94] Luke 5:39.
[95] Matt. 15:26.
[96] Matt. 21:28–32.
[97] Matt. 18:23–35.
[98] Luke 18:9–14.
[99] Luke 10:30–37.
[100] Matt. 25:1–13.
[101] Matt. 25:14–30; Luke 19:11–27.
[102] Luke 16:10–31.
[103] Luke 7:44.
[104] John 10:1–16.
[105] Mark 9:34.
[106] Luke 14:11.
[107] Matt. 22:14.

better for them to be converted by miracles than to remain altogether in their unbelief. St. Paul says that signs were given to unbelievers [108] that they might be converted to the faith.

By His miracles Christ engendered in the hearts of the multitudes faith in Himself and in His doctrine. After narrating the miracle at the wedding feast in Cana, St. John says, "This beginning of miracles did Jesus in Cana of Galilee, and manifested His glory, and His disciples believed in Him." [109] In speaking of the Jewish pasch, when Jesus drove the buyers and sellers from the temple, the evangelist adds, "Many believed in His name, seeing His signs which He did." [110] After the cure of the ruler's son, the father "himself believed, and his whole house." [111] After relating the miracle of the resurrection of Lazarus, John remarks, "Many therefore of the Jews, who were come to Mary and Martha, and had seen the things that Jesus did, believed in Him." [112] The divine Master Himself appealed to His miraculous works as a conclusive proof of His divine mission. When St. John the Baptist sent his disciples to Christ with the question, "Art Thou He that are to come, or look we for another?" the Saviour's answer was, "Go and relate to John what you have heard and seen. The blind see, the lame walk, the lepers are cleansed, the deaf hear, the dead rise again, and the poor have the gospel preached to them." [113]

Secondly, Christ's miracles were proofs and evidences of His Divinity. His miracles surpassed the entire capability of created power and could be effected only by divine power. For this reason the man whose sight had just been restored said, "From the beginning of the world it hath not been heard that any man hath opened the eyes of one born blind. Unless this man were of God, he could not do anything." [114] Indeed, no man, even though he be possessed of extraordinary skill and ability, has ever of himself raised the dead to life, given sight to the blind, calmed the waves or driven the evil spirit from a possessed body. He who accomplished such wonderful deeds was Cod. Again, Christ performed miracles by His own, and not by a delegated, power, as did Elias and Eliseus. He performed them in His own name and by a mere word or move-

[108] I Cor. 14:22.
[109] John 2:11.
[110] John 2:23.
[111] John 4:53.
[112] John 11:45.
[113] Matt. 11:4, 5.
[114] John 9:32, 33.

ment of His will. A "virtue went out from Him and healed all." [115] This power of working miracles was so proper to Him that He communicated it to the Apostles, who in turn worked miracles in His name.

Christ's miracles may be divided into three groups: miracles over the evil spirits, miracles over diseases and death, and miracles over irrational or inanimate creation. Each one of these three categories had a pedagogical value. In the first place, Christ came to rescue from the power of the demon those who believed in Him. Hence, it was fitting that among other miracles He should deliver those who were obsessed by demons.

Again, Christ came as the Redeemer of men and Conqueror of death. In the present order, diseases, death and corruption of the body are consequences and penalties of original sin. Christ came as Physician of both the soul and the body. Although death will not be fully vanquished until the final resurrection, it was fitting that Christ should reveal His power over it by miraculous cures of diseases of the body, by raising others from the dead and by His own resurrection.

Finally, the pagans admitted the existence of "many gods" and assigned a divinity to almost every object in nature. Christ by His miracles over celestial and earthly bodies – over the sun, winds and sea – showed that all things in heaven and on earth are subject to Him. Speaking of the sidereal phenomena which occurred at His birth and death, St. Thomas says, "Then above all, there was need for miraculous proof of Christ's Godhead, when the weakness of human nature was most apparent in Him. Hence it was that at His birth a new star appeared in the heavens. But in His Passion yet greater weaknesses appeared in His manhood. Therefore, there was need for yet greater miracles in the greater lights of the world." [116]

Christ's miracles often confirmed His teaching. Thus He wrought miracles on the Sabbath day to prove to the Jews that the law of charity was more important than their law of sabbatical rest.[117] When curing the man who had been let down through the roof into the midst of the crowd which surrounded Him, Jesus said to the

[115] Luke 6:19.
[116] *Summa Theologica*, II a, q. XLIV, a 2, ad 3[um].
[117] Matt. 12:11, 12.

bystanders, "That you may know that the Son of Man hath power on earth to forgive sins (He saith to the man sick of the palsy), I say to thee, Arise, take up thy bed, and go into thy house." [118]

In no instance was the probative power of a miracle so great as in the case of the resurrection. When the Jews pressed our Lord on the question of His divinity, when they demanded a sign or a proof of His divine mission, He, to convince their mind and confound their incredulity, referred them to His future resurrection. "An evil and adulterous generation," He once said to the Jews, "seeketh a sign; and a sign shall not be given it, but the sign of Jonas the prophet. For as Jonas was in the whale's belly three days and three nights, so shall the Son of man be in the heart of the earth thre days and three nights."[119] And again Christ said, "Destroy this temple and in three days I will raise it up."[120] If Christ, after having uttered this prophecy, had not risen from the dead, belief in His divinity would have been destroyed, and doubts as to the Father's acceptance of Christ's work would have arisen. Christ's words would have become a falsehood, and Christian faith, a phantom. But if after this prophecy Christ did rise, it follows that what He said is true, that He is God and one with the Father.

Why is the confirmatory value of miracles so great? Why are miracles in Christian apologetics called the most certain signs of revelation? Why is a doctrine confirmed by a miracle necessarily from God and God's? Because God who is Omniscience, Supreme Truth, and Holiness cannot perform a miracle to confirm an error or falsehood. This principle is well expressed by St. Thomas: "Since those things which are of faith surpass human reason, they cannot be proved by human arguments, but need to be proved by the argument of divine power: so that when a man does works that God alone can do, we may believe that what he says is from God; just as when a man is the bearer of letters sealed with the king's ring, it is to be believed that what they contain expresses the king's will." [121]

Our Lord's miracles were occasionally accompanied by exhortations to and approval of virtue. In connection with several miracles

[118] Luke 5:24.
[119] Matt. 12:39, 40.
[120] John 2:19.
[121] *Summa Theologica*, III a, q. XLIII, a 1.

He inculcated the lesson of humility; He forbade those cured to make known the miracle, thus desiring to avoid the applause and admiration of men. "He charged them strictly that no man should know it." [122] In connection with a large number of miracles, we find, among the accompanying statements of Christ, words such as "Thy faith hath made thee whole" [123] and "Thy faith hath made thee safe, go in peace." [124] Frequently, in order to impress the witnesses with the necessity of faith, He first questioned the sick man to afford him an opportunity of professing his belief.[125] On the other hand, He emphatically refused to perform the miracles solicited by the tempter, by Herod and by the Scribes and Pharisees because they lacked the proper dispositions. After calming the tempest, the Master rebuked the Apostles with the words: "Where is your faith? [126] When Peter, walking on the waters, became frightened and began to sink, Christ said to him, "O thou of little faith, why didst thou doubt?" [127] In His own country Our Lord "wrought not many miracles there because of their unbelief." [128]

The miracle frequently supplied a concrete starting point for the statement of a religious truth and at the same time strengthened and illustrated the truth. After Christ had wrought the cure of the ten lepers He profited by the occasion to teach the lesson of obedience to authority; since only one of them returned to give thanks for the favor, Christ at the same time inculcated the lesson of gratitude.[129] He miraculously exposed the sins of the Scribes and Pharisees who brought to Him the woman taken in adultery by writing with His finger on the ground; then by way of reproach and to teach them the lesson of forgiveness He said to them, "He that is without sin among you, let him first cast a stone at her." [130] His miracle of the multiplication of the loaves strengthened, illustrated and made more intelligible to the multitudes His Eucharistic discourse.[131] To teach the Jews that even heathens who trust lovingly in God are more worthy of favors than the Jews who emphasized only outward observances, Christ wrought the cure of the

[122] Mark 5:43; cf. Luke 8:56.
[123] Mark 10:52.
[124] Luke 7:50.
[125] Matt. 9:28, 29.
[126] Luke 8:25.
[127] Matt. 14:31.
[128] Matt. 13:58.
[129] Luke 17:14–18.
[130] John 8:7.
[131] John 6.

centurion's servant.[132] He taught confidence and perseverance in prayer by His cure of the Canaanite woman, who, despite the seeming repulses of the Saviour, continued to beseech Christ until the request was granted.[133] When healing the servant's ear which Peter cut off, He taught the lesson of forgiveness and of resignation to God's will.[134] The raising of Lazarus illustrated the consoling doctrine that those who have faith in Christ will rise on the last day.[135] The underlying principle in all these examples is the same: the concrete action or work served as a means of teaching a supernatural and heavenly truth.

6. *Explanation.* To impress the truth more deeply upon the minds of His hearers and to clear up any misunderstandings, our Lord occasionally — though rather rarely — interprets the various details of the parable. The idea is readily understood and assimilated; its meaning is deepened, when the relation between it and the thing or action — which stood for it in the parable — is established. Let us note, for example, our Lord's explanation of the parables of the sower, the cockle, and of the defilement.

a. *Parable of the Sower.*

(1.) *Presentation* (Matt. 13:3–8).

3. "And He spoke to them many things in parables, saying: Behold the sower went forth to sow.

4. And whilst he soweth some fell by the wayside, and the birds of the air came and ate them up.

5. And other some fell upon stony ground, where they had not much earth: and they sprung up immediately, because they had no deepness of earth.

6. And when the sun was up they were scorched: and because they had not root, they withered away.

7. And others fell among thorns: and the thorns grew up and choked them.

8. And others fell upon good ground: and they brought forth fruit, some an hundredfold, some sixtyfold, and some thirtyfold."

(2.) *Explanation* (Matt. 13:18–23).

18. "Hear you therefore the parable of the sower.

19. When any one heareth the word of the kingdom, and understandeth it not, there cometh the wicked one, and catcheth away

[132] Matt. 8:11–13.
[133] Matt. 15:22–28.
[134] John 18:11.
[135] John 11:25, 26.

that which was sown in his heart: this is he that received the seed by the wayside.

20. And he that received the seed upon stony ground, is he that heareth the word, and immediately receiveth it with joy.

21. Yet hath he not root in himself, but is only for a time: and when there ariseth tribulation and persecution because of the word, he is presently scandalized.

22. And he that received the seed among thorns is he that heareth the word, and the care of this world and the deceitfulness of riches choketh up the word, and he becometh fruitless.

23. But he that received the seed upon good ground, is he that heareth the word, and understandeth, and beareth fruit, and yieldeth the one and hundredfold, and another sixty, and another thirty."

b. *Parable of the Cockle.*

(1.) *Presentation* (Matt. 13:24–30).

24. "Another parable He proposed to them, saying: the kingdom of heaven is likened to a man that sowed good seed in his field.

25. But while men were asleep, his enemy came and oversowed cockle among the wheat and went his way.

26. And when the blade was sprung up, and had brought forth fruit, then appeared also the cockle.

27. And the servants of the good men of the house coming said ti him: Sir, didst thou not sow good seed in thy field? whence then hath it cockle?

28. And he saith to them: an enemy hath done this. And the servants said to him: Wilt thou that we go and gather it up?

29. And he said: No, lest perhaps gathering up the cockle, you root up the wheat also together with it.

30. Suffer both to grow until the harvest, and in the time of the harvest I will say to the reapers: gather up first the cockle, and bind it into bundles to burn, but the wheat gather ye into my barn."

(2.) *Explanation* (Matt. 13:37–43).

37. "He that soweth the good seed is the Son of man.

38. And the field is the world. And the good seed are the children of the kingdom. And the cockle are the children of the wicked one.

39. And the enemy that sowed them, is the devil. But the harvest is the end of the world. And the reapers are the angels.

40. Even as cockle therefore is gathered up, and burnt with fire: so shall it be at the end of the world.

41. The Son of Man shall send His angels, and they shall gather out of His kingdom all scandals, and them that work iniquity.

42. And shall cast them into the furnace of fire: there shall be weeping and gnashing of teeth.

43. Then shall the just shine as the sun, in the kingdom of their Father. He that hath ears to hear, let him hear."

c. *Parable of the Defilement.*

(1.) *Presentation* (Matt. 15:10–11).

10. "And having called together the multitudes unto Him, He said to them: Hear ye and understand.

11. Not that which goeth into the mouth defileth a man, but what cometh out of the mouth, this defileth a man."

(2.) *Explanation* (Matt. 15:15–20).

15. "And Peter answering, said to Him: Expound to us this parable.

16. But He said: Are you also yet without understanding?

17. Do you not understand, that whatsoever entereth into the mouth, goeth into the belly, and is cast out into the privy.

18. But the things which proceed out of the mouth, come forth from the heart, and those things defile a man.

19. From the heart come forth evil thoughts, murders, adulteries, fornication, thefts, false testimonies, blasphemies.

20. These are the things that defile a man. But to eat with unwashed hands doth not defile a man."

7. *Key to the Parables.* a. Since Our Lord was dealing with adults and not with children, He ordinarily did not interpret His parables. As He proceeded with the similitude, the disciples were able to translate the phrases of the parable into the terms of the supernatural truth which He wished to teach. They passed step by step from the known to the related unknown, from the concrete picture to the abstract truth. They gradually linked one idea with another until they grasped the full import of His teaching. The parable in itself was only a means to an end. Frequently the various details of the parable contained no special meaning but were intended to place in relief the supernatural truth which Christ wished to teach. We shall now briefly indicate the central theme of the principal parables and thereby supply a key to their understanding.

b. *Parables of the Kingdom of Heaven.*

(1.) *The Sower.*[136] (a) Men hear the word of God with various dispositions of mind and heart.

(b) The truths of the Gospel profit only when received in a good heart.

(2.) *Seed Cast into the Ground.*[137] The spiritual life in man's soul grows secretly, slowly and constantly until it reaches full maturity.

(3.) *The Tares or Cockle.*[138] The good and evil coexist in the world; they will be definitely separated on the day of judgment.

(4.) *The Mustard Seed.*[139] The humble beginning, rapid extension and universality of Christ's kingdom.

(5.) *The Leaven.*[140] The supernatural efficacy and transforming power of the Gospel.

(6.) *The Hidden Treasure.*[141] The Christian must give up whatever may hinder his acquisition of salvation.

7.) *The Pearl of Great Price.*[142] We must seek the kingdom of heaven and give up all that hinders its attainment.

(8.) *The Fishing Net.*[143] The wicked will be separated from the good on the day of judgment.

(9.) *The Great Harvest and the Few Laborers.*[144] The Christians must pray to God the Father that He would send new zealous workers to labor among the many still awaiting admission into God's kingdom.

(10.) *The Bridegroom and the Wedding Guests.*[145] The Apostles and disciples of Christ must rejoice while the Master is visibly present among them. After His death and during the troubled times following His Ascension, mourning and fasting will be suitable.

(11.) *The Old Garment and the Old Wine Bottles.*[146] (a) The

[136] Matt. 13:3–9, 18–23; Mark 4:3–9, 13–20; Luke 8:5–15. Cf. L. Fonck, *The Parables of the Gospel* (New York, 1915).

[137] Mark 4:26–29.

[138] Matt. 13:24–30, 37–43.

[139] Matt. 13:31, 32; Mark 4:30–32; Luke 13:18 ff.

[140] Matt. 13:33; Luke 13:20 ff.

[141] Matt. 13:44.

[142] Matt. 13:45, 46.

[143] Matt. 13:47–50.

[144] Matt. 9:37, 38.

[145] Matt. 9:14, 15; Mark 2:18–20; Luke 5:33–35.

[146] Matt. 9:16, 17; Mark 2:21, 22; Luke 5:36–38.

disciples of Christ, accustomed to a less severe mode of living, cannot immediately undertake a new life of fasting.

(b) The Old Law and the Gospel cannot be combined, because they are fundamentally different.

(c) The Jewish form of worship is to be superseded by Christian rites and ceremonies.

(12.) *Old and New Wine.*[147] Men abondon slowly the traditions to which they cling.

(13.) *Wayward Children.*[148] The incredulous generation is like unto morose children who are never satisfied and refuse to join in the games of others.

(14.) *Real Defilement.*[149] Food and the stains which adhere to unwashed hands — being something material — cannot defile man's soul. Evil, in its manifold forms, as it proceeds from a sinful will and corrupt heart, alone can really defile man.

(15.) *Uprooted Plants and Blind Leaders of the Blind.*[150] (a) Men (the Scribes and Pharisees) who follow their own spirit instead of the Spirit of God will be ejected from God's kingdom.

(b) Men (the Scribes and Pharisees) who follow those who have closed their eyes to divine light walk in spiritual darkness, and both will meet with eternal damnation.

(16.) *Children and the Dogs.*[151] (a) The benefits of the Messias and of His Kingdom are to be allotted, in the first place, to the Chosen People.

(b) At times God does not immediately answer our prayers because He wishes to try our faith and make us pray with greater earnestness, confidence and humility.

(17.) *Kingdom of Heaven and of Satan.*[152] Satan cannot join a league against himself and expel his own satellites. Satan is subject to a stronger one — to Christ — who by His divine power can cast him out. Men cannot remain neutral but must choose between Christ and Satan.

(18.) *Laborers in the Vineyard.*[153]

[147] Luke 5:39.
[148] Matt. 11:16–19; Luke 7:31–35.
[149] Matt. 15:10, 11, 15–20; Mark 7:14–23.
[150] Matt. 15:13, 14; Luke 6:39.
[151] Matt. 15:22–28; Mark 7:27, 28.
[152] Matt. 12:22–30, 43–45; Mark 3:23–27; Luke 11:17–26.
[153] Matt. 20:1–16.

(a) Heaven will always exceed our merits.

(b) Salvation is of grace, not of merit.

(c) The measure of celestial rewards depends not on the length of time spent in the Catholic Church but on the zeal and fervor in co-operating with grace.

(19.) *The Two Sons.*[154] Notorious sinners, whose actions were at first rebellious, afterwards repented at the preaching of St. John and entered the one fold. The Pharisees, who externally professed to obey God, internally rejected the Baptist's teachings.

(20.) *The Wicked Husbandmen.*[155] (a) The Jews will be rejected, and the Gentiles will be admitted into Christ's Church.

(b) Punishment will overtake those who reject Christ.

(21.) *The Marriage of the King's Son.*[156] (a) The Jews will be rejected, and the Gentiles will be admitted into Christ's Church.

(b) Sanctifying grace is necessary for salvation.

(22.) *The Great Supper.*[157] (a) All mankind is invited to eternal life, but the salvation of each one depends on his acceptance of the invitation.

(b) Temporal affairs must be sacrificed when they are an obstacle to salvation.

(23.) *The Signs of the End.*[158] When Christ's disciples will see all the predicted signs, they will know that the glorious advent of Christ the Judge is near.

(24.) *The Body and the Eagles.*[159] All men will – as by a divine impulse – perceive the presence of Christ the Judge and forthwith assemble at the place of judgment.

c. *Parables Concerning the Members of God's Kingdom.*

(25.) *The Barren Fig Tree.*[160] If men do not profit by the opportunities of repentance, which God in His mercy offers to them as He did once to the Jews, His judgment will inevitably overwhelm them.

(26.) *The Good Tree and the Bad.*[161] As a man's virtues are a

[154] Matt. 21:28–32.
[155] Matt. 21:33–46; Mark 12:1–12; Luke 20:9–20.
[156] Matt. 22:1–14.
[157] Luke 14:16–24.
[158] Matt. 24:32, 33; Mark 13:28, 29; Luke 21:29–31.
[159] Matt. 24:28; Luke 17:37.
[160] Luke 13:6–9.
[161] Matt. 7:16–20, 12:33–35; Luke 6:43–45.

proof of the goodness of his heart, so his vices are a proof of its corruption.

(27.) *The Pharisee and the Publican.*[162] We should practice humility and especially pray with humility.

(28.) *The Last Place at the Feast.*[163] Every one that exalts himself shall be humbled, and he that humbles himself shall be exalted.

(29.) *Poor Guests.*[164] Good works done from a natural motive only have their reward in this world; those proceeding from a supernatural principle will have a reward in the next world.

(30.) *The Rich Fool.*[165] We must avoid covetousness, and lay up to ourselves treasures in heaven by leading a charitable and virtuous life.

(31.) *The Vigilant Servants.*[166] We must always be prepared for the coming of Christ the Judge.

(32.) *The Thief in the Night.*[167] The time of death and of the judgment is uncertain; the Judge's coming will be sudden and unexpected.

(33.) *The Faithful Steward.*[168] Ecclesiastical superiors must use aright the divine gifts conferred upon them, watch carefully over the flock entrusted to their care and prepare for Christ's coming.

(34.) *The Ten Virgins.*[169] We must always watch and prepare for Our Lord's coming.

(35.) *The Closed Doors.*[170] (a) The Jews, who were called first, will be preceded by the Gentiles, who were called later.

(b) Many who began to serve God early but lost their first fervor will be surpassed in virtue and merit by those who began to serve God later but were zealous.

(36). *The Five Talents.*[171] (a) Our lot at the judgment will depend upon the use we have made of God's gifts and graces.

(b) Condemnation of sloth.

(37.) *The Pounds.*[172] (a) Our lot at the judgment will depend upon the use we have made of God's gifts and graces.

(b) God's justice and eternal punishment will ultimately overtake His enemies who rebelled against Him.

[162] Luke 18:9–14.
[163] Luke 14:7–11.
[164] Luke 14:12–14.
[165] Luke 12:16–21.
[166] Mark 13:33–37; Luke 12:35–38, 39, 40.
[167] Matt. 24:43, 44.
[168] Matt. 24:45–51; Luke 12:41–48.
[169] Matt. 25:1–13.
[170] Luke 13:25–30.
[171] Matt. 25:14–30.
[172] Luke 19:11–27.

(38.) *Unprofitable Servants.*[173] We must not be elated over our good works because God has a right to our services and because in serving Him we are only fulfilling our duty.

(39.) *The Good Samaritan.*[174] Our love of neighbor must embrace all men without distinction, especially those who need our assistance.

(40.) *The Unjust Steward.*[175] The Christian should be as wise in spiritual matters as worldlings are in securing what is to their own advantage.

(41.) *The Rich Man and Lazarus.*[176] (a) Those who misuse riches will go to hell.

(b) Those who remain unmoved by the ordinary means of salvation would be equally unconvinced by the testimony of miracles.

(42.) *Serving Two Masters.*[177] The commands of God are absolutely opposed to the demands of mammon.

(43.) *The Unmerciful Servant.*[178] Man must forgive his neighbor his little faults if he wishes God to forgive him his own great faults.

(44.) *The Mote and the Beam.*[179] We must not reproach others with lesser faults when we ourselves are guilty of greater.

(45.) *Pearls before Swine.*[180] Do not dispense holy things to men who are hostile and obstinately perverse.

(46.) *Son Asking for Bread.*[181] If men who are sinners and who are hard and difficult to deal with, give good things to their children, how much more the heavenly Father, who is absolutely good and powerful, will give good things to those who ask Him.

(47.) *Friend Coming at Midnight.*[182] We must persevere in prayer, even when God at first seems to reject our petitions.

(48.) *The Unjust Judge.*[183] "We ought always to pray and not to faint."

(49.) *The Two Debtors.*[184] There is a proportion between the sins forgiven and the penitent's love of Christ.

(50.) *Salt of the Earth.*[185] The preachers of the Gospel must by their example, teaching and sanctity of life counteract the moral corruption of the world.

[173] Luke 17:7–10.
[174] Luke 10:30–37.
[175] Luke 16:1–9.
[176] Luke 16:19–31.
[177] Matt. 6:24; Luke 16:13.
[178] Matt. 18:23–35.
[179] Matt. 7:3–5; Luke 6:41, 42.
[180] Matt. 7:6.
[181] Matt. 7:9–11; Luke 11:11–13.
[182] Luke 11:5–8.
[183] Luke 18:1–8.
[184] Luke 7:41–43.
[185] Matt. 5:13; Mark 9:48, 49; Luke 14:34, 35.

(51.) *Lamp on the Lamp Stand.*[186] The teachers of the Gospel must by their doctrine, exemplified and confirmed by their good actions, dispel the intellectual darkness of the world and move men to glorify the Father.

(52.) *The Builder, the King Going to War.*[187] The folly of not calculating what the service of Christ involves, the danger of precipitation and rashness.

(53.) *Disciples, Servants of the Household.*[188] The followers of Christ must not expect better treatment than the Master.

(54.) *Prudent Householder.*[189] The Christian teacher must have a rich and varied knowledge and must propose divine truths in a manner adapted to the understanding of different men.

(55.) *House Built on Sand – on a Rock.*[190] A Christian, whose spiritual life is based on a living faith and strengthened by good works, will be unmoved by the calamities, temptations and persecutions of this world.

d. *The Head of the Kingdom.*

(56.) *Light of the World.*[191] Christ by His examples, doctrine and grace enlightens the mind darkened by original sin. Men, whose deeds are evil, resist the truth which condemns them.

(57.) *Grains of Wheat.*[192] Christ by His death will multiply believers in Himself and will save men.

(58.) *The Vine.*[193] Christ as Head of the Mystical Body is the source of grace for its mystical members.

(59.) *King's Son Free from Tribute.*[194] Christ as the natural Son of God and of the King of Kings was not bound to pay tribute for the temple of His Father.

(60.) *The Physician.*[195] Christ in His mercy came to heal and save sinners.

(61.) *The Good Shepherd.*[196] Christ is the model for the pastors of His Church in all ages.

[186] Matt. 5:14–16; Mark 4:21; Luke 8:16, 11:33.

[187] Luke 14:28–33.

[188] Matt. 10:24, 25; Luke 6:40.

[189] Matt. 13:52.

[190] Matt. 7:24–27; Luke 6:47–49.

[191] John 3:19–21, 8:12, 9:5, 12:35, 36, 46.

[192] John 12:24, 25.

[193] John 15:1–8.

[194] Matt. 17:23–26.

[195] Matt. 9:12, 13; Mark 2:17; Luke 5:31–33.

[196] John 10:1–6.

(62.) *The Lost Sheep; The Lost Coin.*[197] God in His love seeks to save all, especially those who have strayed from the fold and are helpless. The recovery of an anxiously sought sinner causes more heavenly joy than the tranquil possession of many just.

(63.) *The Prodigal Son.*[198] (a) Christ loved sinners notwithstanding the murmuring of the Pharisees.

(b) God, like a tender father, is always ready to receive and pardon His erring children.

(c) Man cut off from God can never find true happiness in the slavery of sin.

8. *Permanence of Christ's Teaching.* Our Lord strives to engrave His teachings permanently upon the minds and hearts of His hearers by means of repetition. He does not immediately set aside a new truth after teaching it to His followers nor does He look upon it as completely mastered after one presentation. On the contrary, He recalls a truth over and over again to the minds of His hearers until it is thoroughly assimilated.

Our Lord repeatedly emphasizes the need of prayer and mortification. He reiterates at least three times the prediction of His sufferings and resurrection. He frequently repeats certain striking maxims and solemn sayings as, for example: "He who shall exalt himself, shall be humbled," "the first shall be last, and the last first," "many are called but few are chosen." He recalls past events in order to base new doctrines upon them: "Remember My word that I said to you, the servant is not greater than his master"; [199] with this introduction He amplifies His previous teaching and warns His followers that they must be prepared for suffering. The Saviour also harks back to past events in order to make more intelligible the doctrine which He is enunciating.[200] These repetitions were not tiresome and monotonous tautologies. Frequently, they were amplifications of some doctrine previously enunciated and which continued to satisfy the interest and curiosity of the listeners. Their suitable and varying form rendered them pleasant and enabled them to exercise a profound and lasting influence on His hearers. When the Saviour was not understood, He repeated the same doctrine in a more intelligible form.[201]

[197] Matt. 18:12–14; Luke 15:3–7, 8–10.
[198] Luke 15:11–32.
[199] John 15:20; cf. Luke 22:35; John 14:4, 13:33.
[200] Matt. 16:21.
[201] E.g., John 8:27, 10:6.

Psychology tells us that man assimilates a given subject gradually and not in one act. He does not grasp an object — presented to the mind for the first time — integrally and intuitively but only imperfectly. It is by gradual advances that he is introduced to and grasps the inner nature — the deeper and essential characteristics — of an object. This is all the more the case if the new doctrine runs counter to certain settled prejudices in the mind.

These principles are exemplified in a special manner in the Eucharistic discourses of Our Lord. From the miraculous multiplication of the loaves Christ gradually leads the thoughts of His hearers to a heavenly and incorruptible Bread. When questioned by the Jews as to how one may obtain this Bread, Christ requires faith as an indispensable preliminary condition. The previous mention of the "bread from heaven" also recalls to the Jews the manna of the desert. Christ now seizes the opportunity to point out the difference between the two: whereas the effects of the manna — and of the bread which He had multiplied — are material and temporary, those of the new Bread are spiritual and eternal. Our Lord then makes a further advance in His teaching by pointing out that He Himself is the Bread. Finally, He declares — and repeats in six different ways — that this Bread is His Flesh and Blood and that all must partake of it if they wish to have life everlasting.[202]

Christ impresses His teaching indelibly upon the consciousness of His hearers because He adapts it to the capacity of His disciples and uses illustrations the significance of which they can readily appreciate. If He perceives persons of different professions and capabilities in His audience, Christ utters one parable after another, until the apperceptive masses of each class have been touched and the lesson driven home to all who listened to Him. In the thirteenth chapter of St. Matthew's Gospel the topic of Christ's discourses, namely, the "kingdom of heaven," is repeated — conformably to the calling of His hearers — seven times and in seven different pictures. To the parable of *the sower* Christ adds those of *the cockle*, of *the grain of mustard seed*, of *the leaven*, of *the treasure hidden in a field*, of *the merchant seeking good pearls*, and of *the net cast into the sea*. Although all these parables deal with the kingdom under its internal, external and eternal aspects, the repe-

[202] John 6:1–59.

tition is a pleasing variation and not a monotonous reiteration of the same idea.

There is a gradation in the thoughts presented to His hearers. The parable of the sower describes the various dispositions of mind and heart with which men receive the Gospel of the kingdom; the second illustrates the action of the forces of evil; the third describes the humble beginnings, rapid extension and universality of the kingdom; the fourth exhibits the supernatural efficacy and transforming power of the Gospel; the fifth and sixth indicate the immense sacrifices which are necessary for the attainment of the kingdom; the last denotes the good and wicked members in the kingdom.

The rejection of the Jews and admission of the Gentiles into the kingdom is taught in three parables – the parables of *the wicked husbandmen, the great supper,* and *the marriage of the king's son.* But here, too, there is a pleasing variation of images as well as gradation of ideas. The first describes the treatment accorded the messengers of the kingdom; the second, the various excuses for not accepting the invitation to enter the kingdom; and the third, the heavenly glory of the just.

9. *Maxims and Proverbs.* The custom, in our Catholic schools, of writing a short religious saying on the blackboard – which is to serve as the child's thought for the day – finds in its essential purpose a firm support in the practice of our Lord. Christ frequently introduced proverbs, maxims and pithy sayings into His discourses. Proverbs, and pithy sayings are the result of reflection and experience. They express the general judgment of the people and the utterances of celebrated and holy men. They make a religious truth clearer and more perspicuous, are easily caught on account of their brevity and pithiness and, together with the religious truth connected with them, remain a long time in the memory. That they have a convincing, determining influence on man's will and action is evident from the manner in which crowds are often guided or misled by a simple slogan.

Our Lord's religious instruction frequently culminated and was crystallized – and this point is of importance to the catechist – in a proverb or saying. Let us indicate here a few parables the principle thought of which was summed up in an apposite concluding sentence: parable of *the wayward children* – "And wisdom is justified by her children,"[203] parables of *the laborers in the vineyard* and of *the closed doors* — "So shall the last be first, and the first last,"[204] parable of *the marriage of the king's son* — "For many are called but few are chosen,"[205] parable of *the good and the bad trees* — "Out of the abundance of the heart the mouth speaketh,"[206] the parables of *the last place at the feast* and of *the Pharisee and the publican* — "Every one that exalteth himself, shall be humbled, and he that humbleth himself, shall be exalted."[207] parable of *the faithful steward* — "Unto whomsoever much is given, of him much shall be required, and to whom they have committed much, of him they will demand the more,"[208] parable of *the pounds* — "To everyone that hath shall be given, and he shall abound; and from him that hath not, even that which he hath shall be taken from him."[209]

Apart from these pithy sayings Christ tried to appeal to the minds of His listeners and make an impression on their will and emotions by such forceful and urgent sayings as the following: "No servant can serve two masters,"[210] "No man lighting a candle covereth it with a vessel, or putteth it under a bed, but setteth it upon a candlestick that they who come in may see the light,"[211] "Not every one that saith to Me, Lord, Lord, shall enter into the kingdom of heaven, but he that doth the will of My Father who is in heaven,"[212] "Where your treasure is, there will your heart be also,"[213] "If the blind lead the blind, both fall into the pit,"[214] "They that are in health need not a physician, but they that are ill,"[215] "A prophet is not without honor, but in his own country, and in his own house,"[216] "Physician, heal thyself,"[217] "The foxes have holes and the birds of the air nests, but the Son of Man hath not where to lay His head,"[218] "The servant is not greater than his master,"[219] "For in this is the saying true: that it is one man that soweth, and it is another that reapeth,"[220] "If in the green wood they do these things, what shall be done in the dry?"[221] "These things ye ought

[203] Matt. 11:16–19.
[204] Matt. 20:16.
[205] Matt. 22:14.
[206] Luke 6:45.
[207] Luke 14:11, 18:14.
[208] Luke 12:48.
[209] Luke 19:26.
[210] Luke 16:13.
[211] Luke 8:16.
[212] Matt. 7:21.
[213] Luke 12:34.
[214] Matt. 15:14.
[215] Matt. 9:12.
[216] Mark 6:4.
[217] Luke 4:23.
[218] Matt. 8:20.
[219] John 15:20.
[220] John 4:37.
[221] Luke 23:31.

to have done, and not to leave those undone." [222] Occasionally Our Lord appeals to the sayings of Holy Scripture, as for example: "All that take the sword, shall perish with the sword" [223] and "Go then and learn what this meaneth, I will have mercy and not sacrifice." [224]

At times Christ incites His hearers to thought and reflection and arouses their feelings by such sharp expressions as the following: "It is not good to take the bread of the children, and to cast it to the dogs,"[225] "Give not that which is holy unto dogs; neither cast ye your pearls before swine,"[226] "Blind guides, who strain out a gnat and swallow a camel,"[227] "Cast out first the beam out of thine own eye and then shalt thou see to cast out the mote out of thy brother's eye." [228] To this category belong also the terrible woes which our Lord on numerous occasions pronounced against the Pharisees.[229]

The hyperbole – an expression which says more than the speaker intends and which is not to be interpreted verbally and equivalently but according to its inner meaning – is likewise of frequent occurrences in Christ's method of teaching. Here are some examples of this rhetorical figure used by Christ: "If thine eye scandalize thee, pluck it out and cast it from thee," [230] "It is easier for a camel to pass through the eye of a needle than for a rich man to enter the kingdom of heaven,"[231] "He that hath not, from him shall be taken away also that which he hath,"[232] "Lay not up to yourselves treasures on earth, where the rust and moth consume,"[233] "To him that striketh thee on the one cheek offer also the other," [234] "The last shall be first and the first last." [235] These hyperboles made His hearers reflect and prevented His words from becoming lifeless forms. His followers pondered these sayings more seriously and thus gained a deeper insight into their import.

Training of the Will and Heart

1. *Application to Conduct.* Our Lord was an educator as well as an instructor. He wished men to embrace His teaching not merely intellectually but also – and especially – affectively. He knew that

[222] Matt. 23:23.
[223] Matt. 26:52.
[224] Matt. 9:13.
[225] Matt. 15:26.
[226] Matt. 7:6.
[227] Matt. 23:24.
[228] Matt. 7:5.
[229] Matt. 23.
[230] Matt. 18:9.
[231] Matt. 19:24.
[232] Matt. 13:12.
[233] Matt. 6:19.
[234] Luke 6:29.
[235] Matt. 20:16.

the will is the driving power of the soul and that an undisciplined will often misguides an enlightened mind. Hence all His efforts were directed toward a correct orientation of the will and toward a proper training of the heart, emotions and appetitive faculties. This spiritual growth of the will was not to be one-sided — it was not to take place in utter isolation from the mind — but was to be stimulated by the bright rays of faith streaming upon it from a supernaturally enlightened intellect. Our Lord made energetic efforts in this regard because of the low educational and moral standards of his hearers — standards which were permeated by the Pharisaic spirit of externalism and personal righteousness. He strove unceasingly to counteract the evil disposition of the Jews who were prejudiced against His doctrine and presented a serious obstacle to the permanence of His teaching.

Our Lord frequently emphasized the necessity of applying in daily conduct the truths which He is enunciating. At the close of His Sermon on the Mount He says, "Everyone therefore that heareth these My words, and doth them, shall be likened to a wise man that built his house upon a rock." [236] If one's life is built upon the rock of Christ's teaching, it will remain unshaken amid the storms of life's temptations. Man builds upon Christ, however, only when he receives Christian truths into his innermost being and embraces them with his will, heart and emotions. He, on the contrary, "that heareth these My words, and doth them not, shall be like a foolish man that built his house upon the sand." [237] Men's application of His teaching to their conduct is always our Lord's primary concern: "Blessed are they who hear the word of God, and keep it" [238] and "My mother and My brethren are they who hear the word of God, and do it." [239] Because He aims ultimately at influencing action and conduct, He leaves vain and useless questions unanswered or gives them a practical turn.[240]

Our Lord earnestly desires that divine doctrines should be incorporated into and become a vital part of our daily life, and bring forth fruit a hundredfold. The just man must live by his faith: "Not in bread alone doth man live; but in every word that proceedeth from the mouth of God." [241] Faith, it is true, is the root and

[236] Matt. 7:24. [237] Matt. 7:26. [238] Luke 11:28. [239] Luke 8:21.
[240] Luke 13:23, 19:11; John 12:34.
[241] Matt. 4:4.

foundation of justification, the very basis of Christian morality and perfection. Yet, even though our faith in Christ were strong enough to operate miracles, if it does not result in works, it will not avail us unto salvation. Our faith must be expressed in deeds as well as in words: "Not everyone that saith to Me, Lord, Lord, shall enter into the kingdom of heaven, but he that doth the will of My Father." [242] Above all, our faith must issue in a love of God and love of neighbor, for "on these two commandments dependeth the whole law and the prophets." [243] And love, in turn, will involve sacrifice and self-denial: "If any man will come after Me, let him deny himself, and take up his cross daily, and follow Me." [244]

A truth which is not incorporated into the mind and heart in such a way as to bring forth fruit will rise up on the last day in condemnation against us: "Every tree therefore that doth not yield good fruit, shall be cut down, and cast into the fire." [245] In the parable of the barren fig tree, the owner of the vineyard addresses the following words to the dresser, "Behold, for these three years I come seeking fruit on this fig tree, and I find none. Cut it down therefore: why cumbereth it the ground?" [246] Nowhere, perhaps, does our Lord express this idea in such forcible terms as in the parable of the talents: "Wicked and slothful servant, thou knewest that I reap where I sow not, and gather where I have not strewed; thou oughtest therefore to have committed my money to the bankers, and at my coming I should have received my own with usury. Take ye away therefore the talent from him . . . and the unprofitable servant cast ye out into the exterior darkness." [247] That the Saviour did not consider His exhortations to a moral life as mere formalities is clear, too, from His reiterated and emphatic references to the judgment: "The Son of Man shall come in the glory of His Father with His angels, and then will He render to every man according to his works" [248] and "they that have done good things, shall come forth unto the resurrection of life; but they that have done evil, unto the resurrection of judgment." [249] From all these examples it is clear that revelation was given to us, not merely to perfect our reason and increase our knowledge but also, and above all, to transform our hearts and wills.

[242] Matt. 7:21.
[243] Matt. 22:40.
[244] Luke 9:23.
[245] Matt. 3:10.
[246] Luke 13:7.
[247] Matt. 25:26–30.
[248] Matt. 16:27.
[249] John 5:29.

2. *Christ's Example.* The child tends by natural impulses to imitate the examples set before it. The first step it takes and the first word it utters are the result of imitation of parent or teacher. In writing, drawing and singing the child exercises himself on given models. In language lessons he has the correct sentences of the teacher and of the schoolbook for a model. When his mental view has broadened, when he has passed out of his first surroundings, his inspirations are drawn from examples of the past as set forth in history, biography and literature.

What is true of secular branches applies also to religion. Man is moved to live according to the doctrines of morality through exalted examples and models — especially the supreme Exemplar, Christ. Examples are stronger than words and teach better than precepts; "Words move but examples draw." Whereas oral instruction appeals to and acts upon the intellectual faculties, example stimulates the appetitive faculties and the powerful innate imitative instinct. Moral ideas become doubly attractive where they are exemplified in the activity of a living personage. Christ's teaching undoubtedly had an intrinsic beauty which compelled universal admiration. At the same time its efficacy was enhanced by His example and by the perfect harmony between His words and His conduct. His life prepared the way for — it illustrated and exemplified — His teaching and at the same time confirmed it. He first began to *do* and then to teach. "I have given you an example that as I have done to you, so you do also."

To enumerate and describe all the virtues of Our Lord would be to compose a life of Christ.[250] We can here touch on only a few of them. St. Paul emphasizes Christ's generosity as manifested in His Incarnation: "You know the grace of our Lord Jesus Christ, that being rich He became poor, for your sakes; that through His poverty you might be rich." [251] The virtue of humility was in a special way peculiar to Christ: "Learn of Me, because I am meek and humble of heart." [252] His whole life was likewise characterized by obedience: "I seek not My own will, but the will of Him that sent Me." [253] "He humbled Himself, becoming obedient unto

[250] Cf. John 13:15. The virtues of our Lord are extensively treated in F. Nepveu's *L'Esprit du Christianisme*, Eng. tr., *Like Unto Him or the Spirit of Christianity*, (New York, 1923).

[251] II Cor. 8:9. [252] Matt. 11:29. [253] John 5:30.

death, even to the death of the cross." [254] He gave us the greatest possible proof of fraternal love: "Greater love than this no man hath, that a man lay down his life for his friends." [255] His charity manifested itself in His compassion for the miseries of others: "I have compassion on the multitudes, because they continue with Me now three days, and have not what to eat, and I will not send them away fasting, lest they faint in the way." [256] Just as the sun sheds its light and heat everywhere, so our Lord scattered on every side His graces and blessings; He "went about doing good, and healing all." [257] His meekness was that of a lamb remaining silent in the hands of his shearers: "Who, when He was reviled, did not revile; when He suffered, He threatened not; but delivered Himself to him that judged Him unjustly." [258] He gave us on the cross a supreme proof of His patience and foregivingness when He prayed for the pardon of His enemies and offered an excuse for their awful crime: "Father, forgive them, for they know not what they do." [259]

The list, as we already pointed out, could be expanded indefinitely. The only virtues which we may not predicate of Christ are those which would be incompatible with His sinlessness and His enjoyment (already while on earth) of the beatific vision – as, for example, faith, hope, penance, continency, and servile fear.

3. *Mastery of Emotions.* Our Lord's mastery over the feelings and affections of others made His words doubly effective and constituted, perhaps, the highest triumph of His eloquence. This mastery was a consequence of His perfect humanity. Endowed with an exquisite sensitiveness, He could feel in a perfectly human way. Although always calm, noble and dignified, He nowhere and never conducted Himself as a Stoic. With majestic calm He spoke of eternity, of His divinity and of the divinity of His teaching. He marveled at the faith of the centurion [260] and wondered because of the unbelief of the people of Nazareth.[261] He was troubled and groaned at the sepulcher of Lazarus,[262] complained touchingly and wept over the estrangement and blindness of Jerusalem.[263] His farewell address [264] and His high-priestly prayer [265] are inimitable

[254] Phil. 2:8. [256] Matt. 15:32. [258] I Pet. 2:23. [260] Matt. 8:10.
[255] John 15:13. [257] Acts 10:38. [259] Luke 23:34. [261] Mark 6:6.
[262] John 11:33–38.
[263] Luke 19:42; Matt. 23:37. [264] John 14–16. [265] John 17.

models of tender affections and indirect pathos. No passage, perhaps, better expresses the affectionateness which pervades His teaching than the following: "Come to Me, all you that labor, and are burdened, and I will refresh you. Take up My yoke upon you and learn of Me, because I am meek and humble of heart; and you shall find rest to your souls. For My yoke is sweet and My burden light." [266] What a powerful incentive to the emotional life of the Jews which had been well-nigh smothered by Pharisaical externality and by countless unbearable minutiae!

Frequently our Lord tried to inspire His audience by means of impressive modes of speech. Examples of such formulae are the following: "He that hath ears to hear, let him hear," [267] "Lay you up in your hearts these words." [268] "Hear ye Me all, and understand,"[269] and the impressive formula, "Amen, Amen, I say to you." At times He gave added emphasis to His teaching by raising His voice and "crying out." [270] Whether the Saviour made use of the oratorical actions is not clear. Luke 7:44 ff., seems to suggest such a procedure. It is clear, at all events, that He made frequent use of an inspiring look. A glance animated by a warm and natural affection exercised a powerful influence on the emotions of His hearers. Christ looked encouragingly up to Zacheus,[271] He looked quietingly upon the Apostles who in their despair asked the question — "Who then can be saved?" — and answered, "With men it is impossible but not with God. For all things are possible with God." [272] When Peter had denied Him the third time, "The Lord turning looked on Peter." [273] He looked with satisfaction at those about Him of whom He could say, "Behold My mother and My brethren." [274] A loving look from the Saviour was the recompense of the young man who had kept the commandments from his youth.[275] But He looked with anger and sorrow round about on those who in a hostile spirit were watching the Sabbath healing.[276]

The permanence of His teaching was facilitated by the power and authority with which He — a divine Legislator and not a mere interpreter — enunciated His doctrines. "The people," St. Matthew tells us, "were in admiration at His doctrine. For He was teaching

[267] Matt. 13:43; Luke 8:8, 14:35; Mark 4:9.
[266] Matt. 11:28–30.
[268] Luke 9:44.
[271] Luke 19:5.
[274] Mark 3:34.
[269] Mark 7:14.
[272] Mark 10:27.
[275] Mark 10:21.
[270] John 7:28.
[273] Luke 22:61.
[276] Mark 3:5.

them as one having power, and not as the Scribes and Pharisees." [277] The God-man spoke with great power because His words flowed from the depths of His heart and penetrated deeply into and transformed the hearts of His listeners. Men were readily persuaded by Christ's words because they saw the complete harmony between His doctrine and His conduct. He taught the ways of God forcibly, too, because with Him there was no acceptation of persons. He did not hesitate to say to Israel's representatives, "Amen I say to you, that the publicans and the harlots shall go into the kingdom of God before you." [278] The crushing force of His eloquence was especially felt in His woes against the Pharisee.[279] and in His warning against scandal. He did not hesitate to speak of the last things of man, of judgment and of hell – realities of which no biblical personage spoke more often and more forcibly than He.

4. *Christ and Children.* How highly the Incarnate Word esteemed childhood is clear from the fact that He became a child Himself. He could have come in the form of an angel; He could have appeared on earth as a full-grown man like Adam – but no! He became a child. When the Prophet Isaias was scanning the horizon for some sign of the future Messias, he caught a glimpse of Him under the form of a child: "A *child* is born to us." [280] Nothing is so touching, too, as the predeliction with which the evangelists refer to Him as a child. St. Matthew tells us that the Magi followed the star in quest of the "Child": "The star which they had seen in the East, went before them, until it came and stood over where the *Child* was. And entering into the house, they found the *Child* with Mary His Mother." [281] When addressing Joseph, the angel likewise speaks of Christ as a child: "Arise and take the *Child* and His Mother, and fly into Egypt." [282] Referring to a somewhat later period, St. Luke adds that the "*Child* grew, and waxed strong, full of wisdom, and the grace of God was in Him." [283] Evin in His twelfth year the evangelist still refers to Him as a "child": "The *Child* Jesus remained in Jerusalem, and His parents knew it not." [284]

The child has a special attraction for the crib, and Christmas is

[277] Matt. 7:28, 29. [278] Matt. 21:31.
[279] Matt. 23; 18:6; Mark 9:41 ff.
[280] Isa. 9:6. [281] Matt. 2:9–11. [282] Matt. 2:13. [283] Luke 2:40.
[284] Luke 2:43.

rightfully considered as the feast of childhood. Yet it is not the sensible appeal which is here the determining factor. The baptized child whose soul is endowed with the virtue of faith feels — as by a sort of supernatural instinct — all that Christ did and meant for childhood. For one needs only to read history to see how pitiable and deplorable was the lot of the child in pre-Christian times. Under Achaz and Manasses — to quote only one example — horrible rites in honor of the pagan god Moloch were performed south of Jerusalem. An immense hollow brass idol, containing a powerful furnace, was placed at the entrance of a ravine and into its red-hot arms the Israelites cast their children. Elsewhere in the pagan world the child fared no better. Christian apologists and historians as well as pagan poets and philosophers testify to the eagerness of ancient peoples to sell or expose the child or to dash its head against a stone.

The atmosphere was still tainted by this prejudice against the child when our Lord began His public ministry. Even the Apostles, thinking that the Master had interests far more important than those of children, attempted to impede the children's free approach to Him. It was then that Christ uttered those words which renewed the face of the earth and filled the hearts of mothers with hope and joy: "And they brought to Him young children that He might touch them. And the disciples rebuked those that brought them. Whom when Jesus saw, He was much displeased and saith to them: Suffer the little children to come unto Me, and forbid them not, for of such is the kingdom of heaven." [285] These few words — so simple and yet so beautiful — proclaim the eternal truths that the child is made in the image and likeness of God, that he has an immortal soul capable of participating in sanctifying grace and that he is destined for the beatific vision. Here, then, we have the first reason for Christ's great esteem of childhood.

Christ became man in order to redeem all men — including children — and make them brothers and sisters in His Blood. In Christ's Mystical Body "There is neither Jew nor Greek, there is neither bond nor free, there is neither male nor female. For you are all one in Christ Jesus." [286] Hence, the risen Lord rebuked Saul because in persecuting the Christians he was persecuting Christ Himself.[287] And at the last judgment the King will say to the elect:

[285] Mark 10:13, 14. [286] Gal. 3:28. [287] Acts 9:4, 5.

"As long as you did it to one of these My least brethren, you did it to Me."[288] Among these "least brethren" are to be numbered the children, for we are told that it is Jesus Christ Himself – full of grace and charm and made a "child" for us – whom we receive when we receive children: "And taking a child, He set him in the midst of them. Whom when He had embraced, He saith to them: Whosoever shall receive one such child as this in My name, receiveth Me, and whosoever shall receive Me, receiveth not Me but Him that sent Me."[289]

Thirdly, Christ esteemed childhood because the child typifies and possesses the qualities necessary for entering the kingdom of heaven – namely, simplicity, humility and docility. The disciples had only an imperfect notion of the kingdom which Christ came to establish; they visioned it as temporal and material, as one in which each can advance his own personal ambitions. They failed to understand Christ's predictions of future sorrows. And hence on the way to Capharnaum they broke out in rivalries and disputed who should be the greatest in the kingdom: "And there entered a thought into them, which of them should be greater."[290] When they came into the city and were in the house, our Lord asked them: "What did you treat of in the way?[291] And they answered: "Who thinkest thou is the greater in the kingdom of heaven?"[292] Thereupon Christ called a little child and placed him in the midst of His astonished and attentive disciples, and said, "Amen, I say to you, unless you be converted and become as little children, you shall not enter into the kingdom of heaven. Whosoever, therefore, shall humble himself as this little child, he is the greater in the kingdom of heaven."[293]

How highly Christ esteemed childhood is evident finally from the woes which He pronounced against those who by word, deed or example would turn the child from the path of virtue: "He that shall scandalize one of these little ones that believe in Me, it were better for him that a millstone should be hanged about his neck, and that he should be drowned in the depth of the sea."[294] Indeed, death of the body is a much lesser evil than the death of the soul of the person scandalized and the penalty of eternal death which

[288] Matt. 25:40.
[289] Mark 9:35, 36.
[290] Luke 9:46.
[291] Mark 9:32.
[292] Matt. 18:1.
[293] Matt. 18:2–4.
[294] Matt. 18:6.

awaits the scandalizer in the next life. Take heed, our Lord again warns us, because their guardian angels are powerful in heaven and will avenge them: "See that you despise not one of these little ones, for I say to you that their angels in heaven always see the face of My Father who is in heaven." [295]

Children and mothers were not long in feeling the warmth of Christ's love for them. Mothers knew that by elevating childhood our Lord was at the same time ennobling motherhood. Hence mothers brought their children in full confidence to Him, besought Him graciously to touch them, to bless them, to lay His hands on them, and to pray for them: "Then were little children presented to Him, that He should impose hands upon them and pray." [296] "And embracing them, and laying His hands upon them, He blessed them." [297] Yes, the Saviour gathered in His Sacred Heart His tenderest and most powerful prayers and said them over the children in order to preserve their souls pure and untarnished.

The children responded spontaneously to the Saviour's love. They felt that they were loved, they came with full confidence, as when one knows he is specially loved. Forgetting the needs of life for three days, they followed Him into the heart of the desert; when our Lord miraculously multiplied the loaves to feed the fainting crowd, we find that in this crowd were many children. The Gospel, enumerating those who had been marvelously fed, adds, "beside children." [298] We find them again at our Lord's triumphant entry into Jerusalem on Palm Sunday; they mingled their cries with the acclamations of the people; their faces were aglow with the simplicity and excitement of their age; their cries echoed even in the Temple, "Hosanna to the Son of David." [299] When the Pharisees in their indignation attempted to silence the children, Christ justified them: "Have you never read," He said to the hypocrites, "out of the mouth of infants and of sucklings Thou hast perfected praise." [300] Some of these children must have been with their mothers, when these women were weeping for the suffering Saviour, and when our Lord, kind and compassionate even to the end, said to them: "Weep not over Me, but weep for yourselves and for your children." [301]

The study of Our Lord's attitude toward children impresses

[295] Matt. 18:10. [296] Matt. 19:13. [297] Mark 10:16. [298] Matt. 15:38. [299] Matt. 21:15. [300] Matt. 21:16. [301] Luke 23:28.

upon us several important lessons. In the first place, the catechist must reproduce in his life – at least in some measure – Christ's love for children. If he loves children, he will win their love in turn. As the flower opens its petals to the warm rays of the sun, so the children will open their minds and hearts to a catechist whom they love. But if he is harsh and cold, he will not produce lasting results. As St. Gregory says, "Those who are not loved are not willingly listened to." The catechist's love must be based principally upon supernatural motives. He must see in his little charges souls made in the likeness of God and redeemed by the Blood of Christ. He must see in the little sons of men sons of God and partakers of the divine nature who are destined one day to enter into possession of the eternal inheritance. He must see in them members of that Mystical Body of which Christ is the head. He must always consider it the greatest calamity if anyone should give a sinful bent to the child's plastic mind and heart or corrupt those on whom the future of the Church depends.

If the catechist's conduct is motivated by considerations such as these, he will become childlike with the children but not childish. He will become weak with the weak and make himself all things to all men, in order that he may gain all. Notwithstanding all his kindness a certain gravity will be visible in him and win for him reverence and respect.

The example of Christ shows us, secondly, that instruction should begin with little children. The child's mind is like wax which can easily receive an impression and be molded at will. Early instruction lays a firm foundation for the whole life. In its early years the child is more easily impressed by moral lessons than in later years. As the popular proverb says, "As the boy, so the man." And Scripture testifies, "A young man according to his way, even when he is old he will not depart from it."[302] If religious instruction is delayed until the child reaches mature age, his evil inclinations will in the meantime become deeply rooted and blunt his perceptions. He will become affected by the cares and prejudices of life, and it will become as difficult to reform him in his grown-up state as it is to bend a full-grown tree.

5. *Christ's Love for Men.* Christ's love embraced men of all conditions, creeds and callings. His love, in fact, was the mainspring

[302] Prov. 22:6.

and source of that burning zeal which manifested itself in so many different ways. The Saviour strove to make full use of every opportunity to teach. He taught the multitudes publicly in the synagogues and in the temple.[303] Yet it was with no lesser zeal that He preached privately, frequently to only one individual. Fatigued and hardly sat down on Jacob's well,[304] He opened a conversation with the Samaritan woman and shows Himself in the most perfect way the Good Shepherd seeking the lost sheep. In the house of Lazarus, Mary was His only auditor, yet He defended her against Martha's complaints and affirmed that Mary had chosen the better part. The force of this zeal showed itself in His shrinking from no difficulty and in His withdrawing from no one – not even from the sinners, publicans, Scribes and Pharisees. He left mother and country,[305] always faithful to His fundamental principle that He came to call sinners and not the just. The nobility of this loving zeal manifested itself in a great patience and in a perfect obedience to His Father's will, despite His certain knowledge that this zeal would be the eventual cause of His death.

The divine Educator strove above all to assure Himself of the love of His disciples and to banish from their hearts all self-interest. For in the measure that we possess a man's love, to that extent we enjoy an influence over his will and actions; love is the root of all affections, emotions and inclinations. Never is there to be detected in Christ's disciples a trace of fear which is not inspired by the inmost love of Him. When at the Transfiguration the three disciples heard the heavenly voice and in terror fell upon their face, "Jesus came and touched them, and said to them: Arise and fear not." [306] His first salutation to those who were frightened by His presence was, "Fear ye not." [307] Men's fear of Our Lord, whenever it arose, was due to the fact that they did not immediately recognize Him. St. John tells us that the disciples rejoiced to see the Lord [308] – not to satisfy their curiosity as Herod did,[309] but because of their love for Him.

Since love produces love – *quis amantem non redamet?* – Christ gave His disciples freely of His own divine love; He did so by word and deed, by His patience and meekness,[310] by His entering inti-

[303] Mark 1:21; Matt. 4:23, 26:55; Luke 4:16; John 18:20.
[304] John 4:6.
[305] Matt. 13:57; Luke 4:43.
[306] Matt. 17:7.
[307] Matt. 14:27; Luke 24:36.
[308] John 20:20.
[309] Luke 23:8.
[310] Matt. 21:5.

mately into all their temptations and weaknesses,[311] by praying for them [312] and by defending them against others.[313] His love for them was also manifested by the titles which He assigned to them on different occasions. He called them brothers, friends, *Filioli.* He pours forth the love of His Sacred Heart especially in His farewell discourses and comforts His disciples who are saddened by His imminent departure.[314] We can well understand the evangelists when they tell us that the disciples could not bear to be separated from Him even for a few hours,[315] that they were ready to die with Him [316] and that they remained attached to Him even after they realized that He would not establish an earthly kingdom. Christ's condescension and affability, coupled with a great love for them, necessarily produced in His disciples a great confidence and respect.

To what extent the teaching of the Saviour had captivated the interest of His followers is evident from the words of St. Peter, "Lord, to whom shall we go? Thou hast the words of eternal life." [317] On the evening of the first Sabbath which He spent in Capharnaum after the beginning of His public ministry, still captivated by what they saw and heard in the synagogue, "all the city was gathered together at the door." [318] And when on the next morning He went into the desert place to pray, "Simon and they that were with Him, followed after Him. And when they found Him, they said to Him: all seek for Thee." [319] After the cure of the leper, the crowds were so great that "He could not openly go into the city, but was without in desert places; and they flocked to Him from all sides. And again He entered into Capharnaum after some days. And it was heard that He was in the house, and many came together, so that there was no room: no, not even at the door; and He spoke to them the word. And they came to Him, bringing one sick of the palsy, who was carried by four. And where they could not offer him unto Him for the multitude, they uncovered the roof where He was; and opening it, they let down the bed wherein the man sick of the palsy lay." [320]

When He was warning the Apostles for the second time of the

[311] Matt. 26:41; Heb. 4:15. [312] Luke 22:31, 32.
[313] Matt. 12:2, 15:2; Luke 5:33; John 18:8.
[314] John 14–16. [316] John 11:16. [318] Mark 1:33.
[315] Matt. 14:22. [317] John 6:69. [319] Mark 1:36, 37.
[320] Mark 1:45, 2:1–4.

leaven of the Pharisees, "great multitudes stood about Him, so that they trod one upon another."[321] In his description of the first multiplication of the loaves St. Mark adds the following detail: "For there were many coming and going, and they had not so much as time to eat. And going up into a ship, they went into a desert place apart. And they saw them going away, and many knew: and they ran flocking thither on foot from all the cities, and were there before them. And Jesus going out saw a great multitude; and He had compassion on them, because they were as sheep not having a shepherd, and He began to teach them many things."[322] The multitudes were full of respect[323] and even His enemies were obliged to confess, "Behold, the whole world is gone after Him."[324]

The interest of the people maintained itself despite the severe truths which He taught them. They saw His earnestness and zeal; they understood clearly that He came to seek and to save what was lost; they knew that their salvation was the sole desire of His Sacred Heart. That the people listened to Him gladly is evident from the fact that great multitudes constantly pressed around Him. The evangelist explicitly tells us that in the synagogue of His native city "all gave testimony to Him, and they wondered at the words of grace that proceeded from His mouth."[325] In the midst of a discourse "a certain woman from the crowd, lifting up her voice, said to Him: Blessed is the womb that bore Thee, and the paps that gave Thee suck."[326] At the very beginning of His public ministry He is said to have "taught in their synagogues and was magnified by all."[327] After His solemn entry into Jerusalem He began to teach and "a great multitude heard Him *gladly*."[328] While He was expounding the Scriptures to the disciples of Emmanus, their hearts were burning within them.[329] Verily, as St. John says, "Never did man speak like this man."[330]

[321] Luke 12:1.
[322] Mark 6:31–34.
[323] Mark 9:14; Matt. 20:29, 31.
[324] John 12:19.
[325] Luke 4:22.
[326] Luke 11:27.
[327] Luke 4:15.
[328] Mark 12:37.
[329] Luke 24:32.
[330] John 7:46. Cf. William A. Russell, *Jesus the Divine Teacher* (New York, 1944); Edward A. Pace, "How Christ Taught Religion," in *Catholic University Bulletin*, Dec., 1908.

CHAPTER II

ST. PAUL

The Dignity of the Catechist's Office

The teacher of the Gentiles was in very deed the "Apostle of Jesus Christ." The conversion of St. Paul, while it changed his earliest and most fundamental convictions, did not destroy but only gave a new object and new direction to his impulsive zeal and impetuous temperament. In one supernatural flash the thoughts and affections of the pitiless persecutor were brought into loving subjection unto Him whom it was Saul's most passionate desire and most active purpose to destroy.

In fact, the manner in which St. Paul speaks of Christ, whose death had always been a scandal and stumbling block to the haughty Pharisee, is a phenomenon which, humanly speaking, seems to contradict all laws of psychology and all analogies of history. Notwithstanding that rigid monotheism which was hopelessly refractory to deification and considered the adoration of man as the abomination of desolation, he now freely accepts Christ as the Son of God and does not suffer that the Lord be compared to any created being. He tells us that Christ eclipses all by His splendor, fills all with His plentitude, exists before all the ages.[1] To Him every power must be subject, before Him every knee must bow.[2] He is the image of the invisible God,[3] the brightness of His glory.[4] By Him everything was made, by Him everything subsists, and toward Him everything converges.[5] He is the end of

[1] Ephes. 1:21–23; Col. 1:18–20.
[2] Phil. 2:9–11. [3] Col. 1:15. [4] Heb. 1:3.
[5] I Cor. 8:6; Heb. 1:2, 10; Col. 1:16, 17.

the law,[6] the corner stone and foundation without which no building can stand.[7] He was yesterday, He is today, and the same for all the ages.[8] Henceforth St. Paul's sole desire will be to spend himself and be spent for Christ; his sole glory, the cross of Christ; his sole knowledge, Christ crucified. The powers which formerly were used for destruction will now be used unto edification. As formerly he execrated the name of Christ so now he says anathema to anyone who does not love Our Lord Jesus Christ.

This lofty Pauline ideal must always be the guiding norm of the Christian catechist. The mission of the Christian teacher, of the priest-catechist, is a supernatural one. It sets him apart from the rest of men and stamps him with a character which is plainly superhuman. Christian teachers are ministers of Christ and the dispensers of His heavenly mysteries. They are ambassadors of Christ, God as it were exhorting by their mouths. They have the honor of collaborating in the spread of the Gospel in virtue of a divine power. Their office is derived not from men but from God through Jesus Christ.[9] They are the depositories of a divine doctrine which they must preserve unaltered.

This Pauline doctrine concerning the supernatural origin of the Christian teacher's mission is of supreme importance both for the training of the child and for the life of the catechist. The child's faith must be based on God's word and authority and on the testimony of the Church. God wishes supernatural faith to be spread among men, not by ordinary teachers who establish their doctrines by means of arguments from reason and human authority, but through the agency of messengers and witnesses, empowered by God and testifying to objective facts.[10] It was the will of the Supreme Founder of the Church that truths of revelation should be taught and preserved by witnesses whose testimony should be believed because they had seen and heard what they preached, by delegates to whom He had promised the never-failing assistance of the Holy Spirit to preserve them from all error. The Apostles and their successors, the pope and the bishops, exercise the teaching office as the direct representatives of God. Through their word faith comes, is nourished and spread. The priest-catechist is directly the delegate of the Church, and indirectly the

[6] Rom. 10:4. [7] I Cor. 3:11; Ephes. 2:20. [8] Heb. 13:8.
[9] I Cor. 4:1; II Cor. 5:20; II Tim. 1:8; Gal. 1:1. [10] Acts 1:8.

delegate of Christ Himself, and must plainly tell his listeners that he is the messenger of God and of the Church.

This consciousness of the Christian teacher's divine mission must be the law of his moral attitude, the first rule of his thoughts and discourses, the basis of all his activity. It must arouse in him the sentiments of his duty and dignity and counteract the ennui of daily routine. In the life of St. Paul it created two sentiments, two passions, one might say: a high-mindedness without pride and a devotion without reserve. Paul is not ashamed of the Gospel but preaches it with a bold and proud enthusiasm.[11] Far be it from him to teach the Gospel with a humiliated, timid and pusillanimous air, to ask, as it were, indulgence for it. This would pain the faithful and merit contempt from the enemy. This high-mindedness of St. Paul is not a native disposition but the fruit of grace. It is a divine gift which his beloved converts are asked to obtain for him by prayerful supplication with God.[12] St. Paul is a minister and an ambassador as little proud of his person as he is firm in sustaining the rights of the Master, attributing to Him alone the honor of his ministry and the courage and success in fulfilling it.

Rarely was man devoted to a cause as St. Paul was to his. He tells us that because of his supernatural calling he no longer belongs to himself. His mission made him a debtor to all; Greeks and barbarians, the learned and the ignorant – all have a claim upon him.[13] He was become a servant of all for the sake of Christ: [14] "For whereas I was free as to all I made myself the servant of all, that I might gain the more." [15] "For if I preach the gospel, it is no glory to me for a necessity lieth upon me; for woe is unto me if I preach not the gospel." [16] His was an indefatigable zeal. "Preach the word; be instant in season, out of season; reprove, entreat, rebuke in all patience and doctrine." [17] – thus does St. Paul entreat his helpers and thus, too, does he do himself. By word and pen, in the synagogue, in the hall, in the small artisan's house, by the riverside, on the ship, in prison, wherever willing hearers could be found, he puts up his pulpit and teaches the word of God. He preaches at all times, during the day and during the night, sometimes entire nights.[18] All audiences are welcomed to him: Jewish colonies in the Diaspora, a group of soldiers at

[11] Rom. 1:16.
[12] Col. 4:3, 4.
[13] Rom. 1:14.
[14] II Cor. 4:5.
[15] I Cor. 9:19.
[16] I Cor. 9:16.
[17] II Tim. 4:2.
[18] Acts 20:6–13.

Philippi, the Areopagus at Athens, Nero and his court – all are embraced within his great love and zeal. He is indeed the sower of that word which he characterizes as the sword of the spirit [19] and as the chief weapon in our struggle with the spirits of darkness.

St. Paul was above all personal hatred and animosity. He loved man as man because he saw a vision of all humanity in God. In dealing with his own countrymen he speaks of them, it is true, in words of unusual exasperation. Yet, if he hates them because of their sins, he does not exclude them from God's plan of universal salvation. He says that for the sake of the fathers the Jews were most dear to God whose gifts are without repentance. If blindness in part happened in Israel it was that the fullness of the Gentiles might come in. If some of the branches were broken off, it was in order that the wild olive might be ingrafted and made partaker of the root and of the richness of the olive tree. In fact, diminution of the Jews became the riches of the Gentiles, their loss the reconciliation of the world. Yea, St. Paul declares – in language that has ever been the stumbling block of religious selfishness – that he could wish himself to be an anathema from Christ for his brethren, his kinsmen according to the flesh.

St. Paul's devotion to his sublime task resulted in a complete and heroic disinterestedness. Although as a man of God he had a right to live by his ministry, he taught the Gospel without any human reward [20] and boasted of the glorious independence in which his habits of poverty had placed him.[21] Though a good patriot, he gives up all exclusive predelictions of race and country and becomes "all things to all men" in order to save all.[22] Above all vain glory, he does not recognize any earthly judge and considers human opinion as nothing.[23] He gives up the joys of personal action and the pleasure of being the first or the only one in the performance of good deeds.[24] When in Rome some of the Jews preached Christ merely out of base motives, thinking to insult him and make his bonds more galling, the Apostle resorts to no denunciation, no invectives. After all, he says, that in every way, whether with masked design or sincerity, Christ is being taught, therein I do – aye, and whatever angry feeling may try to rise in my heart – I will rejoice.[25] Thus does he trample upon the snake of personal

[19] Ephes. 6:17.
[20] I Cor. 9:18.
[21] Phil. 4:10–20.
[22] I Cor. 9:22.
[23] I Cor. 4:3.
[24] Phil. 1:18.
[25] Phil. 1:14–18.

annoyance before it strives to hiss in his heart. As spiritual father of those whom he begot to the supernatural life, he had a claim upon the recognition and gratitude of his converts. Yet, if they seemed forgetful and indifferent, he did not complain. He knew that those souls belonged to the Lord and Redeemer and that his own reward was stored up in heaven and would be rendered to him by the Just Judge.[26] He affirms that he would be willing to accept even a delay of the beatific vision if the spiritual interest of those entrusted to him demanded it.[27]

The mainspring and sustaining power of all his activity was his supernaturally infused love of Christ. In fact, Paul became wholly fascinated with the Person of Christ and entirely absorbed in preaching "among the Gentiles the unsearchable riches of Christ." [28] From his pre-Christian career, there is no souvenir so bitter to him as the thought that in his erring obstinacy he persecuted Christ in the person of His Mystical members, that he once used all the tyranny of his intolerance to break the bruised reed and quench the smoking flax, that he endeavored by the infamous power of terror to compel some gentle heart to blaspheme its Lord.[29] I am the least of the apostles," he tells the Corinthians, "who am not worthy to be called an apostle, because I persecuted the church of God." [30] And even when the shadows of a troubled age began to close around him, keen in the sense that he was entirely forgiven through Him who "came into this world to save sinners of whom I am the chief," [31] he cannot forget that though in ignorance he had once been "a blasphemer, and a persecutor, and contumelious." [32] These aberrations of youth, however, were expiated by an apostolate which became only too familiar with the persecutions he once made the Christians undergo. The powers which were once used for the ravaging of the Church were now enlisted for the upbuilding of Christ's Mystical Body: "the things that were gain to me, the same I have counted loss for Christ." [33]

When he pondered over all the blessings which were his since his conversion, there frequently escaped from his lips – spontaneously, as it were – those grateful and affectionate cries, so well known to the readers of St. Paul. "He loved me and delivered Him-

[26] II Tim. 4:8.
[27] Phil. 1:23–25.
[28] Ephes. 3:8.
[29] Acts 22:4, 26:11.
[30] I Cor. 15:9.
[31] I Tim. 1:15.
[32] I Tim. 1:13.
[33] Phil. 3:7.

self for me,"[34] "God forbid that I should glory save in the cross of our Lord Jesus Christ,"[35] "Who then shall separate us from the love of Christ",[36] "for me to live is Christ, and to die is gain,"[37] "If any man love not our Lord Jesus Christ, let him be anathema."[38]

This personal fervor of the catechist plays a very important role in impressing religious truths upon the minds and hearts of his listeners. If the teacher remains cold in the presence of the truths and facts of faith, the instruction becomes dry and uninteresting. If the teacher is indifferent, the pupils will hardly become fervent. In order to be able to give a thing to others, one must possess it himself. Burning words cannot come from a frozen heart. Children instinctively doubt the reality of something treated in a perfunctory manner. They quickly detect if the catechist really means what he says. A teacher who does not do what he teaches pulls down with one hand what he builds up with the other. The religious instruction itself becomes disagreeable to him, since his words are a constant reproach to his conduct. If, on the other hand, the catechist's heart is gripped with enthusiasm for the ideals of religion, this inward fire will soon become manifest and inspire the hearts of the children. A few words from the mouth of a teacher who has himself experienced the sweet and comforting power of religion have a greater influence on children than the finest discourses of another.

The Difficulties of the Catechist

The catechist and teacher who becomes weary and discouraged because of the dullness, ignorance, indifference and ingratitude of his pupils and listeners will find a solution for many of his difficulties in the doctrine and life of St. Paul. His drooping spirits will be revived and his zeal inflamed by contact with the Apostle's ardent charity and inspiring example. For St. Paul's loving zeal has to its credit a catalog of sufferings beside which that of the most zealous catechist and the most afflicted saint shrinks into insignificance. In that "Iliad of woes," the Second Epistle to the Corinthians, he recalls how he was "in many more labors, in prisons more frequently, in stripes above measure, in deaths often. Of the Jews five

[34] Gal. 2:20.
[35] Gal. 6:14.
[36] Rom. 8:35.
[37] Phil. 1:21.
[38] I Cor. 16:22.

times did I receive forty stripes save one. Thrice was I beaten with rods, once I was stoned, thrice I suffered shipwreck, a night and a day [under moonless and leaden skies] I was in the depth of the sea. In journeying often; in perils of waters; in perils of robbers; in perils from my own nation, from the false brethren and from the Gentiles; in perils in the city, in perils in the wilderness, in perils in the sea. . . . In labor and painfulness, in much watchings, in hunger and thirst, in fasting often, in cold and nakedness. Besides these things which are without; my daily instance, the solicitude for all the churches." [39]

Nor was this all. Coupled with the spread of error by his enemies were the worst controversial weapons, namely, surreptitious sneers and personal slanders. The Judaizers persistently tried to undermine the Apostle's influence and systematically disparage his authority. He was mean of person, they said, miserable and sickly in appearance, untutored and inefficient in speech, bold in letters and at a distance, a weakling walking according to the flesh. He was vaccillating in purpose, always shifting about, now saying one thing and now another, with the obvious intention of pleasing men. He was not one of the original Apostles, and his Gospel was not the real Gospel. His teaching was a revolt against the fathers, a breaking down of that hedge about the Law, the thickening of which had been the lifelong task of eminent rabbis.

In the face of these sufferings, calumnies and dangers, St. Paul's heart did not sink within him. He did not fold his hands in utter despair and pronounce his life and teaching a melancholy failure. No, such was not the attitude of the indomitable man. In the strength of God he triumphantly stems the overwhelming tide of afflictions and dauntlessly continues to cast himself into the never-ending battle. Flung to the earth, chained like a captive to the chariot wheels of his Lord's triumph, haled, as it were, from city to city as a deplorable spectacle, amid the incense which breathed through the streets in token of the victor's might, he yet glories in his infirmities and rejoices that he can "fill up those things that are wanting of the sufferings of Christ." [40] Mobbed, maltreated, depressed by poverty and illness, he yet travels for the foundation or confirming of churches, carries on the duties of a laborious and

[39] II Cor. 11:23–28.
[40] Col. 1:24.

pastoral ministry, bears the anxious burden of the churches, continually takes his place like a general on a battlefield with his eye on every weak and endangered point, and amidst it all finds time to write the letters which would engage the attention of thousands.

The ministers indeed are weak, he writes to the Corinthians, but the ministry, glorious. Their treasure of light was in earthen vessels in order that the glory of their victory over the world and its idolatries might be God's not theirs. This was why they were at once weak and strong – weak in themselves, strong in God. This was why St. Paul could boast that "in all things we suffer tribulation, but are not distressed; we are straitened, but not destitute; we suffer persecution, but are not forsaken; we are cast down, but we perish not; dying, and behold we live; as chastised, and not killed; as sorrowful, yet always rejoicing; as needy, yet enriching many; as having nothing, and possessing all things." [41] While we bear about in our bodies the mortification of Jesus and are always delivered unto death for His sake, he says, the life of Jesus is made manifest in our mortal flesh. Death is working in us, life in you; the trials are mainly ours, the blessings yours. "We know, if our earthly house of this habitation be dissolved, that we have a building of God, a house not made with hands, eternal in heaven. . . . For that which is at present momentary and light of our tribulation, worketh for us above measure exceedingly an eternal weight of glory. While we look not at the things which are seen, but at the things which are not seen. For the things which are seen, are temporal; but the things which are not seen are eternal." [42]

In public as well as in the solitude of his sad imprisonment Paul's life was hid in God. No epistle so clearly reveals this joyful peace amid suffering as that to the Philippians. Amid the trials and suspense of a bitter imprisonment it manifests to us the existence of a deep happiness – a peace as of the inmost heart of the ocean under the agitation of its surface storms. It was dictated by a worn and fettered Jew, the victim of insult and gross perjury, and yet its substance may be summed up in the words *gaudeo, gaudete, iterum dico, gaudete.*

Even in that testament of Christ's dying soldier – the Second

[41] II Cor. 4:8, 9, 6:9, 10.
[42] II Cor. 5:1, 4:17, 18.

Epistle of Timothy—there is none of that weariness and disappointment so frequently characteristic of waning life. His last letter is far more of a paean than a *miserere*. Even in the midst of natural sadness his letter to Timothy is all joy and encouragement. It is the young man's heart, not the Apostle's, that has failed. It is Timothy, not Paul, who is in danger of yielding to languor and timidity. Fan up the flames of your zeal and courage, he tells Timothy, be a good soldier, a true athlete, a diligent toiler. With a smiling and encouraging farewell he hands to his disciple the torch of truth.

As for himself, the day's work in the Master's vineyard is well-nigh over, the battle finished, the race run, the treasure safely guarded. At Antioch and at Jerusalem he vindicated forever the freedom of the Gentiles from the yoke of the Levitic Law. In his letter to the Romans and Galatians he had proclaimed alike to Jew and Gentile that they are not under the Law but under grace. He rescued Christianity from the peril of dying away into a Jewish sect. Laboring as no other apostle labored, he preached the Gospel in the chief cities of the world from Jerusalem to Rome.

As for the rest he knew that his times were in God's hands and that, whether life or death awaited him, all things were his and he was Christ's, and Christ was God's. It was no earthly reward that he sought, no posthumous success for which he sacrificed his life. His one aim was to be utterly true to the best that he knew; his one desire, to leave the Church more glorious and Christ better known among men than before. Though God seemed careless of his earthly happiness, he would be the last to complain. Even though God should slay him, he would yet trust in Him. One might refer to him in a sense the words which he himself applied to the great heroes of God: "All these died according to faith, not having received the promises, but beholding them afar off, and saluting them, and confessing that they are pilgrims and strangers on the earth. . . . But now they desire a better, that is to say, a heavenly country. Therefore God is not ashamed to be called their God, for He hath prepared for them a city." [43]

The catechist, too, encounters many difficulties. With his higher education he finds it hard at times to stoop to the level of the child's

[43] Heb. 11:13, 16.

mind and to enter into his thoughts and feelings. Frequently — especially on the missions — he is obliged to teach while he is weary and exhausted by fatigue. Then again there are the difficulties which arise from the nature of the subject matter taught. It is rightly said that it is far more difficult to teach religion than the secular branches. Whereas in the latter visible, concrete objects are studied and made use of, in the former the realities discussed cannot be perceived by the senses or readily grasped by the understanding. Finally, the children are often flighty and inattentive, gross, dull and irregular in attendance. They have a limited vocabulary and do not easily understand and grasp things. All these difficulties are frequently augmented by the carelessness and indifference of the parents.

In circumstances such as these the catechist must approach his work in the spirit of St. Paul and consider the bright side of things. He must remember that solid religious instruction will be a benediction to the child, to the parents and to future generations. He is only the sower; God will give the increase. The fact that he does not immediately perceive the desired results does not prove that his efforts have been in vain. He must keep in mind, too, the reward which God has in store for those who labor zealously in behalf of children. On the other hand, he should reflect on the harm that is caused when religious instruction is neglected or poorly given — a harm which can never be remedied. Every catechist, finally, who fulfills carefully the duties of his vocation must be prepared — even as Our Lord and St. Paul were — for opposition and contradiction.

Contents of Catechization

The difficulty of determining the contents of catechization according to St. Paul's epistles arises from the peculiar character of these writings. St. Paul's epistles were not deliberate treatises and systematic expositions of Christian religion. They were not something studied and literary. They were simple letters — pastoral and not personal — written on a specific occasion and to a particular body of converts. They were suggestions in regard to local difficulties or arrangements, or words of counsel, encouragement and consolation. They were subsidiary to the ordinary teaching and rarely contained anything which was not a matter of advice, controversy or difficulty. Hence they were not evoked by any inward purpose or necessity on the part of the Apostle to formulate his thought, but each of them was called forth in response to particular conditions in the community to which it is addressed. The contents and form are often due to the Apostle's vivid realization of the situation to which he is addressing himself.

The particular situation, then, determines in each case the central idea of the epistle. The Epistle to the Romans is the epistle of redemption and justification; that to the Galatians, the epistle of freedom from bondage to the Mosaic Law. The First Epistle to the Corinthians is the solution of practical difficulties in the light of eternal principles; the Second, a defense of the Apostle's impugned authority, his *apologia pro vita sua.* Hope is the keynote of the Epistles to the Thessalonians; joy, of that to the Philippians; emancipation, of that to Philemon; consolation and encouragement, of that to the Hebrews. Christ's Person is most prominent in Colossians; Christ's Body, His Church, in Ephesians. The First Epistle to Timothy and the Epistle to Titus are manuals of a Christian bishop; the Second Epistle to Timothy, the noble and tender testament of a dying soldier of Christ.

The second difficulty of determining the contents of catechization from the epistles alone is due to the fact they they were preceded by what is known as the primitive catechesis — a fund of doctrines common to all the Christian churches. That there were catechists in the primitive Church who were either authorized by competent authority or who spontaneously assumed the task of instructing converts, that there were converts to whom was taught the word of God *par excellence*, the Gospel of Christ, that there was a catechesis with which both catechists and catechumens were familiar, is evident from the following passage: "And let him that is instructed in the word, communicate to him that instructeth him, in all good things." [44] The catechumens were probably both the candidates for baptism and the neophytes whose training was still incomplete. The Pauline epistles are addressed without exception to persons already familiar with the ideas of the Gospel. Dogmas are mentioned occasionally and fragmentarily and as something well known. The epistles are by no means intended to

[44] Gal. 6:6.

give a first or complete instruction to their readers. If their recipients were strangers to the elements of the Christian faith and especially of Christology, Paul's letters would stand forth as an insoluble enigma.

This primitive catechesis was not left to the inspiration of the individual but was identical in its tenor and uniform in its content. It imposed itself imperiously as a rule of faith on both the teacher and the faithful: "You have obeyed from the heart unto that form of doctrine into which you have been delivered." [45] When Paul returned to Jerusalem from his first apostolic mission among the Gentiles and explained to the leaders of this church the essential elements of his gospel, the "pillars of the church" extended to him the "right hand of fellowship," indicating thereby that, though the destination and manner of explaining the Gospel may be twofold, in itself the Gospel of Christ is essentially one.[46]

Paul incidentally gives us a summary of this primitive catechesis when he announces to the Hebrews that he is about to leave the first elements of revelation in order to pass on to a consideration of higher realities: "Wherefore leaving the word of the beginning of Christ, let us go on to things more perfect, not laying again the foundation of penance from dead works, and of faith toward God, of the doctrine of baptism, and imposition of hands, and of the resurrection of the dead, and of eternal judgment."[47] A specimen of the Apostolic catechesis is found in I Cor. 15:1–11, a section which begins with the following words: "Now I make known unto you, brethren, the gospel which I preached to you, which also you have received, and wherein you stand, by which also you are saved, if you hold fast after what manner I preached unto you, unless you have believed in vain." An analogous statement is found in the section on the Eucharist: "For I have received of the Lord that which also I delivered unto you, that the Lord Jesus, the same night in which He was betrayed," etc.[48] These passages indicate that the facts concerning the Saviour's life held a more important place in the Apostle's preaching than in his writings, for he transcribes only a part of his oral gospel. They presuppose, further, that the first instruction was precise and stereotyped after the manner of a Catechism. Paul expressly says that on these fundamental

[45] Rom. 6:17. [46] Gal. 2:7 ff. [47] Heb. 6:1, 2. [48] I Cor. 11:23.

points the teaching of the Apostles and the faith of the Christians were identical: "Whether I, or they, so we preach, and so you have believed." [49]

In brief, the primitive catechesis, according to all indications, comprised a fourfold element: the *historical,* dealing with the actions, miracles and doctrine of Our Lord; the *dogmatic,* comprising a rudimentary *credo* with a trinitarian impress; the *liturgical,* stressing the mystical signification and value of Baptism, Confirmation and the Eucharist, and containing specific regulations in regard to the recitation of the Lord's Prayer; the *moral,* containing a precise and fixed moral code popularly known as the "way." [50]

The epistles of St. Paul contain only a few indications as to the positive contents of catechization. The catechist must, in the first place, meditate upon and fill his soul with the doctrines of divine revelation, for "All scripture, inspired of God, is profitable to teach, to reprove, to correct, to instruct in justice." [51] Secondly, alongside of Scripture must stand Tradition: "But continue thou in those things which thou hast learned, and which have been committed to three, knowing of whom thou hast learned them";[52] "Hold the form of sound words, which thou hast heard of me in faith, and in the love which is in Christ Jesus. Keep the good thing committed to thy trust." [53] The teacher should offer his hearers sound dogmatic and spiritual food, "embracing that faithful word which is according to doctrine, that he may be able to exhort in sound doctrine and to convince the gainsayers." [54] Sound dogma must be accompanied by apposite ethical and ascetical exhortations: "But speak thou the things that become sound doctrine: that the aged men be sober, chaste, prudent, sound in faith, in love, in patience. The aged women, in like manner, in holy attire, not false accusers, not given to much wine, teaching well, that they may teach the young women to be wise, to love their husbands, to love their children, to be discreet, chaste, sober, having a care of the house, gentle, obedient to their husbands, that the word of God be not blasphemed. Young men, in like manner, exhort that they be sober." [55] In all these things let the teacher's example be the guiding light: "In all things show thyself an example of good

[49] I Cor. 15:11. [50] I Cor. 4:17. [51] II Tim. 3:16. [52] II Tim. 3:14.
[53] II Tim. 1:13; I Tim. 6:20. [54] Tit. 1:9. [55] Tit. 2:1–6.

works, in doctrine, in integrity, in gravity, the sound word that cannot be blamed; that he, who is on the contrary part, may be afraid, having no evil to say of us." [56] The times need sound instruction more than ever: "For there shall be a time when men will not endure sound doctrine. But according to their own desire they will heap to themselves teachers, having itching ears, and will indeed turn away their hearing from the truth, but will be turned unto fables." [57]

St. Paul also gives specific instructions as to what the Christian teacher should avoid. Subtleties and uncertain novelties are rarely conducive to a good life: "But avoid foolish questions, and genealogies, and contentions, and strivings about the law. For they are unprofitable and vain." [58] Still less should purely secular subjects be dragged into holy discourses: "Shun profane and vain babblings, for they grow much toward ungodliness." [59] All questions debated in theological circles should be avoided; the faithful should not be drawn into disputes in which there is mostly question of things that are uncertain and cannot be proved: "Avoid foolish and unlearned questions, knowing that they beget strifes. But the servant of the Lord must not wrangle, but be mild toward all men, apt to teach, patient." [60] We must guard against controversy with those who differ from us. A refutation of the opinions of others may be inevitable now and then, but on the whole the words hold good: "What have I to do to judge them that are without?" [61] And if a refutation is necessary, it must always remain objective and not descend to the level of our opponents in their abuse of us: "A man that is a heretic, after the first and second admonition, avoid: knowing that he is, that is such an one, is subverted, and sinneth, being condemned by his own judgment." [62]

Catechetical Method

1. *The form and the spirit of the catechesis.* In proposing Christ's message to his listeners and converts St. Paul deliberately refrained from all human wisdom and flattering eloquence. Of exaggerated rhetoric, of oratorical dignity and winning elocution the Apostle thought little. Approaches such as these lay for him

[56] Tit. 2:7, 8.
[57] II Tim. 4:3, 4.
[58] Tit. 3:9.
[59] II Tim. 2:16.
[60] II Tim. 2:23, 24.
[61] I Cor. 5:12.
[62] Tit. 3:10, 11.

under the ban of revelation. Mere human wisdom had not led the world to a knowledge of God nor saved the world from the crucifixion of Christ. The influence from above, it is true, augmented the power of the Apostle's word and appeal. But it did not refine or polish his style; it left intact his peculiar traits of mind and heart. This providential disposition of things placed in a proper light and perspective the supernatural which alone can save souls. It enabled men to understand that the conversion of the world was to be wholly supernatural and would owe nothing to the persuasive words of human wisdom.[63] It was to be a merciful revenge upon and a providential punishment of that scientific and philosophical pride which inclines too easily toward atheism and idolatry. Since man failed to recognize God by the light of natural reason, it was becoming that he should be at once confounded and saved by the folly of a preaching which in its form and contents was intended to humiliate man's proud spirit.[64]

The apostolic word was to be simple, too, in order that it might attain directly the multitudes, especially the poor and the humble – those privileged souls of grace. Unlike human wisdom which descends from the learned to the masses, Christ's message ascended from the simple to the learned.

St. Paul demands a catechesis which is above all Christian and orthodox. Its unique foundation must be Jesus Christ.[65] It must know Christ alone and refer all knowledge to Him. It must not be a transformed Christ suited to human fantasy and fancy, but the true Christ – Christ crucified.[66] This severe orthodoxy must be patient and learned,[67] nourished by reading and meditation,[68] scrupulously exact in language,[69] avoiding all profane novelty.[70] Abreast of the times and satisfying the legitimate desires of the heart and mind, it must not flatter pride nor the intellectual whims of the moment. It must not accept half truths or eviscerated transitory doctrines. Powerful and authoritative, supple and adaptable,[71] it must at the same time avoid idle curiosity and vain disputes[72] and never leave itself open to the attacks of the adversary.[73]

[63] I Cor. 2:4.
[64] I Cor. 1:21.
[65] I Cor. 3:10, 11.
[66] I Cor. 2:2.
[67] II Tim. 4:2.
[68] I Tim. 4:13.
[69] II Tim. 1:13.
[70] I Tim. 6:20.
[71] II Tim. 4:2.
[72] Tit. 3:9.
[73] Tit. 2:15.

The catechization must be informed and animated by various virtues. The whole instruction must proceed from *love of God* and *love of souls*; without this all will remain cold.[74] Where there is love, the necessary power of persuasion and the right accent which reaches hearts will always be present. The catechesis should breathe *unselfishness*;[75] to make the word of God subserve our vanity, ambition or lust of power is to desecrate a holy office and rob God of His gifts for our own personal advancement. The catechist must instruct "in all *patience*."[76] Many explanations will not be understood; many warnings will remain unheeded; many evil conditions will continue to grow apace. But the catechist must continue to work unwearied, trying if possible to correct these defects, laboring for those souls who listen to him with a holy hunger after justice: "Therefore I endure all things for the sake of the elect, that they also may obtain the salvation, which is in Christ Jesus, with heavenly glory."[77]

St. Paul demands that the catechist teach with power and conviction: "These things speak . . . with all authority."[78] The catechist must not give way to any fear of men: "Be instant in season, out of season, reprove, entreat."[79] He should say to himself with the great Apostle: "To me it is a very small thing to be judged by you, or by man's day."[80] He must seek to please God rather than men: "If I yet pleased men, I should not be the servant of Christ."[81] He must propound the word of God with a consciousness of power, and not like a petitioner who is grateful when his hearers listen to his words. The catechist stands before the multitude as God's messenger.[82] He should teach with emphasis and with the full conviction of his high mission and of his right to conquer. He must proceed with determination and courage, especially when men "will not endure sound doctrine."[83] He must not hold back solemn and bitter truths, "for God hath not given us the spirit of fear; but of power."[84]

Although St. Paul despised human wisdom and worldly eloquence, he was not a dull teacher. He made exquisite use of feeling and emotions and was in every sense a natural orator. Every one of his sentences is animated with fire, life and love.

[74] I Cor. 13:1.
[75] II Cor. 2:17.
[76] II Tim. 4:2.
[77] II Tim. 2:10.
[78] Tit. 2:15.
[79] Tim. 4:2.
[80] I Cor. 4:3.
[81] Gal. 1:10.
[82] II Cor. 5:20.
[83] II Tim. 4:3.
[84] II Tim. 1:7.

As an admirer of the great Apostle has well said, he runs with playful ease up the whole scale of feeling. At one time it is a deep and touching earnestness; at another, melancholy and sadness; at another, touching apprehension and deep-felt sympathy; at another, gentle complaint and earnest threatening; at another, a tender love and intimate wooing; and finally, a glowing enthusiasm, bright joyousness and an exultant feeling of triumph and victory.

2. *Immanent Correlation.* St. Paul's method is characterized by a synthetic correlation of dogmatic truths with one another and with moral principles. The Apostle constantly points out the connection between dogmatic truths and emphasizes their practical bearing on our spiritual life. His epistles evince a powerful, magnificent and almost painful effort to express in a few words that doctrinal unity of which he bore in himself the conception and passionate taste. He stresses an aspect of Christian doctrine which no catechist can afford to neglect. For the unity of Christian truth is such that no particular opinion can be adopted, and no particular dogma changed or rejected, except by modifying the whole of that truth. Christian doctrines are not a collocation of isolated conceptions without influence on one another; they have an internal connection and coherence binding them into a whole, so that none can be tampered with or altered without injury to the rest. Peculiarly is this the case with the doctrine concerning sin – so basic in St. Paul's epistles – on which is based the correlated doctrine of man's indispensable need of Redemption and spiritual renewal. If the facts of sin are inadequately studied or misconceived, the all-important work accomplished by Christ's passion and death will be necessarily and proportionately misjudged and misrepresented. Again, to indicate the connection between theoretically correlated truths as well as their practical bearing on the religious life of the listener, gives the pupil a much clearer understanding of the truths, stimulates his self-activity, aids his memory and strengthens his religious convictions.

St. Paul's doctrine is plainly Christocentric. Were Christ removed from the pages of his letters, his teaching would become absolutely unintelligible. St. Paul considers the Person of Christ less in its intimate being than under the aspects whereby it enters into the divine plan of salvation. It is Jesus Christ as Head of the human race, restoring to us especially on Calvary and at the sepulcher our lost heritage, who is the object of the Apostle's love. Occasionally, it is true, Paul casts a glance into the past, upon that humanity which was "without Christ." He sees there heathen society plunged into intellectual darkness and vain speculation and gradually sinking into unnatural depravity. He sees the Jews committing the very sins which they condemned in the Gentiles.[85] He sees the ever-expanding empire of sin and reign of death which he traces regressively through concupiscence and original sin back to Adam and to the tempter. But those pre-Christian scenes were for the Apostle a mere preparation for the Redeemer, a mere prelude to Calvary. They were for him the prehistory, as it were, of Christ meditating in God's bosom His merciful designs, a prehistory of the Church divinely prepared by her Spouse. If St. Paul speaks of Adam's solidarity with the human race in order to explain the reign of Satan and of sin, it is only to show that where sin abounded, grace through Christ did the more abound. Occasionally, too, the Apostle lifts his eyes from Calvary's observatory toward the future in order to contemplate there the accomplishments of God's designs and the consummation of the ages. He can see there Christ's Spouse, the Church, gradually attaining its full stature and maturity, and reaching its complete configuration as determined by divine predestination. But the future interests him only insofar as it is a fruit of the Passion and a corollary of the cross.

The habitual subject of Paul's meditation is the Second Adam's work of restoration on Calvary and at the sepulcher. For it is there that Christ strikes a mortal blow at sin, the flesh, death and the devil, and becomes a "vivifying spirit"; there that He assumes by right of conquest the headship of regenerate humanity; there that He becomes Master of the spirit-powers who henceforth are powerless to overcome man by their insidious onslaughts; [86] there that He assumes preeminence over the angels; [87] there that He, as "the first-born of the living and of the dead," becomes Head of the Church.[88] It is on Calvary that Christ reconciles all, pacifies all, unifies all. The Apostle thus sees Christ descending upon earth in

[85] Rom. chapters 1 and 2. [86] Ephes. 6:10–12. [87] Ephes. 1:20, 21.
[88] Ephes. 1:22, 23; Col. 1:18; Rom. 14:8, 9, 8:29.

order to assume primacy over all things. He sees the new Adam appropriating us unto Himself and incorporating us into His Mystical Body. All humanity, the prolongation and complement, as it were, of Christ, is thus drawn up with Him even into the presence of the Blessed Trinity, and made to "sit together in the heavenly places." [89]

St. Paul was not slow in correlating these sublime doctrines with the Christian's daily life. For could he, the greatest of preachers, be unacquainted with the power of the Gospel as an ethical appeal? The mystery of the cross, he tells us, was the greatest proof of divine love: "God commendeth His charity toward us, because when as yet we were sinners . . . Christ died for us."[90] "He spared not even his own Son, but delivered Him for us all."[91] Since love demands love in return – *quis amantem non redamet?* – Paul was not slow in reciprocating: "God forbid that I should glory, save in the cross of our Lord Jesus Christ," [92] "Who then shall separate us from the love of Christ," [93] "If any man love not our Lord Jesus Christ, let him be anathema."[94] He often exhorts his converts to imitate the self-sacrifice of Christ: "Christ died for all, that they also who live may not now live to themselves but unto Him who died for them and rose again." [95] Of this mysticism the Apostle himself is a living example: "And I live, now not I, but Christ liveth in me. And that I live now in the flesh, I live in the faith of the Son of God, who loved me and delivered Himself for me." [96] Even as Christ died and rose again, so also the Christian who died with Christ in Baptism ought henceforth live with Him a new life exempt from all sin.[97] To defile the flesh by sin is unbecoming to those who were redemed and bought at so great a price.[98] The Christian must always bear about in himself the "mortification of Jesus" [99] so as to present his body "a living sacrifice, holy, and pleasing to God." [100] In the fifteenth chapter of his First Epistle to the Corinthians St. Paul traces the moral consequences which would follow upon a denial of the dogma of the resurrection.

Again, the same love of Jesus, the Redeemer and Head of hu-

[89] Ephes. 2:6.
[90] Rom. 5:8, 9; Ephes 5:2, 25.
[91] Rom. 8:32.
[92] Gal. 6:14.
[93] Rom. 8:35.
[94] I Cor. 16:22.
[95] II Cor. 5:15.
[96] Gal. 2:20.
[97] Rom. 6:1, 11.
[98] I Cor. 6:20.
[99] II Cor. 4:10.
[100] Rom. 12:1.

manity, ought to move us to love our brethren: "Destroy not him with thy meat for whom Jesus died." [101] Those that are stronger ought to bear the infirmities of the weak and not please themselves because Christ likewise "did not please Himself, but as it is written: the reproaches of them that reproached thee, fell upon me." [102] The Apostle beseeches the Corinthians through the "mildness and modesty of Christ" [103] not to despise his apostolic authority. When writing to the same church of Corinth, he tells his converts that the churches of Macedonia, afflicted as they were, yet with a spontaneous liberality and affectionate enthusiasm for his wishes subscribed large amounts for the collection of the saints; so too the Corinthians, abounding in so many gifts and graces, should abound in this; he would not order them, but only asks this as a proof of their love even as Christ had set the example of enriching others by His own poverty: "For you know the grace of our Lord Jesus Christ, that being rich, He became poor for your sakes, that through His poverty you might be rich." [104] In striving to urge upon the Philippians the example of humility and unselfishness as the only possible basis of unity, St. Paul sets before them the divine lowliness which had descended step by step into the very abyss of degradation, yea, even to the death on the cross.[105] Finally, love of neighbor and interest in his spiritual and temporal welfare are demanded by our membership in the same Mystical Body: "And if one member suffer anything, all the members suffer with it; or if one member glory, all the members rejoice with it. Now you are the body of Christ, and members of member." [106]

How can the catechist apply this priciple of immanent correlation, so admirably exemplified in St. Paul's epistles? In the first place, he must correlate every doctrine with Our Lord and with the Church. For the Christian religion is a harmonious system of divine truths whose central point is the Redeemer and whose only infallible teacher on earth is the Church.

Secondly, the catechist should correlate the Catechism with Bible History, Church History, and the Liturgy. The doctrines, historical events and institutions of the Church form one organic whole and are most intimately connected. These branches simply present different views of Christian doctrine. They are organic

[101] Rom. 14:15.
[102] Rom. 15:3.
[103] II Cor. 10:1.
[104] II Cor. 8:9.
[105] Phil. 2:6–9.
[106] I Cor. 12:26, 27.

parts of the same body of religion. In this doctrinal correlation any religious truth can become the means of refreshing in the memory the other connected truths which are then like the firmly joined stones of a building, all supporting and holding fast one another.

Thirdly, doctrines of faith should be correlated with moral doctrines. In treating of a doctrine of morality the catechist should show what corresponding dogma is the reason of the moral law and motive of its observance. A moral doctrine without dogma is devoid of strength. Works without faith have no merit for heaven. On the other hand, doctrines of faith without those of morals produce no fruit — faith without works is dead.

Finally, the catechist should correlate religion with the secular branches. Since God is inseparable from the universe as a whole, He is also inseparable from its parts which for the sake of convenience we study in the so-called secular branches and special sciences.

3. *Adaptation.* St. Paul became all things to all men in order that he might save all: "For whereas I was free as to all, I made myself the servant of all, that I might gain the more. And I became to the Jews, a Jew, that I might gain the Jews. To them that are under a law, as if I were under the law, that I might gain them that were under the law. To them that were without the law, as if I were without the law, that I might gain them that were without the law. To the weak I became weak, that I might gain the weak. I became all things to all men, that I might save all." [107] In all his instructions the Apostle is careful to touch the apperceptive masses of his listeners and to engraft the new doctrines upon those which formed a part of the acquired mental content. In explaining the Christian process of justification he frequently employs terms and expressions current in his day. When instructing the Jews of the Diaspora he usually "reasoned with them out of the Scriptures." [108] In arguing against the Judaizers he shows from abundant Old Testament quotations that Abraham was justified by faith, that his justification was a gratuitous gift, that his spiritual paternity was independent of works and that the promise was superior to the Law. He makes his arguments doubly forceful by drawing upon the psychological experience of the Jews and by showing how the

[107] I Cor. 9:19, 22.
[108] Acts 17:2.

Law was a cause of the knowledge of sin, of actual sin, of divine wrath and of death. When pointing out to Jewish converts the superiority of Christ's Sacrifice and Priesthood he is again careful to compare the New Dispensation with the Old.[109]

A rather unique example of adaptation is found in St. Paul's speech on the Areopagus – a discourse which came to serve as a catechetical model for Christian missionaries in pagan countries for centuries to come.[110] In this speech St. Paul insists on the following points: the existence of one God, Creator of heaven and earth, the necessity of rejecting idolatry and paganism, and the need of repentance with a view to the future judgment by the glorious Christ. In courteous expressions and conciliating arguments, recognizing their piety toward their gods and enforcing his views by an appeal to their own poets, he manages with the readiest power of adaptation to indicate the fundamental errors of every class of his listeners. The inscription on the nameless altar served as a basis for his claim that his auditors were at least partial sharers in the teaching which he was striving to enunciate. His hearers believed that the universe had resulted from chance combination of atoms – he tells them that it was their Unknown God who by omnipotent power created the universe and all therein. They believed that there were many gods far removed from mankind and careless of men – he tells them there is but one God, Lord and Preserver of heaven and earth. They despised all foreigners as barbarians and clung to their racial superiority – he tells that God "hath made of one all mankind." Around them arose a circle of temples as beautiful as human hands could make them – he tells the multitude that God who is One does not dwell in their toil-wrought temples but in the temple of His own creation.

4. *Perspicuity.* The parable, which is the outstanding characteristic of our Lord's catechetical method, is absent from the pages of St. Paul's epistles. This is all the more surprising since the surroundings in which St. Paul labored constituted an excellent setting for such mode of instruction.

His interest lay in the crowded street where the Lord had many people. His was a soul in which the burning heat of a great purpose permeated every other thought, desire and admiration. The power

[109] Epistle to the Hebrews.
[110] Acts 17:24, 31.

and importance of Christ's truths which it was his mission to proclaim prevented him from showing any delight in the scenes of beauty amid which he lived and traveled. His favorite illustrations are those which exemplified the Christian's interior spiritual life and his own restless desire to attain Christ. He draws his imagery from the stadium in which he looked with sympathy on the grace and swiftness of many a youthful athlete; from the race and boxing matches, from the spectacle of the Roman triumph, from the shows of the theater, and from the fading garland of Isthmian pine.

In the Epistle to the Philippians written during the Roman captivity, he likens himself to one of those charioteers – of whom his guardsmen so often talked to him when they had returned from the Circus Maximus – leaning forward in his flying car, forgetting every peril and every competitor as he pressed on to the goal where sat the judges with the palm garlands that formed the prize. "Brethren, I do not count myself to have apprehended. But one thing I do, forgetting the things that are behind, and stretching forth myself to those that are before, I press toward the mark, to the prize of the supernal vocation of God in Christ Jesus." [111] And when at Ephesus and Corinth he saw those fair youths do and suffer so much to win a poor withering wreath of pine and parsley, of which the greenness had faded before the sun had set, he would think of that unfading amaranthine and incorruptible crown of eternal glory which each and all might equally win in Christ: "and they indeed that they may receive a corruptible crown; but we an incorruptible one." [112]

How beautifully in particular does he apply the image of armor to Christian warfare. "Stand therefore, having your loins girt about with truth, and having on the breastplate of justice. And your feet shod with the preparation of the gospel of peace; in all things taking the shield of faith, wherewith you may be able to extinguish all the fiery darts of the most wicked one. And take unto you the helmet of salvation, and the sword of the Spirit (which is the word of God)." [113] Daily the coupling chain, which bound his right wrist to the left of the Roman legionary, clashed as it touched some part of the soldier's arms.

[111] Phil. 3:13, 14.
[112] I Cor. 9:25.
[113] Ephes. 6:14, 17.

Another favorite metaphor of St. Paul is derived from the customs of a Roman triumph. On such occasions the chief captives were paraded before the victor's path, and sweet odors burnt in the streets as his car climbed the Capitol. But when he reached the foot of the Capitoline hill there was a halt; at that spot the captives ceased to form a part of the procession but were led aside into the rocky vaults of the Tullianum and strangled by the executioner in its depths. Thus the sweet odors which to the victor and to the spectators were a symbol of victory were to the wretched victims an odor of death. St. Paul for a moment fancies the Gospel of Christ as that burning incense of which the perfume filled the triumphant street, and which to the well-disposed was a tiding of gladness but to the hardened and impenitent a tiding of wrath and doom. "We are the good odour of Christ unto God, in them that are saved, and in them that perish." [114] And then another passing fancy strikes him: he pictures himself as a captive before Christ's chariot making known the fame of the Victor; thanks be to God, he says, who always leads us everywhere in triumph in Christ. Little perhaps did it occur to St. Paul as he penned these words that the triumph of Christ in which he was being led along from place to place as a willing victim would one day also culminate in a similar death.

The Pauline doctrine of the Redemption has an equally concrete and interesting setting in the ancient processes of slave-liberation. Among the different legal forms according to which in antiquity the liberation of a slave could take place, we find the solemn rite of a fictitious purchase of the slave by a god. The former master conducts the slave to the temple, sells him to the deity, and receives from the temple-treasury the purchase money. The inscriptions of Cos designate this process of liberation by the term "redemption" while the Oxyrhynchus Papyri of A.D. 86–107 denote the price of the word "ransom." Once liberated the slave became the property of the divinity, not its temple-slave but rather a protégé. In regard to men and to his former master he was absolutely free, and in many records it is forbidden under severe penalty to reduce the ransomed slave to his former condition. It goes without saying, of course, that there was an immense difference between these fictitious liberations and the Redemption which the Apostles an-

[114] II Cor. 2:15.

nounced. The God who redeemed the Christian payed the ransom with His own blood, and the liberty which He acquired for him is not that of doing what he pleases [115] but the liberty of the children of God. Christ's Lordship over the Christian is absolute; [116] the pagans, on the other hand, could acknowledge many gods and many lords.

Although the analogy, like every other analogy, limps in certain respects, it served St. Paul's purposes admirably. It is very probable that the Apostle, writing to Christian communities where slaves were numerous, had these ancient processes of slave-liberation in mind when he announced to his converts a new redemption, a liberation from the bondage of sin, of death, and of Satan. From these oppressive powers we were ransomed by the Blood of Christ: "You are bought with a great price." [117] He warns the Galatians against the "false brethren unawares brought in, who came in privately to spy our liberty which we have in Christ Jesus, that they might bring us into servitude." [118] They must not be "held again under the yoke of bondage": [119] because "you are bought with a price, be not made the bondslaves of men." [120] The Christians are bondsmen of Christ, they have become "servants of God and of justice." [121] They must "abide with God"[122] and "attend upon the Lord without impediment." [123]

St. Paul makes abundant use of concrete imagery when he comes to describe the union of Jew and Gentile in the one Mystical Body of Christ. The Gentiles are described as citizens in the holy state, the commonwealth of a people consecrated to God.[124] They enjoy a rank of dignity not inferior to that of the Jews and need not be circumcised. Whereas formerly they were "strangers" and "foreigners," now they are "fellow citizens of the saints" with full rights. They are intelligent participators in a common corporate life consecrated to God. Whereas formerly the Gentiles were "atheists," they are now the "domestics of God," they belong to the family of God and share in the blessings of His household. In this supernatural family they are sons and not servants, heirs and not slaves.

[115] Gal. 5:17.
[116] I Cor. 8:6.
[117] I Cor. 6:20, 7:23; Gal. 4:5.
[118] Gal. 2:4, 4:31, 5:13.
[119] Gal. 5:1.
[120] I Cor. 7:23.
[121] Rom. 6:22, 18.
[122] I Cor. 7:24.
[123] I Cor. 7:35.
[124] Ephes. 2:19, 20.

They are being built together into a building or sanctuary in order that God may dwell therein. Of this holy structure the foundation stones are the Apostles and the prophets, and its "chief corner stone" is Christ Jesus.

From the metaphor of a building the Apostle passes to that of a living organism. The Church as a visible organization of men, can be what it is – the commonwealth of God, His household, and His sanctuary – only because it is pervaded by the Life of Christ. The members of this household are not merely the stones of the building, placed side by side, but they are the branches of a living tree, the limbs of a living body. The same idea of life underlies the Apostle's conception of the Church as a Mystical Body: "You are the body of Christ, and members of member . . . for in one Spirit were we all baptized into one body." [125] The union between the Head and His mystical members is so intimate that the Apostle compares it to that which exists between husband and spouse.[126]

Like our Lord, St. Paul strives occasionally to obtain perspicuity and clarity of ideas by means of striking contrasts and artful antitheses. The following comparisons are outstanding in St. Paul's epistles:

"It is sown in *corruption,* it shall rise in *incorruption;*
It is sown in *dishonor,* it shall rise in *glory;*
It is sown in *weakness,* it shall rise in *power;*
It is sown a *natural body,* it shall rise a *spiritual body;*
This *corruptible* must put on *incorruption;*
This *mortal* must put on *immortality.*" [127]

"By *honor* and *dishonor,*
by *evil report* and *good report,*
as *deceivers* and yet *true,*
as *unknown* and yet *known,*
as *dying* and behold we *live,*
as *chastised* and *not killed,*
as *sorrowful,* yet always *rejoicing,*
as *needy,* yet *enriching* many,
as *having nothing,* and *possessing all things.*" [128]

[125] I Cor. 12:27, 13.
[126] Ephes. 5:22–30.
[127] I Cor. 15:42–53.
[128] II Cor. 6:8–10.

"What participation hath *justice* with *injustice*? or
what fellowship hath *light* with *darkness*? and
what concord hath *Christ* with *Belial*? or
what part hath the *faithful* with the *unbeliever*? and
what agreement hath the *temple of God* with *idols*?" [129]

"When you were *dead* in your sins . . . he hath *quickened* together with him." [130]

"You were heretofore *darkness*, but now *light* in the Lord." [131]

"The *night* is passed, and the *day* is at hand." [132]

These Pauline contrasts together with the Apostle's designation of the Church's moral teaching as the "way" probably give rise to the concept of the twofold way – the way of life and the way of death – which we find developed in the *Didache*. The way of life [133] consists in the observance of the twofold gospel precept of love and of the golden rule; the way of death [134] consists in committing the various sins enumerated by the author. The *Didache* constitutes a model of a catechesis addressed to the catechumens before the conferring of Baptism. Although the catechesis [135] of the book does not comprise anything explicity dogmatic, it certainly presupposes a renunciation of paganism and an elementary acquaintance with the fundamental doctrines of Christianity. The *Didache* should be studied in connection with the Epistle of Barnabas, the first Apology of Justin Martyr, and the *Exhortation to the Heathen* of Clement of Alexandria, which also give us some idea of the moral and dogmatic doctrines taught the candidates before Baptism, and which – to some extent, at least – have been inspired by the great Apostle.

[129] II Cor. 6:14–16.
[130] Col. 2:13.
[131] Ephes. 5:8.
[132] Rom. 13.12.
[133] Chapters 1–4.
[134] Chapters 5, 6.
[135] See p. 2, *supra*.

CHAPTER III[1]

ST. AUGUSTINE

Introduction

St. Augustine's catechetical principles, outlined in this chapter, are taken principally from his work *On Instructing the Unlearned (De Catechizandis Rudibus)*.[1] This treatise was composed at the request of Deogratias, a deacon of Carthage. Although a successful catechist — as is evidenced by the fact that many prospective Christians were brought to him for instruction — Deogratias was desirous of further help and guidance in the ministry of catechizing. He inquired of St. Augustine with what period Bible History should begin and how much matter it should include. He was eager to know whether an admonition should be added to the narration or whether a brief statement of Christian moral precepts would suffiice. At the same time, the deacon complained of the weariness and difficulties proper to the catechist's office and revealed a consciousnes of his own utter insufficiency. St. Augustine's reply to these queries and problems constitutes the treatise *On Instructing the Ignorant.* In complying with the deacon's re-

[1] This treatise is drawn from the same traditional catechetical outline as that found in the *Constitutiones Apostolorum,* VII, 39, VIII, 12 (*P.G.*, I, 1038 ff.) and in the *Demonstration of the Apostolic Preaching* of St. Irenaeus. We find this method used by St. Clement of Alexandria (*P.G.*, VIII, 58–68), St. Cyprian (*P.L.*, IV, 583–604), St. Basil (*P.G.*, XXXI, 1523–1526), St. Cyril of Jerusalem (*P.G.*, XXXIII), St. Gregory Nazianzen (*P.G.*, XXXV, 26), and St. Gregory of Nyssa (*P.G.*, *XLV*, 23, 34, 60, 86). Its influence is felt in St. Ildefonsus of Toledo (d. 669) (*P. L.*, XCVI, 3); Amalarius, Archbishop of Treves (d. 815) (*P.L.* XCIX, 894); Rabanus Maurus, Archbishop of Mainz (d. 856) (*P.L.*, CXII, 1193–1203); and Hugh of St. Victor (d. 1141) (*P.L.*, CLXXVI, 41).

quest, St. Augustine rendered a signal favor not only to the church of Carthage but to the Church at large.

It was fortunate that Deogratias applied to St. Augustine, for St. Augustine was not only a renowned writer and theologian but also a master of the various catechetical methods. He was familiar with the methods employed in Africa and had attended catechetical lectures both at Rome and at Milan. His generous response to Deogratias's modest request took the form of a treatise which was a boon not only to the deacon but to the whole Church. It was a contribution at once to the subject matter and methods of catechization and a manual for the catechist and catechumen. The treatise enunciates the following important educational principles: not to confuse the candidate with too much matter; to explain a little, clearly and concisely; to have but one central theme – the love of God; to give as far as possible individual instruction; to look to the candidate's bodily comfort; to adapt the instruction to the candidate's intelligence; to keep up interest, cultivate cheerfulness, and combat weariness. These pedagogical principles of St. Augustine's treatise have proved of perennial value and have inspired almost all subsequent works on catechetics.

After these preliminary remarks, let us now discuss the Augustinian method itself. Let us explain St. Augustine's principles, first, insofar as they have to do with the matter to be taught; secondly, insofar as they refer to the method; and, lastly insofar as they affect the catechist himself.

The Contents

1. St. Augustine has determined the contents of catechization with considerable clearness and precision. The narration – the historical exposition at the beginning of the catechetical instruction – should begin with the first verse of Genesis and continue down to the present time. St. Augustine gives us the following rules for selecting the material:

a. We are not to repeat verbatim the whole of the Bible; time would not suffice for this nor does need demand it. We must present all the matter in a general and comprehensive summary, choosing the most salient points which are heard with pleasure and which constitute the cardinal points in history. Only in this way will we secure and hold the listener's attention. The remaining details should be woven into one narrative in a rapid survey, to constitute the background for the more important features.

b. The catechist should not abandon the course of the narration and permit the heart and the tongue to stray into the more tangled mazes of controversy.

c. The catechist should narrate in such a way as to account for and explain the causes of each of the facts and events that he relates. Augustine would, therefore, have the catechist present an interesting philosophy of history.

2. In addition, since the Old Testament is a preparation, a type and a foretokening of the New, St. Augustine insists that the two testaments be intimately connected and inter-related. The various events of the Old Testament must converge upon Christ as upon their central point: "And, in truth, for no other reason were all the things that we read in the Holy Scriptures written before our Lord's coming than to announce His coming and to prefigure the church to be, that is to say, the people of God throughout all nations, which church is His body, in which are included and numbered the just who lived in this world even before His coming and who believed that He would come as we believe that He has come . . . [Christ] sent before Him in the persons of the holy Patriarchs and Prophets some part of His body, with which as with a hand He foretokened His future birth."[2]

3. As St. Augustine evolves his model biblical lesson, he constantly correlates important biblical incidents with Christ and with the Church. Here are a few examples of this correlation. The flood, wherein the just were saved by the wood of the ark, is a symbol of the future Church which Christ buoyed up above the flood in which this world is submerged. The chosen people, especially those who thought on the rest to come and sought a heavenly home, prefigured the Church, the Mystical Body to which by faith they already belonged. The passage of the Jews through the Red Sea, in which their enemies were completely destroyed, is a symbol of Baptism whereby the faithful pass over into a new life and whereby their sins like enemies are totally blotted out. The paschal lamb is a figure of Christ's Passion: "And with the sign of His Passion and cross, you today are to be signed and sealed upon your forehead, as it were upon a door-post; and so are all Christians

[2] *Op. cit.*, III, 6.

signed and sealed." [3] The Law was written on tablets of stone to typify the hardness of the hearts of the Jews who were not to fulfill it. The land of promise was a figure of the spiritual kingdom; the city of Jerusalem, of the heavenly Jerusalem. In that earthly kingdom of the people of Israel, King David stood out most prominently as a prefiguration of Christ the King. The captivity of the Jews in Babylon is a figure of the subjection of the Church to the kings of the world. The seventy years signify the end of the foreordained time, at which the Church is delivered from the confusion of this world, as was Jerusalem from the captivity of Babylon. Even as on the sixth day man was made in the likeness of God, so with the coming of Christ the sixth age begins in which through the Holy Spirit the mind of man is renewed in the image of God and the law is fulfilled out of love of God.

Augustine well knew that education does not consist merely in a training of the intellect. He understood that education consists in inflaming the heart with love of virtue and in inclining the will toward the good. Hence, when he comes to the New Testament, he lays added emphasis on the relation of truths to daily life. He refers to the doctrines of the bodily resurrection, final judgment and the beatific vision as powerful motives for right conduct. The various lessons of the Incarnation are summed up in a passage which is a masterpiece of prose and tender piety.[4]

The Method

In expounding his method of teaching, St. Augustine insists that the instruction must at all times be adapted to the capacities, needs

[3] *Op. cit.*, XX, 34.

[4] *Op. cit.*, XXII, 40. The whole passage deserves to be quoted in full:

"And therefore I say, did Christ the Lord, made man, despise all the good things of earth, that He might show us that these things are to be despised; and endured all earthly ills that He taught must be endured; so that neither might happiness be sought in the former nor unhappiness be feared in the latter. For, inasmuch as He was born of a mother who, although she conceived, was untouched by man and always remain untouched, a virgin in conception, a virgin in childbirth, a virgin in death, was yet espoused to a workman, He put an end to all the inflated pride of carnal nobility. Inasmuch as He was born, moreover, in the city of Bethlehem, which among all the cities of Judea was so insignificant, that even today it is called a village, He did not want anyone to glory in the exaltation of any earthly city. He, likewise, became poor, to Whom all things belong and by Whom all things were created, lest anyone believing in Him should dare to be unduly exalted be-

and circumstances of the listener. This principle of adaptation is admirably formulated by St. Augustine in the following passage:

"I can testify to you from my own experience that I am differently stirred according as he whom I see before me waiting for instruction is cultivated or a dullard, a fellow-citizen or a stranger, a rich man or a poor man, a private citizen or a public man, a man having some official authority, a person of this or that family, of this or that age or sex, coming to us from this or that school of philosophy, or from this or that popular error, and in keeping with my own varying feelings my discourse itself opens, proceeds, and closes. And since the same medicine is not to be applied to all, although to all the same love is due, so also love itself is in travail with some, becomes weak with others; is at pains to edify some, dreads to be a cause of offense to others; stoops to some, before others stands with the head erect; is gentle to some, and stern to others; an enemy to none, a mother to all." [5]

St. Augustine has left us two model lessons in which he has embodied the principles which he recommends. The essential characteristic of his method – the distinctive note of Augustinian catechetics – is the historical exposition or the narration; if you have to teach your hearers, he says, you must do so by narration. "The narration is complete when the beginner is first instructed from the text 'in the beginning God created heaven and earth' down to the present period of church history." [6] In this narration, the efforts of the teacher must be bent upon understanding doctrine, not upon memorizing formulas; in all our discourses we must

cause of earthly riches. He refused to be made king by men, because He was showing the way of lowliness to those wretches whom their pride had separated from Him, and yet the whole creation bears witness to His everlasting kingdom. He hungered Who feeds all, He thirsted by Whom all drink is created, He, Who is spiritually both the bread of them that hunger, and the well-spring of them that thirst; He was wearied with earthly journeying Who has made Himself the way to heaven for us; He became as it were one dumb and deaf in the presence of His revilers, through Whom the dumb spoke and the deaf heard; He was bound Who has freed men from the bonds of their infirmities; He was scourged Who drove out from men's bodies the scourges of all pains; He was crucified Who put an end to our torments; He died Who raised the dead to life. But He also rose again, never more to die, that none might learn from Him so to despise death as though destined never to live hereafter."

[5] *Op. cit.*, XV, 23.

[6] *Op. cit.*, III, 5.

try and endeavor above all, to reach the intelligence of our hearers, through the clearest manner of speaking possible. "All that I myself understand, I wish to make understood by my hearers." [7]

At the same time, Augustine warns the teacher not to present too much matter to the listener at one time. He insists that it is much better to present a little at a time but to explain this well. Finally, if we inquire why the narrative method wins souls so easily, the answer is also given by St. Augustine; It so happens, he says, that the very facts, by themselves, stir the hearer so deeply that no further endeavor of oratory is needed to stir him.

In these days when project methods are so much in vogue and when traditional methods are frequently disparaged, it is well to call attention to this distinctive feature of St. Augustine's method; namely, the exposition of historical facts. This "narration" of St. Augustine's method has its roots deep in Christian antiquity and in the Sacred Scriptures themselves. During the centuries before Christ the true religion was preserved not by writing but by oral tradition. Fathers narrated to their children the wonders which they had seen with their own eyes or heard from the lips of their parents. The children, in turn, were to transmit these accounts to their posterity. This method was followed by the patriarchs and prophets, the psalmists and the moralists of the Old Testament. The proclamation of the New Alliance did not alter this ancient method. The discourses of St. Peter, St. Paul, the other Apostles and St. Stephen, the dispute of the Christians with the Jews, were all basically a narration of facts. This same narrative method was from the very beginning adopted by the Eastern and Western Fathers. St. Augustine's treatise represents the fullest development of a catechetical method which we find in one form or another in the writings of St. Irenaeus, St. Clement of Alexandria, St. Cyprian, St. Basil, St. Cyril of Jerusalem, St. Gregory Nazianzen and St. Gregory of Nyssa. St. Augustine's method influenced the whole subsequent history of catechetics .Through Rabanus Maurus, Bishop Fénelon, Abbé Fleury, Gruber, and the exponents of the Munich Method it continues even up to modern times.[8]

[7] *Op. cit.*, II, 3.

[8] The great Bishop Fénelon tells us that "in former times, it was through Bible History that children were taught. The magnificent method which St. Augustine ordered to be used for unlearned people was not a method ar-

What role, it might be asked, did the question-and-answer method play in St. Augustine's catechetical system? The original meaning of "catechize" was to instruct orally. There is nothing in the etymological history of this term to show that questions and answers constituted an essential element in catechetical instruction. There can likewise be no doubt that catechesis consisted essentially in oral instruction. The primary concern of the "unlearned" was to hear and learn the truths of revelation which from the very fact that they were revealed, could not admit of Socratic discussion. Secondly, Augustine used the acroamatic or lecture method in catechizing as the method best adapted to the narration. However, occasionally during the narration he made use of the erotematic or question-and-answer method, not to impart instruction but to ascertain whether or not the listener was following him. Thirdly, before beginning the narration, Augustine interrogated the prospective candidate in order to ascertain his dispositions and ability. This questioning enabled Augustine to determine his subject matter and to adapt his discourse to the capacity and peculiarities of the candidate. Finally, it must be remembered that the "unlearned" were obliged to answer the questions of the profession of faith put to them before their formal admission into the catechumenate. This profession of faith was gradually designated as the catechesis, and eventually the notion became current that all

ranged by him, but was the very method practised everywhere in the Church from the beginning" (*Oeuvres de Fénelon* [Paris, 1843], II, col. 489). The Abbé Fleury speaks in the same approving manner of Augustine's treatise (*Catéchisme Historique* [Lyon, 1747], p. 20). In Germany there appeared in 1779 Felbiger's Catechism, which refers specifically to St. Augustine in its title (*Grundsätze des Katechisierens aus den Schriften und Beispielen der heiligen Väter, vornehmlich des hl. Cyrillus und hl. Augustinus*). In 1832 Archbishop Gruber of Salzburg brought out his Catechism, which was based, as its title also indicates, on Augustine's treatise (*Praktisches Handbuch der Katechetik für Katoliken oder Anweisung und Katechisationen in Geiste des hl. Augustinus* [Salzburg, 1832]). In 1905 J. Eising showed conclusively that the well-known Munich method of catechizing is modeled on this treatise (*Die katechetische Methode vergangener Zeiten in zeitgemässer Ausgestaltung* [Wien, 1905]). This array of authorities might fittingly be closed with a quotation from Leo XIII, who notes as an old ecclesiastical tradition the fact that "in the catechetical and theological schools, commonly established in the various sees—among which those of Alexandria and of Antioch were most famous—the whole teaching system consisted almost exclusively of the narration, the explanation and the defence of Holy Scripture" (*Providentissimus Deus*, 1893).

catechesis consisted in instructing by means of questions and answers.

The catechist should motivate his teaching throughout with the love of God. St. Augustine establishes the foundation for this motive *par excellence.* He says that Christ became incarnate principally in order that we might learn how much God loves man. When as yet enemies, Christ died for us. God first loved us, and spared not His only Son but delivered Him up for us all. Christ came that man might begin to glow with love of Him by whom he was first loved. If hitherto man found it irksome to love Him, now, at least, it should not prove irksome to return that love. There is nothing that invites love more than to be beforehand in loving. With how much love is the inferior fired when he discovers that he is loved by Him who is superior. Love is more welcome when it is not burnt up with the draught of want but issues from the overflowing stream of beneficence. The former springs from misery; the latter, from mercy. We must also love our neighbor at the bidding and after the example of Him who in love made Himself our neighbor when we were wandering far from Him. Even as He laid down His life for us, so may we lay down our life for the brethren.

The Catechist

1. The first quality which St. Augustine demands of every catechist is in intense love of God and of his fellow men. When the teacher is on fire with love of God, some of that fire will invariably spread to his pupils. Indeed, as we said before, love of God should be the principal aim of all catechization. And, of course, the most effective way to enkindle this love in the immortal souls of men is to remind them of the eternal love of God for them.

The catechist must also be a man of prayer. The catechist's prayer is far more important than his actual instructing. St. Augustine tells us that when he instructs an unlearned person, he tells that person little but tells God much.

Although much of the instruction has to be done with a group, Augustine warns that the catechist – in order to bring into play the personal element – should give as much individual instruction as possible. In group instruction one of the main duties of the teacher is to make his lecture interesting. Augustine realizes that this is a very difficult task and points out that the weariness and apparent failure of the catechist are due to one or several of the following causes:

a. The inferiority of speech to thought, the inability to express in words what the mind silently perceives and admires.

b. The inability to express truths as well as they have been expressed by others, the fear of the uncertain issue of our discourse because of the uncertain gesture of the hearers, and the consequent desire to hear or read what has already been well said or written.

c. Weariness of repeating again and again the elementary truths which the mind has outgrown.

d. Discouragement due to lack of any interest on the part of the pupil.

e. The dejection and irritation which arises out of a sudden transition from interesting and important occupation to a work which requires great tranquillity of mind.

f. Paralysis of enthusiasm due to the report of some scandal.

2. Having pointed out the obstacles which impede the catechist's work, St. Augustine then indicates the remedies:

a. The teacher should not allow the dullness of his own instruction to discourage him, for, perhaps, the audience enjoyed it even though he did not. And in a confidential tone, Augustine tells us that he was almost always discouraged with his lectures. "It is not in our power," he says, "to bring forth those imprints which intellectual apprehension stamps upon the memory and, as it were, submit them by the sound of our voice to the perception of those listening, in any way parallel to the open and evident expression of the face. For the former are within, in the mind; but the latter is without in the body."[9] In this world we cannot even perceive truths as we desire, much less express them for "we see now through a glass and in a dark manner." This inability, however, should not discourage the catechist but spur him on to greater effort. Cheerfulness on the part of the catechist is absolutely necessary. People listen to us with much greater pleasure when we ourselves take pleasure in the same work of instruction. The thread of our discourse is affected by the very joy which we ourselves experience.

b. If our knowledge seems to be inadequate and our words ill-suited to the occasion, we should do the best we can. The teacher

[9] *Op. cit.*, II, 3.

need not worry, provided his mind does not wander from substantial truth. But if, though setting out with the best of purposes, he strays through human frailty from the paths of truth, he should discreetly and humbly correct his errors when opportunity presents itself. If there are any who – blinded by insane jealousy – rejoice that we have erred, let them furnish us an occasion for the practice of forbearance. If our teaching is contrary to a long-standing erroneous belief and practice, and if the listener is curable, he should be cured by an abundance of reasons and authorities. But if he draws back and objects to being cured, let the teacher take comfort in the well-known example of our Lord, who, when men were offended at His word and shrank from it as a hard saying, spoke to those who remained: "Will you also go away?"

c. In prescribing a remedy for the third cause of weariness, St. Augustine reveals his two outstanding virtues, namely, a burning love of God, and an all-embracing love of his fellow men whose feelings he has analyzed better perhaps than any writer before his time or since. The best way to overcome tedium – which arises from a constant repetition of well-known truths – is to have sympathy for our listener. If we link ourselves to children with brotherly love, things which will be new to them will also be new to us. When we are showing to our close friends certain lovely expanses of space whether of town or countryside, to which we ourselves have grown accustomed and pass by without any pleasure, our own delight is renewed by their delight at the novelty of the scene. What is new to our listeners becomes new to us, because of the bond of love between the two. With what greater joy, then, ought we be renewed in the newness of the things which pertain to God on whose account all things are to be learned. Again, if we pass through streets which are most familiar to us, we, nevertheless, gladly point out the way to one who had been in trouble through losing his way. With what greater alacrity and joy should we point out the way – although quite familiar to us – in matters of salutary doctrine and conduct the soul to God's kingdom of light and life.

d. The apathy of the learner may be due to several reasons: he may be overawed; he may be too bashful to express his opinion; he may fail to understand, or he may not agree with the teacher. He should be dealt with accordingly, for no stereotyped form of instruction will do for all alike. The teacher must do his best to dislodge the hearer from his hiding place: "We must drive out by gentle encouragement his excessive timidity, which hinders him from expressing his opinion; we must temper his shyness by introducing the idea of brotherly fellowship; we must by questioning him find out whether he understands; and we must give him confidence so that if he thinks there is an objection to make he may freely lay it before us. We must at the same time inquire of him whether he has ever heard these things before, and so perhaps they, as being things well-known and commonplace, fail to move him."[10] Lack of interest is frequently due also to physical fatigue and exhaustion.

St. Augustine is also careful to indicate the procedure in regard to the backward pupil: "But if he is slow witted . . . we should bear with him in a compassionate spirit, and after briefly running through the other points, impress upon him in a way to inspire fear the truths that are most necessary concerning the unity of the Catholic Church, temptations, and the Christian manner of living in view of the future judgment; and we should rather say much on his behalf to God, than say much to him about God."[11]

e. If we consecrate our time and our endeavors to God's glory, our being interrupted in the midst of more congenial work will not annoy us. If anything unavoidable happens to disturb our order, let us bend readily to it, so that we may make our own that order which God has preferred to ours. For it is more proper that we should follow His will rather than He, ours. No one plans for the better, unless he is readier to leave undone what is forbidden by Divine Power than eager to do what is devised by human thought.

f. Grief at the presence of scandal among the Church's members must not cause us to desist from catechizing. So great should be our love toward those for whom Christ died, desiring to redeem them from the errors of this world, that the very fact that someone stands in need of instruction should have the effect of dispelling our grief. The joy over gains must alleviate grief over losses. When we warn our hearers against imitating their weak brethren, our discourse has more fervor because actual grief supplies the fuel. And thus the emotions of the heart do not pass away without bearing fruit. If, finally, we are saddened by our own sins and errors, let us keep in mind that catechizing is a work of great mercy which will quench the fire of passion and expiate the penalty of sin.

[10] *Op. cit.*, XIII, 18. [11] *Loc. cit.*

CHAPTER IV

LEADING CHILDREN TO CHRIST: JEAN GERSON

Although he was the chancellor of the University of Paris, Jean Gerson devoted his spare time freely to the instruction of children. When his associates contended that it was ill-becoming for a man of his position to waste his time on children, he replied, "If I am blameworthy, it ought to be more on account of my presumption than of my too great condescension, since, in instructing sinless children, I dare to meddle with the work of deeply spiritual men. I am really in the position of a land turtle seeking the company of the feathered tribe. . . . And when it is further objected that I should devote my time to more important duties, I answer that I cannot conceive of any sublimer work that my insignificant personality could perform to any advantage." [1] In order to justify his conduct he composed a small treatise entitled *De Parvulis ad Christum Trahendis.*[2] In this work, which we shall now analyze, Gerson advocates the early religious training of children, dwells on the evil results of neglecting the children, speaks of the means to be employed zealously for bringing children to Christ and extols the noble character of the catechist's office.

Early Religious Training of Children

Since children and the young always constitute a considerable portion of the Church, Gerson concludes that they must necessarily have been among the objects of those divine constitutions which

[1] Cf. "*Joannis Gersonii Opera Omnia*", 5 vols. (2nd ed.; M. Lud, Ellies du Pin, Paris, 1728), III, 287. All references in this chapter are to this edition of Gerson's works.

[2] *Op. cit.*, III, 277–291.

were to direct the universal course of the Church. Far from neglecting children, Christ rebuked those who in their folly and pride hindered children from coming to Him. Addressing Himself to the disciples who surrounded Him, and through them to all future generations, Christ said, "Suffer the little children to come to Me, and forbid them not. For of such is the kingdom of God. Amen I say to you, whosoever shall not receive the kingdom of God as a little child, shall not enter into it. And embracing them, and laying His hands upon them, He blessed them." [3] In obedience to this admonition of Christ we too must lead children to Him; we must do so by means of instructions adapted to their age and mental capacity. While avoiding coarse and vulgar language, we must not be afraid to stammer, as it were, with them, after the manner of mothers and nurses who know how to formulate a language intelligible to the little ones. To encourage children to come to Christ, to teach them how to come to Christ, to remove scandals from their path – this, according to Gerson, is the noble work of every catechist.

The task of bringing children to Christ, says Gerson, must begin during the child's tenderest years, for increase of grace and consequent formation of character depend upon coöperation with initial graces. The more completely one coöperates with grace, the more abundantly does one receive it and the more thoroughly does it penetrate and fortify one's soul. He who rejects graces, who abuses the gifts of God and neglects the talents of the Sovereign Master, will by a just judgment of God find it extremely difficult to return to Jesus Christ. Far from being able to persevere and be saved, such a man will be in danger of eternal damnation. If children who are innocent cannot of their own natural powers attain to virtue, how much more difficult will it be for those youths who are burdened with sin and vicious habits and who are enemies of God!

God has "perfected praise," as the psalmist says, "out of the mouths of infants and of sucklings." [4] Just as the first flowers of the springtime are eagerly sought and cherished, so the homage of innocent children is dearer to God than the honor of men who abandon their sinful ways only when years and decrepitude have come upon them. Let us offer to God the bloom of youth and not

[3] Mark 10:14–16.
[4] Ps. 8:3.

the faded flower of that advanced age when sin begins to forsake us instead of our abandoning sin.

Finally, no period is so important for the formation of habit — which Aristotle calls our "second nature" — as that of childhood. Nor is anything so important for one's career as the acquisition of good habits. Philosophers and poets are in full agreement with theologians concerning the necessity of young people contracting good habits; Cicero, Ovid and Horace have written with much penetration and skill on the subject. If sin and sacrilege testify to the terrible force of a bad habit, how great, on the other hand, is the power and efficacy of a good habit, especially when it is aided by grace! Dissolute men of Gerson's time scoffingly repeated the pagan proverb: "A man angelic in youth becomes satanical in old age." [5] If this be true, Gerson replies, what then is to be expected of a satanical young man? The proverb, however, is an untruth intended to excuse and protect the corrupt youth of Paris from criticism and derision. The fact remains, say Gerson, that children whose minds have not been obscured by pernicious novelties and whose hearts are free from the contagions of sin, are best qualified to assimilate the principles of right conduct. They are the vessels destined to receive exquisite fluids, young plants which readily obey the hand which cultivates them.[6]

Scandalizing the Little Ones

Our Lord Himself indicated the reasons why we should avoid giving scandal to the little ones: "See that you despise not one of these little ones." And why? "For I say to you, that their Angels in heaven see the face of My Father who is in heaven," and furthermore, "of such is the kingdom of God." [7] Terrible punishment necessarily awaits those who disregard the warning of Our Lord: "He that shall scandalize one of these little ones that believe in Me, it were better for him that a millstone should be hanged about his neck, and that he should be drowned in the depth of the sea." [8] These words of Our Lord, says Gerson, are to be understood in a real and not a mystical sense. They do not refer to spiritual children, but to those little beings on the thres-

[5] "Angelicus juvenis senibus satanizat in annis" (*Op. cit.*, III, 279).
[6] *Op. cit.*, III, 278, 280. [7] Matt. 18:10; Mark 10:14. [8] Matt. 18:6.

hold of life for whom scandal is far more dangerous than it is for others. Gerson finds that Our Lord's admonition was foreshadowed in several pagan authors. According to Horace, a child at this age is like unto soft wax and easily lends itself to vice; once deformed, it cannot be easily restored to the form of virtue. Juvenal, wishing to prevent the scandalizing of children, taught that the greatest respect is due to them and that nothing sinful should be done in their presence.[9]

Gerson defines scandal as a word or an act which lacks rectitude and which is an occasion of spiritual ruin for another. He distinguishes two kinds of scandal, indirect and direct. One commits scandal indirectly if one fails to prevent evil when in virtue of one's authority and duty one should and could do so. One also commits scandal indirectly when, in spite of one's desire to prevent it, one is deterred by fear of gossip or of harm. Others keep children from going to Christ by deriding and calumniating their teachers and accusing them of working only through cupidity and hypocrisy. Such men are either lying supine in religious tepidity or are being tormented by a consuming jealousy of those whose conduct is a reproach to them.

Direct scandal is given by those who glory in their wicked deeds and who, because of diabolical perversion, try to increase the number of accomplices in their crimes and of companions in their damnation. Such men respect neither the innocence of character nor the purity of childhood. Hence it is that the thoughts and imagination of men are so prone to evil, since from childhood, in addition to the primordial corruption of nature, they have been imbibing the poison of sin. Parents and teachers frequently show no solicitude for the moral education and preservation of children. What wonder, then, that children fall so easily as they proceed along the journey of life, where they are continually exposed to the temptations of Satan, without guide or counsellor! Gerson, quoting from Juvenal, warns that domestic examples corrupt children more quickly and thoroughly, since they are endowed with greater authority. For, what son does not wish to do what his father does? Frequently no later remedy is of any avail, since vice has become a second nature.

[9] *Op. cit.*, III, 280.

Means of Leading Children to Christ

Gerson enumerates several different methods of directing children to Christ. Public preaching, private admonition, direct instruction – all these have proved useful. In Gerson's estimation, Confession is the best means of bringing children to Christ. It is there that a wise, prudent, and patient confessor detects the hidden maladies of sin, applies apposite remedies and gives salutary admonitions for the future. For youths who had been given over to sin but who have repented, Gerson advocates a detailed, frank and sincere Confession of their whole life. Such an act will at once unburden the soul of its crimes and fill it with an indescribable peace. In questioning the child, the confessor must inspire horror of all sin and be careful not to suggest new sins.[10]

The confessor must impress the child with his discretion as a confessor and with his consciousness of his sacred obligation not to reveal by word or sign the secrets of the sacred tribunal. The penances must not be too severe. "I impose no penance," says Gerson, "which cannot be performed immediately, for I prefer, after the example of William of Paris, to send men to purgatory with a light penance which they will accomplish voluntarily, rather than to hell with a penance which they will not perform." [11] The confessor must not despise his penitents, no matter how heinous their sins, but must consider them as beloved brothers in Christ who in confidence have shown him the festering wounds of their souls and who have been restored to the purity and innocence of the children of God. He must assure those who experience confusion in avowing their sins that this very embarrassment contributes to the remission of the penalty due to their offenses. Those who complain of experiencing no sensible consolations in their devotion must be taught to love not only the consolations of God but also the God of consolations.

Gerson tells us that he tried to impress the following four points on his young penitents:

1. They must beware lest they become an occasion of ruin and damnation to others (*si non caste, tamen caute*).

2. Those who have had accomplices in sin must discreetly seek out such as have been scandalized and try to bring them to repent-

[10] *Op. cit.*, III, 282.

[11] *Op. cit.*, III, 289.

ance; for, after having played the role of a demon, they must fulfill the office of an angel.

3. Should they have the misfortune of falling back into their vices, let them speedily seek a proper antidote to sin in a sincere and integral Confession.

4. Let them say a *Pater* and an *Ave* every morning and evening in order to satisfy for their past sins and to obtain sufficient graces to avoid sin in the future.

In advocating this remedy Gerson found himself confronted with the following oft-repeated contention of his contemporaries: "It is sufficient if the children go to Confession only once or twice a year." To this assertion Gerson always had a ready answer: the children of light must be as wise in spiritual things as the children of this world are in temporal things; the former must be as diligent in caring for the soul as the latter are in caring for earthly things. This, however, did not satisfy his adversaries, who urged a further difficulty: children often quickly return to their sins. Gerson again answers that many older persons, even those advanced in the ways of perfection, fall back into their old sins, but they do not for that reason cease going to Confession. What kind of a sailor, he asks, would he be who after emptying the water from the ship would cease to work because new water rushes in? The fact that we soil our hands daily does not make us cease washing them. We combat vices to overcome them, and not to be overcome by them. If the child shows insincerity in the confessional, the confessor must by prudent questioning and sound advice correct such a fault.[12] The teacher must be especially vigilant to guard against the possibility of children contaminating one another, for no creature is so subject to infection as a child.

Defense of Gerson's Ministry

The art of arts, says Gerson, is the care of souls, and nowhere is this art so necessary as in the instruction of children. Inexperienced priests, who attempt the latter without being perfected in the former, are blind men leading the blind, and disaster will be the

[12] Gerson apparently did not realize that this dishonesty among the children was occasionally created by the regime of distrust and espionage which prevailed in the schools of his time. Cf. his "*Instruction for the Children of Paris,*" *op. cit.*, IV, 717–720.

inevitable result. Many consider catechization as beneath the dignity of a renowned theologian, littérateur or high ecclesiastic. Gerson knows that he himself, as chancellor of the University of Paris, will be ridiculed and that his reputation will suffer because of his ministry among children. But he is consoled by the thought that those whose viewpoint is determined by the example of Christ and by His great love of souls adopt a different attitude. Such men know that the greatest Master and Doctor did not consider it beneath His dignity to deal in terms of a divine familiarity with those little creatures of God. Their outlook is wholly supernatural, their conduct is guided by the maxim of St. Paul: "Brethren, if a man be overtaken in any fault, you, who are spiritual, instruct such a one in the spirit of meekness, considering thyself, lest thou also be tempted." [13]

When his enemies alleged the distance which separated him from little children, Gerson declared that he would not hesitate to come down to a child's level. Must not one stoop down in order to raise a fallen man? Can majesty and love share without a struggle the same crown? Yes, he will strip himself of all dignity and power; he will become little with the little ones in all things except sin. For if our teaching is to be effective, he says, it must be animated by love. Children are captivated and molded more by caresses than by threats. Children, especially the timid ones, will not open their hearts to a confessor or teacher whom they hate or fear. They will not trust him unless they are assured of his kindness and discretion. They are drawn only towards him who is affable and cheerful and who has become their friend and brother.

Gerson finds an admirable exemplar of these qualities in St. Paul. When the Apostle writes that he became all things to all men,[14] he surely meant to include children. Had he despised relations with the young, how could he command fathers to treat their little ones humanely and not provoke them to indignation or make them fainthearted? [15] St. Paul himself dispels all doubt concerning his attitude when he says, "We might have been burdensome to you, as the apostles of Christ; but we became little ones in the midst of you, as if a nurse should cherish her children." [16] How potent, indeed, has the example of Our Lord been upon the life

[13] Gal. 6:1. [14] I Cor. 9:22. [15] Col. 3:21; Eph. 6:4. [16] I Thess. 2:7.

of St. Paul and of countless other men.[17] How often have sinners corrected and amended their ways because of the meekness and kindness of others! Did not St. Ambrose by his benevolence captivate the heart of St. Augustine?

Every action of Christ embodies a precept as formal as His words. When He commanded the Apostles to allow children to come to Him, when He embraced and blessed them and imposed His hands on them, He intended to teach us an important lesson. If He who is the God of ages,[18] and in whom are hidden all the treasures of wisdom and knowledge,[19] extended His arms in benediction over children, how can any one of us be ashamed of his interest in the little ones?

Hence, when Gerson's adversaries contend that a man of high position ought to be busy with more important things, the chancellor answers that he knows of no work more momentous than to tend, with the help of God's grace, these beautiful plants in God's garden. He could, it is true, attempt to obtain the same results by means of public preaching. He could do so with more pomp, but hardly with more efficacy. Besides, if Christ spoke to the vast multitudes, He also deigned to speak at length with individuals, such as, for example, the sinful Samaritan woman. As to the rest, Gerson clearly foresaw from the beginning that he would be criticized and that his motives would be misjudged. He has undertaken nothing without the approval of his bishop, and the results obtained are open to the inspection of all. If the fruits are good, he asks that no one condemn the tree as evil.

We take it as a matter of course, says Gerson, if a man, without any regard for the hour or the day, draws a beast out of a well or ditch into which it had fallen. Why then accuse of foolishness and indiscretion him who, animated by a Christ-like zeal, tries to save the souls of youths? The public lavishes unqualified praise upon a physician who exercises his art gratuitously, or upon a lawyer who pleads cases without a stipend, upon any one, in fact, who freely places himself at the service of another without demanding a recompense. What a sad spectacle, then, to see artisans and physicians of souls criticized, calumniated and thwarted in their zeal, when they are laboring spontaneously for the salvation

[17] Matt. 11:28–30. [18] I Tim. 1:17. [19] Col. 2:3.

of others! Living temples and sanctuaries of God are constantly threatened with danger and spiritual ruin. Are we to stand by idle, and tremble before the forces of evil? Such surely was not the attitude of Christ, whose love for souls is compared to the anxious care of a hen for her chicks.[20]

The catechist of today may well reflect on this sublime teaching of Gerson. Some priests who devote a long time to the preparation of a sermon spend no time in preparing for catechetical instruction or for hearing children's confessions. "Anything is good enough for children," they say. "Anyone can ask questions and listen to answers." Such men stand in sharp contrast to Gerson as well as to all great catechists of the Church. "Can anything vie in importance with this art," asks St. John Chrysostom, "the aim of which is to train the mind and fashion the heart and character of youth? He who is charged with this task must exhibit greater zeal than any painter or sculptor."[21] The ceaseless warnings of ecclesiastical authority regarding the necessity of religious instruction show only too clearly that its importance cannot be overestimated. The Church knows well that the office of the catechist is deserving of all esteem. By Baptism a child is made an heir of heaven; it depends principally upon the catechist whether the child will attain its supernatural destiny. In working for this sublime end the priest has at his disposal means which are not within the reach of parents, lay-teachers or Sisters, namely, the canonical mission from the bishop and a supernatural authority with which he is invested by ordination as a minister of Christ. The treasures of graces and truths, prayer and good example, are freely at his command. In being faithful to his office of catechist, he knows he is assuring the future of the Church, because the children of today are the men of tomorrow. He knows that, if Christ pronounced terrific woes against those who scandalize children, he has also prepared ineffable rewards for those who lead children to Him.

[20] *Op. Cit.*, III, 282.
[21] "*In Matthæum*," hom. ix.

CHAPTER V

ABBÉ CLAUDE FLEURY

Abbé Claude Fleury, a friend of Bousset and Fénelon, was born in Paris in 1640. Being a son of a lawyer, he devoted himself to legal studies and when eighteen years of age was called to the bar. This manner of life, however, did not suit the disposition and inclinations of young Claude, who by nature was gentle, peaceful and benevolent. He abandoned law for theology and embraced the ecclesiastical state. His deep piety and solid theological learning soon won for him the admiration of those in high places. Louis XIV, who was well qualified to discern great and useful talents, made him preceptor to the Princes of Conti whom the king wished to be educated with the Dauphin. His position as tutor aroused his interest in educational psychology and pedagogy. In 1675 he wrote his *Traité du choix et de la méthode des études.*[1] Later on he made a practical application of his educational principles in three works: *Les mœurs des Israëlites,*[2] *Les mœures des chrétiens,*[3] and finally the work the underlying principles of which we shall explain in the following pages, namely, the *Catéchisme historique.*[4]

Ignorance of Religion

In the opening pages of his introduction to the *Catéchisme* the abbé deplores the universal ignorance of religious truths in his

[1] Published in Paris in 1686.

[2] Published in Paris in 1681. The second London edition, published in 1832, contains an account of the life and writings of Abbé Fleury (pp. 9–14).

[3] Published in Paris in 1682.

[4] Published in Paris in 1683. The full title runs as follows: "*Catéchisme historique, contenant en abrégé l'histoire sainte et la doctrine chrétienne.*" The edition used in preparing this chapter is that of Lyons of 1747.

time. Not only peasants and laborers, but also men with a liberal education, men of letters, devout people versed in spiritual and ascetical literature, are ignorant of the essentials of religion. Nay, there are even priests and theologians, who, although intensely interested in the questions debated in theological schools, are frequently unacquainted with the Scriptures and the beauty and intrinsic coherence of divine truths and are quite unprepared to instruct children and to oppose the onslaughts of the enemies of the Church. Laymen rest contented with the thought that they once learned their Catechism, not realizing that long since they have forgotten the fundamental truths of religion or perhaps never thoroughly understood them. Others are too proud to avow their ignorance, too sophisticated to adopt the simplicity and humility of children in their quest for the kingdom of God. Finally, certain ecclesiastics, who prefer their own interests to those of Christ, consider catechization as undistinguished, toilsome and fruitless; they prefer to establish a reputation by eloquence in the pulpit and by popularity in the confessional, forgetting that their work cannot be supernaturally fruitful unless Christians have first been grounded in the essentials of faith.

This darkness of the mind, says the learned abbé, must necessarily result in a weakening of the moral fibre and in a corruption of the heart. The Catholic religion does not consist merely in ceremonies and external worship; it is also a body of doctrines, a science. The faithful were called disciples before they received at Antioch the name of Christians. The bishops were called doctors by all the ancients. When founding His Church, Our Lord said to His Apostles, "Go and teach." [5] It is impossible to be a genuine Christian while remaining in utter religious ignorance. He alone is a genuine Christian who thoroughly knows and practises the Christian religion. Although it is possible to know one's religion without practising it, it is impossible to practise it without first knowing it; every affection presupposes its intellectual coefficient. Unless devotions are based on dogmatic principles and deep convictions, they will at best be superficial. While knowledge of Christian doctrine spontaneously results in an admiration of its intrinsic beauty and love of its precepts, religious ignorance tends ultimately to a contempt of religion itself and to sin.

[5] Matt. 28:19.

Causes of Religious Ignorance

Before seeking out an apposite remedy, the abbé strives to determine the causes of the ailment which he sets out to cure. The causes of religious ignorance are, in his estimation, the following:

1. *Psychological Laws.* Ignorance is born with us and is one of the consequences of our psychophysical constitution. At birth the child's soul has neither innate nor infused knowledge but, on the contrary, is devoid of all knowledge. To be born in the bosom of the Church and of educated parents avails little. The gradual moulding and perfecting of the child's mind must be the untiring labor of parent and pedagogue, who should always remember that nothing can enter the mind unless it first strikes the senses. In religious instruction the teacher must, in addition, enlist the powerful aid of grace, since there is question not only of abstract spiritual truths which are difficult to contemplate but also of supernatural truths which cannot be assimilated by our unaided native powers.

2. *Spiritual Sloth.* The abbé enumerates various excuses by which the Catholics of his time tried to justify their religious lethargy and to drug their conscience: "My knowledge far exceeds what I care to practice. . . . My knowledge of the Catechism is all-sufficient. . . . I prefer submissive, respectful belief to a study and scrutiny of religion which might prove to be dangerous" — and so on. The abbé emphatically asserts that the true religion need have no fear of being known, because it teaches nothing which cannot be sustained in the full light of day. The same divine Scriptures which command us to receive with submission the revealed truths of God, to bring into captivity our understanding and to obey the faith, also expressly command us to meditate upon the law day and night, to apply all our powers to a study of wisdom and science and to strive all our lives after a more perfect knowledge of God's will.

3. *Lack of Adaptation.* There are almost endless treatises on various aspects of religion, but they are not sufficiently adapted even to the best-intentioned Christians. Theological works are written in a style which is inaccessible to those without a Scholastic training and often deal with queer and abstruse questions of which the faithful have no need. Scripture commentaries are too long and are frequently unintelligible to laymen. The lives of the saints

present only particular aspects of virtue. Spiritual books presuppose the Christian to be sufficiently instructed in the essentials of religion and by their style and bulkiness repel the active and busy man of the world. The Sunday sermons are detached one from another and treat of various subjects according to the whim of the preacher. There is no coherent exposition of the biblical and dogmatic facts which are fundamental in our religion.

4. *Ignorance of the Liturgy.* Many do not understand the meaning of even the most frequently recurring phrases of the Mass, and few make use of missals or of translations. The public readings of the scriptural passages, which form a great part of the Liturgy, fail to instruct those for whom they are primarily intended. They fail to instruct, because the laity are not sufficiently acquainted with the sacred books whence these lessons are derived, and because the faithful do not read these biblical lessons in their proper sequence. These defects should, of course, be remedied in the sermons. But how often does the explanation of the Gospel consist in choosing an expression or a word from it and deriving from the phrase all that one momentarily wishes! People may follow the services and listen to sermons for years and yet be ignorant of the elements of Christianity.

5. *Catechism Texts and Instruction.* The Catechism is an abridgment, and, although it contains the necessary truths, it must, to be brief, omit the numerous concrete facts on which its answers are based or from which they flow as abstract conclusions. The original authors of the Catechism were Scholastic theologians who did little more than extract important definitions and divisions from each theological treatise and translate them into the vernacular without altering their style. The Scholastic method is felt even in the attempt to make the child understand the *raison d'être* of the sequence of particular religious truths. These men, who had studied for a long time and were well versed in the subtleties of a science, did not sufficiently reflect on the psychological state and on the ignorance of those whom they wished to instruct. To speak the language of scholastic philosophy to those who do not as yet fully know any language and who have not acquired ideas of the common things of life, is naturally the height of folly.

Abbé Fleury does not wish to minimize in the least the historical importance and role of the Catechism. Present ignorance of religion, he says, is as nothing compared to what it would have been without Catechisms. But the fact remains that the style and form of Catechism have little attraction for those who use it. The teacher wearies of repeating the familiar abstract formulas and perseveres in his difficult task more out of charity than out of pleasure. The child, too, finds it difficult to assimilate the dry answers of the Catechism. Since the child's mind at this period is unusually plastic, these first impressions are often lasting, and many children retain an abiding secret aversion to the instructions which so fatigued them in infancy. All religious talks strike them as mournful and tedious. Religion appears to them as a hard law which is to be followed more out of fear than of love. Many, prejudiced by the severity of the Catechism and the simplicity of the women who first taught them, drop religion altogether. These impressions revive with increasing force and vividness at a period when their waxing passions and evil habits render religious truths distasteful to them and when, in their effort to appease the remorse of conscience, they would fain destroy all religion.

The Narration Method

A good catechetical method takes into consideration not only the intrinsic nature of the religious truths to be taught but also the intellectual capacity of those to be instructed. In the determination of the method which is best adapted to the nature of man, the experience of the ages ought to prove a decisive factor. Fleury finds that men, even in the remotest periods of history, have followed practically the same method of teaching religion. They made use of narration and of a simple deduction of facts, and on these based the dogmas and precepts of morals.[6] The narration of history always preceded instruction and exhortations. In both the Old and New Dispensation the historical books precede the doctrinal and moral treatises. The abbé proves his thesis from the Old and New Testament, from the Fathers and from reason.

1. During the two centuries before Christ the true religion was preserved by oral tradition. The fathers narrated to their children the divine wonders, which they had seen with their own eyes or heard from the accounts of their parents, and which in turn their pious children were to transmit to their posterity. This method

[6] *"Catéchisme historique,"* pp. 15–16.

was followed by the patriarchs and prophets; it was the method of Adam, Noe, Abraham, Moses, Josue, Samuel, Esdras, and the Machabees. Scripture did not set aside this ancient custom but rather established it more securely. The duty of parents to transmit the sacred truths of God to their children and to their children's children continued to be emphasized especially in the Psalms and the moral books of the Old Testament.

2. The proclamation of the New Alliance did not alter this method of secular standing. The discourses of St. Peter, the other Apostles, and St. Stephen, the controversies of the Christians with the Jews, and the preaching to the Gentiles, were all basically a narration of and a deduction from facts. The Jews had to be reminded of God's wonderful intervention in behalf of their fathers, in order that they might the better understand the fulfillment of the divine promises in Christ. To the Gentiles it was necessary to narrate that God created the world, that He governs it by His Providence and that He will judge it through His Son risen from the dead.

3. The numerous catechetical instructions for converts found among the works of the Fathers are for the most part also based on facts. The body of the discourse is generally a narration of God's mercies toward the human race from the beginning of the world to the proclamation of the Gospel. St. Augustine continually speaks of narration as a method of instruction and illustrates it by two examples.[7]

4. The existence of God, the immortality of the soul and the freedom of the will can, it is true, be proved by convincing arguments. The Fathers used this method of instruction in dealing with unbelievers and pagan philosophers, and St. Gregory of Nyssa gives us an excellent model of such a catechization. But children and the majority of men find it difficult to follow abstract arguments. Besides, no one can by his unaided powers arrive at a knowledge of mysteries; they must, therefore, be narrated before they can engender faith. The objectivity of these supernatural truths is beyond dispute, since God confirmed them by signs and miracles. Even a child readily grasps the force of this motive of credibility. It must be God who spoke through these men of old, since in His name they raised the dead and performed works which

[7] "*De catechizandis rudibus.*"

He alone can do. It was thus that the man born blind reasoned; so, too, Nicodemus, a doctor in Israel.

Unsatisfactory Substitutes

Many, realizing the value of concrete facts and stories as a means of making the instructions agreeable, and not finding or not knowing how to find apposite stories in the Scriptures, draw upon uncritical lives of the saints. They think that these fantastic and visionary stories are good enough for children. And what will be the result? When the same children grow up, says Fleury, they will, without distinguishing the true from the false, acquire a contempt for all that they have learned in the religion class. Surely, the word of God, which is often taught before God's altar, should not be adulterated with anything that could not be sustained before the most learned men or which is unworthy of the majesty of religion.

Others abandon the Catechism for an abridged illustrated Bible History. But the selection of stories in the latter is often haphazard and the method defective. The stories are not sufficiently Christocentric, and the sequence and relation of events are seldom clear. Pictures increase the cost of the book, and instructions given solely with a view to explain the picture become vague once the illustration is withdrawn.

An indiscriminate reading of the Bible itself would likewise, in the estimation of Fleury, prove unsatisfactory. Many would experience difficulties in understanding the biblical manner of speech, Oriental customs, and the Hebraisms inevitable in the best translation. Again the books of the Bible, though useful, are not all equally necessary for our salvation; certain sections of the Old Testament have been abrogated by the coming of Christ. Finally, some scriptural passages are obscure and must be interpreted by specialists trained in exegesis.

The practice of correlating the Bible with the Catechism, although not without merit, likewise fails to satisfy the demands of Fleury. Biblical events would be more pleasing and attractive if they were told successively in their natural order and with reasonable length. In mere correlation they are narrated according to the order of the Catechism and, as it were, in passing, as if the teacher feared and regretted the loss of time in so doing.

Fleury's Catechism

Fleury's aim is to give us in the form of a narration a summary of the principal doctrines of the Bible. He wishes his Catechism to be a model of instruction, a book which is to be imitated, varied and adapted to different persons and times. He draws up two Catechisms, one for children and the less instructed, the other for the better instructed and the more capable. The second repeats to some extent the matter of the first; this is not only consonant with the method of Scripture, but also serves to make the truths the child's abiding possession. Parental instruction, the "Small Catechism," the "Large Catechism" – these are the three concentric circles of catechization which should impress the truth indelibly upon the child's mind.

Fleury's method, then, is predominantly scriptural. When his contemporaries doubted the possibility of explaining dogmas without Scholastic terminology, the abbé replied, "The Fathers of the early centuries, who were obliged to explain all the truths of the Christian religion, did not use the language of Aristotelian philosophy but of Sacred Scripture. Let us follow their example. Let us imitate, as far as we can, the style of Our Lord, of the Apostles, and of the Prophets. They spoke the common language of men; their expressions were simple, obvious, clear and appealed to the imagination. Let us use, too, the language consecrated by the Church's decrees, prayers, and professions of faith, a language which the Church wishes us to put in the mouth of all the faithful. In trying to avoid difficult and abstract terminology, we must beware, however, lest we fall in the opposite extreme. To make ourselves understood, it is not necessary to acquire the child's improprieties of language. We must at all times safeguard the majesty of religion and command respect for the word of God. A careful study of Scriptures will enable us to be simple and yet dignified."

In Fleury's "Small Catechism" the biblical narrative is followed by a series of questions and answers dealing with the subject-matter of the chapter. This arrangement is based on the conviction that a child must first hear about supernatural truths before he can be questioned about them. The purpose of the questions is to ascertain how much the child has retained, to correct what he has learned inaccurately, and to stimulate him to greater activity if he has been negligent. The questions and answers aim at simplicity and brevity and admit of only one answer. Answers of a mere "yes" or "no" are carefully avoided, lest the children become indifferent as to what they affirm or deny. In the "Large Catechism" the questions and answers are omitted; the children who use this book are older and more attentive and see better the utility and necessity of what they learn.

Fleury counsels the same proportion, sobriety and reserve in the practice of religion as in the teaching of it. We must be satisfied with the practices authorized by the Church's usage and not strive after new and uncommon devotions. Morning and evening prayers should be modelled as far as possible after Prime and Compline, or at least after their spirit; in all other exercises the Missal, Breviary, and Ritual must be our norm and guide. The abbé does not wish to disapprove of current formulas (such as the acts of faith, thanksgiving, contrition, etc.), but he would rather establish them on a more solid basis. For all these acts are contained in ecclesiastical prayers. The entire Symbol is an act of faith, and contains as many acts of faith as it does articles. The *Confiteor* and the Seven Penitential Psalms contain excellent acts of contrition. The orations which follow the Litany of the Saints are all model prayers. The *Gloria Patri* is an act of adoration; the *Deo Gratias,* an act of thanksgiving. The Psalms are so many examples of the most perfect acts of religion and have been intimately incorporated into the Church's Liturgy. Hence, whoever participates in liturgical prayer practises his religion in an excellent degree.

The abbé urges the catechist to proceed with discretion in determining the details of morning and evening prayers and in regulating the Christian's daily life. The catechist must not leave the faithful under the impression that they commit sin if they omit certain favorite formulas or fail to assume particular bodily attitudes during prayer. He must strive to counteract any tendency which would make religion a matter of mere mechanical routine. His primary aim must be the development of the inner life; if these inner sentiments are present, words and external signs will soon be forthcoming; and if they are not, God will hear us nevertheless.

The catechist himself must be well grounded in the Scriptures, in theology and in solid piety. During religious instruction he must supply those details and facts which the Catechism narrative in its brevity had to omit. He must be careful not to mingle pious legends and theological opinions with dogmas and biblical truths. While restraining useless questions and idle curiosity on the part of the child, he himself must avoid all the theological quibbling. In dealing with abstract truths he must use concrete comparisons and examples adapted to the listener. Since burning words cannot come from a frozen heart, the catechist must be animated with a great love of God and of his neighbor; he must see in his charges images of God and members of Christ's Mystical Body. This enthusiasm of the teacher for the things of God will soon be communicated to and absorbed by the child's plastic mind and receptive heart.

The method of Abbé Fleury is a reflection and continuation of an important element in traditional and especially Augustinian catechetics. In fact, in a modern work Fr. Tahon sets out to establish the following principles concerning the Scripture-narration method: "The method of the Apostles for teaching beginners was simply the process of first presenting the facts of sacred history and then drawing out from these facts the doctrinal elements of religion. This method of teaching through sacred history may be called the narrative or Scriptural method. This method at once became the traditional method in the Church, and was formulated *ex professo* by St. Augustine, precisely as the method for teaching the ignorant. This method was the only one known and used in the Church for centuries till the troubles of the Reformation came to introduce a most unfortunate change." [8] The narration method is adapted to the nature of the truths to be taught. Supernatural truths can neither be discovered nor fully comprehended by reason. The Supreme Founder of the Church ordained that revealed truths should be transmitted by witnesses whose testimony would be believed because they had seen and heard what they preached, and by messengers to whom He had promised the never-failing assistance of the Holy Spirit to preserve them from all error. The Church knows and always knew of only one way by which men can come into possession of divine truth – to receive

[8] "*The First Instruction of Children and Beginners*" (London, 1930), p. 25.

it from her, to acknowledge and believe it on her infallible authority.

But it is questionable whether the method should be used to the exclusion of those pedagogical devices and projects which are so admirably adapted to the child's nature and which appeal to his senses and stimulate his self-activity. Teachers know only too well that a continuous uninterrupted discourse will not hold the children's attention very long. Furthermore, the narration method should not be used as a means of disparaging the Catechism. The Catechism in its present form came providentially into vogue during the Protestant revolt when the Faith was threatened most and when Catholics began to feel the dire need of a more thorough religious instruction. The prevalence of error in our day demands a clear-cut presentation of Christian doctrine. The Catechism secures unity, thoroughness and purity of doctrine. In an historical presentation of faith it would be necessary in the end to formulate, after the manner of the Catechism, the doctrinal contents of Bible History.

CHAPTER VI

PRINCIPLES OF CHILD EDUCATION: BISHOP F. FÉNELON

Francis de Salignac de la Mothe Fénelon (1651–1715), celebrated French bishop and author, was eminently fitted both by nature and experience to discuss the religious education of children. By nature he was gifted with "the defiance, the disdain, the horror of common ideas." [1] For this reason he could break away from the artificial, pedantic educational ideas of his day.[2] At the same time he possessed great talent. At the age of twelve he was already proficient in Latin and Greek, and at the age of fifteen he preached a public sermon with remarkable success. Such ability was soon put to good use after his ordination. As a priest of the community of St. Sulpice, he preached and catechized for three years, and thus prepared himself to advise so pointedly on the religious education of children. Treating of Fénelon's early years, Cardinal F. L. de Bausset writes: "An invaluable advantage which Fénelon derived from the ecclesiastical ministry was . . . (the) prodigious and unbelievable facility which he acquired of speaking and writing with an exuberance which aroused the wonder and admiration of his contemporaries." [3]

At the age of twenty-seven Fénelon was appointed superior of the "Nouvelles Catholiques," an organization of women who were

[1] F. Brunetière, "Fénelon," in *La Grande Encyclopédie* (Paris), XVII, 174, col. 2.

[2] The wonderful and false pretence of knowledge so common in the seventeenth-century France was cleverly pictured in Moliére's comedies, *Les Precieuses Ridicules* and *Les Femmes Savantes*.

[3] *Histoire de Fénelon* (2nd ed., Paris, 1809), I, 46.

converted from Protestantism or who were still following the necessary preliminary instructions. For ten years Fénelon devoted himself to this task of religious education. While thus engaged in practical catechization, he composed his first important work, *Treatise on the Education of Girls.*[4] The treatise was written as a simple token of friendship for the Duchesse de Beauvilliers, who desired advice for the education of her eight daughters. It would seem Fénelon later allowed its publication only with reluctance.

A careful study of this treatise will go a long way towards giving us a clear picture of Fénelon as a catechist.[5] Within its thirteen chapters he has enclosed his general principles of pedagogy, valuable because so detailed. More than that, he has formulated very practical principles for the guidance of the teacher of Bible History and the Catechism. However, to extract from the work these general principles of pedagogy and special principles of catechetics, a task which we propose to undertake in the following pages, is not an easy matter. Bausset made the attempt and admits that "little by little, our extract had grown to be the entire work: we were made aware that it belongs to the small number of perfect books to which one can add nothing and from which one can deduct nothing without changing its spirit and exactness." [6] It is with a profound realization of the truth of this statement that the present work is undertaken.

General Principles

1. *The whole process of education is to be made as pleasant and agreeable for the child as possible.* "The way which I point out," says Fénelon, "however long it may seem, is the shortest, because it leads directly whither one wishes to go; the other way, which is that of fear, and of a superficial culture of minds, however short it may appear, is exceedingly long; for by it one hardly ever arrives at the true goal of education, which is to train minds and to inspire a sincere love of virtue." [7] With these words Fénelon indicates quite clearly the double purpose of education. The aim of education is not merely to develop the intellect, but also to form the will to virtue. How is this to be done? In such a way, says Fénelon, as will make education a pleasure.

[4] *De l'Education des Filles,* in *Œuvres de Fénelon* (Paris, 1843), II. All references and quotations are from this edition.

[5] Brunetière, *loc. cit.*, pp. 177–178. [6] *Op. cit.*, I, 67. [7] P. 512, col. II.

The idea that the process of learning must afford pleasure to the child is fundamental in Fénelon's pedagogy. "Notice," he says, "the great fault of ordinary education: men put all the pleasure on one side, and all the ennui on the other; all the tedium in study, all the pleasure in recreations. What can a child do, except impatiently endure this method, and run eagerly after games? Let us, then, try to change this order: let us make study agreeable; let us conceal it under the appearance of liberty and pleasure; let us allow the children sometimes to interrupt study with little outbursts of amusement; they have need of these distractions to relax their mind – then lead them quietly back to the point." [8] If the teacher has something distasteful to propose or demand, let the child understand that the task will soon be followed by something pleasurable. Let the pupil always see the utility and practical application of everything that we teach him.[9]

Fénelon demands that the lessons be as informal as possible. A teacher can insinuate countless other ideas besides the lesson itself, if he proceeds in a lively and cheerful manner. The children themselves will retain interest in subjects the teaching of which was accompanied by pleasurable experiences.[10] The learning process ceases to be a pleasure if too great an exactitude is required of the child. Frequently the teacher demands of the pupil a degree of seriousness, silence and bodily composure of which he himself would be incapable. He forgives children nothing and forgives himself everything. This naturally produces in the child a critical and hostile attitude. The ancients understood better the bright and overflowing nature of the child; it was by the diversion of verses and music that the principal sciences, axioms, virtues and elegance of manners were introduced among the Greeks and Egyptians.[11] Finally, intimidation should find little room in a correct system of education. A child who has to be threatened before he performs his duty is evidently finding little or no pleasure in the performance of that duty. If a child is asked to abide by a rule, he should see the convenience of doing so at that particular time and in that particular place.[12]

2. *The relation between teacher and child should be one of frankness, kindness and mutual confidence.* Fénelon demands of

[8] P. 484, col. II. [9] P. 482, col. I. [10] P. 484, col. I.
[11] P. 481, Col. II; p. 483, col. I. [12] P. 488, col. I.

the teacher a high degree of natural virtue. All the teacher's words must inspire the child with a love of truth and a hatred of dissimulation. The teacher must use no subterfuge in order to control the children or make them accept what he teaches. A teacher who is unkind, dishonest, deceitful in his relations with the children, and unwilling to trust them, can do an infinite amount of harm.[13]

In like manner there should be no austerity on the part of the teacher, no imperiousness, no rigorism, no excessive appeal to authority. The engendering of servile fear should be assiduously avoided. Fénelon's directions in this regard are pointed: "Never, except in extreme necessity, adopt an austere and imperious air, which makes the children tremble. Frequently this affectation is pedantry in those who govern; as far as the children are concerned, they are ordinarily but too timid and shy. You will seal up their heart, and take away from them that confidence without which no fruit can be expected of education. . . . Let them never fear to allow you to see their faults. To succeed in this, be indulgent to those who do not disguise themselves before you. Do not appear either astonished or irritated at their evil inclinations; on the contrary, sympathize with their weakness." [14] In fact, Fénelon counsels the teacher not to conceal his manifest personal failings but to try sincerely to correct them; he will thereby not only prevent contempt of his person but also edify the child and encourage him to correct his own faults.[15]

If confidence and reasonable persuasion are not strong enough, authority must make itself felt. Fénelon gives the following practical advice concerning the correction of the child: "Await the moment when the mind of the child will be disposed to profit by the correction. Never rebuke him, either in his first impulse or in yours. If you do it in yours, he notices that you act with ill-humor and haste, and not with reason and good-will; you lose your authority irretrievably. If you rebuke him in his first impulse, he has not a mind sufficiently free to acknowledge his fault, to overcome his passion, and to feel the importance of your advice; it is even exposing the child to the danger of losing due respect for you. Always show him that you exercise a perfect self-control; nothing will make him see it better than your patience. Wait for your chance, even for several days if it is necessary, in order to make a

[13] P. 478, col. II. [14] P. 482, col. II. [15] P. 482, col. I.

successful correction. Never reproach the child for a fault without indicating the means of overcoming it." [16] Punishment should be recurred to only in the last resort and should be characterized by those qualities which will sting the child with shame and remorse.[17]

3. *The instructor must make generous use of sense-subjects in order to appeal to the child's curiosity and imagination.* Whereas the two preceding principles had to do primarily with the child's will, the third principle is concerned principally with the intellect. It applies to the teacher as pedagogue and expounder of doctrine. It is based on the sound psychological principle that in our present state the proper object of the intellect is derived from concrete sensible things, that intellectual cognition depends upon concomitant sensible activity. Fénelon would say that we can do no better than follow nature. In the early years of the child's life impressions are of unusual intensity and often bear an important relation to his whole life. "One must hasten to write in their mind," says Fénelon, "while the characters easily form themselves therein. But one must choose carefully the images which he is to engrave there; for one must pour into a reservoir so small and so precious only choice things; one must remember that at this age one must pour into their minds only that which one wishes to remain during their whole life." [18] Coupled with this plasticity of the child's mind and heart is an unusual curiosity. The catechist should take advantage of this penchant of the child's nature and enrich his memory with noble impressions.[19] In short, whatever affords pleasure to the imagination, makes study easier. Hence, the books should be well-bound, even gilt-edged, with beautiful illustrations and letters well formed.[20]

Our facial expression and the very tone of our voice frequently influence a child's conduct. If the words of the catechist are accompanied by certain tones and gestures, they will easily incline children "to be with honest and virtuous persons whom they see, rather than with other senseless persons whom they may be in danger of liking; again, you can, by the different expressions of your countenance and by the tone of your voice, represent to them

[16] P. 483, col. II.
[17] P. 483, col. II.
[18] P. 480, col. II; cf. p. 477, col. II.
[19] P. 479, col. II; p. 481, col. I.
[20] P. 484, col. I.

with horror the people whom they have seen in anger or in some other misbehavior, and take the kindest tones with a face more serene to represent to them with admiration the good and modest things which they have seen." [21] Fénelon would strive to make the same impression upon children by means of sensible object-lessons or dialogues between two catechists.[22]

4. *The good example of the teacher and of other men is of prime importance: protect the child against bad example.* The substance of Fénelon's teaching on evil example is contained in the short fourth chapter of the *Treatise* and is entitled, "Imitation to be Feared." Children who as yet have acquired no bad habits and who are still ignorant easily tend to imitate whatever they see. Hence the importance of offering them only good models, especially in the person of their teachers. Bad examples, however, are inevitable; despite the precautions that one may take, children will see many things that are evil. One must, therefore, call their attention early to the contemptibility of certain vicious and senseless persons in whose character there is nothing respectable. One must show them how despicable and miserable is he who does not cultivate his reason but abandons himself to his passions. One must not hesitate to open their eyes to the faults and weaknesses even of persons whom they respect. In this way we can, without training them in irreverence, develop their taste and make them sensitive to true decorum. At the same time, we must teach them to bear one another's burdens, not to exaggerate the faults of their neighbor, and to appreciate the good which is in others.

Children frequently fall into bad habits through a playful mimicry of odd characters. Fénelon warns against this: "It is also necessary to keep them from mimicking strange people; for these mocking and comic manners have about them something low and contrary to good sense; it is to be feared lest the children acquire them, because the heat of their imagination and the suppleness of their body, coupled with their playfulness, make them easily assume all sorts of forms to represent that which they consider odd." [23] The most solid bulwark against the influence of bad example, according to Fénelon, is the mental attitude which appreciates the beauty of virtue and of virtuous people at the same time

[21] Pp. 477–478. [22] P. 480, col. II. [23] P. 480, col. I.

that it despises everything evil. If the child acquires a dull and somber idea of virtue, if license and irregularity present themselves to him in an agreeable form, all is lost and we labor in vain.

5. *Praise and rewards are to be given with discretion.* Fénelon has not much to say apropos of rewards and praise. He advises teachers not to promise clothes or dainties as rewards. This would bring about a two-fold evil: it would inspire them with an esteem for things which are, after all, secondary, and would deprive the teacher of the means of establishing other, more useful rewards. One can more profitably reward the children with certain games, which are innocent and accompanied with a certain amount of skill, by outings in which conversations may become very instructive, by small gifts which have the semblance of a prize, such as colored pictures, medals, books, etc.

Fénelon's advice concerning praise is no less pointed. One would run the risk of discouraging the children if one never praised them when they have done well. Since encomiums at times lead to vanity, we must use them in such a way as to stimulate the child without puffing him up. We must not only avoid all exaggeration and flattery but must also trace all good back to God as to its source.[24] Fénelon also devotes some space to particular types of children who cause endless trouble because of their abnormalities. We deem it sufficient for the purposes of this study merely to indicate these various types: the listless, backward child,[25] the hypocritical child,[26] the overpassionate child,[27] the child who lacks good will,[28] and the child with special idiosyncrasies.[29]

Special Principles: [30] *Bible History*

1. *Value of Bible History.* Fénelon's attitude towards Bible History is in harmony with all that he has said concerning the necessity of making the learning process pleasant, agreeable and interesting. To his mind, stories, especially Bible stories, are invaluable. Children are passionately fond of interesting stories. One can see them daily either transported with joy or shedding tears at the recital of adventures which appeal to them. The catechist should not fail to profit by this propensity of the child.

[24] P. 488, col. I. [25] P. 485, col. II–p. 487, col I. [26] P. 487, col. I.
[27] P. 487, col. II. [28] P. 478, col. I. [29] Pp. 501–505.
[30] Chapters VI–VIII.

The value of the story in religious education is attested to by God Himself. "God, who knows better than anyone else the mind which He has created, has consigned religion into well-known facts which, far from overburdening the simple folk, help them to understand and to retain the mysteries. For example, tell a child that in God three equal Persons are but one sole nature; by dint of hearing and repeating these terms, he will retain them in his memory, but I doubt that he perceives their meaning. Relate to him that, when Jesus Christ came forth from the waters of the Jordan, the Father caused this voice to be heard from heaven: 'This is My beloved Son in whom I am well pleased: hear ye Him,; add that the Holy Ghost descended upon the Saviour in the form of a dove; you make him find the Trinity in a sensible manner in a story which he will not forget. There you have three Persons whom he will always distinguish by the difference of their actions; you have only to teach him that altogether they make but one God. This example suffices to show the utility of stories; although they seem to lengthen the instruction, they abridge a good deal and take away from it the dryness of the Catechism where the mysteries are detached from facts. Also let us see that in olden times stories were used for purposes of instruction. The admirable manner in which St. Augustine wishes us to instruct all the ignorant, was not a method that this Father alone had introduced; it was the method and the universal practice of the Church. It consisted in showing, through the sequence of history, that religion is as old as the world, that Jesus Christ was expected in the Old Testament, and that Jesus Christ is reigning in the New; this is the foundation of Christian instruction."[31]

2. *Technique of Story-telling.* Here Fénelon's practical experience appears at its best. His observations are so minute as to leave no doubt that he practiced what he preached. Biblical stories, such as those of creation, the fall of Adam, the deluge, the call of Abraham, the sacrifice of Isaac, the adventures of Joseph, the birth and flight of Moses, not only arouse the child's curiosity but establish firmly in his mind the origins and foundations of religion. For it is through a series of historical facts that we trace the establishment and perpetuity of religion; it is in them that we find the truths to be believed and the precepts to be observed.[32]

[31] P. 489, col. II.

[32] P. 488, col. II; p. 489, col. I.

Fénelon's technique in the actual telling of stories is based on a keen psychology. The appeal must always be to the child's curiosity and imagination. Enliven your accounts, he tells the catechist, with brisk and familiar tones, paint glowing word-pictures of biblical events. Make all the personages speak; children who have a lively imagination will believe that they see and hear them. Tell, for example, the story of Joseph; make his brothers speak as brutal men; Jacob, as a tender and afflicted father. Let Joseph himself speak; let him take pleasure in being master of Egypt, in concealing himself from his brothers and then in disclosing himself. This naïve representation, coupled with the marvel of the story, will charm the child, provided that we do not burden him with too many similar narrations. Occasionally the teacher can put off to another day the telling of the sequel of the story, in order to hold the children in suspense and make them impatient to see the end. The teacher should not oblige the child to repeat the stories for fear of embarrassing the child and taking away from him all liking for these narrations. The catechist may, however, designate some person who will be free with the child and who will appear to wish to learn of him the story. The child will be delighted to repeat the story and thus gradually accustom himself to recitation and to accuracy.[33]

Where the catechist has a large class, he can train the children little by little to play the part of the personages of the stories. One can take the rôle of Abraham; the other, of Isaac, etc. These performances will charm them more than the other games, accustom them to think and say serious things with pleasure, and impress these stories indelibly upon their memories. Fénelon also advocates judicious questioning as to the children's individual opinion concerning the personages and events. He says: "It will not be useless to make the children pronounce upon the different characters of these holy people, in order to ascertain whom they like best. Some will prefer Esther, others Judith; this will stir up among them a little debate which will impress these stories more forcibly on their minds and develop their judgment."[34] Finally, pictures with strong colors and majestic figures will also leave a deep impression on the child's imagination.[35]

3. *The Bible and the Child.* To tell the children the stories of the

[33] P. 489, col. I. [34] P. 490, col. I. [35] P. 491, col. I.

Bible is not enough. They should also be trained to read intelligently the Sacred Books. To make the mysteries, the actions and the maxims of Jesus better understood, one must prepare young people to read the Gospels. One must train them early to read the word of Jesus Christ, just as one prepares them early to receive in Holy Communion the Body of Jesus Christ. The principal foundation of this training must be the authority of the Church, the Spouse of the Son of God and Mother of all the faithful. It is she to whom we must listen, because the Holy Spirit enlightens her to explain the Scriptures for us. She and she alone is the authentic interpreter of Scripture and the principal rule of faith and morals. We cannot go to Jesus Christ except through her.[36]

Special Principles: Catechism

Fénelon considers the following truths as fundamental in the Christian religion: (1) man is composed of a soul and body, the two being distinct; (2) the soul is more precious than the body. Fénelon devotes several pages to the method of imparting these truths to children. A natural sequel to these doctrines is the belief in the resurrection of the body. "I would try," he says, "to give them profound impressions concerning the resurrection of the body." And he immediately indicates some methods of inculcating this truth. "Teach them that nature is only a common order that God has established in His works, and that miracles are only exceptions to these general rules; that, accordingly, it does not cost God more to perform a hundred miracles than (it does) me to leave my room a quarter of an hour before my accustomed time. Then recall the story of the resurrection of Lazarus, then that of the resurrection of Jesus Christ, and His familiar appearances during forty days before so many persons. Finally show them it cannot be difficult for Him who has made men to remake them. Do not forget the comparison of the grain of wheat which one sows in the earth and which one causes to decay in order that it may revive and multiply."[37]

Although Fénelon accepts the traditional fourfold Catechism contents (Creed, Sacraments, Commandments, Prayer) as the matter of religious instruction, his ideal is a Christo-centric religion

[36] P. 495, col. II; p. 497, col. I.
[37] P. 495, col. I.

and life. The teacher must constantly place before the children Him who is the center of all religion, the "finisher of our faith," and our unique hope. The teacher must reform all the judgments and actions of the child after the example of Christ who took upon Himself our human nature in order to show us how to think, live and die. Teach the child to represent to himself what Christ would think and say of our conversations, of our amusements, and of our most serious occupations, were He still visibly among us. What would be our astonishment were He to appear suddenly in our midst, at a moment when we are profoundly forgetful of His law? Yet, it is just this which will happen to each one of us at death, and to the entire world when the secret hour of universal judgment will have come.[38]

In dealing with the Commandments Fénelon stresses the necessity of the internal element in the observance of God's law. Repeat often, he admonishes the catechist, that the letter kills, but that the spirit vivifies. God wishes to be honored not only by the lips but also by the heart. Not those who cry "Lord, Lord," will enter the kingdom of God, but those who possess genuine, inner sentiments of the love of God, of renunciation of earthly things, of self-denial and hatred for the world.[39]

Fénelon also demands a thorough initiation into the Liturgy of the Sacraments. The catechist should use the concrete sensible elements of the Sacraments as a stepping-stone to the spiritual and abstract. He should inspire the children with a desire to know the reason for the ceremonies and words which make up the Divine Office and the ritual of the Sacraments. The children should witness a Baptism, and be present at the consecration of the Holy Oils on Holy Thursday and at the blessing of the baptismal font on Holy Saturday. They should often be reminded of the promises and exorcisms of Baptism. To hear Mass properly the children should be told to unite themselves to Jesus Christ sacrificed for us and to apply His sacrificial spirit in their daily lives. Ceremonies and rubrics are not worship, but only an expression and stimulation of it. And what is true of Baptism and of the Mass is true also of the other Sacraments; through the visible things of sense the child should attain the invisible things of spirit and of grace.[40]

In fact, Fénelon demands that the catechist should always

[38] P. 498, Col. I. [39] U. 498, col. II. [40] P. 497, col. II; p. 499, col. I.

present abstract truths through the medium of sense objects or vivid word pictures. Fénelon exemplifies this principle in the lesson on creation: "One must show the children a house and accustom them to understand that this house did not build itself. The stones, you will tell them, were not raised without someone bringing them up. It is well, likewise, to show them the masons who are building; then make them look at the sky, the earth, and the principal things that God has made there for the use of man; tell them: 'See how much more beautiful and better made the world is than a house. Did it make itself? No, without doubt; it is God who has built it with His own hands.'"[41]

The reasoning powers of the child must be developed in accordance with his age and ability. The child must be convinced in his own way of the truth of the various Christian doctrines. Argumentation, if used excessively, is apt to arouse doubts in the child's mind, and hence must be employed with discretion. The best way of developing the child's reasoning power is the conversational question-and-answer method.[42]

Fénelon once more calls for sincerity on the part of the teacher. There is nothing so dangerous as to speak to the children of contempt for worldly things without at the same time making them see by every detail of our conduct that we are in earnest. Example has an unusual power over men at all stages of life. In the case of children it is all-powerful, since children are by nature imitators. For the same reason Fénelon warns the catechist most solemnly against jesting about religious things in the presence of the child.[43]

Finally, the catechist should enable the child to make a correlated synthesis, a sort of a philosophy of religion, of all his religious knowledge: "When the child will have made the reflections necessary for knowing himself and God, add (to them) the facts of history in which he has already been instructed; this melange will enable him to correlate in his mind all the doctrines of religion; he will notice with pleasure the relation between his own reflections and the history of the human race. He will have recognize that man has not made himself, that his soul is the image

[41] P. 491, col. II; for an illustration of the same principle in Fénelon's proof of the immortality of the soul, cf. p. 493, col. I.

[42] Cf. p. 492, col. II, where Fénelon illustrates this method in regard to the existence of the soul.

[43] P. 495, col. I-II.

of God, that his body has been fashioned with so many admirable powers by a divine industry and power; immediately he will recall the history of creation. Then he will consider that he is born with inclinations contrary to reason, that he is deceived by pleasure, swept away by passion, and that his body carries his soul against reason, as an impetuous horse carries away a rider, whereas it is his soul which should govern his body; he will perceive the cause of this disorder in the story of the sin of Adam; this story will make him await the Saviour, who is to reconcile men with God. Behold the whole groundwork of religion." [44]

Conclusion

In reading the *Treatise on the Education of Girls* one must bear in mind that it was originally intended for the Duchesse de Beauvilliers and her eight daughters. Fénelon seems to have before his mind's eye the private governess with one or a few children under her charge. The correct purpose of education is apparent throughout the entire *Treatise*. Religious instruction should not only train the mind but should also inflame the will; in fact it should transform the whole man. In appealing to the intellect one must follow the penchant of the child's nature; one must appeal to the child's senses, curiosity and impressionable nature. The old Scholastic axiom, "Nihil est in intellectu quod non prius fuerit in sensu," underlies Fénelon's entire scheme of education. For the proper development of the will, Fénelon requires a constant sincerity and good example on the part of the teacher, a sound application of the truths learned to the child's life, and a relation of mutual confidence and charity between pupil and teacher. The body, likewise, must be correctly developed. Although it must be trained to moderation from the very beginning, it should not be sacrificed to intellectual prowess and an excess of moral stability.

One may be inclined to ask whether all that Fénelon advocates is workable. His own record as an educator is, perhaps, the best recommendation of his principles. "The Duc de Beauvilliers, who had been the first to test in his own family the value of the *Traité de l'éducation des filles*, was in 1689 named governor of the grandchildren of Louis XIV. He hastened to secure Fénelon as tutor of the eldest of these princes, the Duke of Burgundy. It was a most

[44] P. 495, col. II.

important post, seeing that a formation of a future King of France lay in his hands; but it was not without great difficulties, owing to the violent, haughty, and passionate character of the pupil. . . . The results of this training were wonderful. The historian St. Simon, as a rule hostile to Fénelon, says: 'De cet abîme sortit un prince, affable, doux, modéré, humain, patient, humble, tout appliqué à ses devoirs.' "[45] No kinder testimonial could be given to Fénelon, no higher praise to his principles of child-education.

[45] A. Degert, "Fénelon," in *Catholic Encyclopedia*, VI, 36.

CHAPTER VII

THE METHOD OF ST. SULPICE: ABBÉ JACQUES OLIER AND BISHOP DUPANLOUP[1]

No one has contributed so effectually to the revival and spread of catechization in France as Abbé Jacques Olier, the disciple and friend of St. Vincent de Paul. The large parish of St. Sulpice in Paris, of which he took possession in 1642, was at that time the very sink of immorality (*l'égout de Paris*). It was reputed the most vicious parish, not only in the French capital, but in all Christendom. The enormity of the evils seemed to have killed all hope of reformation.

But Abbé Olier did not despair of the mercy of God. He set out to evangelize the parish, first of all, by means of Catechism classes, for the depravity of morals was quite equalled by the ignorance of religion. His aim was to help especially the young. Several Catechism classes were established at the Church of St. Sulpice itself and about twelve others in different parts of the parish. Each of these classes was in charge of two ecclesiastics from the seminary. The bread of truth was thus dispensed to about four thousand children. As a result of the priestly zeal of Abbé Olier and of his successors, the Faubourg St. Germain was gradually converted into a flourishing religious center.

The Catechism classes of St. Sulpice are to this day much as they were when founded by Abbé Olier and his venerable co-laborers.

[1] Cf. P. F. Lagrange, "*Life of Monseigneur Dupanloup*" (London, 1885); Charles E. de Vineau, "*Bishop Dupanloup's Philosophy of Education*" (Washington, 1929); Sister M. Albert Lenaway, "*Principles of Education according to Bishop Dupanloup*" (Washington, 1942).

The same rules, the same customs, consecrated by long experience, are still preserved. Their influence for good is not limited to the single parish of St. Sulpice but extends to a great number of parishes in different dioceses of France, and even of foreign countries. True, Catechism classes cannot be organized everywhere in the same manner; the locality, the efficiency of individual catechists and the aptitude of the children have to be taken into account. Again, the Sulpician Method was devised without any reference to parochial schools as known in the United States. But, if we disregard the accidental and accessory features of the method, we shall easily perceive that its essential and primary principles can be of perennial value to the teacher of religion.

The Method of St. Sulpice strives not merely to instruct children, but also, and above all, to touch and convert their hearts, to make them love God and Jesus Christ, to root out of their souls sins and to inspire them with a horror of evil and the love of good. This high ideal cannot be attained by a dry and cold instruction, no matter how thorough and solid it may be. The Method of St. Sulpice combines and emphasizes a few simple exercises which, as experience itself has amply shown, interest and delight the children and attach them strongly to their religion and to the Catechism. The principal exercises, the very foundation of the Catechism classes, are the recitation of the letter of the Catechism, the instruction, the reading of the Gospel and the homily. Besides these, there are certain secondary exercises, though quite as important as the first, namely, admonitions, singing of hymns and prayers. At the same time various rewards and attractions supply the *condiment* of the class, and maintain a spirit of emulation among the children.[2]

Recitation

After the children have sung two or three stanzas of a hymn, the repetition of the Catechism or the *questioning* begins. The catechist calls the child by his name and surname. The child immediately stands up, makes the sign of the cross, saying the words

[2] This exposition of the Method of St. Sulpice is based on the well-known translation from the French, "*Method of St. Sulpice*" (London, 1896); Bishop Dupanloup, "*The Ministry of Catechizing*" (New York); J. Bricout, *L'Enseignement du Catéchisme en France*" (Paris, 1922); P. Boumard, "*Formation de l'Enfant par le Catéchisme*" 2 vols. (Paris, 1927).

aloud, and answers the Catechism question. It is important to know the names of the children by heart, and pronounce them correctly. If the catechist mispronounces a name, his audience will begin to titter, and the child will feel mortified and acquire a dislike for the class. If a child has a queer or unusual name, it should not be called out openly; better to put a question to his neighbor and, when he has answered, simply say, "The next."

The questioning should be quick, lively and animated. The catechist, while he is questioning one child, must be prepared with the next question as well as with the name of the next child he intends to question. A child who has not answered well may be questioned a second time to see if he remembers the answer which another has given. A child may be asked again if he has been given a difficult question, such as only the most advanced could answer; this privilege granted to the most forward may lead the others to be more attentive, so that they in turn may deserve to be questioned oftener. If a child is conceited and answers well, he should immediately be given a question which he cannot answer and then be told that there are many things which he does not yet know. Shy children should not be discouraged by being blamed too sharply; it is well sometimes to give such a one a very simple question (one to which he has only to answer yes or no) and then immediately give him a word of praise.

In the Catechism classes of St. Sulpice three ways are employed to excite the emulation of the child during questioning.

1. *Praise.* An intelligent catechist can thus set up a sort of rivalry or opposition between the attentive and inattentive.

2. *Good marks.* The catechist announces the mark which each child has gained by his recitation and immediately writes it opposite his name on the list. Marks are also given for good behavior.

3. *Game of good points* (*jeu de bons points*). This exercise, approved by St. Francis de Sales, consists in proposing to one of the children, who has won nine or ten points, a series of short, clear and definite questions upon a mystery, a proof or some fundamental truth of religion which we wish to engrave on his mind and heart. The questions are put one after another to the child, according to his capacity, and in a lively, animated way, as if a kind of challenge. There results from this a sort of combat, in which sometimes a clever child is pressed almost further than he

can go. When the catechist knows how to keep up interest, all the audience may be seen taking part, their attention redoubled, holding their breath in the uncertainty of the victory. If a child succeeds, he receives the *bon point*, a holy card. Sometimes for the sake of variety the catechist can set up a sort of battle between several champions. For the success of the game *de bon point* it is important to prepare beforehand and to write down the questions which are to be put to the children. The catechist must at all times be master of himself and know how to vary the manner of proposing questions in order to avoid monotony. Above all, he must refrain from all idle and subtle questions, questions which might awaken in the child's mind a dangerous curiosity and doubts concerning his faith.

Instruction

In this exercise the catechist must fix the attention of the children – most of them very restless – on most serious subjects, both of dogma and morals. He must bring the most abstract truths and highest mysteries within the reach of these young and volatile minds and engrave them indelibly in their memory. Finally, he must make these truths dear to the children's heart and induce the children to take these great truths as the rule of their conduct. The catechist who would really instruct his audience must observe the following points:

1. *Brevity*. Lengthiness, vagueness and superfluous details generally come from a lack of preparation. "When the vine makes much wood," writes St. Francis de Sales, "then it bears less fruit." The mind of the children, says Fénelon, is like a vessel with a very narrow opening, which can only be filled drop by drop. "Believe me," says St. Francis de Sales to the Bishop of Belley, "I tell you this from experience, from long experience; the more you say, the less they will retain; the less you say, the more they will profit; by dint of burdening your hearers' memory, you break it down, just as lamps are extinguished if we put too much oil in them, or as plants are suffocated if we water them too much."

2. *Clearness*. To attain this essential quality, the catechist not only must prepare and grasp thoroughly what he intends to say, but he must be able to put himself in the place of his hearers. He must avoid figurative or confused expressions, big words, exagger-

ations, digressive phrases or parentheses, and all technical expressions. He should avoid all terms which convey nothing to the hearer, remembering that the children usually do not feel free to ask for explanation. Respect for the Word of God, on the other hand, forbids the catechist to employ jokes or slang or to use expressions grammatically incorrect.

3. *Method.* After recapitulating clearly and briefly the subject and divisions of the last instruction, the catechist should give out, with the same clearness and very slowly, the subject and divisions of the new instruction. The children themselves, moreover, must perceive the method and follow the catechist with the help of the division. Otherwise, the catechist will put a strain on the young intellects; they will try in vain to follow him and, finally, no longer knowing where they are or understanding what is said to them, lose interest altogether.

4. *Proofs.* It is not well to give a great many proofs, for such a procedure would confuse the children's mind. One or two — three at the most — are sufficient. The most indisputable proofs are those drawn from Sacred Scripture; when we use the sacred writings, it is God Himself who speaks. Next, the catechist may employ those furnished by the words and sayings of the Fathers, but he should choose those which are short, definite and forcible, as, for example: "He who made you without yourself, will not save you without yourself" (St. Augustine). Thirdly, a simple and strong proof from reason is sometimes effective.

In adducing arguments, we should make frequent use of *comparisons* and parables that appeal to the senses; the comparisons, however, should be brief, apposite and clear. However, we must not have too many comparisons; they should be so used that the listener is not aware of the art employed; finally, they should not all take one form. *Examples* drawn from Sacred Scripture, from the lives of the saints, from nature, and occasionally from profane history, likewise leave a profound impression on the child. Dialogues should not be introduced between the persons of the story, unless they are in the words of Sacred Scripture or unless they are quite probable.[3]

5. *Application.* An important way of gaining the children's attention, though too often forgotten, is to work on their emotions,

[3] Cf. Bricout, *op. cit.*, pp. 38 ff.

set these in motion, and turn them towards virtue and truth as readily as they are inclined to evil. The catechist must carefully watch his young audience, study their feelings and, if possible, read their very hearts, without the children, however, being aware of it.

The instruction itself may be given in two ways. First, it may be given as a continuous discourse. An inexperienced catechist ought not to make use of this method, because he will not be able to keep up the children's attention for any length of time; besides, since the children are not afraid of being questioned, many do not listen to what he says or make any effort to follow him. Secondly, the instruction may be given by way of frequent questions. The subject and the divisions of the instruction are given out and repeated by one of the children. Then the catechist gives the first part of the instruction with its proofs, and, when he has finished, he calls upon a few children to repeat the proofs. Then he passes on to the other parts, which also he is careful to have repeated. This plan is more successful, because it sustains the children's attention and makes them hear the instruction twice over without their suspecting it. But they must repeat the lesson in a lively and interesting manner, lest the class suffer through monotony.

The Gospel

The followers of the Sulpician Method watch for the first glimmer of the children's dawning reason in order to fix their thoughts on the Gospel and by the study of this sacred book to sanctify their earliest recollections. Accordingly, in all the Catechism classes of St. Sulpice the children are made to learn with care and repeat with great reverence the Gospel for the day, which serves also as the text and groundwork of the homily. In the older Catechism Classes of Perseverance, one of the four evangelists is sometimes chosen for each year and learned from one end to the other.

The principal object of the *homily* is to form the children's conscience and by earnest and vigorous words to excite the fear of God in these young souls. The homily turns on a single truth, which it brings into full light and sends all burning and glowing, like a dart, into the souls of the children. Its subject may be either the main point in the mystery which is celebrated on that particular day or the fact narrated in the Gospel. The personal application of the mystery must never be omitted, since the object of the homily is, above all, the moral conversion and improvement of the children. The fundamental truths, the last things, the great virtues and sins — these are the most frequent topics of the homily. The children are exhorted to avoid occasions of sin, to correct even their smallest faults and to root out their evil habits. Since all impressions, however strong, last but a short time with children, it is necessary to present the same truths under different forms and to recall them frequently.

Hymns (Cantiques)

Though a secondary exercise, the singing of hymns usually produces a deep impression upon the child's soul. A hymn well sung often does more for the conversion of children than the most fervent exhortation. Besides being a prayer, a hymn contains the two great means of religious training, namely, instruction and exhortation. Truths of faith, great moral precepts, motives for avoiding evil and doing good, are to be found on almost every page of a hymnal. At the same time the children also elicit different religious acts — acts of faith, hope, love, contrition and good resolve. Sacred singing has this additional advantage and value that in it every one instructs and exhorts himself, as St. Paul says (Col. 3:16), the words being helped by that powerful influence and charm which music exerts over the senses, imagination, feeling, in fact, over the whole being. "It was by the singing of hymns," says Bishop Dupanloup, "that I could do something even with the most hopeless child. . . . When we were uneasy about an entire Catechism class or First Communion, when the great work of converting all these young souls was not being accomplished according to our desires, we redoubled our zeal, not only in instructing and exhorting them, but also in making them sing the hymns well."[4] The children, needless to say, must be made to understand the hymns, see their beauty and feel their force and unction.

Prayer

One of the greatest services which a catechist can render to his children is to teach them prayer, properly so-called. If the children

[4] *Op. cit.*, p. 183.

pray well, they will never forget the holy truths of religion or lose the consciousness of God and of divine things. If they pray, though it be only imperfectly and without much fervor, they will always draw upon themselves some grace and favor from God. They may even grow careless and fall, but sooner or later they will return to the Lord's house and be saved. To attain these desirable results, the meaning of the ordinary as well as of the liturgical prayers must be explained to them, and they themselves must be asked to explain the meaning of every word. Only in this way will the children instruct themselves and respond to the devout feelings expressed in the prayers; their heart will follow their ears and tongue; they will enter into the spirit of prayer, and prayer itself will take possession of them.

Admonitions (Les Avis)

The few words spoken by the head catechist before or after prayer, at the beginning of the Catechism class, after the instruction, or at the end of the Catechism, are known as the "admonitions." These admonitions often turn on the Catechism itself; then, going on, on the faults and virtues of children, on the most essential practices of the Christian life, on the duties of children to parents. It is in these admonitions that children are congratulated on their progress and industry, or reproved for their giddiness, idleness, absences, etc. This is also the time for proposing to them little cases of conscience, suggested by what one has heard about the children during the week. These admonitions must be well prepared and to a certain extent arranged according to a plan drawn up beforehand so that nothing essential may be omitted. In an admonition, as in every other discourse, there is one chief and essential point on which depends the desired result. Frequent and almost always unexpected, coming each time at the opportune moment, carried straight to those whom they concern, the admonitions have an unusual power for direction and correction. They are extremely difficult to give well and demand a rare tact, for there is question of striking a sure blow, of conquering such and such a difficulty, of making an attack on the innermost soul. It is like a hand-to-hand fight or duel with evil, so necessary is it to strike home, sometimes even to pierce deeply.

"Condiment" of the Catechism Class

In order that the purpose of the Catechism class may be fully attained, there is need of something which will give to its lessons and exercises a sort of taste or aroma, something that will penetrate and animate them and make them lived and enjoyed by the pupils. Children are very susceptible of pleasant impressions, of everything that is lovable and charming. Thanks to their bright and overflowing nature, it is easy to touch their hearts and imaginations. If their first impression of the Catechism class is one of weariness and dislike, they may acquire a secret and even insurmountable aversion to religion. It would, consequently, be a mistake and want of skill to present Christian Doctrine to them in a dry, cold and austere manner. The means employed by the Method of St. Sulpice to make catechization attractive are the following:

1. *Rewards.* Rewards serve to win the hearts of the children and excite them to do well. Only offer them prizes (devotional pictures, books, medals, etc.), and the task is changed into a pleasant and agreeable occupation. The answers by which the children have gained rewards remain deeply engraved in their memory. St. Francis de Sales considered rewards so important for the success of the Catechism class that he was accustomed to carry little gifts in his pockets. St. Robert Bellarmine used also to try to interest the children by the attraction of rewards.

2. *Fêtes.* The feasts celebrated in a special manner by the Catechism classes are those of the Birth of Our Lord, Holy Family, All Saints, Immaculate Conception, and the children's saints. These festivals break the monotonous uniformity of the classes and by their novelty excite the longing and curiosity of the children. When the day arrives, the church and altar are decorated in such a way as to charm the child and produce pleasant impressions upon him. On such occasions one of the following exercises takes place:

a. *Billets* are read and explained. These *billets* — the admirable invention of the great catechist, Père Romillon — are short Christian reflections in the form of question and answer, relating to the character, history and object of the festival. They are recited by children distinguished for their industry and good behavior (sometimes dressed as angels bearing a message from heaven). They are afterwards briefly explained by one of the priests, and moral conclusions and practical resolutions are drawn from them. The *billets* are brief and precise, compiled and rehearsed with great care, and not more than six are recited on the same day.[5]

b. *Dialogues.* This exercise, which particularly interests the children, turns on a subject of devotion, dogma or morals. In it the children themselves express what they think concerning certain subjects or explain what they admire most about the character or virtue of a saint.

c. *Conferences.* This exercise consists in treating a religious subject in the form of objections and answers between two catechists. To remove all danger of confusing the audience, nothing is discussed in the controversy which is not agreed upon beforehand. So too, nothing is said that would be inconsistent with the reverence due to the Word of God. The questions must not be too subtle nor the objections more easy to remember than the answer. The objections bear not on the truth itself but on doubtful points which need explanation.

Emulation

The young hearts of children are particularly sensitive to emulation. Love of self is a disposition quite as natural to children as to older people; in both cases it is from it that jealousy springs. This inclination, if skillfully guided, can be changed into a remedy against the natural carelessness and indolence of children. St. Jerome, in a letter on the education of a young child, recommends that she have companions who will excite her jealousy, whose successes will be to her like goads, piercing her to the quick.[6] But, as Fénelon says, we must animate the children without intoxicating them, being always careful to sanctify their motives.

1. *Dignitaries of the Catechism Class.* In every Catechism class there are various dignitaries (prefects), chosen from among the older children, who are entrusted with special duties, enjoy certain privileges and occupy places of honor in the class. This excites the emulation of the children and makes them ambitious of the same.

[5] The catechist puts the question to the children; they answer by reading the *billet.*

[6] *"Ad Gaudentium de Pacatulæ infantulæ educatione."*

The parents themselves feel greatly flattered when their children are raised to some office. However, no children are chosen for these honors who absent themselves from the Catechism class or who come late; nor those who do not know their Catechism lessons or who answer imperfectly; nor those who are giddy or rude, who talk to those next to them or make them talk; nor, finally, those who give any cause for complaint to their parents or teachers, because all such children will give bad example to the others instead of edifying them. The dignitaries are not chosen permanently but are periodically changed; this again is another way of exciting emulation.

2. *Analyses.* An analysis is the written account of the instruction, compiled and prepared by the child from notes taken during the instruction. It is also called a *diligence,* because the labor it entails is a most certain test of the diligence of the children and of their zeal for the Catechism. Children who are engrossed in taking notes are necessarily attentive in class and regular in their attendance. The direct and personal coöperation of the child in his own religious formation is thus also enlisted. A pupil who prepares his analysis is deeply impressed by his subject, and, if the analysis is made (for instance) concerning the avoidance of some fault, he will be angry with an indignation which is truly in his own soul. The analyses are always concluded by a resolution and a prayer: a resolution, defective though it may be at first, which the child draws out from his very self, and a prayer, though for a long time it be only the lisping of the soul, which is not only on his lips but comes from his heart. In this way the child is initiated into the most serious work of the Christian life, and the great secret of the spiritual life begins revealing itself to him.

Seals of different shapes and colors, impressed on the first page of these analyses, show the different degrees of merit. The grand seal, the seal of honor, is given to the analysis which seems best in every way. Care is to be taken lest the children copy from other books or have the parents dictate the diligences to them. The catechist should always correct the analyses in order to see if the children have misunderstood him on some point.

3. *Distribution of Pictures.* About five or six times a year pictures are distributed to the best-behaved children. Before the distribution, the catechist examines the subjects represented in the pictures

so as to be able to explain them to the children and draw moral application from them.

4. *Solemn Distribution of Prizes.* This takes place every year in all the Catechism classes and is without doubt the best way to awaken the zeal of the children and excite their emulation. This distribution should be surrounded with a good deal of ceremony. Those who have not won a prize ought to receive some beautiful image, with the seal of the class, as a remembrance. For all ought to go from such a meeting happy, contented and encouraged for the coming year.

5. *Visits of the Pastor.* The pastor, if he does not personally undertake the charge of the parish Catechism classes, occasionally holds a visitation of them. The children are told that the pastor upon questioning will be informed who are well-behaved and industrious, so that he may think well of them and prepare for them suitable rewards.

6. *Punishments* are used rarely and with discretion. The children should be convinced that we are sorry to punish them, that we only do it for their greater good and because we dearly love them.

Divisions of the Catechism Classes

1. The Method of St. Sulpice has adopted the following division of the Catechism class, based on the difference in age, circumstances and needs of the children:

a. *The Little Catechism.* The "little Catechism" class is intended for children from six or seven to ten years of age. Its contents consists principally of Bible History and the life of Our Lord.

b. *The More Advanced Catechism.* Children are not admitted to this Catechism class until they are ten years old. Thereafter the children are initiated into the Catechism class according to all the detailed regulations of the Method of St. Sulpice.

c. *Week-Day Catechism.* This Catechism class is held on two days of the week for about three months.[7]

d. *Catechism Class of Perseverance.* The purpose of this class is to ensure the perseverence of children, to give them a more extended knowledge of Christian Doctrine and to inspire them with a sincere and lasting love of virtue. The more likely they are to

[7] Cf. Boumard, *op. cit.*, pp. 141 ff.; Bricout, *op. cit.*, pp. 62 ff.

lose the grace of God in the midst of worldly dissipations and bad examples, the more important it is to strengthen them in those good habits in which they were trained at a more tender age. Public instruction and exercises cannot satisfactorily attain this end; being intended for all, they do not contain anything which pertains to the vital problems of young boys and girls. In the Catechism Class of Perseverance the course usually extends over three years. This time is deemed sufficient, it being supposed that there are thirty meetings each year, independently of the summer months and of the festivals. The first year is devoted to the exposition of dogma; the second, to morals; the third, to the Sacraments and to all that concerns public worship. The Catechism Class of Perseverance also fosters frequent Communions and frequent retreats.[8]

2. The *place* of the Catechism class, it might be noted in this connection, receives special consideration in the Method of St. Sulpice. The school of Jesus Christ, where the secrets of eternal life are revealed to the children, must be suitable for its purpose. If, failing a proper place in the parish church, the class is to be held in a sacristy, in some large room at the presbytery, at a school, or elsewhere, the place must be adapted to the sacredness of the work to be accomplished there. It must be transformed, at least for the time of the class, into a chapel. The image of Our Lord, the crucifix, the images of the Blessed Virgin and of the saints, must beautify and adorn it. As far as possible, there should also be a small, suitably prepared altar, a statue, hangings, etc. These objects help to fix the child's attention during prayer and check his restlessness. If, on the other hand, the children sit on the same chairs or at the same desks where a little while before they went through a lesson which wearied or vexed them or where they received a rebuke, they are apt to become as antagonistic to religious instructions as to the other classes.

3. Finally, the Method of St. Sulpice demands that the catechist, who would labor profitably for the sanctification of children, be endowed with the following virtues:

a. *Gentleness and love for the children.* He must avoid both weakness and harshness. It is not by force, but by kind suasion and

[8] Cf. Msgr. Gaume, "*Catéchisme de Perseverance*" (10th ed., Paris, 1872; Engl. tr., Dublin).

fatherly tenderness, that he will win the child's heart and draw him to Jesus Christ.

b. *Zeal for the salvation of children.* The catechist must love his children with a love which is pure and supernatural and which leads him to devote himself to the instruction solely on account of their salvation. With the weak he becomes weak; he makes himself all things to all men, that he may gain all. It is only by being animated with true zeal that he will be able to make a stand against all sin, repress all disorder and enforce the observance of all commandments.

c. *Spirit of piety and prayer.* The zeal of which we just spoke can be attained only by fervor, union with God and entire dependence on grace. Nothing but a sound, enlightened, generous and constant piety can touch and convert the children and supply those holy exhortations which are necessary for forming them in a virtue. Burning words cannot come from a frozen heart.

4. The Method of St. Sulpice is better adapted to summer vacation schools and Catechism classes than to religion periods in a parochial school. The Method recommends itself because of the variety of its subject-matter and the manifold self-activity which it demands on the part of the child. By its insistence on the careful learning and reverent repetition of the Sunday Gospel, it gradually acquaints the child with New Testament Bible History. The celebration of the festivals and the practice of the *billets* initiate the child into the liturgical year. The *Arbeitsprinzip* (work principle) is applied in the game of good points (*bons points*), the taking of notes during the class, the analysis, *billets,* dialogues, etc. The result of all these factors is the sustained interest of the child at religious instruction.

The heart of the child is unusually plastic and receptive towards every noble feeling. Whatever is implanted in the child's mind at an early age takes deep root and becomes a permanent acquisition. Men rarely lose the first impressions received in childhood. In no department of education is this verified to such an extent as in that of religious training. If religious instructions have vexed and wearied the child, if he has formed a sad and somber idea of virtue, he will likely bear a secret aversion to religion during his whole lifetime and even incline to unbelief. If religion seemed to him a mere formality or a hard law, if he applied himself to it from necessity and not from love and joyous enthusiasm, the labors of the teacher will be to a great extent in vain. If he finds weariness in study and pleasure in his games, is it to be wondered that he submits impatiently to the one and runs eagerly after the other? The Method of St. Sulpice, although it seems to exaggerate the use of rewards and prizes and, consequently, is in danger of introducing a wrong motive, has nevertheless accomplished a good deal in forestalling such undesirable consequences. In attempting to make catechization attractive, it avails itself of all the natural inclinations of childhood (even of its faults), and tries to bring them into the service of the good and true.

CHAPTER VIII

THE PSYCHOLOGICAL OR STIEGLITZ METHOD

The psychological method in catechetics is fostered in a special manner by a group of experienced catechists in southern Germany, who, dissatisfied with the hitherto superficial procedure on the part of the catechist, the difficult and abstract language of most catechisms, and the wrong order of presentation, struck out in this relatively new direction. The method is known as the "Stieglitz Method" from its chief exponent, or as the "Munich Method" because it originated among the members of the Society of Catechists of Munich. The monthly organ of this Society, the *Katechetische Blätter,* became the best exponent of this system.

Fundamental Principles

The Munich Method considers the following principles as basic:

1. The supernatural does not destroy but is based upon nature: hence correct catechetical methods cannot be opposed to the pedagogic rules established for profane science. However, since he deals with mysteries and the supernatural order, the catechist must also rely on the virtue of faith and the assistance of divine grace.

2. By reason of the substantial union of body and soul, intellectual cognition depends upon concomitant sensible activity: *Nihil est in intellectu quod non prius fuerit in sensu.*[1] In our present state the proper object of the intellect is derived from sensible material objects. A good method, therefore, as Aristotle already remarked,

[1] St. Thomas, *Summa Theologica,* Ia, q. lxxx, art. 1.

proceeds from the known to the unknown, from the concrete to the abstract.[2]

3. A child does not grasp an object at first intuitively or integrally but only in its external outlines, not in one act but only gradually. First there is apprehension, then understanding or conviction, and finally practice.[3] These three stages of learning presuppose three corresponding teaching modes: presentation, explanation and application.

4. Every conscious and deliberate act implies the coöperation – more or less intense – of the sense, imaginative, intellectual, volitional, emotional and bodily faculties of the child. The Munich Method, as will be shown presently, gives due consideration to all of these.

Planning the Lesson

The Munich Method demands that each religion lesson should constitute a methodical *catechetical unit* – that is, revolve around one theme. A catechetical unit is determined not by time but by internal reasons. It demands that everything that is intrinsic to a doctrine should be associated, correlated and treated in connection with it. This procedure will aid the child's understanding of a doctrine and exercise a more profound influence upon his life.

A catechetical unit does not mean that only one catechismal question should be made the subject of a lesson. It is possible that two different topics may be taught in one period, but they are clearly differentiated, and the lesson comprises in reality two catechizations. Conversely, the treatment of one topic may extend over two consecutive periods. Secondly, catechetical units are not independent units but must all be referred to, and correlated with, Christ, the center of our salvation; in other words, catechization must be *Christocentric*. Thirdly, catechetical units are not all of the same and equal importance, to be treated perfunctorily one after another; for it is obvious that prayer, contrition for sins, and reception of the Sacraments influence the Christian life more profoundly than certain other doctrines.

[2] *Physica*, lib. I, cap. 7; *Metaphysica*, lib. I, cap. 2.

[3] Cf. M. Gatterer, *Katechetik* (Innsbruck, 1924), pp. 195–197. This chapter follows the outline of the Munich Method as found in Fr. Gatterer's treatise.

Two Preliminary Steps in the Lesson

1. The *preparation (Vorbereitung)* requires that the catechist show the connection between the new subject matter and information previously received. Association of new images with those latent in the child's mind is always an important part of the learning process. The catechist must always proceed to the unknown by means of the known. Hence, a brief repetition or review of knowledge previously acquired should preface the new lesson.

2. Indication of the *aim (Zielangabe)* immediately follows this introduction. In order to arouse the child's interest and attention from the very beginning, to awaken in him a desire for instruction, the subject should be announced in a clear, distinct and captivating manner. This goal, says Stieglitz,[4] is like a star which will lead the child to the promised land.

First Essential Stage: Presentation (Darbietung)[5]

In presenting the new doctrine to the pupil the teacher must pay special attention to the following points:

1. *Perspicuity (Anschaulichkeit).*[6] The psychological principle that all intellectual cognition – especially in the case of a child – depends upon concomitant sensible activity must be all the more taken into consideration when the mind is to gain knowledge of entirely spiritual objects. Hence the catechist's exposition must be such that the children see, if not with their eyes, at least in their imagination, that which the teacher expounds. Perspicuity may be obtained by showing the *things themselves* (liturgical objects), by exhibiting *copies of things* (maps, colored and dignified pictures). Recourse may also be had to *projects* and drawing (crib, altar, symbols, diagrams, sketches). Finally, explanations are more

[4] *Ausgeführte Katechesen über die katholische glaubenslehre* (11th ed., Munich, 1922).

[5] Cf. Wolff-Habrich, *Die Volksschulunterricht* (Freiburg im B., 1917), p. 41; H. Schmitz, *Die religiöse Unterweisung der Jugend* (Cologne, 1920), p. 30; G. Grunwald, *Philosophische Padagogik* (Paderborn, 1917), p. 129; A. Weber, *Die Munchener* Methode (Munich, 1905).

[6] Cf. M. Gatterer, *op. cit.*, p. 160; F. Krus, *Pedagogische Grundfragen* (2nd ed.; Innsbruck, 1920), p. 321; J. B. Hartman, *Anschaulichkeit in Religionsunterricht* (Munich, 1907); L. Nolle, "Sense of Sight in Religious Education", in *Catholic Educational Review* (1914), p. 406, "The Sense of Hearing in Religious Education", *ibid.* (1915), p. 26.

readily grasped when written on the *blackboard* with the important words underscored.

2. *Language* (throughout instruction). As means of visualizing abstract religious truths the Munich Method has frequent recourse to historical materials. These historical narratives are drawn from Holy Writ, which is energized in a special manner by the grace of God; from the history of the Church, of the saints and of Christian life in general. Profane history is used only in so far as it can be made a hand-maid of faith. Imaginary and fairy tales are avoided as apt eventually to jeopardize the teacher's authority. The stories should not be surcharged with details nor too long, lest the child miss the main point. In the use of language the catechist must neither overrate nor underestimate the child's intellectual ability. Unintelligible verbose formulae will become inoperative memory loads and soon expelled. Incomplete presentation of a truth gives rise to erroneous notions. The sublime character of the truths which he is imparting forbid the catechist to use slang, colloquial, grammatically incorrect and undignified expressions. The simplest method of acquiring an appropriate language is to read good catechetical books and commentaries.

3. *Questioning* (throughout instruction). The catechist may use questioning throughout the instruction, always aiming at one or several of the following objectives: to counteract the passivity of the pupils; to arouse their attention; to stimulate them to personal activity; to ascertain if he has been understood; to make them humble and ready to learn, after acknowledging their ignorance; to recapitulate the lesson after it has been fully explained; to draw out certain religious and moral truths. However, it is well to keep in mind that the Apostles and their successors were sent to preach and to announce authoritatively Christ's doctrine, and that faith, consequently, comes by hearing, not by questioning.

In questioning the catechist should observe the following rules: he should in time interrogate all pupils, both the bright and the dull; the more difficult questions may be reserved for the brighter pupils in order to stimulate their zeal; the question should be addressed to the whole class, and then, after all have had time to think, let one child be called upon; the catechist must at all times avoid questions which might awaken doubt in the child's mind concerning his faith.

The Second Essential Stage: Explanation (Erklärung)

Catechists of the old school were wont to follow the *analytic method*: The catechist read, or had some one read, the Catechism text, resolved it into its component parts, explained and analyzed each in succession and then combined the parts into a whole. The followers of the Munich Method follow the *synthetic method*: from the interesting, concrete story set before the child in the Presentation they proceed to deduce the abstract elements of the doctrine and, by combining these in a final summing up, obtain substantially the answer of the Catechism. Finally, the Catechism text is read and its wording and phrasing explained.

With the younger children the authority of the priest or teacher and the words of the Catechism carry complete conviction. The maturer children, however, should be given proofs. The Catechism answer is an abstract and brief summary of facts drawn from the teachings of the Church, Holy Writ, Tradition and the Liturgy. The catechist must supply these divine arguments which the Catechism in its brevity cannot offer. The catechist must always keep in mind that the proofs drawn from the divine deposit are primary and essential; those from reason, only secondary. The first are the objects of faith; the second pave the way for faith and shield it against the attacks of atheists and heretics. The second must never be substituted for the first; the argument from the life and death of Christ, for example, is a far more powerful argument for the immortality of the soul than the most subtle discussion of the soul's simplicity and spirituality.

The Third Essential Stage: Application (Anwendung)

Children learn for life and not for school. Hence the Christian doctrines must become the abiding, permanent possession of their mind and heart.

1. The truth must be impressed, first of all, upon the *mind*. This may be done in the following ways:

a. *By memorizing.* Children should memorize the Catechism answers only after the matter has been thoroughly explained; memorizing thus properly becomes the finishing touch rather than the initial step in the catechization process; the Catechism text should be memorized literally and correctly, because infallible and immutable truths demand an accurate and definite expression.

b. *By reviewing.* The last five or ten minutes of an instruction may be devoted to a short review of what was learned in the lesson. This review may include not only the explanation but also the examples and application. The catechist should encourage the pupils to explain in their own words how they understood the doctrine and how they would practice it. The answers of the children will show how well the catechist has explained the doctrine in question.

c. *By immanent recapitulation.* One may review at the same time not only the subject but also the doctrines and practices correlated with it.

d. *By examinations.* In the case of well-trained Catholic children, examinations are of great value. But they also have their drawbacks. The principal thing in religion is a life in accordance with revealed truth.

2. The divine truth must above all be impressed upon the child's *heart* and made vital and operative in his daily life and conduct. It is well to remember that increase in knowledge does not necessarily imply progress in virtue. Intellectual culture in itself does not mean civilization, nor does morality go hand in hand with intellectual advancement. The training power of mere knowledge is very limited. Revelation has been vouchsafed us, not merely for the greater illumination of our understanding, but above all for the uplifting and complete conversion of our hearts. Revealed truth was communicated to us with a divine purpose, namely, the salvation of souls. In other words, religion is not a mere *formula;* it is *life.*

Hence the catechist should constantly apply all Christian truth to the concrete occurrences of the child's everyday life and draw from it practical consequences suited to the age of the child. Just as the application of the rules of grammar and syntax develop proficiency in a language, so also the constant application of supernatural truths and rules intensifies the Christian life. The application should follow naturally from the doctrine and not be dragged in by force. It should refer not only to the present but also to the later life of the child. Important applications should be repeated on different occasions and in different ways until the child's conscience becomes responsive to the doctrine in question (prayer, contrition, commandments, etc.). The catechist must use discretion in the selection of applications. He should guard against an accumulation of resolutions; saints are not made in a day. It would be better to choose one virtue and over a period of days and even weeks impress it deeply on the child's heart.

3. In this process of moral transformation the catechist should carefully develop the child's faith. He should remember that there is in the child an infused supernatural disposition inclining the child to assent to supernatural truths and that this infused virtue, like the natural faculty of reason, should grow in a threefold manner: in extent, in intensity, and in time. Secondly, he should base the child's faith on God's word, on God's authority, on the testimony of the Church. The Church knows only one way by which men come into possession of supernatural truth: to receive it from her and believe it on her infallible authority. In conformity with this principle many Catechisms of the Middle Ages assigned the question to the child and the answer to the teacher. Hence the catechist must plainly tell the children that he is a messenger of God and point out how the teaching authority descends from Our Lord to the Apostles, bishops, priests, lay teachers. Finally, he must carefully avoid anything that would arouse doubts in the child's mind; excessive and inappropriate questioning, subtle and abstract distinctions beyond the child's grasp, a constant endeavour to prove everything – all these may do more harm than good. Let the catechist – without being antagonistic – explain simply and clearly the objections which a child is apt to meet; the mists of error will be dissipated by the light of truth.

4. The catechist must have a great reliance on *prayer*. Since the means must be proportioned to the end, man's natural faculties of intellect and will cannot elicit a supernatural act unless they are first elevated to the supernatural order by grace. Children cannot make an act of faith or observe the Commandments without the help of grace. The Catechism lesson is an occupation on which depends the salvation of many precious souls fashioned after God's image and redeemed by the precious Blood of Christ. Such a task surely demands the assistance of the Holy Spirit [7] and should always be preceded by a fervent prayer.

5. The catechist's *personal fervor* also plays an important role. If the teacher remains cold in the presence of the truths and facts of faith, the instruction will become dry and uninteresting. One can

[7] Cf. J. Rutché, *Saint Esprit et l' Éducation* (Paris, 1928).

hardly expect great fervor on the part of pupils when they see their teacher indifferent. Children instinctively doubt the reality of something treated in a perfunctory manner. If, on the other hand the catechist's heart is gripped by enthusiasm for the ideals of religion, this inward fire will soon become manifest and inspire the hearts of the children.

6. Exponents of the Munich Method warn the catechist against the excessive use of *natural or utility motive*, the endeavour, namely, to cultivate morality in the children by pointing out to them the temporal benefits or evils consequent upon a given action. Such training eventually develops astute egoists who will not shrink from duplicity and injustice. It turns the impressionable heart of the child from God and centers it on a debasing selfishness. Worldly calculations often miscarry. Men who serve God only for earthly rewards will in time of misfortune and hardships become disappointed, revolt against God and lose their faith. Temporal advantages accruing from the practice of virtue, and the evils consequent upon sin, should be mentioned only as secondary factors. They should be regarded as partial rewards and punishments preliminary to the full retribution of eternity. It should always be made clear that even if virtue is not rewarded and evil punished in this life, they most certainly will be in the next life. These principles should be kept in mind especially when instructing the children concerning the Fourth and Sixth commandments.

All catechization should aim at making the children understand how much God loves them and desires in turn to be loved by them. A pure and stainless heart is more easily influenced by a feeling of love than by any consideration of eternal damnation. Since self conceit and pride are the great obstacles to divine love, the catechist must at an early date strive to cultivate humility in his children by recalling to their minds the examples of abnegation and humility of the Saviour. A simple explanation of the Incarnation and Redemption will spontaneously draw the hearts of the children to the Saviour.[8]

[8] For an exemplification of the Psychological Method in catechismal instructions, consult J. J. Baierl, *The Creed Explained* (Rochester, 1919), *The Commandments Explained* (Rochester, 1920), *The Sacraments Explained* (Rochester, 1921), *Grace and Prayer Explained* (Rochester, 1921); J. Bern-

An Appreciation

The Munich Method has gained numerous followers, not only in Germany and Austria, but all over the Catholic world. The good results which it has brought about cannot be overestimated. Inquiries into present conditions have been stimulated, widespread interest in catechetical work has been aroused, and a general demand for better-trained catechists — teachers capable of developing the mind as well as forming the heart — has arisen. Owing to the Munich Method, Catechisms are being revised according to the accepted laws of pedagogy. Kinkead's series of Baltimore Catechisms, for example, seems to be influenced by the principles of the Munich Method. Fr. Yorke's textbooks of religion are likewise an application of the principles of the Munich Method to the teaching of the Catechism; the child is led by a story, explanation and picture to the abstract catechismal formula, which is then memorized.

In so far as it is based on well-known and firmly established psychological principles, the Munich Method is unimpeachable. And why, after all, should religious training follow its own individual way and not profit by the latest profane didactic methods? We readily grant that the doctrines of Jesus Christ and profane learning cannot be placed on the same level, and that the religious teacher, while making use of profane didactic means, must also rely on the assistance of divine grace. But it is also true that grace does not destroy nature and that, consequently, correct catechetical methods cannot be opposed to the didactic rules established for profane science. Now, in what manner is religious instruction often imparted to our children? Frequently, it is a mere process of

---

beck, *Katechetische Skizzen* (Munich, 1909); K. Buhlmayer, *Ausgeführte Katechesen für das erste Schuljahr der katholischen Volksschule* (3rd ed.: Munich, 1922), *Ausgeführte Katechesen für das zweite Schuljahr* (2nd ed.; Munich, 1923); H. Steiglitz, *Ausgeführte Katechesen über die katholische Glaubenslehre* (11th ed.; Munich, 1923), *Ausgeführte Katechesen über die katholische Sittenlehre* (10th ed.; Munich, 1922); *Ausgeführte Katechesen über die katholische Gnadenlehre*, 2 vols. (8th ed.; Munich, 1922). A series of lessons according to the Munich Method on Bible History will be found in A. Urban, *Teacher's Handbook to Bible History* (New York, 1905); K. Raab, *Der Weg Gottes*, 2 vols. (Donauworth, 1924). For Church History, consult K. Buhlmayer, *Ausgeführte Katechesen über katholische Kirchengeschichte* (Munich, 1925).

cramming the memory and of a scrupulously accurate reproduction of verbose and abstract formulas, which the children can hardly pronounce, much less comprehend. Many children repeat answers of the Catechism in the same glib and thoughtless way as the altar boy recites the *Confiteor* and strikes his breast. Their hearts and wills are left as cold and untouched by these daily intellectual drills as by the multiplication table. Nay, the worst rascals often give the best answers in Catechism. Frequently these exercises of verbal memory, instead of developing in the child the right Catholic instinct, end in making religion itself an insufferable bore. The abstract forms, instead of promoting growth, turn out to be non-functional memory loads and dead accumulations which paralyze and crush the mind. Would any one try to make adults believe that they can grasp the sense of a statement, not by an exercise of reason or understanding, but by an exercise of memory? "The child will retain the words," it is said, "and later, as his intelligence matures, he will realize the force of them." One might as well feed a piece of solid food to a mere infant, and say that when he grows up, he will digest it.

We would not for a moment wish to imply that modern theorists were the first to recognize and apply the psychological principles of education and that catechetics should be brought into exact line with the teaching of secular subjects. The truth is that educators are coming to adopt the principles of a method which, not only the Catholic Church, but Christ Himself followed. In fact, nothing is more surprising than, for example, the frequency with which Christ prepares His hearers by a parable for the literal statement of a sublime truth. Christ could have proclaimed His doctrine in exclusively literal terms, or in formulas more precise than the most technical language ever used by a theologian. But no! He usually introduces His hearers to a profound spiritual lesson or truth by means of a parable, which He draws from the facts of nature or from ordinary human experience. To the lawyer's literal inquiry, "Who is my neighbor?" (Luke 10:29) He answers with a parable He meets in the same manner the unuttered question in the mind of Simon the Pharisee concerning the sinful woman (Luke 7:41). He appeals to the most vital interests of His hearers' minds and hearts. He speaks to the shepherd of the sheepfold; to the vine-dresser, of the vine; to the fisherman, of his nets; to the lawyer, of the law; to those steeped in prophecies, of their fulfillment; etc. In this way the interest of His hearers was gradually aroused, an attitude of expectance created, their desire to know stimulated, until unconsciously they were prepared for the enunciation of the spiritual truth. Thereafter, every new experience and contact with the objects and events of the parable served to impress more deeply upon their hearts the truth of Christ's message. These experiences, furthermore, were proper not only to the times of Christ but to all ages; if they served as vehicles of sublime spiritual truths then, why should they not be used as means of teaching the same unchangeable truths today?

It is true that the enthusiastic supporters of the Munich Method have in certain cases exaggerated the use of the parable. The abundance of examples and comparisons may lead the catechist to pay more attention to variety than to unity, to appearances than to reality. In view of the intellectual greediness of the child, clear, correct and thorough instruction may give way to amusement. Hence the repeated insistence of the Munich School that the story be truly illustrative, that the details be not too numerous nor emphasized to the extent of absorbing unduly the child's attention – in a word, that the story be a means to an end, and not an end in itself. Furthermore, the Munich Method does not in any way minimize the value of memorizing. A religious lesson directed by the Psychological Method should naturally and logically issue in the catechismal answer. The terse and concise formulas of the Catechism are more easily impressed upon the mind, and misunderstanding and errors are thereby more easily avoided. In fact, it would be impossible to give a satisfactory survey of Bible History unless its salient features were summarized as they are now in the Catechism.

It is also objected at times that under the Munich Method, at least up to the Application stage, the child is almost entirely passive and receptive. The tendency of modern pedagogy is to ingrain ideas less through reasoned expositions than through the child's cooperation and self-activity. Meaning of concepts and truths is built up by actual experiences. Learning by listening is supplanted by learning through doing. Subject-matter is presented as experience to be lived rather than as formula to be memorized. Unlike the Munich Method, which engages only the senses of sight and hearing, the defenders of the *Arbeitsschule* (the Franch *école active*) appeal to the whole child with all his senses and faculties. The development of the intellectual powers must progress with the development of the physical powers. By striving to educate the children for life, the *Arbeitsschule* may in truth be considered as a *Lebensschule*.[9]

The exponents of the Munich Method, however, are the first to realize the value of the *Arbeitsprinzip: Lernen durch tun* ("learn by doing"). Action, according to Gatterer,[10] has a twofold purpose in the *Lebensschule*: it is the beginning and the end of the instruction; action leads to understanding and understanding to action. In so far as the children actively and personally cooperate in the acquisition of a truth or concept, action has a didactic value. When the truth or knowledge attained is applied to conduct and life, action takes on an educational value. Catechization, the same author tells us, must be thoroughly an *Arbeitsund Lebensschule*.[11] The *Arbeitsprinzip* must enter not only into the application, but also into the stages of Preparation and Presentation.[12] The truths of revelation were vouchsafed us, not merely to increase our knowledge, but also and above all, to convert our hearts and transform our conduct. The *Arbeitsprinzip* will aid the catechist in attaining the twofold end of catechization, namely, knowledge and practice of the faith.

But the *Arbeitsprinzip* also has its limitations. To handle all catechetical material according to this principle would demand much more time than is or can be alloted to religious instruction. Again, it is questionable whether the principle as such ought to be applied in teaching such doctrines as the Trinity, Incarnation, Sacraments, etc.[13] Furthermore, faith comes by authoritative teach-

[9] Cf. F. Weigl, *Buildung durch Selbsttun*, 2 vols. (Munich, 1923).

[10] *Op. cit.*, p. 183.

[11] *Ibid.*, 185.

[12] *Ibid.*, pp. 221, 234.

[13] The author of *Religion Hour* (Chicago, 1928), pp. 14–15, correctly remarks: "Dramatization will be conspicuous by its infrequency, if not, indeed, by its absence. This form of expression has taken a firm hold in some places, including at the present time a so-called dramatization of the Sacraments. I am unable to feel that the Sacrament of Baptism, for example, means more to the six or seven-year-old boy who has impersonated a priest, poured water upon a doll's head, and substituted cold cream for holy oil. It is agreed by many students of child psychology that only those things should be used for

ing and by learning, not by playing. Whereas secular education emphasizes and is satisfied with external activity, in catechization the invisible grace of the Holy Spirit and the inner acts of virtue are of primary importance. Without these all external catechetical activity would be mere hollow semblance. To be effective in catechization, the *Arbeitsprinzip* must unite the mind and heart to God. It must impress supernatural truths upon the soul in such a way that the child, whether at school or at home, whether in private or in public life, will be guided by the thoughts and maxims of faith, derive strength and comfort from them, and, in a word, live by them.

---

class-room dramatization which will not suffer in any way from the crude handling of children. Is there a danger that dramatization of the kind that I mentioned will render that which is sublime, ridiculous in the eyes of our children? From what I hear, I fear so."

CHAPTER IX

THE EUCHARISTIC METHOD

The principal points of the Eucharistic Method have been synthesized and clearly presented by the saintly Belgian priest, Dr. Edward Poppe (1890–1924), in his work, *la Méthode Eucharistique*.[1] This work places its fundamental principles within easy reach of priest, catechist and teacher. While a student at the Séminaire Léon XIII in Louvain, Abbé Poppe became imbued with the liturgical spirit at the Benedictine monastery of Mt. César. There he learned to understand and appreciate the essence of liturgical worship, the value of the Missal for prayer and meditation, the meaning of ceremonies and the beautiful arrangement of the ecclesiastical year. Later on, as a priest and catechist, he frequently conducted the children to church and carefully explained to them the various sacred objects, books, vestments, etc. He translated and explained to them the liturgical prayers, so that the little ones might better understand the grandeur and beauty of the Mass. He exhorted the children to receive Holy Communion frequently, for it is an integral part of the Mass.

The promoters of the Eucharistic Crusade in Belgium, and especially the Premonstratensian Abbey of Averbode, were inspired by the Eucharistic Method in organizing their apostolate of Frequent Communion. By the spoken and the printed word they instructed their followers and members in Eucharistic life and practice. Their untiring devotion is being crowned with remark-

[1] "*La Méthode Eucharistique*" (2nd ed., Averbode, Belgium, 1924); cf. also B. Van Havere, "*Une Ame-Apôtre*" (Termonde, Belgium, 1926), "*Manuel du catéchiste eucharistique*", "*La direction spirituelle des enfants*" and "*L'Ami des Petits*" (Averbode, Belgium).

able success. The Eucharistic spirit is being gradually introduced into various Belgian associations and schools. This widespread acceptance of the Eucharistic Method is due to the fact that it does not try to supplant current catechetical systems, but rather to animate them with a supernatural spirit, endow them with supernatural energies and bring men to a realization of their supreme destiny.

Strictly speaking, there is nothing new in the Eucharistic Method as regards its means and procedure. The supernatural means which it utilizes – the Holy Mass, Holy Communion, the Sacraments and sacramentals – are as old as the Church. The Method is called "Eucharistic" because of its special effort to apply in the Catholic education of youth the pontifical decrees concerning frequent Communion. Its pedagogical procedure, which is inspired by the law of the specialization of effort, is likewise intimately connected with Catholic ascetical tradition. The method does away with the barrier existing between the Sacraments and natural pedagogical procedure.

Christian education is defined by Dr. Poppe as the "methodical reformation of the child, deformed because of original sin, in order to comform him to Christ." [2] The Eucharistic Method is based on the principle that the actual condition in which we must work out our salvation is one of fallen and repaired human nature. Christian training is the gradual restoration in us of the divine image defaced by sin. This gradual conformation of the child to Christ must be both external and internal; it must affect the child's private as well as public life. In his strictly religious relations with God and the saints, in his domestic relations with his parents, brothers and sisters, in his social relations with his classmates, friends and enemies, in his civic relations with fellow-citizens and civil superiors, in his parochial relations with the clergy and the faithful, the child must learn to conform his mentality to Christ's doctrine and his conduct to Christ's precepts, counsels and examples. Because this conformation to Christ's image is a supernatural task, Christian education must be supernatural both as to its means and its ends. Without the grace of the Holy Spirit, our natural efforts would remain absolutely inefficacious. "Without Me you can do

[2] *Op. cit.*, 17.

nothing."[3] The catechist must, therefore, recommend his children to God in his daily Mass and prayers. He must not only speak to the children of God, but he must also speak to God about the children.

Dogmatic Principles

The primary source of all graces, and especially those necessary for education, is the Most Blessed Trinity. The meritorious source is the Supreme Sacrifice of the God-Man, the Great High and Unique Priest, Jesus Christ, born of the Blessed Virgin Mary. The Sacrifice of the Cross, so frequently recalled to us by the sign of the cross, is verily the source of all graces. As High-Priest forever, Christ conferred on Peter, on His Apostles, and on their successors, His mission and His powers, especially the powers of teaching, sanctifying and governing all men. Throughout the ages Christ continues to teach, sanctify and govern by means of the hierarchial priesthood. Though the ministry of the sacerdotal hierarchy, the graces of Calvary are renewed and applied to us in the Holy Sacrifice of the Mass. The Mass is the center of the Liturgy and of our Christian life. In the words of St. Thomas,[4] it is the end and consummation of all the Sacraments. It renews the Passion and Sacrifice of Christ in virtue of which the Sacraments operate. The priestly hierarchy is also the direct and official heir of the educative mission of Christ. The educators exercise their apostolate dependently on His doctrine, precepts and graces. The lay catechist and the Sister have the great honor of being the collaborators and helpers of the priests.

Catholic education must, therefore, be characterized by a hierarchical and Eucharistic spirit. In the church, in the confessional, in the pulpit and at catechetical instruction, the children must see in the priest the representative of Christ. Again, just as the Sacrifice of Calvary is the center of all history, so the Holy Mass must be the center and source of all the supernatural and educational energy in our lives. The life of the pupils, as well as of the educator himself, must be centered in the Holy Sacrifice of the Mass. The children should realize that they should assist at Mass not only on Sundays, but also on weekdays whenever possible. They should be

[3] John 15:5.
[4] *"Summa Theologica,"* III, Q. lxv, art. 3; Q. lxxiii, art. 3.

taught to direct their thoughts to the Sacrifice of the Mass continually being offered in different parts of the world and to unite their actions with it. The most intimate manner of participating in the Sacrifice of the Mass, the most effective means of profiting educationally by the Holy Sacrifice, is Holy Communion, an integral part of the Mass and the most noble of Sacraments. The children should, therefore, be urged to receive Communion frequently, to prepare themselves for it worthily and to profit by its graces fully.

Grace itself, however, is not sanctity and perfection; it is only the principle of sanctity and perfection. It must be applied to the child's conduct and developed according to his temperament and capacities. It must be used methodically for the correction of the child's defects and for the acquisition of Christ's spirit and virtues. Only in this way will the graces of the Mass, of Communion, and of the other Sacraments obtain their full efficacy and render the child externally and internally conformable to the life of Jesus Christ, his Model. But by what pedagogical processes are these graces to be applied to the child?

Pedagogical Principles

Pedagogy and ascetical theology tell us that it is impossible to acquire simultaneously all virtues or to correct simultaneously all defects. The energies of grace as well as the attention and forces of the individual must be applied to a particular determined point of life, namely, a dominant defect or the virtue opposed to it. The particular point is determined and controlled by the conduct cards (*cartes de conduite*), the weekly accounts (*billets de la semaine*), and the weekly examination of conscience (*revue hebdomadaire*). The "particular point" is applied, not only in direct, but also in occasional instructions. Let us briefly describe these pedagogical aspects of the Eucharistic Method.

1. *Conduct Cards* (*Cartes de Conduite*).[5] The teacher has a number of cards printed or typed and gives one to each child. Each card bears an appropriate message under the form of a wish from Jesus:

> My child,
>
> Jesus demands of you this week:
> that you obey promptly in school.

[5] Cf. "*Les series de cartes de conduite*" (Averbode, Belgium).

These conduct cards enable the teacher to find and determine the "particular point." School discipline and the conduct of the child at home, on the street and in the church, can successively be the subjects of these cards. The cards printed for the Belgian schools by the Abbey of Averbode are adapted to the liturgical seasons and to the occupation of the child. The different series concern the following points:

a. Conduct at church (Mass and Holy Communion).
b. Mortification (Lent).
c. the Dead (November).
d. Conduct at home (vacation).
e. Discipline at school.
f. Principles and truths (doctrinal points.)

On a determined day in the week the particular series of cards is placed in a beautifully decorated basket. The children draw a card from the basket but refrain from reading it until each child has drawn his or her card. When the drawing is completed, they turn over the card, and each reads his in silence. The teacher then recites a prayer that each child may successfully apply the particular point to his daily conduct. The card is then carefully put away in the desk. From time to time, either before the morning exercises or before dismissing the pupils, the teacher reminds the children of the card and its particular message. The children may be taught to express and write their particular point in the form of a maxim or ejaculatory prayer. If the particular point is "meekness," the maxim will be: "Be meek," and the ejaculatory prayer: "Jesus, meek and humble of heart, make my heart like unto Thine." To maintain an intimate correlation between education and the sources of grace, the teacher encourages the children to recall the particular point especially during Mass and Holy Communion. The good resolutions connected with the Sacrament of Penance should also center around the particular point.

2. *The Weekly Account* (*Billet de Semaine*).[6] The *billet de semaine* is a written account of the child's personal conduct during the week. It initiates the children into the examination of conscience which they will practice later on. By means of this exercise the children learn to control the particular point as well as their

[6] Cf. "*Les billets de semaine*" (Averbode, Belgium).

spiritual life and to correlate their conduct with Mass and Holy Communion. The aim of the *billet* is to center their whole life and all their spiritual exercises around the center of the Liturgy, the Holy Eucharist.

The exercise is carried on with the greatest discretion and without flattery or hypocrisy. The children are encouraged to write the *billets* sincerely before the eyes of the omnipresent and omniscient God. The children never sign the *billet,* and the teacher never refers to an individual fault written thereon. After the *billets* have been distributed and filled, they are gathered in a box and placed before the statue of the Sacred Heart, of the Blessed Virgin or of St. Joseph. On the first Friday of the month and during the Forty Hours' Devotion they are placed before the Blessed Sacrament. A word of exhortation is then addressed to the children and an appropriate prayer said. The *billets* are later on burned, or cut into pieces and strewn before the Blessed Sacrament during processions.

3. *Weekly Examination of Conscience* (*Revue Hebdomadaire*).[7] The *revue hebdomadaire* is a collective examination of conscience in the form of a conversation with the Eucharistic Christ. It is an efficacious method of replacing the *billet de semaine*, when the latter cannot be applied with success. The exercise is thoroughly explained before it is applied, and the director illustrates by examples how each one in the secrecy of his heart is to answer the questions. At the opening of the exercise the director reminds the audience and children that they are in the presence of God. Only a few apposite questions are chosen for each exercise. They are adapted and supplemented by the director according to the needs of the participants. The ultimate aim is to enable the pupils to make an examination of conscience without the aid of a director or questionnaire. This collective exercise is made preferably before the Blessed Sacrament. It is during these precious moments that the Eucharistic Christ coöperates most efficaciously in the renewal of our spiritual life.

The Particular Point

The procedure of the "particular point" must be intimately correlated with all catechetical training and with Catholic education

[7] Cf. "*Les statuts de C. E. pour adultes*" (Averbode, Belgium).

in general. The Eucharistic Method comprises in different proportions three inseparable elements: explanation, application and the aid of the supernatural factor (Eucharist, Sacraments). In every educational process we explain, apply and furnish the means of carrying out the application. The practical direction or application of the lesson to the pupil's conduct is realized through the method of the particular point. The particular point must be designated and concretely determined in all direct teaching, in occasional instructions and in the teacher's individual relations with the pupils and parents.

1. *Direct Teaching.* a. *The Catechism.* The Catechism lesson is from the very outset correlated with the Eucharist. The teacher reminds the pupils of the morning Mass and Communion and points out that those children who have participated in the Sacred Mysteries will understand the lesson more easily. Those who have failed to do so should supply the deficiency by a Spiritual Communion and correlate the prayers before class with the particular benefit they hope to derive from the lesson. In explaining the lesson the teacher aims to be dogmatically correct and accurate. He has frequent recourse to the so-called intuitive processes, to narrations and descriptions. From time to time he conducts the children to church in order to explain to them the altar and the various sacred objects used in the liturgical services. He exhorts the pupils to deduce from the lesson explained particular resolutions applicable to themselves. The best resolutions are written on the blackboard, and one point of general application is chosen for the whole class. The teacher than reads aloud the other points, pauses after each one and lets the children choose in silence the resolution best suited to them. This individual application is made only once a week, and the children are urged to offer up their Mass for the intention of living conformably to the lesson and resolution.

b. *History.* The events narrated from Old Testament *Bible History* are correlated with the future Messias and with the New Testament. The children are taught to judge Old Testament facts and events from a moral and Christian viewpoint and to apply the lesson to themselves. In other respects the procedure, especially for New Testament Bible History, is the same as in the Catechism lesson. The facts and events of *profane history* are likewise considered from a moral and Catholic viewpoint. The teacher strives to arouse the aversion of the children for reprehensible acts and to excite in them a desire to imitate beautiful and noble deeds. The teacher is always careful to correlate the good resolutions with the prayers after class and with the Mass and Communion of the morrow.

c. *Profane Subjects.* The other profane subjects are likewise intimately correlated with religion. In *arithmetic* the teacher introduces problems of everyday life and suggests moral and Christian solutions and applications. In *geography* the teacher frequently refers to the Creator, the First Cause of all things, and strives to arouse in the children gratitude towards God. He points out the missionary countries and the civilizing and uplifting influence of the Church, indicates the apostles and saints of a given region, and describes with the aid of pictures the notable sanctuaries in a particular locality. In *reading, writing* and *penmanship,* the teacher is careful to introduce from time to time maxims and subjects of a moral and religious nature.

2. *Occasional Instruction.* Whether it be the child's personal life with its daily responsibilities and little contrarieties, or family life, or social life, or parochial life, the children are taught to consider every event and situation from a supernatural and Christian viewpoint. They are directed to correlate all events and problems with their interior and exterior apostolate and with their life vocation. They are urged to offer up their Mass and Communion, their prayers and mortifications for the satisfactory solution of the problems of the day. They are exhorted to discuss those same problems with one another and with their parents, but always from a supernatural viewpoint. They are asked to reflect how they would proceed, or how they intended to proceed, when confronted by similar difficulties.

3. *Relations with Pupils.* In his *individual relations with the pupils* the catechist should base all encouragements, counsels, reprimands and punishments on the supernatural motive of love for Jesus. In dealing *with the children's parents* he should exhort them to coöperate by their vigilance, examples and prayers in the work of the Christian education of their children. If the conduct of a pupil is unsatisfactory, he should call upon his parents personally and impress upon them the importance of their coöperation and aid. Before vacation he should warn the parents of the

dangers of this period of liberty. He should remind them of their obligation to send their children to Mass, Confession and Communion. He should induce them to supervise the children's amusements. From the pulpit he should occasionally address words of exhortation to parents and to women's sodalities, etc.

The methodical influence which the Eucharistic Method exercises over children is sustained and intensified by a group or *nucleus of the élite*. The nucleus is public or secret according to the mentality and dispositions of the pupils and the will of the superior. By its apostolate it assures a Christian spirit and good habits among the mass of students. The number of members is very restricted and the conditions of entrance severe. The members must carefully observe all the regulations and rules of the school, live in peace with their companions, hear Mass daily, receive Communion weekly, etc. In order to exercise efficaciously this supernatural apostolate among their companions, members of the group receive additional spiritual instruction outside of class at special reunions. The spiritual director and confessor who knows his penitents intimately likewise exercises an important part in the spiritual formation of these élite. The nucleus of the Eucharistic Crusade considers Eucharistic life as the principal means of the apostolate. All groups consider grace as the indispensable element of all success.

The success of the method depends to a large extent also on the spiritual life, exemplary conduct and willing coöperation of the *educator himself*. Holy Mass and Communion, devotion to the Blessed Virgin Mary, daily meditation and even mortifications must be to him invaluable resources in his sublime work. His motto must be the words of the Divine Pedagogue, Jesus Christ Himself: "He that shall *do* and teach shall be called great in the kingdom of heaven" [8] and "For them do I sanctify Myself, that they also may be sanctified in truth." [9]

In our description of the Eucharistic Method we have frequently noted the constant correlation of its pedagogical principles with the graces of the Eucharist. In conclusion, we would call attention to what may be considered an extrinsic association of education with the Eucharist, namely, the "Dial of Sacrifice (*Cadran du Sacri-*

[8] Matt. 5:19.

[9] John 17:19.

fice).[10] The "Dial of Sacrifice" is a pedagogical means of teaching the child to refer to the Sacrifice of the Mass all the exercises, actions and sufferings of the day. The dial, no matter at what time of the day, reminds them of the country where Christ is being offered for us and where He is dispensing light, strength and grace. The Sacrifice of Christ, continually offered all the day long, becomes the center of the child's life and exercises a powerful influence over his mind and heart. A glance at the Dial of Sacrifice is often sufficient to procure silence, attention and the proper demeanor among the children. How often children suddenly stop a dispute, when struck by the thought that at that moment Jesus is renewing His great sacrifice in some missionary country, and place their little sacrifices and mortifications on the paten actually being raised by the priest! Christ thus becomes for them the Universal Mediator through whom they offer up their prayers and actions to the Heavenly Father. Their desire to assist at the Mass actually being celebrated becomes spontaneously a Spiritual Communion. The Dial leads them to appreciate better the value of the Mass, and inspires them with a desire to assist at it more worthily and more frequently. In this way the children are gradually conformed to Christ, their Model, in both their internal and external life. Holy Church, the Mystical Body of Christ, becomes itself conformed to its Divine Head and Chief.

[10] "*Le Cadran du Sacrifice*" (Averbode, Belgium).

CHAPTER X

THE *SOWER* METHOD

The chief exponent of the *Sower* Scheme, which is associated with the educational journal of that name, is the Rev. F. H. Drinkwater.[1] This well-known educator tells us that most Catholic children in England attend Catholic schools where a definite time (sometimes, an hour) is assigned to religious instruction. Ordinarily the process of memorizing began when the child was five years old, and thereafter it was kept up constantly; at stated times the children were questioned by visiting examiners. Teachers who attempted to use this method could not but notice its many disadvantages and difficulties. The Catechism drill was associating religion with a wearisome school task; this was all the more true since the process went on for a long time, covering the same matter several times. The excessive emphasis placed on the memorizing of the Catechism left little time for other equally important things such as church music, Bible History, the study of the life of Our Lord, Church History, and the lives of the saints. Furthermore, it was noticed that the Catechism consists of dry abstract formulas, unintelligible to children even when accurately memorized. The

[1] Cf. "*The Givers*" (London, 1926), "*Religion in School Again*" (London, 1935). We are indebted principally to these two books for our information concerning the *Sower* Method. However, since these books are a collection of articles written intermittently over a long period, we were in doubt at times whether we were reproducing faithfully the author's mind. Furthermore the *Sower* Scheme underwent a revision in 1929 and in 1936. Cf. "*Scheme of Religious Instruction, Approved for Use in the Elementary Schools of the Diocese of Birmingham*" (London, 1936).

Catechism drill itself was found to be psychologically unsound, since it took no account of the child's intellectual capacity.[2]

How were the school supervisors to remedy these defects? Were they to abolish the Catechism altogether? Such a solution would have been too negative. It would have left the teachers without an appropriate substitute. At the same time it would have been too drastic, since definite verbal formulations of divine immutable truths are obviously necessary. Ought they to introduce a shorter and simpler Catechism, written in childlike language, and insisting on the central truths of faith? Such a procedure would have been new in England and would have demanded years of advocacy before it could be put in force. Meanwhile, it was desired to offer immediate help to both teachers and school children. The *Sower* Scheme or "compromise," which was an outgrowth of this state of affairs, accepted the Catechism as it stood, but it decided that only one hundred of the four hundred answers were sufficiently important in their actual wording to be memorized. The rest was to be used as any other schoolbook. The Catechism was to be the textbook only for the four middle years of school life, from the ages eight to eleven inclusive, a period when the child's intelligence is rapidly developing and his memory working at its best. Subsequent experimentation with the *Sower* Scheme led Father Drinkwater, as we shall indicate later, to postpone the use of the Catechism even to a later period.

Religious Instruction

The *Sower* Scheme strives to make religious instruction conformable to the fundamental laws which govern the development of the child's mind and powers of apprehension. It takes into consideration the varied types of mind in children of different ages. It

[2] Fr. Drinkwater, "*The Givers*" (New York, 1926) pp. 131–132, rightly remarks: "Any experienced teacher knows that children of different ages need to be taught quite differently. . . . If we are to build education on interest, differences of age must be taken into account much more seriously and systematically. . . . But no one seems to feel foolish about a system of religious instruction, which uses very much the same matter and methods for children of six and children of thirteen. . . . Only in the teaching of the Faith do we still follow the order of logical development instead of the order of the child's growth in apprehension. Only in the teaching of the Faith do we still demand memorized definitions and analysis from the children of five and six."

demands that the contents and method proper to early adolescence be not anticipated in childhood, much less in infancy. It proposes to divide religious training in schools into three main periods, each stage being in its own way a complete survey of Catholicism and having its appropriate contents, method and discipline. There three stages of religious school-training, according to *The Givers*,[3] are the following: children aged five to eight, children aged eight to twelve and children twelve and upwards. In the 1936 revised *Scheme of Religious Instruction*, approved for use in the elementary schools of the Diocese of Birmingham, the three stages run as follows: infants (five to eight years), juniors (eight to eleven years) and seniors (eleven to fourteen or fifteen years). "Broadly speaking," says Fr. Drinkwater, "in the first stage we play, reverently and lovingly, but still play; in the second we learn facts, and by the help of the will store the retentive memory of childhood; in the third we reason and apply." [4] This concentric syllabus, the same author says elsewhere, "might be compared to climbing a high tower with three successive lookout posts giving an ever-widening view of the same country; and the comparison would be improved if one supposes a pair of field-glasses at each window – each pair more powerful than the one below. The climber would see the same countryside at each stage, but with greater range and greater meaning and also with more detail." [5]

1. *First Period (five to eight years)*. Religious instruction during this period should comprise all the essential points of Catholic life and doctrine, but in a manner as elementary, childlike and simple as possible. During this whole stage, which culminates in First Communion, no Catechism text is used. Prayers and hymns are learned, and religious practices in school and church receive special attention. The methods of instructing are mainly those of pictures, stories, dramatizations, drawings, natural conversations,

[3] Pp. 178, 185–186. The threefold division adopted by the Munich Method is based on the general knowledge and ability of the child: (1) those who are only beginning to acquire, or have very incompletely acquired, proficiency in reading and writing; (2) those who are fairly proficient in reading and writing (intermediate grades); (3) those who are standing on the threshold of life.

[4] *A Scheme of Religious Instruction* (2nd ed.; London, 1922), introduction, p. vii.

[5] *The Givers*, p. 178.

etc.[6] Fr. Drinkwater inclines to Fr. Shields' view that in this early stage there should not be a separate "period" for religious instruction but that religion should rather permeate the entire work of the school. A book recommended to the teacher during this period is Sister Mary Eaton's *The Little Ones.*[7]

2. *Second Period (eight to twelve years).* This stage is again a complete survey of Christian Doctrine, but the Catechism, according to *The Givers,*[8] is now used as a textbook. The answers of the Catechism are first built up in the children's own words, then translated into the phrases of the Catechism, and finally committed to memory. The learning of prayers and hymns continues to receive a prominent place. The play-way methods of the first stage are still used to some extent. The stories take a wider range and comprise much Scripture and Church History. The children are encouraged by reasonable stimuli to fulfill their religious duties, but care is exercised lest they become tired of religion or of its representatives. Books recommended for this period are the English *Catechism of Christian Doctrine,*[9] *Teaching the Catechism,*[10] *Stories in School,*[11] and *Short Instructions on the Mass for Children.*[12] A glimpse into the child's imagination and into his internal spiritual life is afforded us in the interesting little work entitled *The Way into the Kingdom.*[13]

The *Arbeitsprinzip* (work principle) continues to receive due

[6] The Munich Method contends that religious instruction during this period should be given especially and primarily by means of Bible History. The abstract religious formulas of the Catechism are not the appropriate food for the mind and heart of the child at this age. In fact, because the Catechism formulas are so difficult of comprehension, there is danger that the child may grow averse to all religious teaching. They can become intelligible to the child only when presented through the medium of Bible History. The latter, in the hands of a competent teacher, will arouse interest, joy and readiness to listen, and will beget enthusiasm for the examples of virtue and aversion for sin. The Munich Method recommends that the essentials of Bible History be given in the words of the Catechism; in the First Grade, however, the Catechism text itself is not used, but concert repetition of the answers must take place of the book. In the Second and Third Grades the children may be given a Catechism in order to enable them to learn more easily the conclusions of the Bible History lessons.

[7] London, 1923.

[8] P. 180.

[9] London, 1925.

[10] London, 1925.

[11] London, 1923.

[12] Birmingham, 1922.

[13] London, 1922. Cf. also Fr. Drinkwater's booklet, *Doctrine for the Juniors* (London, 1935).

emphasis in this second and middle period. The children are encouraged to learn by doing things. Besides dramatization, the solving of "cases," and the performance of duties in church, etc., the chief expression work of this period is the home-made Catechism which every child is obliged to produce. This Catechism project was inspired principally by three articles of A. M. Scarre in *The Sower*.[14] As the children go along, they make their own Catechisms in close contact with the printed Catechisms. This home-made Catechism may be made in three different ways: first, the children may make the book at a handiwork lesson; second, a suitable note-book with plain and lined leaves, the one for gum-work and the other for writing, may be selected; third, the Catechism text itself may be used; the book is taken asunder; leaves are inserted between the pages of the text and used for comments, illustrations and gum-work.

In the first year, the book is mainly a picture album. The illustrations refer to Catechism teaching or to correlated incidents from Bible History. Appropriate extracts from the Catechism are sometimes inserted beneath the pictures.

In the second year, the content of the book grows: Catechism answers and comments, Bible History, liturgical questions and hymns now receive attention.

In the third year, the book has three divisions: doctrine, the Mass, and Bible History. The doctrinal points are often elucidated by appropriate passages from Sacred Scripture. The Mass and Bible History are frequently illustrated from Catholic booksellers' catalogues. The comments of the child become more personal and individual, revealing his active and thinking mind.

In the fourth year, the book is larger and more elaborate. It is usually written in sections, and covers the Catechism, Bible History, Liturgy and prayer. Sketches, designs, verses, extracts, original compositions, individual remarks etc., make up this volume.

Commenting on this home-made Catechism project, the editor of *The Sower* writes, "Miss Scarre's idea has the simplicity combined with the infinite possibilities which is the mark of a genuine first-class idea. Why didn't we ever think of it before? It has all

[14] "The Middle School. I" (*The Sower,* March, 1921), "The Middle School. II" (*ibid.,* May, 1921), and "The Middle School. III" (*ibid.,* June, 1921).

the characteristics of a real teaching method. The making of the book provides a permanent aim for the religious instruction time (it must not be confused with mere expression work, for it is the work itself). It keeps the children occupied, gives them a chance to be doing something, and doing it at their own pace, gives much scope for individual differences of enterprise and ability, and for the right sort of emulation, and leaves them a sort of leisure for thinking over things (and children do think if they are allowed to). Its advantages to the teacher are just as evident; it relieves him of the strain of many class lessons, or of keeping order in a class which is not properly occupied, and it gives him full leisure to watch and observe and go round the class individually with his suggestions, and hints, and information, and encouragment – in short, to practice the art of incidental teaching under the most favourable conditions." [15]

3. *Third Period* (*twelve years and onward*). The child is now entering on a new phase of living. The period of receptivity is fast replaced by a period of criticism and analysis. Interest in abstract truth is supplanted by a bent towards practical service. Hence, religious instruction must appeal to the child's reasoned judgment and must represent religion chiefly as something to be done. "All the points of The Sower Scheme," says Fr. Drinkwater, "are important, and there is a reason for them all; but if there is one point more essential than any other, it is this point of giving a highly practical bent to religious instruction in the early years of adolescence. As soon as we begin to look at Catholicism as something to be done, as a call to service of God and man, the horizon widens out, and endless possibilities, with endless variations according to individual temperaments, come in sight. Books and words retire to their proper place, and we begin to discover for ourselves (even if we are but beginners, our own share in the Incarnation, our personal concern in the awful and tender mysteries of Advent, and the meaning of the Christmas Angel's word to us: *Ecce evangelizo vobis gaudium magnum.*" [16]

In this third stage the Catechism, according to *The Givers*,[17] is no longer the daily textbook but is retained as an authoritative reference book. All methods are now pressed into service; black-

[15] Editorial Notes, in *The Sower* (June, 1921), pp. 3–4.
[16] *The Givers*, pp. 21–22. [17] P. 181.

boards, maps, pictures, individual researches, and written exercises are used extensively. Most important of all, the children are taught to make orderly notes on the lesson. In fact, the method may be summed up as a constant use of and reference to the note-book (*Arbeitsprinzip*). A good notebook is the only textbook prescribed for the pupil. As the founders of the Sulpician Method already noticed, much of the work done in class is lost unless the child has some adequate reminder. The notebook encourages use of reference books and the looking-it-up habit, and so it satisfies the intense group-spirit of this age, for the children of this period of life delight to go in groups or "gangs" in quest of new material. Additional avenues of activity and "practical service" are offered to the pupils by the altar societies, St. Vincent de Paul Societies and the Catholic Truth Societies.

According to Father Drinkwater's views (expounded in his work entitled *The Givers*), the Catechism is to be memorized – at least in its essentials – in the second period, while in the third period it is to be used as an authoritative reference work. In his more recent work, *Religion in School Again*, the author of the *Sower* Scheme inclines towards postponing the use of the Catechism until the last period. Let us state his position in his own words: "The Sower believes so strongly in the important place of the Catechism in the school that it wishes to have it done under the best possible conditions, that is to say, by children of an age to see more meaning in it, and coming to it as to something fresh and interesting. This means that the parrot-system (by which I always mean the rote learning of statements in scientific language before the mind is ready to receive them) must be avoided. In the Infant and Junior Schools the only way to avoid the parrot-system is to leave the Catechism-text out of the syllabus; in the Senior School we can avoid it by having Catechism answers explained and understood *before* they are learned by heart. . . . Study the Catechism text, then, in the Senior School (from eleven or so, that means), and not before."[18] From that we gather that the complete survey of Christian Doctrine, which is prescribed for every period, is to be correlated with the Catechism formulas not in the second period, as suggested in *The Givers*, but only in the third period.

In the third stage the whole ground of Christian doctrine and

[18] Pp. 177, 178, 176.

practice is covered once more. The aim, however, is not systematic completeness but rather an all-around acquaintance with Catholicism. The course now includes more advanced teaching concerning the spiritual life, the counsels, frequent Communion, etc. The students should be given as vivid and as real an idea as possible of God's nature and attributes, for he who has once obtained the true idea of God's nature will not easily curse, swear, blaspheme, commit secret sins, etc. The children should be shown how the Incarnation and the Mystical Body – so briefly treated in the Catechism – are pivotal doctrines of the Catholic Faith. They must be shown the historical reality of the Gospels, so that if they chance across a rationalistic or modernistic treatise they will not be easily swayed by its specious arguments. They should also be given some Church History; they must become acquainted with the Church's growth and expansion and know that the Church ruled by Pius XII is much more vast than the Church under St. Peter. They should know what to think of the peculiarly English and American heresy – that it does not matter what one believes or what religion one chooses, provided one lives a clean life. They should also be sufficiently acquainted with some of the Old Testament questions and problems which they are sure to meet sooner or later. The great Catholic principles of social justice should be explained to them with special reference to existing conditions. The children should be taught how to participate intelligently in the Liturgy. In brief, they should be introduced to the many aspects of the Catholic faith in such a way that they will continue to have a vital interest in their religion, even amid the countless new interests which await them on leaving school. Books intended to be used during this period are *Twelve and After* [19] and McLaughlin's *Catechism Theology.*[20] The numerous commentaries on the Catechism which have appeared in recent years can likewise be used with profit in this as well as in the middle period.

The aim of the *Sower* method in this period is to enable the child to give an account of the faith that is in him. Principles – and not facts and details – are the chief aim. Though the program may seem vast, Fr. Drinkwater proposes to unify and systematize it by means of the principle of correlation. "Still less are we saying that all the things enumerated above should be treated as separate

[19] New York, 1925.

[20] London, 1922.

'subjects' or divisions of religious instruction. In secondary schools, not to mention our places of higher study, religion is already in danger of being divided up too much into 'subjects' thought of as unconnected. Even the least ambitious school has separate mental pigeon-holes for Catechism teaching, Old Testament history, New Testament history, and the Gospel for the something-or-other local examination; and any additions are usually made in the form of new layers or subjects, with each perhaps its different time or its different teacher: church history, and apologetics, and the Holy Scripture (but that is the unlikeliest of all), and social study. But these things are all one. To divide them off from each other in this way may conduce to logical statement, but it does not make for reality. Bible History and Church History are one uninterrupted story. Catholic history and Catholic liturgy and Catholic doctrine and Catholic apologetics are one – that is to say, they are not really different regions of fact, but at most only different angles from which one observes that living thing, Catholicism." [21]

From the above it is clear that in the *Sower* Scheme the whole doctrinal content of the Catechism is gone through, at least in its main outlines, every two or three years. This concentric method meets the evident differences in children of different ages. It respects the fundamental psychological law that with adults, and even more with children, an object presented to the mind is grasped at first only in its external outline; it is only slowly and by repeated efforts that its deeper and essential characteristics are finally comprehended. The concentric method also makes for a deeper and more thorough comprehension than can be expected from a single study of the matter. Frequent reviews and applications to various states of life are necessary in order to impress truth deeply on the mind and heart. A practical reason militating in favor of the above method is the more or less frequent change of abode on the part of the children. There is great danger of their never being instructed in the whole Christian doctrine, if in a relatively short time it cannot be given to them in its entirety.

The objection is sometimes advanced that the concentric method deadens interest and creates tedium. This objection is undoubtedly based on the mechanical manner and slipshod work of many teachers, who would not attain better results with any other

[21] *The Givers*, pp. 183–184.

method. The concentric method does not favor mechanical repetition but insists that the verities already learned should constitute the foundation on which to rear the remaining parts of the edifice of Christian truth. To manifest so little confidence in the teaching art as to assert that the reviewing of a study after one or two years must prove irksome, is quite out of keeping with the psychological methods of the day. Truths presented with inspiring warmth and supernatural persuasiveness tire no more than recurring liturgical feasts, classic works of art, etc. We must be careful not to allow the children to be infected by the blasé disposition of the modern adult. Finally, we should not lose sight of the fact that quantitative increase and new matter may stimulate curiosity but may not necessarily make for solid piety.

Religious Education

It would perhaps be inaccurate to say that the exponents of the *Sower* Scheme draw a clear distinction between religious instruction and religious education. Yet, the suggestions which some of the handbooks contain may — theoretically, at least, and for the sake of clarity — be classed under the second heading. "Religion," says Fr. Drinkwater, "is an affair in which the heart and will are deeply concerned, or else it is nothing. You can teach writing or arithmetic or French with the easy conviction that in any case they will be useful. But no one would want to teach religious knowledge on the same level, because religion *is of no use* until it is accepted and lived." [22]

1. *Prayer.*[23] Of paramount importance in the formation of Christion character is prayer — that part of the school-time, namely, which is actually spent in religious duties. For when the children are reciting their prayers, they are not merely learning about religion but actually putting it into practice. What is the precise object of having prayers in school? One of three reasons is usually alleged: first, to make sure that the children will memorize at least the ordinary prayers; second, to make sure that the children shall actually get their daily prayers (morning and evening prayers, grace before and after meals) said, at least on school days; third, to ask God's blessing upon the day's work. Of these three reasons

[22] *The Givers,* 49.
[23] *Ibid.*, pp. 186–196; *Religion in School Again,* pp. 102–106.

it is clear, says Fr. Drinkwater, that the last is the only genuine and valid one. To make sure that the children shall know their daily prayers is a matter that pertains to religious instruction, and not to religious practice; memorizing and mere repetition of one's prayers is not of itself a raising up of the mind and heart to God. The mere learning of the prayer formulas ought to be treated as an ordinary school exercise. Secondly, to make sure that the children say their daily prayers is likewise rejected by Fr. Drinkwater as a reason for saying prayers at school. The teacher should teach the children how to say their prayers and remind them frequently about saying them, but he should never do it for them. Otherwise, they will never acquire the habit of saying their prayers themselves at home.

If the children are to acquire the true idea of prayer, everything during prayer must be done as well as possible. The prayers must be short. Occasionally some special prayers may be added, but these must not be too numerous or too long. The teacher should beware of adding to the school prayers all sorts of pious aspirations, which may appeal to him personally but have little meaning for the children. Besides, it is not advisable that public prayers should be converted into a long succession of these ejaculations artificially put together. On the other hand, it would be highly desirable to initiate the children into the liturgical prayers of the Church, which are brief and yet inspiring. Care must also be taken lest the children say their prayers in a mechanical and sing-song manner – a manner which is destructive of all true devotion. This ugly recitation, with its unanimous rise and fall of intonation, which is undesirable even as mere speech-training, perhaps expresses a need on the part of the children for more rhythm and singing. Fr. Drinkwater strongly recommends the singing of a hymn at the beginning of every school session, or at least at the morning session. Even from a merely natural educational viewpoint, much is to be said in favor of opening a session with a hymn; it fills the lungs, clears the mind, tranquillizes the mood and conduces to better work afterwards.

What shall the teacher do during prayer? Should he pray, or should he supervise the conduct of the children, or should he attempt to do both? The third alternative, to try to pray and watch the children at the same time, is to attempt the impossible; at the same time the children are apt to get a very poor idea of the meaning of prayer. If he cannot do both, which of the two alternatives will he choose? To keep an eye on children while they pray is very apt to suggest misbehaviour to them. A good example is likely to have a more permanent effect on the children than the inhibition coming from being watched; hence, the teacher should usually join devoutly in the prayers.

2. *Interest.* The purpose of Catholic schools is to produce good practical Catholics by the proper training of the will. No training, however, will be successful unless it is based upon desire. This atmosphere of desire is produced by reasoning, knowledge, imagination, and emotion; a varying fusion of these constitutes interest. During school age a child is passing through a whole series of interests and aptitudes, and the methods of teaching must either keep pace with these changes or fail. The teacher can win the child's interest if he takes into consideration the age, the present mental content and experience and the dominant instincts of his pupils. The child's hobbies must serve as a *point de depart* of interest in higher things.

Secondly, interest depends on aim and purpose. Things become interesting to a learner if he sees the end they are meant to serve and wants to attain that end himself. The transforming power of conscious purpose cannot be neglected by the religious teacher. For the children are always asking "why," and they are much more interested in a lesson if they see whither it is leading. This purpose, let it be carefully noted, must not be a very general or remote one; to urge young children to learn the Catechism as a means of attaining their final end is too remote a purpose to provide a reason for serious work. Instruction should be related to some immediate and definite purpose, such as Confession, First Communion, Confirmation, etc. Even the more purely doctrinal parts of religious instruction can be properly orientated by pointing out how each dogma fits in with all the rest and how everything converges towards and centers in Christ. In fact, so necessary a part of the learning process is purpose that, where a true purpose is lacking, it is necessary to create a purpose of some kind. This is the common justification for examinations. Emulation which loses sight of the right purpose in learning is a bad thing; certain forms of emulation (such as prizes and class-placing) are a permanent discouragement to children of only average ability. Punishments and rewards are second-rate motives, and consequently make for second-rate work and second-rate discipline.[24]

3. *Authority.*[25] It is certain that schools can also create an atmosphere of antagonism to religion. Fr. Drinkwater says: "Consider Monday morning in many a school. Mass defaulters singled out and stood up like targets; public inquisition as to why they missed, eliciting answers of various degrees of truthfulness and intimate domestic detail; conscientious objurgations by the inwardly sympathetic teacher; pointed reflections on mortal sin and its relation to some of the four last things. The ordeal being over (let us hope that the cane has played no part in it), enter Father So-and-So, and perhaps the whole process has to be gone through once more, with variations." [26] The child thus comes to connect religion with the most embarrassing moments of his schooldays. There is developing in his mind a repugnance to religion which will make him dislike the Sunday Mass for a long time to come. Such disciplinary methods may result in a better attendance at Mass during the school year, but what will happen during the Christmas and summer vacations? What will happen after the child graduates? The same may be said of Confession. Children are sometimes marched to Confession in droves, a procedure which effectively teaches the children that Confession belongs to the school program and should be discontinued after graduation.[27] Fr. Drinkwater does not propose to leave the children entirely to their own initiative. Children of all ages need help and reminders of one kind or another. But what he does propose is that these aids should be gradually withdrawn as the child grows older, so that the child may act of his own accord. When the child graduates from school, he should be as

[24] *The Givers*, pp. 125–128. [25] *Ibid.*, pp. 149–156. [26] *The Givers*, p. 152.

[27] Fr. Drinkwater (*ibid.*, p. 154) makes the following just observations: "When we rely on the pressure of school discipline to bring children to Mass, we are teaching them NOT to come to Mass. When we crowd them together at the far end of a big church to fulfill their obligation, without making sure they understand what it is that goes on at the altar, we are teaching them NOT to come to Mass. When we march them to Confession in platoons and marshal them up to Communion in companies, we are teaching them NOT to come to the Sacraments. When we make them say morning prayers at the beginning of school and night prayers at the end, we are teaching them NOT to say morning and evening prayers. When we say 'grace before meals' before we send them home to dinner, we are teaching them NOT to say their grace."

independent as possible in his religious life. If we expect the child's will to work in different circumstances, we must train him in free self-determination; we must give him suitably varied opportunities for free choice. Otherwise, the things which were intended to be aids may become drawbacks.

4. *Motives.*[28] A habit is formed by the repetition, not of unwilling, but of willing acts. A discipline based on fear, whether physical or moral, will not form habits; it may serve to maintain order for the time being, but it cannot be a training for life.[29] It will develop deceitfulness in both the individual and in the group. It will prejudice children against their lessons and make them look upon learning as an unnatural process. Secondly, discipline should not be based merely on kindness, love or affection. For true discipline implies mastery of all the passions. But love as well as fear is a passion, and to place one passion in charge of the others is to invite chaos. If passions are to be ruled by reason and will, discipline must be based on the fear and love of God. The children must realize that the teacher's authority over them has been communicated to him by the parents, who in turn receive their authority from God. They must see in the teacher's authority God's authority. To obey His authority is always right. When both teacher and pupil obey the same law of God, then discipline is assured.

Being the result of the experience and thought of several Catholic teachers, the *Sower* Scheme cannot but possess many excellent qualities. Its constant application of the *Arbeitsprinzip* brings the method in line with what is best in modern pedagogy. The undue restlessness of the religion hour is converted into various forms of happy activity. The use of the story[30] and picture, especially in the first period, will certainly prove to be of great value; the

[28] *Ibid.*, pp. 157–162.

[29] In regard to physical torture, Fr. Drinkwater (*ibid.*, 170), lays down the following principle: "When physical torture – however slight – is used as a remedy for faults which are more or less scholastic, such as getting exercises wrong, or forgetting things, or inattention, then there are no words of condemnation strong enough." The real remedy, the same author says, is to be found in looking for the cause. Most behavior in children falls under one or the other of the following causes: physical causes, such as defective eyesight or hearing; lack of suitable occupation or environment; desire to create a sensation and be the center of attraction. A hard case, when it does occur, should be treated by segregation rather than by corporal punishment.

[30] Cf. *Stories in School*, introduction, pp. 7–15; *The Way into the Kingdom*, pp. 44 ff.

former makes the Catechism lesson living, vivid, and appealing, while the latter supplies additional concrete details and makes clear what words fail to explain. The second and third periods assign the proper place and role to memorizing. Memorizing should be, not the first, but the last step, the finishing touch to a process of explanation and understanding. The third period also looks towards the life of the child after he leaves school. It is concerned less with equipping the child with innumerable details carefully stored in pigeon-holes than with enkindling enthusiasm for the different aspects of Catholicism. An explanation of the why and wherefore of religious practices is all the more necessary in England and America, where our faith is chilled by constant contact with innumerable sects and creeds. The method does not forget the teacher; its several handbooks supply a variety of material and suggest various ways of using it. Lastly and above all, the method recommends itself because of its constant emphasis on the proper training of the will and heart.[31]

[31] Cf. *Religion in School Again*, pp. 170–180.

CHAPTER XI

TEACHING RELIGION TO RETARDED CHILDREN

The retarded child must be the object of Christ's special predeliction. To children of this group applies in a special way the warning of Our Lord: "Suffer the little children to come unto me, and forbid them not, for such is the kingdom of heaven" (Mtt. 19:14). Made in God's image, redeemed by Christ's Precious Blood, and destined for eternal glory – like the normal child – these children labor under special difficulties in working out their earthly career as well as their eternal end. Of them the Saviour could in His own merciful manner say: "Whosoever shall receive one such child as this in my name, receiveth Me. And whosoever shall receive Me, receiveth not me, but Him that sent me" (Mk. 9:35–36); "As long as you did it to one of these my least brethren, you did it to me" (Mtt. 25:40). To come to the help of these children who are endowed with the same human dignity as others but who are suffering from certain handicaps, is a work most pleasing to God and of all Christ-like works most charitable.

1. *Teacher's attitude*: In teaching children with mental retardation, just as in teaching normal children, the mental attitude of the teacher is important. If the instructor takes all factors into account regarding the specific group that he is to teach, and organizes his material and develops his presentation to meet the specific needs of his group, he will be successful in conveying the ideas he wishes to express. This is assuming that the teacher himself is genuinely interested in the children and in imparting truth to them, so by mental attitude is here meant the knowledge of the specific needs of the group, willingness to help meet these needs, and a genuine love for each person in the group.

No group or no class will have the same specific needs. It is well to remember this. Neither is there any special, infallible method by which mentally retarded children can be most successfully taught. Much will depend upon the teacher's own ingenuity and resourcefulness in adapting general methods to the individual child or the group. It is perhaps in this that the teacher will feel his own limitations. No human being is expected to comprehend all the varying factors and therefore will never be completely successful in his endeavor to impart truth. Nonetheless the interested teacher will try to understand the individuals in his class as well as possible.

Even the limited child will be able to detect a note of insincerity if such exists in the teacher, and such a teacher is wasting both his own and the children's time. The teacher must really care for the children's welfare and be sympathetic with them. He must desire to teach them to know about God in order that they may love God more. Lack of accomplishment will be supplanted by their genuine appreciation. There is so little guile in these children that they most often express just what they think and feel.

2. *The child's capacities*: When teaching religion to the mentally retarded it is helpful to learn the general degree of intelligence of each child, and then group the children according to their chronological ages and mental levels. There is as much difference between a mildly retarded child with an intelligence quotient of about 70 and a severely retarded child with an IQ of 30 as there is between the normal person of average intelligence and the genius. The retarded feel ill at ease if they are placed in a class of children several years younger, especially if there is a considerable difference in physical growth. The retarded child who happens to be small for his age can better adjust with a group of younger children.

Begin where the pupil is by learning as much of the child's individual capacities and achievements as possible, and then work upward from that basis. To do otherwise will doom the child to continued failure and certain discouragement. Tasks should be held within the child's level of comprehension but should be pointed to the peak of his ability. This does not mean that failure of attainment must be avoided at all cost for even the retarded child should learn to accept an occasional failure. To be over zealous in avoiding failure will bring about the opposite evil of gearing the work too low and of not realizing the child's actual potential.

3. *Correlation of ideas*: Make the teaching as concrete as possible and particularly try to relate it to the everyday experiences of the child. Try to help the child to recognize likenesses, differences, and relationship to other situations. One can understandably realize that the mentally handicapped child has a difficult time trying to grasp any speculation, much less profound speculation. If the idea can be geared to something in his life experience it will be a great help to him in both understanding the truth and in remembering it.

When developing the concept of Divine Grace, for instance, if the instructor can inculcate the idea that Sanctifying Grace is really a friendship between God and us, just as there is love and friendship between our parents and ourselves, then a beginning of the concept is formed in their minds. After the retarded pupils seem to have grasped this idea of Sanctifying Grace being a friendship between God and ourselves, the teacher can go further in the explanation, showing that Grace is more than just a natural friendship. They grasp the idea of love and friendship since it is so much of nature that even the most limited feel these needs.

4. *Feeling of success*: When teaching the rearded child it may be necessary to initiate in him the feeling of success, for many of his life activities in the company of normal people will have given him a definite failure complex. Praise should be given on the basis of earnest effort and not on achievement alone. New pupils should have a number of easy assignments so that they may learn to experience success. The teacher should avoid any confusion in his presentation, being careful to connect facts with positive associations, following logical steps, and being careful not to omit points which would make it difficult for the retarded child to follow the sequence of thought. This will give the pupil a better chance to understand and less cause for failure or discouragement.

5. *Making lesson attractive*: Make lessons as agreeable as possible, and expect the child to carry through a task begun. Assigning distasteful tasks for the sake of discipline is imprudent. Especially in the teaching of religion it is important to make the ascertain-

ment of truth and the resulting practice of it something that is joyous and desirable. To tell a class to learn the Our Father and Hail Mary, and to motivate them by fear, would be an unfortunate method. This would make prayer disagreeable and distasteful, leading to indifference or even to despair.

Such tasks as the example given above should be carefully chosen because memorization is particularly difficult for the severely retarded. If such a memory task is selected for a class it ought to be followed through and everyone of the pupils encouraged to accomplish it. The motivation should be out of love of prayer and an understanding of what the prayer means.

6. *Competition*: Competition between the pupils ought to be avoided and the fact that they are competing with themselves should be stressed. They should desire to improve over what they have been doing in the past, regardless of the rate at which fellow-pupils are advancing. This motivation is valid in all branches of the educational program, but more so in the study of religion. To establish a competitive spirit in religion and its practice is to set up a serious handicap for the individuals concerned in developing a fraternal love and sense of community. Emphatically stress that they are not attempting to be better than the person next to them, but to be better now than they were before. No teacher can judge the degree of Grace God has given to a certain individual, nor set up an absolute goal of perfection that the specific person should attain. A continual advance in virtue should be emphasized, the rate of advance varying with the individuals concerned.

7. *Answering child's requests*: Any reasonable request of students should be satisfied. If necessary, the teacher may take time to think it over but he should not fail to give the pupil a reply. When necessary to deny a request help the pupil to see the reasonableness of the denial, pointing out to him that the granting of such a desire would be a real detriment to him. When possible give an alternate choice to the child, as it may be difficult for him to understand an absolute refusal. This depends considerably on the degree of retardation. The more severely a child is retarded the greater the need for an alternate choice because of lack of insight to understand a refusal.

8. *Discipline*: The teacher will attempt to keep the children attentive and well-occupied for two reasons: one is to prevent dis-

orders from arising and the other is to develop the children to their maximum according to the limited talents they may have.

Many discipline problems arise because of failure to keep children occupied with something which demands mental activity. In case of disciplinary problems punishment should be for reformation of the individual or for protection of the common interest. Punishment should never be given for mere retaliation nor in a spirit of anger. Avoid haste in punishing and look for the real cause of the conflict. This may be a mentally disturbed individual who is not acting out of malice but who is unable to adjust to a group situation. Try to prevent conflicts from arising by modifying the environment to avoid trouble, and by substituting desirable for undesirable behavior patterns. If the teacher can gain the confidence of the child, and appeal to him through love and the child's desire to have friends, this is a positive approach. It is well to keep experimenting and be satisfied with gradual improvement, ignoring many of the conflicts that do arise. This makes it possible to concentrate on one objective until that is accomplished.

9. *Respect for authority*: Every child needs to be taught respect for authority and the necessity of obedience. Things of vital importance only should be stated as commands, and these must be insisted upon. If some unforeseen circumstance should change the situation, the reason for the change should be explained to the pupils. Trivial commands for the sake of exacting obedience are inexcusable and are a violation of the person's rights. Many times suggestion, rather than command, brings the best results. In every case respect for authority should be developed out of love rather than fear. If the child is influenced by fear, he will become a problem when the fear is removed since he has not developed true obedience out of love and respect.

10. *The child's home*: The teacher who visits a child's home, or finds out as much as possible about the child's home environment, will have a better understanding of the child and an insight into his behavior. The teacher should try to meet the parents and the best place is in the natural surroundings of the home.

Psychiatrists maintain that every child is a product of his home life and early training and will often act unconsciously in response to that training. Knowledge of home conditions will give the teacher a better understanding of why the child acts as he does, and will make him more kind and sympathetic if the child acts in a certain way which is due to early influences rather than malice.

11. *The curriculum*: Many of the same principles to be followed in the teaching of religion to the mentally retarded also apply to the teaching of so-called normal children. This fact points out that all have human personalities and fundamentally respond in a similar way. Teaching the retarded is like teaching in "slow motion," and the sooner the teacher realizes this the more successful he will be.

The materials of the curriculum must always be specific and detailed, as mentally defective children seldom carry over what is learned to a different situation. They are almost incapable of making general or universal judgments which can be applied to varying situations, and usually need guidance when meeting new or different circumstances.

Due to the fact that the retarded child is quite limited in his power to learn, the curriculum should be free from material which is not of life value to the individual. This fact is doubly true in the teaching of religion. It would be a grave injustice to confuse the simple mind of the child and thus bury his one talent by not allowing him to develop his love of God. Subject matter is to be preferred which meets an immediate need of the pupil and appeals strongly to his interests. The teacher will judge whether or not his immediate needs are properly met, and when a further development of truth can take place.

The curriculum should not be limited to a series of texts, topics, or divisions of instruction, but should be thought of as embracing a large body of habits and attitudes which are of the utmost importance in the education of the child. Although the rate of intelligence can seldom be increased, good habits and behavior can be taught to the mentally deficient child. The child should learn by doing, and by following the good example of those about him. In this manner virtuous habits will be established in the personality pattern of the child and he will reach the level of maturity which is possible to him. It may take the retarded child longer to establish a habit than the normal individual, but once the habit is formed he is less likely to break it. Teachers should therefore be careful to see that the values they have established for the mentally retarded child are correct, and especially that the motive for seeking these values is love.

Religion should form the core of the curriculum, for it is not a question of teaching subject matter but of teaching retarded children how to live so that they may obtain eternal life. Everyone wants to be completely happy. No matter how retarded a child may be, he vaguely seeks happiness. The retarded as well as the normal person is born to live eternally, and therefore the only answer to his desire for happiness is found through the study and practice of religion.

In setting up a religious curriculum which has the reception of the sacraments as its goal, certain facts ought to be kept in mind. The use of reason at the age of seven cannot be presumed. At that age the retarded child may be mentally scarcely beyond the level of an infant. The mental age, or ability to understand, rather than the chronological age is the important factor in judging conditions on which the person is to be admitted to the Sacraments. Holy Baptism and Confirmation are permitted to those who have the intelligence of infancy. In order to receive those Sacraments that require understanding, as Penance and the Holy Eucharist, the person should know the basic idea of the Sacrament to be received and the fundamental truths of religion which are necessary for salvation. As a relative norm, any child with an intelligence quotient less than 25 will be unable to understand sufficiently to receive these Sacraments.

In conclusion, there is no method of teaching religion that will succeed so well as a real love and understanding, manifested by patience, kindness, and prudence. Retarded children understand, and in their childlike simplicity, respond to the example of virtue.

12. *Fundamentals of religion*: The most important part of the program for backward pupils is the prayers, especially the principal ones, together with the acts of faith, hope, charity and contrition. The teacher should strive to make prayer so enter into the life of these pupils that they will never lose the habit of it. While prayer lasts, religion lasts; when prayer is forgotten, religion departs, and with it go grace and salvation.

The explanation of religion should as far as possible be connected with these prayer formulae. The essential points of doctrine to be explained to these children are the following: (1) besides the world in which we live now, God created another world for us after death where we are to see Him face to face in heaven; (2) those who with God's help try to lead a good life will be rewarded in heaven, those who lead a bad life will be punished in hell; (3) there are three Persons in God; (4) the Second Person became Man and died for our sins; (5) the meaning of each of the Seven Sacraments; (6) the essentials of the Sacraments and Penance and Holy Eucharist, together with a simple and easy method of examining one's conscience and going to Confession and Communion; (7) the duties of one's state of life; (8) necessity of avoiding bad companions and occasions of sin.

13. *Catechetical aids*: In this regard the teacher will find valuable aid in the Catechism entitled, "My Guide to Heaven, Essential Religious Doctrine for Exceptional Children" (1953), prepared by the Right Rev. Msgr. James W. Feider, and published at St. Coletta School at Jefferson, Wisconsin. The author has graded the material in the booklet as follows:

1) Questions with the capitalized words comprise the material regarded as essential in preparing the child for First Holy Communion. This material is generally not beyond the ability of first grade children.

2) The additional material designated with arabic numerals (1) is within the scope of the second grade.

3) The questions designated by alphabetical characters (A.) can be used with the groups of third and fourth grade level.

The simple summary of the subject matter at the beginning of each lesson can be profitably used by all.

The teacher will also find valuable aid in the religion booklet, "My Holy Child Book," a book of simple instruction in religion prepared for handicapped children by Sister Miriam Auxilium of Holy Family College, 890 Hayes St., San Francisco. In the simplest of language it covers the Life of Christ, which is correlated with the "Hail Mary" and the "Our Father," and supplemented by appropriate and graded drills for the child.[1]

[1] The author is indebted for the ideas in this chapter to the Christ Child School of St. Paul and to St. Coletta's of Jefferson, Wisconsin. A list of Catholic Schools for Exceptional Children will be in the National Catholic Almanac, 1957 (Paterson, N. J.), p. 495. "Religions Education of Mentally Retarded Children" was the title of a Work Group at the National Congress of the Confraternity of Christian Doctrine at Buffalo, New York, in September, 1957.

CHAPTER XII

CONCLUSIONS

In the foregoing pages we have attempted to give a faithful exposition of contemporary catechetical methods. Being generally built upon sound pedagogical and psychological principles, these methods offer valuable remedies for the shortcomings commonly attributed to catechetical instruction today. We shall enumerate some of these defects, and show how the methods outlined in the preceding pages supply the necessary correctives.

Proceeding from the Known to the Unknown

In the first place, a correct psychological method demands that the teacher proceed from the known to the unknown, from the concrete to the abstract, from the visual impressions to mental pictures and from facts to definitions. The senses and the intelligence form one natural, indivisible whole. In our present state the proper object of the intellect is derived from sensible material objects. Intellectual cognition depends on concomitant sensible activity. Now, when we examine the statements of the Catechism we find that they are abstract, terse and succinct, and that their language is not childlike. To oblige the child to memorize forthwith difficult theological formulas which the child can hardly pronounce, much less understand, is thoroughly unpsychological.[1] The means of bringing the condensed contents of the Catechism within the reach of the child is primarily the oral explanation of

[1] Cf. J. V. Tahon, *The First Instruction of Children and Beginners* (New York, 1930); F. H. Drinkwater, *Religion in School Again* (London, 1935), pp. 87 ff.

the catechist. He must supply the concrete details which the Catechism in its brevity cannot offer.[2] The Catechism answer is much like a theological thesis deduced as a conclusion from a multitude of concrete arguments derived from the Teachings of the Church, Scripture, Church History, and reason.

The Psychological or Stieglitz Method justly deserves the credit for striking out emphatically in the proper direction. Following the example of Christ Himself,[3] of the Church in her Liturgy, of St. Augustine,[4] of Gruber and Bossuet, the Munich Method proceeds from the concrete to the abstract. It begins with a story,[5] preferably a Bible Story or a parable. The story is further illustrated by the aid of pictures,[6] drawings on the blackboard,[7] projects,[8] dramatization, etc. From these concrete elements it abstracts the principal points of the doctrine and by combining these in a final summary, obtains substantially the answer of the Catechism. The Catechism text is then read and its wording and phrasing explained. Once the doctrine is understood, the short abstract text

[2] Cf. J. J. Baierl, *The Catechism Explained,* 4 vols. (Rochester, N. Y., 1919).

[3] Cf. R. G. Bandas, *Catechetics in the New Testament* (Milwaukee, 1934), pp. 18 ff.

[4] *Ibid.,* pp. 119 ff.

[5] In this connection consult D. Chisholm, *The Catechism in Stories,* 5 vols. (London, 1919–1922); Spirago-Baxter, *Anecdotes and Examples Illustrating the Catechism* (New York, 1899); J. D. Hannon, *Teacher Tells a Story,* 2 vols. (New York, 1926); J. J. Baierl, *op. cit.*; J. Fattinger, *Der Katechet erzählt* (Reid in Innkreis, 1934); A. Koch, *Homiletisches Handbuch* (Freiburg im B., 1937). The abundance of examples and comparisons may lead the catechist to pay more attention to variety than to unity, to appearances than to reality. In view of the intellectual greediness of the child, clear, correct and thorough instruction may give way to amusement. Hence the repeated insistence of the Munich School that the story be truly illustrative, that the details be not too numerous, nor emphasized to the extent of absorbing unduly the child's attention – in a word, that the story be a means to an end, and not an end in itself.

[6] Cf. A. J. Heeg, *Bible Picture Rolls on the "Our Father' and 'Hail Mary'* (Chicago) and *Outline Pictures* (Chicago, 1935). St. Anthony's Guild of Paterson, N. J., carries the following pictures: *Catholic Picture Series, Life of Christ Project Pictures,* maps on journeys of Our Lord and the Apostles. The Rev. George Nell of Effingham, Ill., and the Catechetical Guild of St. Paul, Minn., carry pictures on almost every phase of the Catechism.

[7] Cf. O'Connor-Hayden, *Chalk Talks* (St. Louis, 1928); J. Brownson, *To the Heart of the Child* (New York, 1918); J. K. Sharp, *Aims and Methods in Teaching Religion* (New York, 1929), pp. 298–330.

[8] The Catechetical Guild of St. Paul carries numerous projects on the Catechism.

of the Catechism presents no further difficulty. The lively interest which the story immediately arouses could never have been awakened by the dry Catechism text. The attention of the child is stimulated and his heart won from the outset. The method of presentation, then, and the subject matter must be planned to suit the developing mind. Our methods must be adjusted to the steps of the child's natural growth and expression. "God made them [the children]," says Father Drinkwater, "and if we take the trouble to notice after what manner He has made them, we shall know how He intends them to be treated; and if we treat them according, we shall be able to count more on His coöperation, as well as theirs."[9]

The exponents of the Munich Method noticed that up to the stage known as "Application" the child is largely passive and receptive. Modern pedagogy, it was found, tends to inculcate ideas less through reasoned expositions than through the child's coöperation and self-activity. Meaning of concepts and truths is built up by actual experiences. Learning by listening is supplanted by learning through doing. Subject matter is presented as an experience to be lived rather than as a formula to be memorized. The exponents of the so-called *Arbeitsschule* appeal to the whole child with all his senses and faculties. Their aim is to educate the child for life; their *Arbeitsschule* is intended to be also a *Lebenschule.*[10] The *Arbeitsprinzip,* then, as Fr. M. Gatterer tells us,[11] has a twofold phase: it is the beginning and the end of the instruction; action leads to understanding and understanding to action. In so far as the children actively and personally coöperate in the attainment of a truth or concept, action has a didactic value. When the acquired truth or knowledge is applied to conduct and life, action takes on an education value. For the truths of revelation were vouchsafed us, not merely to increase our knowledge, but also, and above all, to convert our hearts and transform our conduct.

The "work-principle" of the German pedagogues is the basic principle in the so-called "active" methods of catechization which

[9] *The Givers* (London, 1926), p. 165.

[10] Cf. F. Weigl, *Bildung durch Selbsttum,* 2 vols. (Munich, 1923); H. Schusslers, *Arbeitsschulmethode und katholischer Religionsunterricht* (Frankfurt, 1922); J. Gründer, *Der Geist des Fuldaer Lehrplans, die Willensbildung und der Arbeitsschulgedanke im kath. Religionsunterricht* (Paderborn, 1927).

[11] *Katechetik* (3rd ed.; Innsbruck, 1924).

predominate now in almost every country.[12] The revision of existing catechetical methods is in the direction of the Montessori School. Religious instruction must supply that environment which is often absent in both the home and the school. It must captivate the whole child, with all his faculties and powers. It must engender an attitude of freedom, spontaneity, activity. It must make the child reflect, love – and live – his religion. Religious instruction must be not merely the assimilation of an abstract formula but the immediate and permanent application of it in daily conduct. A method of vitalizing religion which is becoming increasingly popular in America is the so-called "problem" or "case" method.[13] A hypothetical case from the experience of children is submitted to the child for evaluation. In passing judgment on the problem, in condemning the evil and approving the good which it contains, the child is really laying down a principle of conduct for his own future life.

The Sulpician Method, which still has many exponents in France,[14] demands, after the manner of the Munich Method, that the catechist proceed to the abstract by means of concrete comparisons, examples and parables. "Curiosity," we read is the well-known work, *The Method of St. Sulpice,* "is a natural impulse which leads on half-way to instruction. Now, what is there more fit to excite their (children's) curiosity and to quiet the restlessness of their minds than a comparison taken from sensible things which are all around them, and which come to them through their senses? It speaks to their imagination, and it always interests them, pro-

[12] Cf. M. Fargues, *Les méthodes actives dans l'enseignement religieux* (Juvisy, 1934); F. Derkenne, *La vie et la joie au catéchisme* (Paris, 1935); M. Llorente, *Programa ciclico instruccion religiosa* (Valladolid, 1935); *Tratado elemental de pedagogia catequistica* (Valladolid, 1934); M. Casotti, *La Scuola Attiva* (Brescia, 1937); *Il metodo Montessori et il Metodo Agazzi* (Brescia, 1931); A. Van der Mueren, *Op den weg der wijsheid, Op den weg der liefde, Bij de ware levensbronnen* (Louvain, 1930–1934).

[13] Cf. Sister of Notre Dame, *Before Christ Came* (Milwaukee, 1935) and *The Vine and the Branches* (Milwaukee, 1935); R. G. Bandas, *Practical Problems in Religion* (Milwaukee, 1934); Sisters of Notre Dame, *Teaching the Ten Commandments* (Milwaukee, 1931); E. Constantin, *Recueil de Problèmes catéchistiques,* 3 vols. (Paris, 1904–1912). E. Duplessy, *Le Catéchisme en Problèmes,* 2 vols. (Parish, 1927, 1928).

[14] Cf. P. Boumard, *Formation de l'enfant par le catéchisme* (Paris, 1930); L. Desers, *Instruction et education au catéchisme* (Paris, s.d.); J. Bricout, *L'enseignement du catéchisme en France* (Paris, 1922).

vided that the thing is described to them with animation, and that the comparison is well put before them. As the catechist talks to tem, the picture he is drawing excites their attention, and keeps their curiosity awake; and, when the application comes, their faces glow with surprise and the secret delight of their hearts." [15] That the Sulpician Method as well as the other methods do not neglect the "active" or "work" principle will become evident as our discussion progresses.

Fr. Shields likewise leads the child to the abstract religious doctrine by means of concrete presentations and embodiments of the truth, which touch the child's imagination and arouse his enthusiasm. In his *First Book* and *Second Book*, the "nature study" is followed by a "domestic study," which is reflected in and grows out of the former; both are constructed in such a way as to form an adequate preparation for the religion lesson which follows. The stories are told with an additional fullness by a series of pictures, either in color or sepia, which illustrates the text. The nature study is intended to be dramatized, the domestic study to be lived out in the home.

In the preface to *Stories in School*, the former editor of the *Sower* repeatedly warns that the children are not to be starved of their stories. In another *Sower* publication we read: "To be able to tell a story vividly is a very important accomplishment for a teacher; and the more 'local color' he can introduce, the more truly will he be educating the children and the more he will delight them, for there are few things a child enjoys more than flights of imagination. And if the teacher lacks the power of painting vivid word pictures, there are always picture books – which are, nowadays, almost all that could be desired." [16]

Apprehension, Understanding, Practice

It is an equally fundamental psychological law that a child assimilates a given subject, not in one act, but only gradually. First there is apprehension, then understanding, and finally practice. If a man wishes to start driving a car, he first looks at and feels the various parts, then asks for an explanation of the interrelation of

[15] London, 1896, pp. 76–77.
[16] *The Way into the Kingdom* (London, 1922), p. 47.

the different sections, and finally gets in to attempt to start it and drive it. These three stages are usually present in the acquisition of any new knowledge. In catechization these three stages of learning presuppose on the part of the teacher three corresponding teaching modes: *presentation,* which should produce a distinct and vivid picture in the imagination; *explanation,* which should make clear the "how" and "why" of things; *permanence,* which should impress the truths upon the mind by memorizing and reviewing, and apply them to conduct by drawing consequences suited to the age of the child and the concrete occurrences of his daily life. The Munich Method with its three fundamental stages satisfies the requirements of psychology on this point.

Graded Teaching of Religion

Psychology also tells us that children do not grasp an object, presented to the mind for the first time. integrally and intuitively but only imperfectly. It is only slowly and after repeated efforts that the deeper nature of an object is finally understood. The varied types of mind in children of different ages must also be taken into consideration. The content and method appropriate to early adolescence should not be projected into and anticipated in childhood, much less in infancy. Any attempt to divide mechanically the instructions designed for children from six to fourteen years into eight parts equal in quantity and in essential quality is unpsychological. In the secular branches — in reading and arithmetic, for example — the same textbook is not used throughout all the grades but a well-defined system of graded instruction is followed. To use in the lower grades a text which properly belongs to the higher grades would be considered absurd. Why, then, should not some similar program of studies be followed in teaching religion? How often do we find the same Baltimore Catechism used throughout the eight grades and even in the four years of high school!

The three stages of the *Sower* Scheme meet the evident divergencies noted in the children in these three periods. It has also supplied the teacher with the necessary handbooks for this purpose. In the Munich Method and Fulda *Lehrplan,* the "concentric circles" — a method whereby the whole of Christian Doctrine is surveyed during three successive periods, each time more extensively and thoroughly, in a manner adapted to the child's growing intellectual capacity – likewise answer the demands of psychology. A distinct contribution in this regard has been made by these four religion series: Mother Bolton's *Spiritual Way, The Christ-Life Series, The Highway to Heaven Series* and the *Schorsch or De Paul Series.* The matter is chosen with a view to the child's ability; its distribution is determined by the amount of time at the child's disposal; the terminology is carefully adapted to the child's age; and the teacher is guided in the presentation of the lesson by scientifically prepared handbooks. A graded Catechism, however, which would have the good qualities of similar books in European countries, is still a desideratum in the United States.

Transformation of the Whole Man

Every conscious and deliberate act implies the coöperation, more or less intense, of the bodily faculties, senses, imagination, intellect, will and emotions. This should especially be the case in catechization, since religion should transform the whole man. The Munich Method, as revised in the light of the so-called "active" methods, gives due consideration to all the faculties of the child's nature. By means of the "action" principle (*Arbeitsprinzip*) the exponents of the Munich Method appeal to the whole child with all his senses and faculties. In the *presentation,* the catechist appeals to the sense of sight by means of the things themselves, copies of things, pictures, maps, drawings, etc.; to the sense of hearing by means of examples, stories, comparisons, descriptions, questioning; to the bodily faculties, by means of handiwork and projects. In the *explanation* he appeals to the intellect, and in the *application* to the will and emotions. In this way the catechist makes use of the supplementary aids to instruction so popular in profane pedagogy.

May we add one word here in regard to handiwork and projects?[17] These catechetical tools should be only a means to an end. They should have only one purpose; they should teach the child to know God in order that he might love Him and serve Him. To handle all catechetical material according to this plan might probably demand much more time than can be alloted to religious instruction. Furthermore, faith comes by authoritative teaching

[17] The project method had the hearty recommendation of J. T. McMahon. See his *Some Methods of Teaching Religion* (London, 1928), pp. 191 ff.

and by learning, not by playing. Whereas secular education may be satisfied with external activity, in catechization the invisible grace of the Holy Spirit, faith and acts of virtue are of the greatest importance. Hence, to be effective the *Arbeitsprinzip* must unite the mind and heart to God. It must impress supernatural truths upon the soul in such a way that the child will always be guided by them, derive strength from them and live them.

Proper Emphasis on Memorization

Another defect frequently signalized in our catechetical instruction is over-emphasis on memory. Religious training is often a mere memorizing and a scrupulously accurate reproduction of abstract and unintelligible formulas. The unassimilated abstract forms, instead of promoting religious life, become non-functional memory loads and dead accumulations, quickly to be expelled from the mind. Many children repeat the Catechism answer in much the same mechanical and thoughtless way as the server recites the prayers at the foot of the altar and strikes his breast. Their hearts are left as untouched by these daily memory drills as by arithmetic problems. In fact, the worst-behaved children often give the best answers. At other times, these daily exercises of verbal memory frequently antagonize the children against religion. Would we try to make adults grasp the sense of a statement by a mere exercise of memory? Would we teach history or geography by compelling the pupil to memorize several paragraphs each day?

Religious training should profit as far as possible by approved profane didactic methods. If grace does not destroy nature but rather perfects it, catechetical methods cannot be in opposition to the didactic rules established for profane science. There is only one brain and one mind in the child, and the laws governing the operations of the mind are fundamentally the same whatever be the contents of knowledge. The abstract statements of the Catechism are the conclusions of a whole reasoning process – formulas deduced from a host of concrete facts. to attempt to teach them to the child without supplying the concrete facts on which they are based is to go counter to all laws of psychology.

Hence the insistence of the Munich Method that the children be required to memorize only after the matter has been carefully presented and thoroughly explained. Hence the requirements of the *Sower Scheme* that the answers of the Catechism be first built up in the child's own words, then translated into the phrases of the Catechism, and only then memorized. "Memorizing," says the former editor of the *Sower* in his preface to *Teaching of the Catechism*, "should not be the first step but the last step or finishing touch to a process of explanation and understanding." We are not prepared, however, to discourage memory work in Christian Doctrine to the extent that Fr. Shields does. Divine immutable truths demand accurate and precise expression. The terse and concise formulas of the Catechism are more easily impressed upon the memory, and misunderstandings and errors are thereby more easily avoided.

Application of Religious Truths to Everyday Life

Our present system of catechetical training is frequently criticized for its failure to apply religious truths to the concrete occurrences and events of everyday life. As a matter of fact, a catechist who concludes that his task is done when he has *instructed* his pupils, or when the children have satisfactorily *memorized* the lesson, is sadly mistaken. Mere increase in knowledge does not necessarily mean a corresponding growth in virtue: "For not the hearers of the law are just before God, but the doers of the law." [18] Revelation has been given us not only for the illumination of the mind but also, and above all, for the transformation of our heart. A catechist's instruction must enthuse the children for the ideals of religion and set their hearts aglow with inward fire. An instruction which fails to make the religious truth operative in the child's life is like a meditation which does not issue in an effective resolution.

Standard catechetical methods have never dissociated religious *education* from religious *instruction.* In the Munich Method the former is emphasized in the "Application," in Fr. Shields' "Primary Methods" by the "Thoughts for Us," and in the Sulpician Method by the homily, application and admonitions. These stages set forth the inherent power of these truths to counteract sinful and sensual tendencies and to raise our minds to a love of heavenly things. However, a mere accumulation of applications, instead of contributing to spiritual perfection, might produce the opposite effect,

[18] Rom. 2:13.

namely, a dulling and deadening of the moral sense. Sinful habits are not usually rooted out simultaneously; saints are not made in a day. The Eucharistic Method and the Fulda *Lehrplan* more correctly emphasize the "particular point" (the *Leitgedanke*) which is to be recalled and impressed upon the mind and heart for an indefinite period of time.

Much will depend upon the catechist as to whether the child will make the divine truth an integral element of his life and daily conduct. Hence the catechist should observe, among others, the following rules:

1. Since the converting of hearts as well as the conversion itself of the heart are supernatural works, the catechist must constantly implore divine aid and grace through prayer. He must not only talk to the children about God; he must also talk to God about the children.[19]

2. If the catechist wishes to inflame his pupils with love of God, he himself must be afire with enthusiasm for the ideals of religion. Children detect instinctively the catechist's dispositions. Hence, nothing will counteract the good of the catechist's work so readily as his own lukewarmness and indifference in matters of religion.

3. Supernatural faith is spread among men not by human teachers but by representatives having a commission from Christ. Hence, the catechist must make it plain to the children that he is a representative of God and of the Church, tracing his authority through the bishops and Apostles back to Christ. In this way he will establish the proper foundation for the child's faith.

4. A child's faith is nourished by truth and is weakened by doubt. Hence, the catechist must carefully avoid anything that might arouse doubts in the child's mind – as, for example, engaging in excessive and inappropriate questioning, formulating difficulties which are above the grasp of the children, and giving the impression that everything in the Catholic religion needs to be proved. The fact that Christ says so, or that the Church teaches so, is usually a sufficient argument for both child and adult.

5. The catechist should avoid the so-called "utility" or "natural" motives and should use chiefly supernatural motives. He should not say, "If you lead a good life, God will reward you with temporal blessings; if you sin, God will punish you here below." For the

[19] Cf. J. Rutché, *Saint-Esprit et l'Education* (Paris, 1928).

conditions may be fulfilled, and yet the effects may not follow. The catechist should rather say, "If you lead a virtuous life, God may reward you here below; but whether He does or not, He will most certainly reward you in the next life, etc." The catechist should not say, "Obey your parents, because they feed you, clothe you and provide for you." For what would happen in that case to the child's attitude towards his parents, once he can take care of himself? The catechist should say, "Obey your parents, because parents are God's representatives, because God commands it, because Christ was obedient, etc." The catechist should not say, "Avoid sins of impurity because they will injure your mind and body." For a physically strong person committing sins of impurity may experience none of these effects. The teacher should rather say, "Avoid sins of impurity, because God is omnipresent, because your bodies are temples of the Holy Spirit and are destined for a glorious resurrection, because God in the past has visited this sin with terrible punishments, etc." So too in inculcating obedience to parents, to the Sister in school, to the pastor, to civil authorities, the catechist should make it clear that all authority comes from God and that obedience to legitimate superiors is obedience to God. Natural motives should be used with great caution and only as secondary arguments. The ultimate aim of all motivation should be to show how much God loves us and desires in turn to be loved by us.

Proper Emphasis on Authority

Our catechetical training is also charged with overemphasis on authority — a rather strange criticism in a day and age when authority is so frequently disparaged. Catechists are frequently asked this question: "Why is it that Catholic children, who attend the parochial school and who during the school year attend Mass and receive the Sacraments regularly, think nothing of missing Mass, even on Sunday, during vacation and fail to receive the Sacraments during the summer months?" Is it not because religion has come to be associated too closely with the discipline of the school year? Are not school children, to use the words of Fr. Drinkwater, often "marched to Confession in platoons" and "marshalled to Communion in companies," under the direct and strict supervision of the teacher? Are not their daily prayers often said with them in school? But what will happen at the end of the school year? Will not the child give up his religious exercises in the same way as he discontinued his arithmetic and geography classes, because both have been made equally a matter of class room procedure?

No one has perhaps pointed out the evil of overemphasis on authority so well and suggested such practical remedies as Fr. Drinkwater. This learned catechist does not propose to leave the children to their own responsibility. He realizes that they need aid, guidance and suggestions, but he proposes that the stimuli to obedience be gradually relaxed or withdrawn, so that the child will learn to stand on his own feet. The children should be made to understand why they should perform certain actions even though no one is watching or urging them. They should realize that, while the school classes may come to a close on the first day of June, the practice of religion must continue during vacation and during one's whole lifetime – that the salvation of one's soul must be one's constant concern not only during the school year but during every moment of one's earthly existence. For unless a child is ar far as possible independent in his religious life when he leaves school, he will be easily swayed by a tempter or subversive leader. The exponents of the Munich Method also demand that with the awakening of reason the children be told the motive of their obedience. The main reason is the will of God manifested in the enactments of constituted authority.[20] Only an obedience based on the will and wisdom of God is reasonable, ennobling and becoming to man.

Proper Emphasis on the Natural Virtues

Another defect frequently pointed out in our catechetical training – especially in early home training – is underemphasis of the natural virtues. By natural virtues we mean perfections which belong to rational nature as such, apart from its supernatural destiny. Natural virtuous acts are actions which in their object, circumstances and intention remain intrinsically natural, although they may be directed to a supernatural end. Of course, we are fully aware that theologians insist that the state of pure nature never existed and that we are now in a state of repaired fallen nature. However, our point is that the supernatural is built upon the

[20] Rom. 13:2; I Pet. 2:13–18.

natural and that it perfects the natural and does not destroy it. A child who has not been trained from his very infancy to be kind, considerate, affable and fair will respond only defectively to motives of charity, based on our common membership in the Mystical Body. A child given to dishonesty, duplicity and sneakishness, will hardly observe the Commandments of God and of the Church when left to his own responsibility. And the same is true of a child who is not naturally trustworthy, dependable and faithful in keeping his word. A child who is not trained in refinement of manner, personal neatness, self-reliance and self-respect, will respond only in a feeble manner to the supernatural truths that our bodies are temples of the Holy Spirit and destined for a glorious resurrection, when he is faced with temptations to sins of impurity. How often do we find that, notwithstanding all the supernatural motives put before them in a Catholic school, pupils in these schools will not hesitate to cheat in examinations, steal one another's belongings, disfigure or destroy another's property and commit other secret sins!

Proper Reference to Saints as Models

The failure to appeal to saints as inspiring models for our children is considered another imperfection of our religious training. The child tends instinctively to imitate the example of others. Speaking, reading and drawing are on his part the results of imitation. Now, what better way of satisfying this natural imitative tendency than the lives of the saints? The value of imitation in the teaching of religion was well understood by the Church when she organized the liturgical year. In the *Sanctorale* she places before us men and women who had to face the same temptations and problems as we do and who yet won for themselves a place in God's kingdom. The proper understanding of the *Sanctorale* is possible, however, only if closely correlated with the reading of the lives of the saints.[21]

The Sulpician Method introduces the children to some of the saints by means of the *fêtes* and *billets*. The Munich Method insists upon a close correlation of the Catechism lesson with stories from the lives of the saints. To employ the latter effectively, the catechist

[21] Cf. H. S. Bowden, *Miniature Lives of the Saints*, 2 vols. (London).

must not dehumanize the saints, render men saints effeminate, or invest the saints with unattractive forms of piety. Only strong, living personalities and real models will invite imitation. The delicate, soft and saccharine form under which art frequently represents certain saints (especially St. Aloysius and the Little Flower) will hardly appeal to any real American boy or girl.

Christ: the Way, the Truth, and the Life

Christ is the Way, the Truth, and the Life. In Bible History Christ is represented as the Way, in Catechism as the Truth, and in the Liturgy as Life. The three catechetical branches must therefore be intimately correlated in all religious instruction.[22] Historically, the Church announced the joyful message through these three channels.

First, she announced to men the salient points of the history of salvation contained in the Holy Bible. The sacred books show how the salvation which was promised to Adam came through Christ. Since this instruction was not merely theoretical but also practical, certain special passages calculated to contribute to a moral renovation were chosen.

Secondly, the Church summed up biblical doctrine in certain clearcut formulas, which were to guard the Christian against error and be a sign of orthodox faith. In this way the foundation for the future Catechism was laid. This method of teaching the Catechism by means of Bible History is enjoying considerable popularity in our own day. In France it was initiated by J. R. Maurice Landrieux, Bishop of Dijon,[23] and is being developed and perfected by such catechists as E. Charles,[42] J. Mury,[25] and C. Quinet.[26] The same method is found in the so-called *Religionsbuchlein*[27] of the German-speaking countries. In our own country the method is applied

[22] Cf. "The Libican (Liturgy, Bible, Catechetics) Syllabus of Christian Doctrine," in *Libica* by H. Borgmaan (Baltimore, 1930); M. A. Schumacher, *How to Teach the Catechism*, 3 vols. (New York, 1935).

[23] *Le premier enseignement par l'Evangile* (Marseilles, 1922).

[24] *Le Catéchisme par l'Évangile* (Marseilles, 1933).

[25] *Le Catéchisme dans l'Évangile* (Paris, 1924).

[26] *Pour mes tout-petits. Vingt leçons de catéchisme évangelique par la méthode active* (Paris, 1935).

[27] Cf., for example, the *Katholisches Religionsbüchlein fur die Grundschule, herausgegeben von den bayerischen Bischofen* (Donauworth, 1933).

with special competence by Sister Agnesine, S.S.N.D.,[28] and G. Johnson.[29]

Thirdly, the Church applied the treasures of truth and grace through the celebration of the liturgical year – through her feasts, prayers and blessings, and above all through the Mass and Sacraments. In the Liturgy and sacred chant the condensed contents of Scripture and tradition are prayed, sung, confessed and made a vital part of our lives. The *Opera della Regalità di N. S. G. Cristo* of Milan has published a series entitled *Bibbia e Liturgia*, the purpose of which is to correlate Scripture with the Liturgy. Other contemporary works aim at correlating the Catechism with the Liturgy.[30]

"All branches of learning . . ."

The Religion Course should also form an organic whole with the so-called secular branches. A school which uses textbooks written by non-Catholics, which employs non-Catholic teachers, which admits non-Catholic students, and which calls itself Catholic because of its daily half-hour's class in religion, is Catholic only by extrinsic denomination. Our holy religion, says Pius IX, must be the soul of the entire academic education: "All branches of learning must expand in the closest alliance with religion, and all types of study must be enlightened by the bright rays of Catholic truth."[31] Similarly, Leo XIII proclaims that "religion must thoroughly inform and dominate every subject of instruction."[32] It is not enough to trust to the ingenuity and resourcefulness of the teacher to point out the relation of religion to the other branches of the curriculum. The textbooks themselves should embody this vital connection between religion and the profane studies. It was this that Fr. Shields[33] in our country, A. Manjón[34] in Spain, and L. Vigna[35] and other catechists in Italy, hope to accomplish by their "Religion Books." It is their constant contention that religion is

[28] *Before Christ Came* (Milwaukee, 1934).
[29] G. Johnson, J. D. Hannon, and Sister M. Dominica, *Bible History* for the higher grades (New York, 1935). Consult *Teacher's Manual.*
[30] Cf. Sister of the Visitation, *Le catéchisme dans le missel* (Lophem, 1935).
[31] *Optime Noscitis,* Mar. 20, 1854.
[32] *Militans Ecclesia,* Aug. 1, 1897.
[33] *Primary Methods* (Washington, 1912), pp. 95–96.
[34] *Hojas catequisticas y pedagogicas,* 5 vols, (Grenada, 1920–1931).
[35] *Ai Maestri* (Milan, 1930).

the central, coördinating and dominating element of the child's work in the first years of school and that it must enter the mind along with other knowledge. If religious truths are rigidly restricted to the half-hour's religious instruction, reserved for the Sunday School or deferred till the years of maturity, they will with difficulty be correlated with life will appear as superfluous and exercise an influence on daily conduct.

The Catechist Himself

Realizing the inadequate training in religion of many prospective catechists, several of the methods outlined above – especially the *Sower* Scheme and the Munich Method – have made it their primary aim to supply the teacher with handbooks which are pedagogically sound and doctrinally accurate. All methods, particularly the Eucharistic Method, insist upon the supernatural character of catechization. To reform the child deformed by original sin, to render him more conformable to Christ, His Model, to prepare him for the Beatific Vision and to save his soul, are all endeavors which transcend the power of mere human nature and demand the assistance of grace. Finally, all methods insist upon the exemplary life and sanctity of the catechist. He must be endowed with gentleness and love for children, with zeal for the salvation of souls and with a spirit of prayer and piety. For burning words cannot come from a frozen heart.

INDEX

www.ingramcontent.com/pod-product-compliance
Lightning Source LLC
LaVergne TN
LVHW020528100826
845148LV00010B/1393

* 9 7 8 1 6 0 8 9 9 1 3 4 1 *